SUMMON
THE STARS

SUMMON THE STARS

by Joe Christy
and Page Shamburger

South Brunswick and New York: A. S. Barnes and Company
London: Thomas Yoseloff Ltd

Library of Congress Catalogue Card Number: 78-88254

A. S. Barnes and Co., Inc.
Cranbury, New Jersey 08512

Thomas Yoseloff Ltd
108 New Bond Street
London W1Y OQX, England

SBN: 498 07341 6
Printed in the United States of America

To those who know the sky.
Especially, to those who feel no loneliness
in the lonely, high places
—and sense the reason why.

Contents

8

Foreword

The world's first successful airplane flights—by Orville and Wilbur Wright at Kitty Hawk, North Carolina, on December 17, 1903—proved to be something less than an earth-shaking event. Most Americans simply didn't believe man could fly with artificial wings, and few U.S. newspapers even printed the story. Overseas, the English, who could boast of having a "Royal Aeronautical Society" since 1866, were quite prepared to believe that man could fly; but with typical British procrastination they studied the problem for another five years before producing a plane of their own. The Germans, preoccupied with Count von Zeppelin's huge rigid airships (which took to the air three years before the Wright brothers' success), lagged behind even the British in the development of heavier-than-air flying machines, until the airplane's military potential began to come into focus about 1910. In France, however, things were different. The French, clearly enchanted with the promise of charging noisily about the sky and indulging the anarchy in their souls, embraced the airplane with enthusiasm—and contributed more to its development prior to World War One than all other nations combined (which is why so many present-day aeronautical terms are of French origin: fuselage, pitot, nacelle, chandelle, etc.).

While Frenchmen Louis Bleriot, the Voisin brothers, Edouard Nieuport, Esnault-Pelterie and Armand Deperdussin were daily flying and improving upon a variety of flying machines (and their power-plants), Orville and Wilbur Wright refined their original *Flyer* and spent several years trying to sell it to the U.S. Army.

Meanwhile, other experimenters, including Glenn Curtiss in America and Goeffery de Havilland, Handley Page and A. V. Roe in Britain, began applying themselves to this new art/science and added greatly to man's meagre store of knowledge on the subject.

Finally, on August 2, 1909, the U.S. Army took delivery of its first airplane, the Wright "Model A," and during the next five years bought a total of 24 planes of which ten were destroyed in accidents at a cost of twelve lives, or about one death for every hundred hours of flying time. Then, on July 18, 1914, Congress officially created the Aviation Section of the Signal Corps (authorized strength, 60 officers and 260 enlisted men), and the true parent of today's United States Air Force came into existence. The USAF, however, prefers to regard 1907 as its birthdate, though this is a tenuous claim, apparently based upon an order, dated August 1, 1907 and signed by Brigadier General James Allen, Chief Signal Officer, U.S. Army, establishing an "Aeronautical Division" within the Signal Corps in anticipation of acquiring a motorized gas bag from balloonist T. S. Baldwin. One officer and two enlisted men constituted the total personnel of this division—until one of the men went over the hill and thereby reduced America's aerial might by one-third.

When the United States entered WW-I, on April

6, 1917, the Army, considered by a peace-minded Congress to be an "offensive force" and therefore poorly funded, had 55 airplanes in active service, 334 training planes on order, 35 qualified pilots assigned to aviation duty, plus a handful of ex-barnstormers quickly given uniforms and designated as instructors. The Navy, viewed by Congress as a "defensive force," was relatively fat with appropriations and though the old sea dogs who ran things saw no particular use for a naval air arm, they humored the few junior officers who did, and the Navy went to war with 51 pilots, 6 flying boats, 48 float-planes, 2 balloons and a powered gas bag. At the same time, on Capitol Hill, the people's elected representatives threatened to "blacken the skies over Germany" with America's air fleets, evidently unaware that money alone ($640 million as the spittoons rang and the lawmaker's emotions heated up) was incapable of building air power overnight. An aircraft "industry" that had built less than 200 airplanes since 1903 was asked to produce 20,000 airplanes within a year.

Before the war ended nineteen months later, a billion and a quarter dollars was authorized for American warplanes. Less than half that sum was actually spent, and much of that boondoggled by the automobile interests that had purchased the Wright and Curtiss operations along with most other fledgling plane-makers. When the Armistice was signed, November 11, 1918, the U.S. Air Service had 45 squadrons in the battle zone with a strength of 750 airplanes—most of which were purchased from our Allies.

Less than 1,400 American airmen engaged in combat during WW-I (although nearly 10,000 pilots would have completed training—with an average of 50 hours flight time—early in 1919, and would have been available for combat, had there been planes to equip them); but this small force acquitted itself well. The U.S. Air Service was officially credited with destroying 781 enemy airplanes and 73 balloons while taking losses of 289 airplanes and 48 balloons during the seven months it was in action.

During the years immediately following the First World War, aviation was kept alive in America largely by the itinerant barnstormer flying from the nation's cowpastures selling rides in his surplus Jenny or Standard. Military thinking—and Congressional appropriations—reverted to pre-WW-I levels; and

though Brigadier General William Mitchell, as Deputy Chief of the impoverished Air Service, abrasively campaigned for a strong and separate air arm, and proved in dramatic tests held in 1921 and 1923 that the airplane had made the battleship obsolete, an enervating procession of myopic Congresses, uninformed Presidents and Nineteenth-Century military bosses kept U.S. air power "in an auxiliary position which absolutely compromised our whole system of national defense," to quote General Billy Mitchell.

Mitchell was eventually court-martialed (by order of President Calvin Coolidge) for sassing his superiors, and the truths he espoused went unheeded. However, though we probably didn't deserve it, America was prodded into significant aeronautical developments by another force: The U.S. Post Office Department. Federal subsidies for carrying the mail by air made possible (financially) the first U.S. airlines; indeed, built our airline system, and conditions of these subsidies, carefully controlled by the postmaster general—particularly, President Hoover's postmaster general, Walter Folger Brown—fostered the aerial technology that insured America's air superiority in World War II.*

The promise of profitable airline operations encouraged development of reliable aircraft engines; and the appearance of a truly reliable engine, the Wright *Whirlwind,* was the key ingredient of the aviation boom touched off by Charles Lindbergh's dramatic New York-to-Paris flight in May, 1927. Overnight, the average American "discovered" the airplane, and uncounted millions of dollars were poured into civil aviation. Much of the money went to fast-buck artists, and even more was wasted upon sincere but impractical schemes and inventions. Overall, however, the effect was beneficial, and when the Great Depression of the thirties eliminated all but the most determined and dedicated aviation builders and investors, America had, say, by 1937, a technologically sound if financially weak foundation upon which to build a viable aircraft industry.

Such an industry, far greater in size than anyone then imagined, would soon be essential to our survival.

*The story of American aviation from 1899 to 1939 is detailed in this book's companion volume, *Command the Horizon,* by the same authors.

Acknowledgments

The authors of this work shall be the first to admit that they could not have completed a book of this scope without the aid of many interested people. We are particularly grateful to Gen. (ret.) Richard Mangrum, USMC; the late Gen. Orvil Anderson, USAF; Gladys Wise, USAF-PIO Pentagon; Rowland P. Gill, Historical Reference Section, USMC; Royal Frey, USAF Museum; Lt. M. J. Collet, Naval Historical Foundation; Herb O. Fisher, Port of New York Authority; veteran designer (Curtiss P-36/P-40) Donovan Berlin; N. R. "Bart" Bartimus and Major (ret.) and Mrs. Alfred Fernandez.

Also, Robert T. Smith, Joe R. Reed; Maxine Condon of Lear Jet and our friends in the U.S. military forces who aided with much background material but prefer anonymity. As always, the U.S. aerospace companies provided cheerful and invaluable help, and to our many PR-type friends there we doff our helmet and goggles.

Joe Christy and Page Shamburger

SUMMON THE STARS

WORLD WAR TWO
IN THE AIR

1. Death's Handsomest Machines

The world's first fighter airplane probably was the French Morane-Saulnier *Bullet* of 1914. This single-place mid-wing monoplane became a fighter aircraft (or *avion de chasse,* literally, "hunter airplane") when partners Morane and Saulnier decided, shortly after WW-I began on August 1, 1914, that there must be a more efficient way to down German reconnaissance planes than by tossing bricks at their propellers or exchanging pistol fire at a hundred meters. Therefore, Messieurs Morane and Saulnier mounted a machine gun on the cowling of the *Bullet* and fixed steel deflectors on the plane's propeller blades to protect the prop from the estimated one-in-seven bullets that would not pass between the rotating blades. Equipped with this combination, Lieutenant Roland Garros of *Escadrille* MS23 shot down an Albatross two-seater on April 1, 1915, and thereby presaged the doctrine of air superiority.

Morane-Saulnier's crude installation was not very satisfactory, but it was a serious threat to the Germans who soon countered with a gun-propeller synchronization system—an interrupter gear in which a cam on the prop or prop shaft interrupted the guns' firing—which appeared on the Fokker *Eindecker,* August 1, 1915. The Allies later adopted the hydraulically activated Constantinesco sychronization system which worked very well.

Anyway, the point is, line-of-sight, forward-firing automatic weapons systems perfected (more or less) for airplanes during WW-I spawned the fighter aircraft upon which has since rested the primary obligation of achieving control of the air—and all that *that* implies in modern warfare.

In September, 1939, when WW-II began in Europe with Hitler's invasion of Poland, the United States possessed, in the Army Air Corps,* 489 fighter airplanes: Curtiss P-36's, Seversky P-35's and some obsolete Boeing P-26's and Boeing P-12's. The Army's total heavier-than-air inventory was 2,473 planes. Of these, 754 were trainers. The rest were too old to be useful, except for a few C-33 and C-47 transports (DC-2's and DC-3's), and 22 Boeing B-17 "heavy" bombers, the latter representing America's only really superior combat aircraft.

---

* The Army's air arm functioned as the Aeronautical Division of the Signal Corps from August 1, 1907, until July 18, 1914, when Congress officially established the Aviation Section of the Signal Corps. Then on June 2, 1917, it was re-named the Airplane Division. The Airplane Division was generally called the "Air Service" from September 3, 1917, when Gen. W. L. Kenly took command in France as Chief of Air Service, American Expeditionary Forces. Separation from the Signal Corps came May 20, 1918, with establishment of two new departments, Bureau of Military Aeronautics and Bureau of Aircraft Production. On June 4, 1920, Congress approved the Army Reorganization Bill which officially created the U.S. Air Service as "a separate and co-ordinate branch of the Army" (The U.S. Navy Bureau of Aeronautics was formed August 10, 1921). On July 2, 1926, the Air Corps Act changed the Air Service to the Army Air Corps, and it remained as such until June 20, 1941, when, with a new autonomy under Major General Henry H. "Hap" Arnold, it became the United States Army Air Forces (USAAF). Today's independent United States Air Force (USAF) was created by the National Security Act of 1947, which became effective September 18th of that year. At some near-future date it will probably suffer still another change in name to "United States AeroSpace Force (USASF)."

World's first fighter airplane was the French Morane-Saulnier *Bullet* of 1914. It mounted an 1885 Hotchkiss infantry machine gun in fixed position for forward firing. Pilot Roland Garros depended upon wedge-shaped, steel deflectors (arrow) to protect propeller from the estimated one-in-seven bullets that did not pass between turning prop blades. (Authors' Photo)

General Hap Arnold, Chief of the Air Corps, had shamelessly employed every devious means available to him to obtain even twenty-two heavy bombers. His Army superiors, the President, and the Congress saw no need for a strategic bomber force, indeed, regarded such a force as "provocative" (my, hasn't *that* word a familiar ring). In May, 1938, the adjutant general had directed that Army aircraft development for fiscal years 1939 and 1940 be "confined to that class of aviation designed for the close-in support of ground troops." And when General Arnold doggedly sought funds for more B-17's and modern fighters, he was asked by a congressman, "Just who are we going to fight?" Surely, that reminded Arnold (one of the

Seversky P-35 first appeared in 1936, and was the first U.S. Air Corps fighter fitted with retractable landing gear. The P-35A, delivered to the Air Corps in 1941, was powered with Pratt & Whitney Twin Wasp engine of 1,200 hp, which gave it a top speed of 310 mph. Armament was two .50 caliber and two .30 caliber fixed machine guns. About 50 P-35A's saw combat in the Philippines at the beginning of WW-II. (Photo courtesy USAF)

Army's first aviators) of an earlier lawmaker who snorted, "The Army already *has* an airplane," when similarly petitioned in 1909.

The Navy's air arm was in no better shape than the Army's in 1939. The Navy and Marine Corps could count a total of 2,100 airplanes with 1,300 classified as combat types, but almost none were modern, first-line fighting planes.

The picture had been worse. Just six years before, when, on January 30, 1933, Adolf Hitler took office as Chancellor of Germany following a reign of terror by his Brownshirts similar to that of young American Ultra-lefters in the late sixties, the United States had

a total of 1,752 military airplanes (England had 838 in 1933; France, 1,687; Japan, 1,384; Russia, 1,500. Germany supposedly had none, since the 1919 Treaty of Versailles forbid the building of military aircraft by the Germans). But Hitler's excesses slowly (too slowly) alarmed American leaders—his proclamation of an Aryan "super race," his insane persecution of Germany's Jews, his quick and awesome military build-up and his external aggressions, beginning with occupation of the Rhineland in 1936, Austria early in 1938, and then his September, 1938 demand for the Sudetenland (part of Czechoslovakia), which led to the meeting in Munich where Britain's Prime Minister

Neville Chamberlain, with French approval, appeased the Nazi dictator and sacrificed Czechoslovakia in exchange for "peace in our time." This, and more, convinced President Roosevelt that the Nazis would never stop until they were stopped; and since Britain and France seemed to present an uncertain line of defense, it was high time the United States shored-up her own leaky defenses.

This led to an historic meeting at the White House, September 28, 1938 (actually, while Chamberlain was still "negotiating" with Hitler over Czechoslovakia), attended by cabinet members and top military people including General Arnold, during which President Roosevelt announced, to everyone's surprise, that he wanted an annual production goal of 10,000 airplanes and a capacity for twice that number.

Now, just what changed Roosevelt's mind about the efficacy of air power isn't readily apparent (when Billy Mitchell challenged the Navy to let him prove airplanes could sink capital ships in 1921, Roosevelt, then Assistant Secretary of the Navy, had said, "It is highly unlikely that an airplane, or a fleet of them, could ever sink a fleet of Navy vessels under battle conditions." Later, following Mitchell's demonstrations, Roosevelt was asked by a reporter if he'd changed his mind and Roosevelt said, "I once saw a man kill a lion with a 30-30 rifle . . . but that does not mean a 30-30 is a lion gun"). And perhaps the President had not, at least at that point, modified his beliefs as much as some aviation writers have thought, because, although he did approve Arnold's request for 10,000 airplanes, that proposed air fleet was intended for the defense of the entire Western Hemisphere. The strategic bomber force Arnold wanted was not approved at that time—while the Navy soon got a go-ahead for no less than 34 new battleships and battle cruisers (this program was modified after war began and the aircraft carrier's importance recognized). Therefore, while Roosevelt should be credited with a vague recognition of the need for many more military airplanes, he had not, on the eve of WW-II, suddenly embraced Billy Mitchell's dogma.

However, less than two years later, in the summer of 1940, Roosevelt would up his demand to 50,000 planes per year from American factories as his Secretary of War Henry L. Stimson was noting that "Air power has decided the fate of nations . . . " By that time Poland was gone; Norway, Denmark, Belgium and the Netherlands had fallen to the Nazi conqueror; France was defeated, and the British stood alone—

somehow, both magnificent and pathetic in their awful peril: "We shall go on to the end . . . we shall fight in the seas . . . we shall fight in the air; we shall defend our Island . . . we shall fight on the beaches . . . on the landing grounds . . . in the fields and in the streets, we shall fight in the hills; we shall never surrender . . . " Fortunately for America, they meant every word of it.

The Battle of Britain was won by a fighter airplane force which, at the beginning, consisted of 620 machines (*Hurricanes* and *Spitfires*), and 1,434 pilots. Arrayed against these "few to whom so many owed so much" was a *Luftwaffe* force of 2,618 combat aircraft including 878 Messerschmitt Me-109 single-engine fighters and 220 Me-110 twin-engined fighters.* The balance was made up of twin-engined bombers—mostly Junkers Ju-88A-1's and Heinkel He-111H-3's—and a few reconnaissance craft.

This critical aerial showdown between 3 *Luftflotten* (Air Fleets) of Reichsmarschall Hermann Goering's *Luftwaffe,* and Sir Hugh Dowding's 46 squadrons of the Royal Air Force's Fighter Command, followed the desperate evacuation of British troops from the Continent at Dunkirk (May 30-June 4) and the subsequent fall of France (June 22) by sufficient margin to allow the British time for some build-up of their fighter force or the outcome may well have been different. When the Dunkirk evacuation ended on June 4, 1940, Fighter Command had only 331 *Hurricanes* and *Spitfires.* By August 11th, the eve of "Eagle Day" when the *Luftwaffe* launched its daylight air offensive, this force had been increased to 620 *Hurricanes* and *Spitfires* and production had reached a monthly total of 250 such machines.

Obviously, Hitler should not have given the RAF this breathing spell; but his plan for invading Britain ("Operation Sea Lion") was poorly coordinated and only half-heartedly conceived, because *der Fuehrer* was so certain the English would come to terms after France fell that he was neither prepared to immediately follow-up and press his advantage, nor convinced that it was necessary. Then, once the Nazi leader decided to go ahead with the invasion (against the ad-

* Willy Messerschmitt, designer of these craft, served as design chief for *Bayerisch-fleugzeugwerke* which built them, therefore some writers today identify these planes (correctly) as the Bf 109 and Bf 110. Your authors stick with the "Me-" prefix simply because Allied pilots who fought the Luftwaffe in WW-II so identified this pair of enemy fighters. So, while we may be in a sense technically wrong, we are, more importantly we think, historically right.

The Messerschmitt Me-109 first appeared in 1935. First service model was the Me-109B of 1937, which was powered with a Jumo engine of 900-hp and had a top speed of 295 mph. Among later variants was the Me-109K, fitted with the Daimler-Benz engine of 1,800-hp and possessing a top speed of 450 mph. Armament varied widely, though a typical installation was a 20-mm cannon fired through the prop spinner plus four 7.9-mm machine guns, a synchronized pair in the nose and another pair in the wings. (Photo courtesy USAF)

vice of his best generals), the preliminary air assault against Britain was so badly directed—and later at a crucial stage "re-misdirected" just when it could have, despite much wasted effort, defeated the RAF—the advantage lay with the greatly outnumbered but superbly directed RAF Fighter Command.

The *Hurricane* and *Spitfire* pilots had other, obvious advantages: usually fighting within gliding distance of a friendly airfield, each was not only effective during the entire period of his fuel supply, but was neither out of action long when re-arming and refueling were necessary, nor lost to England in most cases

when he had to bail-out of a crippled airplane or even crash-land. The Me-109 pilots, on the other hand, had to invest 60 minutes of their 80-minute fuel supply in the round trip to England from their airfields on the Continent, leaving them but 20 minutes effective combat time per sortie; while facing the prospect of capture or a grave in the Channel if their craft were disabled in battle. In the end, however, the greatest advantages the British possessed during the battle of Britain were the enemy's tactical errors.

One of the Germans' worst mistakes was their unintentional "conditioning" of the English populace to

Messerschmitt Me-210 was an interim design between the Me-110G of 1941 and the Me-410 fighter-bomber. Engines were 1,475-hp Daimler-Benz and maximum speed was 349 mph. Follow-on Me-410 of 1943 had more powerful engines and was armed with two 20-mm cannon and two 7.9-mm machine guns in nose, plus two rearward-firing 13-mm machine guns in fuselage blisters. (Photo courtesy USAF)

air bombardment which resulted from weeks of token night raids prior to the concentrated air attacks that followed. When the massive air assault began on their cities, the British, having been gradually introduced to this terror, bore it admirably despite heavy civilian losses.

Also during this period (June and July) the Germans struck hard at coastal convoys in the Channel with their vaunted Junkers Ju-87 *Stuka* dive bombers. Shipping losses were not great, but Fighter Command was kept busy and lost nearly 100 planes while knocking down about twice that number of the enemy. The *Stukas,* however, could not live in the sky with *Hurricanes* and *Spits* without heavy fighter escort and were soon withdrawn.

On July 30, 1940, Hitler ordered Goering to begin the daylight air attack against Britain as soon as possible. Goering set the date as August 2nd, but a spell of bad weather forced postponement of *Adlertag* (Eagle Day) until the 12th. At the beginning, German attacks were aimed at RAF airfields and radar sites, a sound enough tactic, and although the *Luftwaffe* lost two planes to the RAF's one, such an attrition rate favored the Germans in the long run. Goering understood that he had to destroy Fighter Command and gain control of the air as a necessary prerequisite to the invasion, but his principal weaknesses were, 1) wildly inflated estimates of British fighters destroyed and the effect of *Luftwaffe* bombs, and 2) his own quixotic switches in tactics. For ex-

British Supermarine *Spitfire* Mk. VII carried a pair of 20-mm cannons in its wings plus two pair of .303 caliber machine guns. The *Spitfire* series, descended from the Supermarine seaplane racer of 1931, the S.6B, contained more than 40 variants with a variety of wings, Rolls Royce engines of 1,230-hp to 2,375-hp. Latter was the Mark 14 model that was capable of 450 mph. Spit Mark IA, which fought Battle of Britain, was fitted with eight .303 caliber machine guns. (Photo courtesy USAF)

ample, after only three days of pursuing a reasonably sound battle plan, he called off strikes against the RAF's radar sites (an almost indespensable link in Fighter Command's defense system). Then, after correctly identifying and attacking the RAF's Sector Stations (the nerve centers from which fighter operations were directed), Goering again turned away from vital tactical targets and, on September 7, began night saturation bombing of London.

The nighttime bombardment of London and other English cities was a terror tactic that failed to work for the reason mentioned, plus, of course, the unimagined courage of the average Briton. And despite terrible casualties (146,777 civilians killed or seriously wounded throughout the war) and countless buildings and homes reduced to rubble, the bombardment of British cities at that time was a blunder of large significance because it took pressure off the defending

Gun camera of Capt. Alvin M. Juchheim, Grenada, Miss., records his victory over an Fw-190, his second for the day. Sequence is presented top-to-bottom left, then top-to-bottom right as enemy pilot bails out of smoking Focke-Wulf. (Photo courtesy USAF)

A formation of Hawker *Hurricane* II fighters over
England. Power was Rolls Royce *Merlin* XX of 1,460-
hp and top speed was 330 mph at 20,000 ft. This
6,000-lb fighter was armed with 12 .303 caliber wing-
mounted machine guns or four 20-mm cannon (as
above). (Photo courtesy USAF)

German Focke-Wulf Fw-190A is shown after being rebuilt by mechanics of the U.S. 404th Fighter Group following its capture. Engine was BMW 801D twin-row radial of 1,760-hp and top speed was 395 mph at 17,000 ft. Though guns were removed from this example, usual armament consisted of two 7.9-mm machine guns and two 20-mm cannon (mounted in wing roots), synchronized to fire between prop blades, plus two 20-mm cannon outboard in wings. (Photo courtesy USAF)

fighters just at the time when "the scales had tilted against Fighter Command," to quote Prime Minister Churchill—at a time when RAF pilot losses were averaging a disastrous 120 per week—and diverted destruction from vital targets to Britain's civilian populace. Thus given another breathing spell at a crucial moment, the RAF fighter force was able to quickly regain its strength, deny the Germans control of the air over England, and render invasion impossible. Operation Sea Lion was at first postponed by Hitler, and later cancelled altogether.

In retrospect, Goering seems to have made some pretty stupid decisions; but these are mitigated to an extent by several factors. In the first place, between July 10 and October 31, the Germans claimed to have destroyed 3,058 British planes, and if Goering accepted this figure (evidently resulting from over zealous *Luftwaffe* reports, perhaps inflated by German Intelligence and reinflated by the propaganda ministry), then he naturally believed that his airmen had knocked out the RAF. But the truth was, actual RAF plane losses for this period totalled 915, and British fighter production, despite the bombings, had, by the end of October, caught up with and exceeded losses so that Fighter Command could count 850 serviceable *Hurricanes* and *Spitfires* available for action.

Another factor sometimes overlooked in evaluating the German air offensive of 1940 is that no such action had ever been tried before against a nation possessing an effective fighter force. The French Air Force had been equipped with obsolete aircraft and was poorly commanded. Poland had possessed 900 combat airplanes, but most were obsolescent and nearly all had been destroyed on the ground. Not until England was directly attacked did the *Luftwaffe* encounter real opposition in the air.

The relative inefficiency of German bombers, aside from the fact that they expended too little effort against militarily important targets, was owed to the lack of a sophisticated bombsight and small bomb loads. Hitler had no strategic air arm and no suspicion that he needed one. His twin-engined He-111's, Ju-88's and Dornier Do-17's were able to reach England with no more than 2,000 pounds of bombs in each machine.

In short, the German war machine, built around *blitzkrieg,* or "lightning warfare" tactics for the conquest of Europe, tied the *Luftwaffe* to ground operations both in concept and equipment. Until the last minute, Hitler never believed the English would fight. When they did, he had no real plan to defeat them and a military structure unsuited for the task.

But in the Messerschmitt Me-109 the *Luftwaffe* did have an outstanding fighter airplane, as American bomber crews and fighter pilots were to learn later in the war. The Me-109 first appeared in 1935, and was battle-proven with the German Condor Legion that fought in the Spanish Civil War. The first service model, the Me-109B of 1937, was fitted with a Jumo engine of about 900 hp which allowed a top speed of but 295 mph; however, the Me-109E which fought the Battle of Britain had the 1,150-hp Mercedes-Benz fuel-injected powerplant and a maximum speed of 354 mph at 16,000 feet. This craft was armed with a pair of fuselage-mounted synchronized 7.9-mm machine guns plus two wing-mounted 20-mm cannon. The Me-109E-3 variant fired a 20-mm cannon through the nose spinner and carried a 7.9-mm machine gun in each wing in addition to a pair of machine guns above the nose. All 109's were difficult to handle on the ground due to their narrow landing gear treads, and about 5 per cent were lost in ground

accidents. Records indicate that approximately 33,-000 Me-109's were built from 1937 through 1945, making it the most widely produced airplane of all time. Its power and armament were repeatedly increased, and the G Model, which appeared late in 1942 fitted with a 1,475-hp Daimler-Benz, had a top speed of 403 mph. The Me-109K of 1944 had 1,800 hp, could do 450 mph, and was armed with a 30-mm Mk. 108 cannon fired through the prop spinner, plus two 13-mm machine guns.

The Supermarine *Spitfire* Mark I evolved from a series of Schneider Trophy seaplane racers built during the late twenties and early thirties, culminating in the Supermarine S.6B of 1931 which attained a speed of 407 mph. Concurrent with designer R. J. Mitchell's Supermarine racers was development of the Rolls Royce V-12 engines which powered them, therefore the *Spitfire* airframe and Rolls Royce *Merlin* engine attained maturity together, and this combination resulted in one of the best all-around fighter aircraft of WW-II. The prototype *Spitfire* first flew in March, 1936, and though the British were aware of its potential, its all-metal, stressed-skin construction required that new production techniques be mastered. That, plus a stingy Parliament and the "shadow factory" scheme for expanding aircraft production, prevented any real procurement of this superior plane until after WW-II began.

Early production *Spitfires* were powered with the 1,230-hp *Merlin* turning a two-blade, fixed-pitch wooden prop which gave a top speed of 360 mph. But three-bladed constant-speed props were fitted to the *Spit* in time for the Battle of Britain, and this greatly improved climb-rate (to 3,000 fpm at 12,800 ft.) and ceiling (37,600 ft.). Armament was 8 wing-mounted .303-in. Browning machine guns.

In the spring of 1941, the *Spitfire* Mk. V, slightly faster and with a little more power than the Mk. I and II, entered service packing four 20-mm wing-mounted cannon, or two cannon plus four .303 Brownings. But appearance of the faster-rolling, speedier Focke-Wulf Fw-190, and the improved Me-109G, dictated that still more performance be wrung from the *Spit,* so, during 1942 most of Fighter Command was re-equipped with the *Spitfire* Mk. IX, and the 415-mph Mk. IX remained Britain's first-line fighter until war's end. Its power came from a two-stage, two-speed supercharger aiding a *Merlin* engine of 1,650 hp, a combination that would take the Mk. IX to 20,000 feet in less than 5 minutes. The

Bell P-39 *Airacobra* had its 1,150-hp Allison buried in fuselage behind pilot to achieve clean aerodynamic lines for a heavily armored fighter mounting a 37-mm cannon to fire through prop spinner, two .50 caliber nose guns, and a pilot well forward for improved visibility. Wings were fitted with two pairs of .30 caliber machine guns. Best speed of the P-39D was 355 mph at 13,000 ft. P-39Q, with Allison V-1710-85 engine of 1,200 hp, had a top of about 375 mph. Slow climb rate and lack of maneuverability made it unsuitable for air-to-air combat and it served mostly as a ground-attack craft. Russia received 4,773 *Airacobras* from the U.S.—for which the Soviets never paid. (Photo courtesy Bell Aerosystems Company)

ultimate *Spitfire,* produced in limited numbers in 1945, was the Mk. 24. Equipped with a 2,375-hp Rolls Royce *Griffon* mightily twisting a six-bladed, contra-rotating prop, the Mk. 24 was capable of 450 mph and had a service ceiling of 43,000 feet. Armament was four 20-mm wing-mounted cannon plus external rocket stores. Altogether, 21,767 *Spitfires* were built.

The less glamorous 340-mph Hawker *Hurricane* Mk. I saw more action at the beginning of the war than did the *Spitfire,* because the RAF possessed more *Hurricanes.* This craft was of conventional (for that time) construction and fabric covered. Designed by

Sidney Camm, the *Hurricane* first flew in 1937 and came from a distinguished family. The H. G. Hawker Engineering Company, formed in 1920 from the T.O.M. Sopwith Company that produced the famed Sopwith Camel of WW-I, produced several good biplane fighters during the twenties and early thirties, including the *Hawfinch* and the *Fury.* Family resemblance was marked, and a good deal of *Fury* could be seen in the *Hurricane.* The *Hurricane* Mk. I was powered with the Rolls Royce Merlin of 1,030 hp. In mid-1943, the armored Mk. IV *Hurricane* went into service fitted with the 1,650-hp *Merlin,* and this version was used as a ground-attack fighter-bomber.

Looking for trouble in the South Pacific, September 12, 1944, is flight of five Chance Vought F4U-1 *Corsairs*. This rugged 2,000-hp, 415-mph six-gunned fighter first went in service in February 1943. The F4U-4, which followed in the summer of 1945, was fitted with a P&W R-2800-18W of 2,325-hp and could top 425 mph. *Corsair* production totalled 12,681 during WW-II, and several later batches were turned out before production ceased in 1953. It served in the Korean War and with the French in IndoChina during the early 50s. (Photo courtesy U.S. Navy)

Curtiss P-36, powered by both the P&W R-1830 of
1,050-hp and the Wright R-1820 of 1,200-hp, had a
top speed of 300–311 mph. Armament was six .303
caliber machine guns. Markings on the P-36 *Hawk*
establish date of this photo as prior to June 1942,
when red center was removed from star insignia, along
with the red/white/blue rudder stripes, on U.S. military planes. Between that time and July 1943, insignia
was a white star on blue circle as on the P-40 and
F4F in accompanying photos. After July 1943, white
rectangular bars were added as on the F4U's in following picture. Finally, in January 1947, a red bar was
added to center of each rectangle and is used today.
(Photo courtesy Donovan Berlin)

Top speed was cut to 294 mph because of a wing festooned with a variety of fittings to accommodate a seemingly endless mix of ordnance. A typical warload was a pair of .303 Brownings and eight 60-lb rockets; or a couple of 40-mm cannon plus a bomb cluster. Total *Hurricane* production was 14,231, of which 1,451 were Canadian-built.

American fighters going into production in 1940 were the Grumman F4F *Wildcat* for the Navy, and the Curtiss-Wright P-40 *Tomahawk* for the Army Air Forces. Other American fighter designs were nearing production status at that time such as the Bell P-39 *Airacobra* (which later proved disappointing), and the Lockheed P-38 *Lightning* (designed in 1936-37, with prototype flight in 1939, it did not go into service until 1942 because of technical troubles). The Republic P-47 *Thunderbolt,* evolved from the 1935 Seversky P-35 via the Republic P-43 *Lancer* of 1939, entered service in 1943—as did the Navy's famed Chance Vought F4U *Corsair.*

The Curtiss-Wright P-40 was a development of the P-36 *Hawk* of 1935 designed by Donovan Berlin. Berlin had served his aeronautical internship at the Army's design and test center, McCook Field, Ohio, from 1921 to 1926. Then, after three years with Donald Douglas, and five years with Northrop (where he was principally responsible for the historically significant Northrop *Alpha and Gamma*), Berlin joined Curtiss-Wright in 1934 as chief engineer at C-W's Buffalo, New York facility. His first creation there was the P-36.

Curtiss-Wright called it the Model 75—*Hawk* 75 —and at first it lost out to the Seversky P-35 in an Air Corps fighter competition. By late 1936, however, it had been de-bugged, and its ruggedness and maneuverability won an Air Corps order for 210 machines (the largest single airplane order placed by the Army since WW-I). The Army's designation for the craft was P-36. The French bought it, too, and it therefore became the first American-built fighter to see action in WW-II when, on September 8, 1939, *Hawk* 75's of *Escadrille* 11/4 shot down the first two Me-109's of the war. Powered by both the Pratt & Whitney R-1830 of 1,050 hp, and the Wright R-1820 of 1,200 hp, the *Hawk* 75/P-36A (*Mohawk* in RAF service) had a top speed of 300-311 mph. More than 800 were built.

In May, 1938, Berlin adapted an Allison V-1710 liquid-cooled engine of 1,150-hp to the P-36 airframe and the happy result was designated the P-40

Tomahawk. The Allison Engineering Company of Indianapolis was formed in the mid-twenties to convert WW-I surplus Liberty V-type (12 cylinder) engines from upright to inverted configuration for use in the Loening Amphibian. Allison became a division of General Motors in 1930, and its own 12-cylinder V-type engine—perhaps inspired by the Rolls Royce engines in the Supermarine racers—was developed by 1937.

The Allison-powered P-40 was superior in all respects to the P-36. It was immediately produced in quantity for the U.S. Army Air Corps, the British and, ultimately, almost every Allied nation. Early production models were the P-40B and C which equipped Chennault's Flying Tigers and were America's standard first-line fighters when the U.S. entered WW-II. Maximum speed of the P-40C was 331 mph. Early armament consisted of four wing-mounted .30 caliber machine guns plus a pair of synchronized .50 caliber guns atop the nose; but this was soon changed to six "fifties." In 1941, the P-40F *Warhawk* (*Kittyhawk* in RAF uniform) appeared with a lengthened fuselage for improved maneuverability, and fitted with a Packard-built Rolls Royce *Merlin* of 1,240 hp which upped top speed to 360 mph. About 2,300 P-40F's were built. Finally, this durable fighter was refined through the K and L models into the P-40N *Warhawk* which was delivered in 1943-44 powered with the Allison V-1710-81 of 1,200 hp. Top speed of the N Model was down to 343 mph, but automatic engine boost and a constant-speed propeller significantly improved performance above 15,000 feet. P-40's served on all fronts throughout the war, and about 13,000 were built, including a number for the Soviets (total U.S. plane deliveries to Russia from June, 1941 to September, 1945, were approximately 15,000 units, largely P-40's, P-39's and A-20's).

The U.S. Navy's F4F *Wildcat* evolved from a prototype conceived in July, 1936, by the Grumman Aircraft Engineering Corporation and was first flown September 2, 1937, at the company's Bethpage, L.I. plant. The Grumman company had been founded in 1929 by Leroy R. Grumman and five associates and their first products were floats and hulls for amphibious aircraft. Leroy Grumman had previously served as general manager for the Loening Aeronautical Engineering Corp. By 1937, Grumman biplane fighters, with wheels retracting into their fuselages, were standard throughout the U.S. Fleet; but when the upstart Brewster Company won a Navy competition for

The 1940 Curtiss-Wright P-40B and C model *Tomahawk* was powered with the Allison V-1710 of 1,150-hp, giving it a speed of 331 mph. The P-40F *Warhawk* followed in 1941, fitted with the Packard-built Rolls Royce *Merlin* of 1,240-hp that upped speed to 360 mph. The P-40 series, developed from the P-36 *Hawk,* served on all fronts throughout the war. About 13,000 were built, many going to Russia. (Photo courtesy Donovan Berlin)

a new fighter with its mid-wing F2A *Buffalo,* Grumman dropped its biplane approach and the first of 7,906 *Wildcats* reestablished Grumman as the Navy's fighter-airplane maker (this love affair was rekindled in 1969 when Grumman was selected to build the F-14A, a Navy air superiority fighter of the seventies).

The WW-II *Wildcat* was produced in more than twenty versions, but the bulk of them were F4F-4's—powered with the P&W R-1830-76 of 1,200 hp; top speed, 318 mph—and the FM-2 built by General Motors, powered with a Wright R-1820 series engine of 1,350 hp giving it a speed of 321 mph. In British service the *Wildcat* was known as the *Martlet.* All variants of the *Wildcat,* whether made by Grumman or GM, were so alike in general appearance that only the practiced eye could tell one from the other. The FM-2, for example, had a slightly taller rudder. Armament was six .50 caliber wing-mounted machine guns. In September, 1943, the tough little *Wildcats,* having carried the Navy's fighter burden during the darkest days of the Pacific War, began their phase-out as the mean and powerful Grumman F6F *Hellcat* arrived eager for battle.

The *Wildcat's* (and *Hellcat's*) principal adversary in the Pacific was Japan's Mitsubishi A6M2 and A6M3 Type "O" Fighter, the *Zero-sen,* called simply the *Zero* by Americans, or the *Zeke,* its official U.S. code name. This nimble craft, designed by Jiro

Horikoshi, came as a shock to American fighter pilots in the days immediately following Pearl Harbor. At that time, Americans were amazingly ignorant of all things Japanese, assumed that Japanese planes were poor copies of older U.S. craft, with engines made of inferior metals, and were piloted by near-sighted fellows with gold teeth, little training and less courage. We were wrong on all counts. The *Zero* was an excellent machine, and a distinctly original design. Like all airplanes, then and now, it represented a compromise. In order to achieve oustanding maneuverability, high speed, rapid climb and the ability to carry a

The principal U.S. Navy and Marine fighter during the early, critical months of WW-II was the Grumman F4F *Wildcat*. Early versions (F4F-3) had nonfolding wings, four guns, and the 1,200-hp Wright *Cyclone* engine. Follow-on F4F-4 built by Grumman and the FM-2 built by General Motors (*Martlet* II in British service) used both the 1,200-hp P&W *Twin Wasp* and 1,350-hp Wright. They had folding wings for efficient carrier handling and six .50 caliber machine guns. Maximum speed was about 320 mph at 21,000 feet. *Wildcat* that is pictured was on Henderson Field, February 9, 1943. Several different pilots had contributed to the 19 victory symbols pointed to by Marine crew chief T/Sgt. R. W. Greenwood. (Photo courtesy U.S. Navy)

The clipped-wing Japanese *Zero* (Mitsubishi A6M3 Type O, Model 32) was given the U.S. code name, *Zeke* 22, but was also called the "Hamp" when it first appeared late in 1942 because U.S. pilots thought it was an all-new design. Actually, it was a *Zeke,* or *Zero-sen,* with a bigger engine and beefed-up airframe. Its 1,130-hp Nakajima supercharged powerplant gave it a maximum speed of 336 mph. Armament was a pair of 20-mm wing cannons and a pair of 7.7-mm nose-mounted machine guns. (Photo courtesy USAF)

heavy fuel load for long-range flying, it sacrificed armor, a heavy structure and self-sealing gasoline tanks. Compared to ruggedly built (and heavy) U.S. fighters, the *Zero* was a fragile airplane; but it could fly circles around a *Wildcat* or *Tomahawk,* and American pilots soon learned to follow a few simple rules when dealing with a formation of *Zeros:* Get above them; build-up airspeed in a dive; strike fast, and don't hang around to tangle with them on their terms.

The *Zero-sen* was ordered by the Japanese Navy in 1937 and first saw action over China early in 1940. The first production models were equipped with the Nakajima *Sakae-12* engine of 950 hp, a twin-row, 14-cylinder radial. Top speed was 316 mph, and its armament consisted of two 7.7-mm machine guns synchronized to fire through the prop plus a pair of wing-mounted 20-mm cannon. The *Zero-sen* A6M3 (U.S. code, *Zeke 22*) which appeared late in 1942 was fitted with the Nakajima NK1F *Zakae-21* supercharged engine of 1,130 hp that gave it a top speed of 336 mph and a climb-rate of 4,500 feet per minute. The *Zero-sen* A6M5 (*Zeke* 52) of 1943 was powered with an up-rated *Sakae* engine of 1,320 hp which allowed a maximum speed of 358 mph at 22,000 feet, and this model carried a pair of 12.7-mm machine guns in the nose along with a 20-mm cannon in each wing. *Zeros* in Japanese Army service were sometimes differently armed; and *Zeros* used for *kamikaze* (suicide) missions may have possessed other gun installations. A total of 10,936 *Zeros* were built.

So, these were some of WW-II's fighter planes, Death's handsomest machines; and though their very reason for existence condemns Man who conceived them, so does their intricate beauty recommend him.

A U. S. Air Force fighter pilot returned to base in Southwest Pacific on 10 September, 1943 with this film in his gun camera, revealing three firing passes at a Japanese *Zero* during a dogfight that ended in flaming defeat for the enemy. Frame at upper left, obviously the initial attack, caught enemy before he jettisoned belly tank. (Photo courtesy USAF)

The Japanese Army fighter, Kawasaki Ki-61 Type 3, was code-named *Tony*. Its 1,175-hp inverted V engine, copied from the German Daimler-Benz DB601A, was never fully de-bugged and penalized an otherwise good design. Top speed was 348 mph and armament consisted of two 12.7-mm nose-mounted machine guns and two 20-mm wing cannon. (Photo courtesy USAF)

Soviet Yakovlev Yak-1 fighter appeared in 1940 and was fitted with a 1,100-hp V-type liquid-cooled engine. Maximum speed was 330 mph. Yak's construction of wood/metal/fabric mix was similar to British *Hurricane*. B-17's in background were flown to Russian airfield on a "shuttle bombing" mission. (Photo courtesy USAF)

2. Pay with Courage

USAF Major (ret.) Alfred Fernandez and his wife Lillian share an unusual distinction. Although separated by almost 5,000 miles of Pacific Ocean, both came under enemy fire on the day Japan launched its surprise attack and plunged the United States into World War II. Ten hours after Lillian stood calmly outside their shot-up quarters at Hickam Field, Hawaii, and aimed her home movie camera at strafing planes ("because I really didn't have anyplace to hide, and I thought pictures might help our intelligence people"), husband Al was diving for a slit trench on Clark Field in the Philippines to escape other Japanese strafers that had just shot the heel off his shoe.

Fernandez was a master sergeant at the time, and a crew chief on a B-17 *Flying Fortress.* "I left Hawaii during the second week in September, 1941," he recalls. "Our airplane was one of a flight of nine B-17D's which made up the 14th Squadron of the 19th Bombardment Group. Our C.O. was Major Emmett "Rosie" O'Donnell. We arrived at Clark Field, near Manila, on the 12th. I left Lillian behind in Hawaii because we had good quarters there; she had a job in the PX at Hickam Field, and I wasn't too sure what the situation would be in the Philippines.

"As it turned out, things didn't look very encouraging. Our nine *Fortresses* were sent to Del Monte, a primitive airstrip on the big Philippine Island of Mindanao, and we lived in makeshift quarters about three miles from the field. During the next two and a-half months, while the Far East Air Force (FEAF) was built up to a total strength of thirty-five B-17's, about a hundred P-40's, perhaps fifty P-35's and some old B-18's and B-10's, we flew some reconnaissance missions, dug air raid trenches, particularly at Clark Field, and speculated over the possibility of war with Japan."

The possibility of war with Japan had been long in the making. As early as 1921 America had demanded that Great Britain terminate England's alliance with Japan as Japanese political and trade influence—backed by a growing military might—seemed destined to dominate all Asia. In 1924, General Billy Mitchell predicted that Japan's expansionist policies would eventually result in war with the United States, and that Japanese air power would strike without warning at Pearl Harbor, the Philippines and Alaska (he also accurately pinned down the time of day such an attack would occur). Mitchell, of course, was scoffed at by U.S. military planners. But following the successful Japanese aggressions in China and Manchuria during the thirties, and Japan's 1940 pact with Hitler and Mussolini which pledged Nipponese entry into the European war on the side of Germany and Italy if the United States should enter on the side of Britain, America at last became alarmed.

Then, when Japan rattled her Samurai Sword at France, demanded and got air bases in French Indo-

China (now Vietnam), and followed up with an invasion of Indo-China, the U.S. decided to blow the whistle on Nippon's ambitions in Asia—and wherever else the Japanese military leaders (the real power in Japan) were covetously gazing.

It seemed a prudent move at the time, because Japan's adventures in international affairs—particularly during WW-I when she declared war on Germany only for the purpose of gaining German-held islands in the Pacific—contributed to a firm belief that her rulers were simply opportunists, and that it would be better for all if Japan were rendered an ineffective neutral. Therefore, the United States, along with Britain and Holland, froze all Japanese credits and embargoed all oil shipments to Japan. Possessing no oil of her own, Japan faced strangulation of her armed forces with only an 18-month petroleum supply in reserve.

Had President Roosevelt and his advisers better understood the Japanese character, it's doubtful that he'd have taken such a drastic step. A nation holding the belief that honorable death in battle—even a lost battle—should be chosen above retreat, was unlikely to retreat before economic sanction, however severe. Thus in that sense, the U.S. unwittingly made war with Japan inevitable when all petroleum shipments to that nation were stopped in July, 1941. Nor did the U.S. leave to the Japanese leaders any face-saving way out, because resumption of oil shipments was tied to demands that Japan pull out of Indo-China, and also give up the expensively won land she had taken in China. Regardless of how just these conditions may have been, they were nevertheless impossible for the Japanese at that late date. So, on November 25, 1941, a Japanese Naval strike force left the home islands bound for Hawaii. The decision had been made; war with America was preferable to a humiliating surrender to U.S. pressure. And though much has been made over the fact that Japanese diplomats continued to talk compromise with U.S. Secretary of State Cordell Hull until bombs were falling upon Pearl Harbor, it now appears that the Japanese emissaries were themselves unaware that Japan's prime minister and military boss, General Tojo, had already given the order to attack American bases in Hawaii and the Philippines.

Much, too, has been made over the fact that enemy planes were able to smash Pearl Harbor, Hickam Field, etc., unexpectedly and almost without opposition—as General Mitchell had predicted 15 years

before. Attempting to discover an answer to this, a prodigious Congressional investigation was launched and its findings, which filled 40 volumes, were published in 1946. Additionally, uncounted other "Monday morning quarterbacks" (including your authors) have sifted mountains of material and interviewed many of the men directly involved while seeking to fix final responsibility for Pearl Harbor's nakedness on the eve of WW-II; and two primary facts always emerge: 1) no responsible American leader, including President Roosevelt, believed the Japanese would dare challenge the overwhelming might of the United States, and 2) *if* Japan should choose such a suicidal course, all were agreed she would strike at the Philippines, which were too far from American shores to be effectively defended, then push southward into Java and Sumatra for the oil she so desperately needed. The statements of a couple of those involved will serve to illustrate the U.S. position at the time: Britain's Prime Minister, Winston Churchill, said (*The Second World War, Volume I,* Houghton Mifflin Co., 1948), ". . . . all the great Americans around the President and in his confidence felt as acutely as I did the awful danger that Japan would attack British or Dutch possessions in the Far East and would carefully avoid the United States . . ." And General Hap Arnold said in his memoirs, "Like most officers in the War Department, I was under the impression that, if a Japanese attack occurred, it would be made first against the Philippines and then would be carried down the east coast of Asia to Singapore, to the Islands of Borneo, Java and Sumatra."

In Hawaii, at the time of the disaster, U.S. Army and Navy planes were lined up in neat rows on their airfields which made them easy to guard against sabotage (and highly vulnerable to surprise air attack), because both Lt. Gen. Walter Short, U.S. Commander in Chief of the Hawaiian Department, and Adm. Husband E. Kimmel, Commander in Chief of the Pacific Fleet, were guided in their attitudes by the thinking of the President and the position of the War Department. This pair of officers, who became the American scapegoats for the debacle at Pearl Harbor, were not so much incompetent as they were poorly led. The fact that President Franklin Roosevelt never admitted a mistake is insufficient proof that he never made one.

The Japanese strike force, under Adm. Nagumo, consisted of six aircraft carriers (Japan had a total of 11 at the time) with their supporting battleships and cruisers. Nagumo kept well to the north of Hawaii, screened by fog and the generally poor weather usual in that part of the Pacific at that time of year, and reached a point about 275 miles north of Oahu, Hawaii, early on the morning of December 7, 1941. At 6:00 A.M. Nagumo began launching his planes.

Meanwhile, a couple of American soldiers, Sgt. Joe Lockard and Pvt. George Elliot, were watching the screen of their primitive radar set atop a lonely hill on Oahu's north coast. They were the only two men in American uniform in position to detect the impending attack. And they did not fail in their duty. At 7:02 A.M. Lockard and Elliot accurately noted a large fleet of planes approaching from 136 miles away at an azimuth of zero to ten degrees. They immediately reported the contact to their watch officer in the valley below by field telephone—and that was the end of it. The second lieutenant who took their call apparently decided it not worth reporting, evidently assuming it to be a flight of B-17's due from the mainland.

At 7:55 A.M. the first wave of enemy planes— 183 fighters and light bombers—struck Pearl Harbor, Hickam and Wheeler Fields. By 8:25 the initial attack was over. Then, an hour later, an additional 170 Japanese carrier-based planes smashed the same targets. The last enemy aircraft was gone by 10 A.M. Behind, the battleship *Arizona* had blown up; the *California* and *West Virginia* rested in the mud on the bottom of the harbor; the *Oklahoma* had capsized, and three of the four remaining battleships of America's Pacific Fleet were heavily damaged. Also destroyed were 87 out of 169 Navy planes and 152 out of 230 Army Air Force planes. Twenty-five U.S. fighters managed to get into the air during the attack and 4 were shot down. A total of 2,467 Americans died (2,086 of these Navy officers and men) that Sunday morning, and at least 1,500 were wounded. Cost to the Japanese was 29 planes. America's sole consolation was that none of her aircraft carriers happened to be in Pearl Harbor when the enemy sneak attack occurred.

Lillian Fernandez wasted little time examining the bullet holes in the walls of her quarters. "There were a lot of fires and smoke was everywhere, and fortunately, I suppose, the smoke concealed the terrible extent of the damage. Most of us had to accept what had happened in degrees," she remembers. "I walked to the PX where I worked and found it a shambles. People were looting it. I went inside, to the offices, and got the money and stuffed it in a big shopping bag then carried it back to our quarters and put it under the bed. Then I went to the hospital because I knew they'd need help. I worked there—gosh, *how* I worked—for four days. Later, I remembered the PX money and turned it in. There was about $25,000 in cash in the shopping bag; but it didn't seem very important then. It's hard to describe how people felt; angry and very purposeful, I suppose. We in Hawaii knew America had been badly hurt, and many expected an invasion, but the general attitude was just a hard determination to fight."

In the Philippines, on the other side of the International Date Line, it was Monday, December 8th. And at 3 A.M. Manila time, during the height of the Pearl Harbor attack, Admiral Hart, commanding the small U.S. Asiatic Fleet, intercepted a message from a Honolulu commercial radio station telling of the disaster. Without waiting for confirmation from Washington, Admiral Hart immediately warned all friendly forces in his area, including the Manila headquarters of General Douglas MacArthur, who commanded all U.S. air and ground units in the Pacific.

As early as 4 A.M. the 3rd Pursuit Squadron, based at Iba Field, took off in their Curtiss P-40's to check a radar report of unidentified planes in the Manila area. They found nothing; but hours later—at 9:30 A.M.—25 Japanese planes attacked Army installations at Tarlac and Baguio in central Luzon, and Tuguegarao to the northeast. And though several isolated contacts with the enemy were reported during the morning by fighter pilots flying the obsolete Seversky P-35's and Boeing P-26's, when the Japanese at last came over Clark Field in force during the lunch hour —9 hours and 20 minutes after word reached the Philippines of the Pearl Harbor strike—it was the story of Pearl Harbor all over again.

But it need not have been. MacArthur's air commander, General Lewis Brereton, was at MacArthur's headquarters by 5 A.M. seeking permission to mount an air strike against Formosa; but MacArthur (who had sat as a juror at Billy Mitchell's trial—and would later face his own Armageddon for his cavalier attitude toward higher authority) was apparently too busy to see Brereton, and Brereton was told by General Southerland, MacArthur's chief of staff, that U.S. air units must not attack until fired upon. This order may or may not have been changed shortly before noon; statements by those involved do not agree.

However, assuming that MacArthur did fail to act decisively in this matter, it probably did not constitute a major blunder, because, although Formosa was, as Brereton correctly assumed, the Japanese base from which air attacks against the Philippines were about to come, it's doubtful if even the most successful preventative raid against Formosa would have done more than prolong the inevitable, for the truth is, following the blow at Pearl Harbor the United States Government wrote-off the Philippines and made no attempt to send meaningful aid to the 100,000 men of the Philippine Army and approximately 20,000 U.S. soldiers, sailors and airmen there.

The decision to abandon the Philippines, correct

Al and Lillian Fernandez each survived the Japanese air attacks that plunged America into WW-II; Lillian was in Hawaii, her husband in the Philippines. When the Philippines fell, Fernandez took to the hills and fought as a guerrilla leader until U.S. forces returned 859 days later. He was one of the few American airmen in WW-II authorized, by a special order from the adjutant general, to wear the coveted Combat Infantryman's Badge along with his Air Force wings. Lillian calmly filmed attacking enemy planes at Pearl Harbor with her home movie camera in an attempt to aid U.S. intelligence officers. (Photo courtesy Maj. Al Fernandez)

(militarily) though it may have been under the circumstances, was no less a betrayal of those valiant men who, lacking numbers and weapons, paid with courage to serve the cause of freedom against overwhelming odds. Their performance stands in sharp contrast to the quality of their leadership and support from Washington. Future generations of Americans should profit from a study of both examples.

Sgt. Al Fernandez was on the flight line at Clark Field when the enemy formations appeared overhead. "I had come up to Clark from Del Monte with a couple of our B17's that needed camouflage paint. The Japs hit us about 12:20 P.M. Most of the Clark Field planes had been in the air as the result of an earlier air raid warning. (Possibly given by an enemy agent. There was some sabotage and a serious breakdown in our communications and air raid warning systems.) The last B-17 was just landing when the

Captured Japanese photo taken at beginning of attack on Pearl Harbor, December 7, 1941, catches Japanese *Kate* (Nakajima B5N Type 97 carrier attack plane) in climbing turn above "Battleship Row" as torpedo explodes against Battleship *Oklahoma*. (Photo courtesy U.S. Navy)

41

Lt. Gen. Lewis H. Brereton (4th from left, front row) assumed command of the Far East Air Force at Clark Field, Philippines on December 7, 1941, only a few hours before Japanese bombers destroyed a major portion of his air strength. Brereton later went on to other commands during WW-II. He is shown above with pilots of the 88th Observation Sqdn., Henry Post Field, Fort Sill, in 1928. He was Post Field C.O. and a major then. Co-author Christy likes this photo because Sergeant-Pilot Chet F. Colby (extreme left, second row) gave Christy his first airplane ride in an Army Douglas O2-H, July 17, 1928, on Christy's ninth birthday; and because Lt. Joe R. Reed (second from left, front row) firmed-up this author's life-long addiction to aviation when Reed opened nearby Lawton's first airport and pioneered airline service. Reed's son, Joe Jr., flew the Hump as an Air Transport Command pilot during WW-II. Others in this photo, some of whose names you may recognize for their later deeds, are: Front row, left-to-right, Lt. H. K. Baisley, Reed, Lt. C. W. Cousland, Brereton, Lt. T. L. Gilbert, Lt. L. D. Fator, Lt. W. E. Bleakley, and Lt. G. V. Holleman. Back row, left-to-right, Colby, Sgt-Pilot W. S. Rosenberg, Lt. K. P. McNaughton, Lt. J. W. McCauley, Lt. R. J. Dugan, and Lt. H. J. Flatequal. (Authors' photo)

bombs began to fall on us. As enemy fighters came strafing down the row of parked planes, I ran for the nearby slit trenches we had dug and a stream of tracers sort of straddled me. I dove into a trench—minus the heel of my right shoe—and stuck my head up to see two guys go down a few feet away. They were all bloated with explosive bullets in them and their skin looked almost transparent. A chaplain was driving by in a Jeep and I shouted to him to get the hell under cover and he kind of smiled and said God would provide his protection. I cursed and said, 'Sir, God *is* providing a damn' good trench here if you've got sense enough to use it!' He just looked at me and kept going, and when I stuck my head up again I saw he had been blasted out of the Jeep and killed by those explosive bullets. I later found one of those bullets and it was in two halves, with a hollowed-out space in the center. I'm not sure of the size, but I guessed it at .58 or .60 caliber—certainly bigger than our .50 calibers, and it sure tore up anything it hit."

Only three P-40's were able to take off during the raid, and although these craft, piloted by Lts. J. H. Moore, R. B. Keator and E. B. Gilmore, shot down four of the enemy, the attacking force of 88 planes—34 of them *Zero* fighters—succeeded in destroying ten P-40's on the ground along with fifteen out of seventeen B-17's and most of the two dozen miscellaneous aircraft which included B-18's, B-10's, O-52's and O-46's. Clark Field hangars, shops, headquarters building and the oil dump were also bombed.

Twenty minutes after the first wave of enemy planes attacked Clark Field, Iba Field, 40 miles away on the opposite side of the mountains, was completely leveled and all but two of the P-40's stationed there were destroyed. Nichols and Del Carmen Fields were similarly hit early the following morning; and the Navy

Two hours after last enemy plane departed the area, the USS *Shaw* explodes in Pearl Harbor while other fires continue out of control. U.S. casualties were 2,467 dead and more than 1,500 seriously wounded. The attacking Japanese lost 29 planes. (Photo courtesy U.S. Navy)

Part of the defending fighter airplane force in the Philippines when war came was equipped with the Boeing P-26A *Peashooter*. This open cockpit, fixed-gear craft was reasonably advanced in design when it appeared in 1933, but was hopelessly outclassed by Japanese fighters in 1941. *Peashooter*'s top speed was 234 mph and usual armament was a pair of .30-caliber machine guns. (Photo courtesy Hudek Aeronautical Collection)

base at Cavite was wiped out on the 10th as Japanese troops began landing in northern Luzon.

Although American and Filipino pilots of the FEAF continued to oppose the enemy with the planes left to them, the Japanese controlled the air above the Philippines. Meanwhile, Admiral Hart, whose Asiatic Fleet actually consisted of nothing more than three cruisers and a dozen destroyers, took his mini-force southward to escape certain annihilation; and on land the untrained and poorly equipped Philippine Army, along with U.S. troops, grudgingly gave ground to superior enemy forces.

By the 15th of December the FEAF consisted of six B-17's and one B-18 stationed at Del Monte on Mindanao; sixteen P-40's, seven P-35's and five O-52's and O-47's operating from Clark Field and several grass auxiliary strips on Luzon—plus a handful of obsolete P-26's flown by the Philippine Air Force. Then, on December 21, the main Japanese invasion force landed in Lingayen Gulf for its march on Manila and General Brereton sent his remaining B-17's to Australia. Brereton left on the 24th aboard a Navy PBY *Catalina* as General MacArthur and his deputy, Major General Jonathan Wainwright, retreated with their men to the Island of Corregidor in Manila Bay and the Bataan Peninsula which enclosed the Bay on the west. U.S. and Filipino airmen without planes took up rifles and joined their fellow fighting men backed up on Bataan.

The remaining American fighter planes in the

Philippines continued to fight from airstrips on the Bataan Peninsula until the day Bataan fell, April 9, 1942. A solitary P-40 was all that was left by then and it prompted a bitter letter, written by a half-starved crew chief, who had long since forgotten about "Tech Orders" and patched airplanes with whatever was at hand: "Dear President Roosevelt," the letter read. "Please send another P-40 to the Army Air Forces fighting on Bataan. The one we have is full of holes. Thank you."

That letter was never delivered; nor was any mail, to or from the Philippines, after December 8, 1941. And too few of the American fighting men there were delivered from death or capture. One who was spared from the final ordeal on Corregidor was Sgt. Al Fernandez. His skill was needed at Del Monte Airfield on Mindanao, which was still in American hands and used by Australian-based bombers as a refueling stop as they struck—futilely—at the advancing Japanese. Al was put aboard a small coastal steamer which managed to run the gauntlet nearly 500 miles southward to Mindanao. The effort at Del Monte, of course, was at best a holding action, and when the survivors in the caves of Corregidor—out of food, medicine and ammunition—at last surrendered on May 6, 1942, the Philippines belonged to the invader—almost.

"Almost," because the 300 American airmen on Mindanao refused to accept defeat.

"We at Del Monte Airfield heard General Wainright's message on the radio that morning," Fernandez recalls. "He ordered all U.S. military forces in the Philippines to surrender. But we knew he was speaking with a Jap pistol at his head, and we knew he'd expect us to disobey if we could. Well, there I was hundreds of miles from Corregidor, and I had a rifle and thirty-seven rounds of ammo and nine hand grenades and, by God, I just *couldn't* surrender!

"We sat around in little groups and talked about it for a while and all of us, the entire remaining personnel of the 14th Bombardment Squadron, decided we'd fight to the end. We also agreed to split up in order to keep the enemy from perhaps getting us all in a single action. I paired off with Sgt. McIntyre who, like me, had almost twenty years' service in the Air Corps. Then, we stuffed our pockets with what food we could carry and walked into the mountains.

"Before we'd gone five miles I was willing to admit that a pair of aging Air Corps sergeants (I was nearly 40 years old) wasn't exactly ideal guerilla material; we had to flop down and rest. We slept that night among the trees and it rained and I was cold and stiff. Worse, I was sick with worry over Lillian because there had been no mail into the Philippines since the first Jap attack, and I didn't know whether my wife was alive or dead—just radio reports that said Pearl and Hickam were hit and there were casualties. But I did know if she had survived, and had faith that I too was alive, and if we were to ever see one another again, I'd have to stay right there in the mountains of Mindanao and kill Japs; I'd have to fight and hide and somehow outwit the enemy until, one day, Americans would return to the Philippines."

And that's what Al Fernandez did. Within days he organized a guerilla force of more than 200 Filipino patriots, and then, for an incredible 859 days, this tiny band fought the invader to a stand-down in northern Mindanao. We'll return to Al in a later chapter for the happy and heroic conclusion of his odyssey.

Although slowed by the stubborn defense of the Philippines, Japanese forces meanwhile had claimed other rich prizes: Singapore and Hong Kong; Malaya, the Dutch East Indies, Borneo, the Andamans and Burma. All were relatively easy conquests with no effective air defenses. And Allied sea power suffered another blow when Britain's proudest battleship, the *Prince of Wales,* along with the heavy cruiser *Repulse,* was caught in the Gulf of Siam without air cover and sunk by Japanese land-based torpedo planes.

Japan had, after five months of fighting and at ridiculously low cost, achieved all her objectives and occupied territory that guaranteed all the oil, rubber and other strategic materials she formerly lacked. She had never intended to fight a war to the finish with the United States. Instead, as in 1895 and 1905 when she gained her ends without defeating either China or Russia, Nippon expected to fight a quick, limited war, taking what she wanted and then standing firm behind a strong defensive perimeter in a war of attrition that her enemies would find too costly to sustain and therefore would end with a negotiated peace—and with Japan in possession of all her booty. She had never seriously considered invading the U.S. Mainland or even Hawaii. Her plan was to quickly neutralize the U.S. Navy and American air power in the Pacific and, with this temporary advantage, grab the riches she coveted along with a string of protective bases to encircle that vast domain from the Indian Ocean and Coral Sea across the Pacific to the Bering Sea. After that, Japan reasoned, the U.S. and Britain, with a major war to fight in Europe (Germany and Italy declared war on the U.S. December 11, 1941, four days after the initial Japanese attack), should recognize the awful cost of pursuing a concurrent war with Japan and seek a negotiated settlement.

But if Roosevelt and his advisers had failed to properly judge the mood of the Japanese, then Japan's General Hideki Tojo and his advisers certainly compounded the felony, because the Japanese sneak attack on Pearl Harbor united the American People in a national anger and determination to fight as no act or exhortation by America's own leaders could have done. After Pearl Harbor, almost no one in America believed (or would openly say) that the United States should settle for anything less than the unconditional surrender of the Imperial Japanese Government; and no U.S. leader ever considered any alternative.

The Douglas B-18 *Bolo* bomber was adapted from the DC-2/DC-3 (C-33/C-47), and 133 entered service with the Army Air Corps beginning in October 1937. Although the early B-17 was flying by that time, Congress preferred a bargain-basement bomber. The B-18 was superior to the 1933 Martin B-10 that it replaced only in range, and the 20 or so B-18's stationed in the Philippines when war came were relatively useless. (Photo courtesy Joe R. Reed Collection)

Anything that could be made flyable was used by
U.S. and Filipino pilots during the early months of
1942 in the Philippines. Men of the 20th Pursuit
Sqdn., having lost most of their P-40's, raised an old
Grumman J2F *Duck* from the harbor at Mariveles
and used it for courier, evacuation, and supply. As
many as nine men were transported at a time in the
2-place *Duck,* though it would not rise above 150 ft.
altitude with such a load. Among those evacuated
from Bataan by *Duck* as the end neared was Carlos
Romulo. (Photo courtesy Grumman Aircraft Engineering Co.)

Japanese "Betty" bomber, Mitsubishi G4M Type 1,
land-based, was principal bomber used against the
Philippines by the enemy. *Betty* was powered with a
pair of 1,850-hp kasei-21 engines, had a top speed
of 270 mph, and by sacrificing self-sealing fuel tanks
and armor plate could carry 2,200 lbs of bombs to
a target 1,000 miles away and return. She did, however, burn easily when hit by Allied fighters. (Photo
courtesy USAF)

When Japan attacked the Philippines about ten hours after the strike at Pearl Harbor (December 8th in the Philippines), the Far East Air Force consisted of 35 B-17's, about 100 P-40's, 50 P-35's, and roughly 80 miscellaneous aircraft, mostly obsolete or at least unsuited to the defensive and makeshift tactics necessary because of enemy air superiority. The Curtiss-Wright O-52 *Owl* observation plane was another of those stationed at Clark Field that was of small value in defending the Islands. (Photo Courtesy Curtiss-Wright Corp.)

The Japanese Nakajima JiMi-S Type 2 was a recon and night fighter. Its 1,130-hp Sakae engines gave it a speed of 315 mph, and its four 20-mm fixed cannons, two firing upwards at an angle of 30 degrees and two firing downwards at a similar angle, made it effective against U.S. night bombing raids in the Southwest Pacific. (Photo courtesy USAF)

3. Welcome the Storm

In March, 1942, while remnants of MacArthur's forces were preparing for their final stand on Bataan and Corregidor, Army Air Force Colonel Caleb V. Haynes was given command of an aerial task force with the code name of *Aquila,* at Patterson Air Depot, Dayton, Ohio. Task Force *Aquila* consisted of thirteen B-17E's, a supporting C-47, the commander's B-24 *Liberator,* and personnel to man and maintain these craft hand-picked by Haynes. Their highly secret mission was to bomb Tokyo from a base in China as a follow-up to a similar mission by sixteen B-25's led by Colonel Jimmy Doolittle, who intended to hit Tokyo from the aircraft carrier *Hornet.* Haynes' force would stage out of McDill Field, Florida, to Brazil then across the South Atlantic to India, Burma and China. But on April 19, after the B-17's had gone as far as Karachi, the plan to hit Tokyo a second time was scrubbed (Doolittle's planes had bombed Tokyo just the day before), and Haynes' thirteen bombers were diverted to General Lewis Brereton's 10th Air Force, then being formed in India.

Caleb Haynes was ordered to Dinjan, in the Assam Valley close to India's northeastern border with Burma, to organize the Assam-Burma-China Ferrying Command, an airlift operation that would supply fuel and ammunition to Colonel Claire Chennault's Flying Tigers in China. Haynes was given two C-47's for the job, and promised eleven more. His pilots were a mixed group of Army Air Force flyers and Pan American Airways personnel. These were the first

"Hump" pilots; the forerunners of a legendary breed who would fly the awesome Himalayas in ever-increasing numbers, carrying ever more cargo, to support not only the Flying Tigers but the USAAF 23rd Fighter Group, which grew from the Tigers, as well as Chinese forces fighting under Generalissimo Chiang Kai-shek. The end result was to keep China in the war on the Allied side and thus tie down many thousands of Japanese, both soldiers and airmen, when the enemy was already over extended.

The men who flew the Hump were, of course, mostly unaware of the strategic importance of their mission. They were often cynical, and lacking in appreciation for the necessity of delivering—at the risk of their lives—say, a grand piano to Madame Chiang Kai-shek, or five tons of beer to their Chinese comrades in arms, when medicine and ammunition and gasoline were needed to sustain forces attempting to slow the Japanese advance across China or pouring into Burma and Thailand. Colonel Robert L. Scott once circumvented what seemed to him a ridiculous priority system and simply flew a few miles from his base in India, asked his crew to open the cabin door, then shoved out his cargo of office equipment. He returned to base, surreptitiously loaded his transport with gasoline drums and .50 caliber ammunition, then delivered it over the Himalayas to a Flying Tiger airstrip.

The Tigers were grateful. So grateful they loaned Scott one of their shark-mouthed P-40's so he could

Generalissimo Chiang Kai-shek and Major General Claire Chennault after Chennault's Flying Tigers were "de-activated" and tough old Papa Tiger was returned to duty with the U.S. Army Air Forces. (Photo courtesy USAF)

do a little hunting between trips over the Hump (later, when the AVG was disbanded and re-formed as the 23rd Fighter Group of the USAAF, Colonel Robert Scott became its first commander).

The original Tigers—officially the American Volunteer Group (AVG)—are hard to accurately describe. In a sense they were mercenaries: American civilians flying Chinese Air Force planes for pay. However, $600 per month wouldn't exactly buy a ticket to Richville, even at 1941 prices, so money alone could not have been the main lure. They were a poorly disciplined lot, given to cowboy attire, complete with pistol belt and beard. To them, danger was a desirable wench to be courted with contempt, and

their arrogance was exceeded only by their ability. But some of them who survived, and eventually grew older and no longer felt the need for a protective shell of bravado, long afterward admitted that they had joined the AVG as a matter of principle: to fight for what they believed in. Anyway, mercenaries, adventurers, patriots, whatever, Claire Chennault's Flying Tigers were supreme in their profession, as deadly a bunch of fighter pilots as was ever assembled.

Actually, the AVG had roots going back to 1937, when Chennault, who was then an Army Air Corps captain, was retired after twenty years' service because of impaired hearing. The legend persists that what the Army really meant by "impaired hearing" was Chen-

This mad-looking P-40 Warhawk likely begrudged the excitement surrounding the arrival of the new P-51 Mustangs in the CBI Theater. After all, P-40s cut the grass of both our defense and offense all alone early in the war. That really is Mustang wing in the Tiger Shark's teeth. They collided on the ground during a "jin-bao" (air raid) and the Mustang came out second-best. The Warhawk was not injured.

51

nault's deafness to warnings from his superiors to halt his campaign for a strong air force and, particularly, stop preaching his "radical" theories on fighter airplane tactics. Whatever the cause, the Army did put Chennault out to pasture. But at midnight on the day of his retirement he left Maxwell Field, Alabama, for China, having accepted an offer from Chiang Kai-shek to re-organize and lead the Chinese Air Force.

This P-40, flown by the American Volunteer Group (A.V.G.), the Flying Tigers in the China-Burma-India theater, clearly shows the original identification of shark's teeth in a blood-red mouth and the Chinese Republic's Bengal Tiger on the fuselage. Just aft of the "Flying Tiger" can still be seen the painted-out British roundel. This group of volunteers, under General Claire Chennault, first flew Tomahawks (the P-40 model with export designation Hawk 81 turned down by the purchaser, the RAF) and later the slightly faster P-40E's with 6 wing guns and provisions for a bomb underneath. The Tigers improvised a home-made bomb rack under their Tomahawks. In only a few days over 6 months, the Flying Tigers were credited with 286 confirmed downed Japanese planes and 300 more probables. Except for the Midway campaign, the Flying Tigers were the only successful fighters for America early in the War.

The original supply lines across the Himalaya Mountains, Able and Baker routes, called for an instrument minimum of 19,000 feet. Sleet, hail, violent turbulence —often with winds of 100 mph or more—"The Rock Pile" was vicious flying at best. On a rare clear day like this, C-46 pilots could only pray the Japanese didn't add to the problems. There was no place to hide when flying an unarmed transport. (Photo Downie and Associates)

By 1941, Colonel Chennault of the Chinese Air Force had a weird sort of staff (apparently not altogether his own choices), a mass of intelligence data on the Japanese Air Force, plus sound plans for effectively opposing that force. He had also learned from bitter experience that he couldn't mold a top combat air unit out of the motley collection of international adventurers that showed up in China looking for jobs. What he needed was a group of experienced professional pilots to start with, then he'd teach them

the tactics that would make them masters of the air in that part of the world. With the Generalissimo's blessing—and $8,900,000 with which to buy fighter planes—Chennault returned to the United States.

His return was well timed. The Japanese had invaded Indo-China the previous September (1940); had signed a tripartite pact with Germany and Italy; were pushing ever southward and westward into China; and Chennault was ready to offer significant resistance to Japan's series of conquests if he could only get planes and men. Aided by Secretary of Treasury Henry Morgenthau, Chennault got what he wanted: one hundred P-40 *Tomahawks,* and permission from President Roosevelt to recruit at U.S. military airfields.

Chennault gathered 100 pilots and 200 ground crewmen from the Navy, Marines, Army and civilian operations. They were hired as employees of the "Central Aircraft Manufacturing Company," and secretly furloughed (in the case of military personnel) for an indefinite period without loss of rank or longevity. Then, disguised as missionaries, doctors, and engineers they left San Francisco early in July, 1941, and traveled by ship, more or less in secrecy, to Rangoon, Burma.

Their planes were waiting, and they were immediately shuttled to a steamy grass strip—an abandoned RAF base—at Kyedaw, 70 miles north of Rangoon, to learn fighter tactics *á la* Chennault. Papa Tiger decided they were ready for combat by late November. He divided his 65 remaining airplanes (the rest had been lost in training accidents, along with 2 pilots) into three squadrons which he constantly moved among half-a-dozen airfields thus leaving the enemy to guess at his true strength and where it would be concentrated at any given time. The two main bases were Rangoon, theoretically defended by the British with some U.S.-built Brewster *Buffalos,* possibly the most inadequate fighter plane of the war, and Kunming, in Yunnan Province of southwest China where

Ramp at an ATC base near Calcutta. C-46 *Commandos* foreground, Douglas C-47's in background. Original AF name for the C-47 was *Skytrain,* but no one in uniform ever called it that. It was most often called *Gooney Bird* during WW-II. (Photo courtesy Don Downie)

A C-47 that didn't make it over the Hump. The Air Transport Command (ATC) or "Assam Trucking Company," as it was called by the crews in India and China, lost 328 aircraft, 910 crew members, and 131 passengers to the "Rock Pile." (Photo courtesy Don Downie)

Chiang's forces were slowly being backed against the Himalayas by advancing Japanese.

Although many people today believe the Tigers fought prior to America's entry into the war, such is not the case. Their first action came on December 20, 1941, when ten unsuspecting enemy bombers attempted to hit "defenseless" Kunming, the eastern terminus of the Burma Road. The Tigers, warned by their mysterious coolie network—which apparently depended upon mental telepathy since they possessed no electronic devices—were waiting, and shot down six of the intruders, listing the remaining four as "probables."

Three days later the enemy struck at Rangoon with 68 bombers and protective fighters. The AVG got ten of them but lost two of their own. Then, on Christmas

Day, the Japanese came again, this time with 108 planes. The Tigers had a turkey shoot that day, downing 25 of the enemy and losing none of their own.

During the next six months, the AVG not only fought the Japanese in the air, where the odds averaged from 5-to-1 to 20-to-1 against them, but bombed and strafed troops, truck convoys—even enemy warships. From December 20, 1941, until the AVG was officially disbanded and the USAAF 23rd Fighter Group born in its place on July 4, 1942, the Tigers were credited with 286 confirmed victories and 300 probables. Twelve Tigers were lost in combat. At no time did Chennault have more than 55 airworthy airplanes. Your authors can add nothing that will describe the Flying Tigers as eloquently as do these simple figures.

Consolidated C-87, a converted B-24 *Liberator* bomber, also was put to work hauling vital cargo over the Hump. This one is approaching for a landing at Texpur. Aerial tanker version of the *Liberator* was the C-109, called the "C-one-Oh-Boom" by aircrews. (Photo courtesy USAF)

Only five of the AVG pilots elected to be sworn into the Army Air Force and remain in China. The rest went back to their regular branchs of service or civilian flying jobs. Tough old Papa Tiger, Claire Lee Chennault, was "re-inducted" into the USAAF as a major general and given command of the China Air Task Force, a part of the 14th Air Force.

In the meantime, the Japanese had overrun Myitkyina and destroyed the hope that the British troops* with U.S. General Stilwell (who served as Chiang's chief of staff) and Stilwell's Chinese forces could hold

the upper end of Burma, including the 800-mile Burma Road that was Chiang Kai-shek's main supply artery linking Kunming with Lashio and the road to Mandalay in central Burma. And it was at this time that Colonel Caleb V. Haynes' Assam Burma Ferrying Command, aided by Chiang's airline, China National Aviation Corporation (CNAC), began to move cargo over the Himalayas in their C-47's and DC-3's.

In April and May, 1942, the airlift over the Hump provided a relative trickle of supplies to Chiang and the AVG because Haynes had but thirteen planes, and the capacities of those were cut in order to struggle over the 16,000-foot peaks of the Able Baker Route across northern Burma. Therefore, some B-24 *Lib-*

* Both Burma and India were part of the British Empire until after WW-II.

Hump crew preparing to start engines of "Polly the Queen" at Chenyi, China. (Photo courtesy Don Downie)

Called everything from "Charlie-46" to "Ol' Dumbo," "Plumber's Nightmare," and the "Greatest Contribution to the Japanese War Effort," the C-46 *Commando* nevertheless opened and maintained the Able and Baker routes over the high Himalayas when nothing else could go that high with that much. This one is landing at Kunming. (Photo courtesy Don Downie)

57

Smoke plume on an unknown peak marks end of an ATC cargo plane and perhaps its crew. If any survived the crash their chances of walking out to friendly territory were slim—but some did. (Photo courtesy Joe R. Reed, Jr.)

Local businessman consents to pose before base operations building at Chenyi, China.

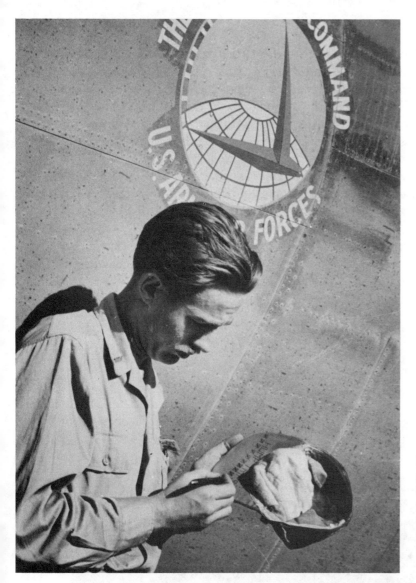

Don Downie, today a well-known aerospace writer, marks off another trip over the Hump. At that time, 600 hours flying transports over the Himalayas, which was classified as "combat" time, was supposed to make one eligible for a flying job with more of a future to it. (Photo courtesy Don Downie)

Douglas C-54 *Skymasters,* flown by both the Naval Air Transport Service (NATS) and the ATC, greatly added to Hump tonnage when they came into service there and could operate over the lower Hump routes as British and American and Chinese ground forces pushed the Japanese southward in Burma. By mid-1945 the C-54's were flying a daily Trojan airlift of medical supplies in and wounded out between Yontan and Guam. (Photo courtesy USAF)

59

erator bombers were hastily taken from the 10th Air Force (under which the AB Ferrying Command operated), converted as cargo carriers as a stop-gap measure, and put to work above the "Rock Pile." These craft were designated C-87's. The same plane, converted to a fuel transporter, was officially known as the C-109; although airmen referred to it as the "C-One-Oh-Boom," because its integral gas tanks too often leaked, and that combined with sparks from its electric flap motors sometimes resulted in a tremendous and fatal "Boom" just after take-off.

Later, the reliable Douglas C-54, designed just before the war as the DC-4 airliner, and during the war the hands-down favorite of all transport pilots, became available for the Hump operation; but in the meantime cargo had to be moved, and the need for an efficient air cargo mover—a real weight-lifter that would be at home above the towering Himalayas—led to the Curtiss-Wright Aircraft Company's St. Louis plant and a quick evaluation of their CW-20 transport.

The CW-20 was originally laid down in 1934 (about the time the first DC-2 appeared) and was intended as an airliner. It was primarily the brainchild of engineer Ken Perkins and was developed under the direction of Chief Engineer George Page. But the big CW-20 (the biggest twin-engined plane in America) lost out to the Douglas DC-3 in the

Curtiss-Wright's production test pilot, Herb Fisher, was sent to CBI as a trouble-shooter on C-46's over the Hump and remained to fly his company's fighter craft, P-40's, accompanying USAAF pilots of the 23rd Fighter Group that grew from the original Flying Tigers. (Photo courtesy Port of New York Authority)

pre-war airline market, and it sort of waited at home, like a marriageable but fat and unwanted maiden, until someone came along that appreciated her.

The prince charming in this case was none other than General Hap Arnold, Chief of the Army Air Forces. It wasn't exactly a matter of love at first sight—General Arnold was desperate—but the hefty CW-20 got a new dress (camouflage pattern), a new name (C-46), and was off to the ball. Both General Arnold and Burdette Wright, general manager of Curtiss-Wright's Airplane Division, knew the risks of going into full production with an unproved airplane; but both felt they had no choice in view of the great need.

Inevitably bugs were found in the C-46. Her unremedied mechanical ills took the lives of many aircrews over the unforgiving Himalayas. But these were frantic days, and there were too few of them for all that needed doing. America was fighting for her life, and almost anything that cut time between production line and firing line seemed justified. Curtiss-Wright's chief production test pilot, Herb Fisher, saved a few minutes' taxiing time on each flight by taking off directly from the factory parking lot. During the course of a day's work that often meant an extra plane okayed for Air Force duty.

However, by late 1943, after significant numbers of C-46's were serving over the Hump, the Air Force saw that it could not accept its losses there. True, some of the unarmed transports had been shot down by Japanese fighter planes; others had simply disappeared. But too many were known to have been lost to mechanical troubles. The Assam Burma Ferrying Command, which had been absorbed into the Air Force's new Air Transport Command the previous December, was losing one airplane for every 218 trips across the Himalayas. Twelve airplanes had already been lost during the month of November, 1943, when General Arnold returned to St. Louis and told Burdette Wright that the C-46's flaws must be found and corrected at once.

Wright called in Herb Fisher* and asked him to take a four-man engineering team, a new C-46, get to India in a hurry and "de-bug" those airplanes.

Fisher was the man to do it. During the past four

* Herbert Owen Fisher; the same "Herb" Fisher who, at this writing, is known to almost everyone in aviation as the special aviation consultant to the Port of New York Authority which operates, among other things, La Guardia and Kennedy International Airports.

years he had tested over 40 types of military planes. Most of all he was experienced in C-46's. Chances were good that whatever could go wrong with a C-46, already had with Fisher at the controls.

Colonel Caleb Haynes had gone from India, and Herb reported to the Air Transport Command's China-Burma-India (CBI) boss, General Thomas O. ("Black Bob") Hardin, a rugged character who had grown up with the air transport industry of the twenties when he ran Texas Air Transport, one of the first airlines. Then Herb immediately began flying the Hump out of Chabua, in the upper Assam Valley, and taking a C-46 pilot along on each trip to make sure the Army flyer fully understood the plane's idiosyncrasies.

Not once during the first five trips did Fisher see the Himalayas beneath because of "normal" Hump weather. But the clouds meant that prowling enemy fighters could not find the transports, so Herb, like others flying the Rock Pile, welcomed the storms. And, like the others, he carried fuel and ammunition; medical supplies, rice, beer, aircraft engines, blasting caps, Jeeps and dart boards, as well as Chinese troops and commuting colonels. Things were seldom dull. One morning Herb was routed from his basha (a type of thatched-roof hut which housed most Hump pilots) and asked by the Chabua C. O., Colonel E. H. Alexander, to take a load of medicine into newly-liberated Myitkyina airstrip in northern Burma. He was to fly a C-47, which was lighter and smaller than a C-46, and determine whether or not the strip at Myitkyina was capable of handling the big *Commando* (some higher-up had given the C-46 the official name, "*Commando*"; though most pilots referred to it as the "pregnant whale").

"Three C-47's were already standing up on their noses in that pig wallow at Myitkyina somebody was dumb enough to call an airstrip," Herb recalls. "The tower, which I found out later was actually the front office of another C-47 which had bellied-in, started yakking and told me they had sniper fire. The Japanese were also lobbing-in an occasional artillery round, he said, and if I insisted on landing to come in from the north, because the south and east quadrants were the snipers' favorites. By then I'd have preferred to initiate that time-honored maneuver known as 'let's-get-the-hell-outa-here,' but Colonel Alexander had said we had wounded down there awaiting evacuation, so I really didn't have any choice.

"I aimed for the north end of the steel mats on that

Many years after WW-II, Hump-Pilot/Trouble-Shooter Herb Fisher (right) renewed friendship with his wartime boss in the CBI, General (ret.) Thomas O. "Black Bob" Hardin. (Photo courtesy Port of New York Authority)

so-called runway, and the Army pilot in my right seat didn't look too happy—or maybe his expression was just a mirror of my own. We had some other crew in the back, but had left Chabua in such a hurry I hadn't met them. Anyway, the old Gooney Bird was running out of landing speed just when we ran out of mats. The tail started up and I thought, 'here comes number four up on its nose,' but she dropped back down and lurched to a dead halt in deep, glue-like mud. It took all the power we had to pull through that goo and park near the trees.

"Just as the engines ticked to a stop, I heard the cabin door flop open and SPLATT! Dammit, somebody was shooting at us. Then I looked back just in time to see our young crew chief slump and fall out

the opening. He was shot dead, right through the chest. The rest of us ducked and all hell broke loose up in the edge of the jungle. That sniper shot alerted our troops and they saturated that area.

"Our ground forces were desperate for supplies, and as soon as they had taken away our crew chief and nurse—we had one of those aboard and I hadn't even known it—hundreds of Wogs (the term common then for Chinese in India) hurried to unload our cargo.

"I walked around to the nose of the old bird paying particularly attention to the mush we were settling in, all the time thinking we'd never get out of there. Then, BBLLLAM! About a thousand feet down the runway the whole damn' mixture of dirt and landing

62

mats blew up. The Japs had an artillery piece up in the hills and were zeroed-in on that strip. They'd lob in a shell and tear up a section of runway, then our Wogs, hundreds of them, would rush out with shovels to fill the hole while hundreds more hauled in new steel mats. They'd half-fix it, then damn' if the Japs wouldn't change trajectory and drop a round on the *other* end! However, the shelling was just an added obstacle. They were carrying wounded aboard my plane and, cripes, I didn't think I could get it out empty, much less loaded, even with perfect timing between the artillery rounds.

"The Chinese workers were still swarming around the last hole when an American soldier ran up to me and saluted (he didn't know I was a civilian, despite my dirty old shirt and lack of insignia) and said we were full and should leave now. 'Oh sure,' I thought. 'Now if somebody'll just tell me *how!*' I looked at the mush between us and the mats; at the Wogs tossing dirt like crazy, and thought, 'God, this is ridiculous.' Then I climbed in the airplane and I saw the litters all lined up and the nurse hanging up those plasma bottles and speaking softly to the white faces and all the eyes turned to me like they expected me to do something. One of them, in the second tier, just a foot or so from where I stood, said very quietly, 'Sir, I'm dying. Can you get me to a hospital?' And suddenly I was angry. I don't know why. Just an anger at my own doubt and fear. 'Don't worry, fellow,' I said. 'We're headed for a hospital in one helluva hurry.'

"Before the Japs gave us another jolt, we blasted that C-47 through the pig wallow with mud chunks hitting the belly and bottom of the wings like cannon fire. We staggered to the mats and then got airborne with small arms fire pinging all around us.

"An hour later, I had those men at the hospital ten miles north of Chabua. My report to Colonel Alexander said that Myitkyina was no place for a C-46— or anything else."

After nearly thirty missions over the Hump, Fisher's employer expected him to return to the factory. Still, the Himalayas continued to claim too many airplanes and crews so Herb chose to stay. Through mid-1944 he rode with any C-46 going either way across the Rock Pile while giving pointers to the pilots. Like Kipling's cat who walked by himself, all places were the same to Herb. In China, he flew from Yunnanyi, Chenyi, Luliang, Kunming and Lumsien; and he returned to all the ATC bases on the India side; from Gaya to Tezpur, from Misamari to Jorhat. And he

learned what was killing C-46 crews; and endlessly preached his remedies.

Engine fires in flight had been a frequent source of trouble, and Herb knew this was caused by deterioration of rubber hose connections at bends in the myriad fuel lines leading into engine nacelles from the C-46's six wing tanks (this was before the time of reliable synthetics for such applications). Rapid, daily changes in environment from the extreme heat and humidity of the Assam Valley to the dry cold above the mountains was literally disintegrating the rubber connections and squirting volatile fuel into hot engine nacelles. The only "fix" for this at the time—if the planes were to be kept flying—was constant, meticulous inspection, and frequent replacement of the hoses. Herb spent countless hours drilling this fact into the heads of pilots and crews. Those who failed to get the message had but one course of action in case of engine fire; bail out. Over the inhospitable Himalayas, perhaps on instruments, that was less than an inviting prospect—although a total of 1,171 men did manage to walk out of those multiple ranges after crashing or parachuting during WW-II.

As the weeks passed, Herb flew with hundreds of different aircrews. In-flight fires were greatly reduced; a problem with the C-46's carburetor heat control was solved, and recurring engine power loss at altitude was traced to air in the fuel lines, the result of very high temperatures in a wing-tank vulnerable to the merciless Assam sun. Then a new and seemingly inexplicable problem arose. Increasingly, night take-offs ended in trees a short distance from the airstrips. Puzzled, Herb switched to nighttime trips exclusively and soon had the solution handed to him—frighteningly—when he found a tree top stuck in the landing gear after a routine flight to China. He reviewed the pilot's take-off technique and had his answer. The victims were simply flying themselves into the ground. Some of them, with too little experience, had picked up the airline habit of easing back on power just after lift-off. This was a fine way to conserve fuel and save engines back in the States when a knowledgable pilot, with a light load of passengers, came out of a well-lighted airport depending upon well-maintained engines and accurate instruments. But off short, jungle strips, in sketchily maintained airplanes, always overloaded, it could spell tragedy. If you are a pilot, you can imagine the sequence of events: As usual, it's a hot night with high humidity. Your C-46 is loaded a good 2,000 pounds over its military gross of 48,-

000. The steel mats bang loudly as you bounce down the rough surface and beyond the mats there is nothing but blackness. You lift off and go on the gauges immediately. Then you ease back the throttles and, to compensate for the loss in airspeed, lower the nose—unaware that both your altimeter and air speed indicator are giving you false readings. Neither instrument has been calibrated since it left the factory. At that point, only luck will keep you out of the trees. But once that danger had been identified, the fix was simple: an order from Black Bob calling for maximum power and a minimum of 130 mph indicated until one had at least 300 feet of altitude during night take-offs.

Altogether, Herb flew 96 missions over the Hump in C-46's. Then he switched to a borrowed P-40 fighter, which was also built by Curtiss-Wright and which Herb had flown extensively as the company's chief production test pilot, and went along with USAAF fighter groups for another 50 missions in the CBI Theater.

In reply to our question about combat as a fighter pilot, Herb grinned. "Heck no, I didn't shoot at any Zeros; a guy could get hurt that way. When my Air Force friends bounced an enemy flight, I just hung around and kept out of the way and watched. I was a civilian and it was my job to try and work out operating procedures that would get a little more speed or range or safety out of the planes my company made. I would have fought if necessary. Truth is, the Air Force didn't need me. Our guys were pretty much in control of the air by that time. I did get carried away one time and went down with my bunch to strafe an enemy truck convoy on the Burma Road."

As the Japanese were at last pushed back in Burma by Allied troops under Lord Mountbatten (including a U.S. Army regiment, "Merrill's Marauders"), the Hump routes moved south to lower terrain and Douglas C-54's took over much of the load. Early in 1945, the RAF and USAAF achieved undisputed air supremacy over Burma and China and the ATC ("Assam Trucking Company," in that part of the world) combined with the Navy Air Transport Service to dispatch a cargo flight out of India every eleven minutes, twenty-four hours per day. Losses dropped to one plane for every 2,309 trips over the Himalayas, making the operation more than ten times safer than it had been just two years before.

In all, 1,314 ATC airmen died flying the Hump while delivering 776,532 tons of cargo. The dollar-cost appears impossible to pin down. One source lists the cost of delivering aviation fuel over the Hump to China at $10 per gallon. Hump pilot Don Downie, now a well-known aviation writer, says a C-46 flight from Chabua to Yunnanyi "cost the U.S. Government around $25,000, give or take an aircrew or two."

The Himalayas are still there. They are awe-inspiring even today, even from the pressurized comfort of a modern jet at 35,000 feet. And when the clouds below momentarily part, and your eye catches the brief flash of sunlight reflected from a crumpled bit of aluminium clinging to a barren peak, there seems a sudden chill in the warm cabin and you realize that you are an intruder, a latter-day tourist trespassing in this vaulted Temple of the Brave.

4. Carrier Shoot-Out at Midway

The turning point of WW-II in the Pacific came with even more suddenness than had the attack on Pearl Harbor; but this time it was the Japanese who were surprised. Within a space of not more than four minutes—10:22 AM to 10:26 AM, June 4, 1942—fifty-four U.S. warplanes so grievously wounded the Japanese Navy it never recovered, and during those hectic 240 seconds, offensive capability in the Pacific passed from the hands of Nippon's Admiral Isoroku Yamamoto to those of Rear Admiral Chester W. Nimitz, commander in chief of the U.S. Pacific Fleet.

The battle, which took place about 130 miles north of Midway Atoll, resulted from a truly classical situation. The enemy, with a greatly superior force screened by bad weather northwest of Midway, made a feint at the Aleutians with a smaller force expecting to attract what was left of the U.S. Pacific Fleet into position to be ambushed. However, Admiral Nimitz had parlayed some excellent naval intelligence work, plus some educated guesses, into a good blueprint of the enemy's intentions. Therefore, instead of the Japanese ambushing the U.S. fleet, it was a weaker, American force in the end that dry-gulched the Nipponese.

The Battle of Midway was at least in part precipitated by a seemingly unrelated event. On April 18, 1942, Lt. Col. Jimmy Doolittle led a flight of sixteen Army Air Force B-25 medium bombers off the flight deck of the aircraft carrier *Hornet,* and headed, just a few feet above the water, for Tokyo, 650 miles away.

Doolittle's raiders struck the Japanese capital during the noon hour. They were almost unopposed, and though their modest bomb loads produced no great damage, the attack did cause much consternation and loss of face among Japan's leaders, particularly when it was established that the raiders were U.S. Army bombers, heretofore believed too big to operate from the limited deck space of carriers (Doolittle's men had practiced "panic" take-offs for weeks).

All but one of the attacking planes were lost. That One made it to Vladivostok, Russia, where it was seized and the five-man crew interned. The rest crashed in China, unable to locate the friendly airstrips supposedly awaiting them because Admiral Halsey, commanding the task force that launched them, failed to signal Washington that he'd sent the Army planes on their mission a full day earlier than planned, and therefore the radio homing-signals in China were silent. The crews of 13 planes—less three men lost in crashes—eventually slipped through enemy-occupied territory to safety in Chungking. Of two crews captured by the Japanese, two men died from crash injuries, one perished in captivity, three were shot (for "bombing schools, hospitals and homes"), and four survived as prisoners of war.

Doolittle believed he had miserably failed in his mission; he had not done significant physical damage to the enemy, and he had lost all his airplanes. The country and the President, however, viewed it differently. The fact that American warplanes were able to strike the enemy's capital city was what mattered, and it resulted in a tremendous morale boost for the American people (it also resulted in the Congressional Medal of Honor and promotion to brigadier general for the surprised Lt. Col. Doolittle).

But of even more importance was the effect of the raid upon Japan's leaders. Basic to their plan for a successful, limited war with the U.S. was the establishment of a strong defensive perimeter across the mid-Pacific to protect territories won and to insure that the home islands of Japan would be immune from assault until peace could be negotiated. To this end, Guam and Wake had been seized in December; Tarawa and Makin in the Gilbert Islands (less than 2,000 miles SW of Hawaii) were taken soon afterwards, while the Marshals, 500 miles to the north, had been a Japanese possession since 1919 and were already fortified. Still, the Doolittle raid clearly established that Japan itself was vulnerable to air attack, at least from carrier-based planes, therefore more and stronger bases were needed to push back Japan's outer defenses. The strategic locations of Midway (about 1,100 miles NW of Hawaii), and of Attu and Kiska, at the tip of the Aleutians, thereby marked those islands as essential bases to Japan's war strategy. Their occupation should also offer an excellent opportunity to draw the remnants of the U.S. Navy into

Scene on flight deck of *USS Lexington* during the Battle of the Coral Sea, May 7–8, 1942. Smoke pours around edges of elevator from internal fires. Planes in foreground are F4F *Wildcats*. (Photo courtesy U.S. Navy)

Crew abandons the "Lady Lex" in Coral Sea after fierce battle that had lasting significance on the outcome of WW-II in the Pacific. Japan lost light carrier *Shoho*. USS *Yorktown* was badly damaged, but by superhuman effort was back in action for the decisive battle of Midway, June 4–7, 1942. (Photo courtesy U.S. Navy)

a battle it could not hope to win—if the trap were properly sprung.

By early May, Yamamoto's plan to seize Midway, Attu, and Kiska was complete, and he assembled a mighty force for the expected show-down with the U.S. Pacific Fleet: 8 aircraft carriers, 10 battleships, 24 cruisers, 70 destroyers, 15 submarines, 8 tankers and 40 transports and other supporting craft for a total of 185 ships and 450 aircraft.

Opposing this armada, Nimitz could muster but 3 aircraft carriers, no battleships, 13 cruisers, 24 destroyers, 25 submarines and 3 tankers for a total of 68 ships and 306 airplanes, including 73 planes based on Midway itself.

Admiral Nimitz was fortunate to have even that much. Until the last minute, he could count but two carriers. Then the bomb-damaged *Yorktown* limped into Pearl Harbor and, with every available shipfitter working until he dropped from exhaustion, a normal two-month repair job was completed in just forty-eight hours and the *Yorktown,* which had taken a hit from an 800-pound bomb during the Battle of the Coral Sea less than three weeks before, was ready to fight once again.

The Battle of the Coral Sea, fought on May 7 and 8, was, taken by itself, a tactical defeat for Rear Admiral Frank J. Fletcher's Task Force 17—which consisted of the fleet carriers *Lexington* and *Yorktown,* escorted by a mixed Australian-American force of cruisers and destroyers—because Fletcher lost the *Lexington* and almost lost the *Yorktown,* while Japanese Admirals Inouye and Kajioka lost only the light carrier *Shoho* and suffered damage to their fleet carrier *Shokaku.* The "Lady Lex" was a poor trade for the little

Shoko. However, this battle temporarily stymied Japan's invasion of Port Moresby in southeastern New Guinea, which would have provided a springboard for attack and invasion of Australia; and it also denied to Yamamoto's Midway Strike Force One, not only the damaged *Shokaku,* but its sister carrier *Zuikaku* whose air group had been seriously mauled in the carrier shoot-out with Fletcher in the Coral Sea. And since those two additional carriers may well have turned the tide for the Japanese at Midway, the Battle of the Coral Sea was doubly significant. It should be noted, too, that if the Battle of the Coral Sea indirectly influenced the outcome at Midway, then the action at Midway in turn wrote the final pronouncement for that earlier battle because, after Midway, Japan's temporary postponement of the Port Moresby invasion became permanent.

Meanwhile, Admiral Nimitz was preparing his battle plan, possessing, as previously mentioned, a reasonably accurate idea as to what Yamamoto was up to because U.S. Naval Intelligence was doing a good job of decoding Japanese fleet messages.* Nimitz could only guess at enemy strength (he under-guessed it), but he did know, days before the battle, that Yamamoto was dividing his fleet into at least two separate forces, with the main one aimed at Midway and the lesser one intended for an assault and probable invasion of the Aleutians. Therefore, Nimitz decided to split his own meagre command and send 3 heavy cruisers, 2 light cruisers and 10 destroyers north to harass the enemy's thrust at the Aleutians. Then, since he had deduced that the Japanese invasion of Midway was set for June 4 to 6, he ordered his forces to begin moving out of Pearl Harbor on May 28 to head for a position—he called it "Point Luck"—350 miles northeast of Midway. Nimitz was certain the enemy's main force would approach Midway from the west or northwest.

The combined American force upon which so much

depended—Task Force 16 under Rear Admiral Raymond A. Spruance, and Admiral Fletcher's Task Force 17—rendezvoused at Point Luck on the afternoon of June 2. Task Force 16 was made up of the carriers *Enterprise* and *Hornet,* 6 cruisers and 9 destroyers. Task Force 17 consisted of the carrier *Yorktown,* 2 cruisers and 5 destroyers. This fleet was, as Admiral Nimitz well knew, a pitifully small force with which to challenge a major part of the Japanese Navy; but the prize was so great he had to take the risk. Nimitz (who directed the whole operation from his Pearl Harbor headquarters) obviously felt that, reduced to its simplest terms, the outcome of the battle should depend upon who first discovered the other's carriers. Nimitz was an old "battleship admiral," but confronted with reality he thrust aside old prejudices and recognized that control of the air meant victory at sea just as it did on land. Aircraft carriers were the new queens of the world's oceans, and the mighty battleships and battle cruisers were relegated to the role of floating anti-aircraft batteries—support vessels dedicated to the protection of the thin-skinned flat-tops.

While the U.S. battle fleet was figuratively lying in the bushes northeast of Midway, Yamamoto was steaming eastward and deploying his forces. His Midway Strike Force One, approaching the atoll from the northwest through a band of stormy weather, was commanded by Admiral Chuichi Nagumo and consisted of 4 carriers (*Akagi, Kaga, Hiryu* and *Soryu*), 2 battleships, 3 cruisers and 12 destroyers. On a parallel course several hundred miles to the south was the Midway Invasion Force which had staged out of Saipan in the Marianas and counted one carrier among its transports and phalanx of escorting warships. Yamamoto's Aleutian Strike Force and Aleutian Invasion Force were many hundreds of miles to the north and divided for a three-pronged thrust to take Attu and Kiska and to attack the U.S. Naval installation at Dutch Harbor. These Aleutian forces had two carriers plus their share of transports and warships. Finally, Yamamoto himself chose to loiter about 300 miles northwest of Midway with a reserve force of one carrier and its supporting vessels, including 3 battleships.

Amateur naval strategists (your authors of course included) have long deplored Yamamoto's seemingly inexplicable divisions of his great sea armada. But the Japanese Navy commander did not know the whereabouts of the U.S. Fleet. He assumed it to be, at least in part, in Pearl Harbor, patching wounds and refitting following the Coral Sea battle—a reasonable

---

* Each nation uses many codes and all are very complex. For example, when groups of numerals are used, the word "ship" which might be represented as "35271" at one point in a message, will not be so "spelled" a second time. Since variants of some codes are employed, the U.S., possessing (probably by espionage) the key to one Japanese code, could have read portions of other Japanese codes belonging to the same family. According to some records, the U.S. was reading the Japanese diplomatic code, or the "winds code" even before Pearl Harbor. The "purple code," perhaps a variant of the winds code, is also mentioned, and seems to have been one of the codes used by the Japanese Navy. But since no U.S. intelligence agency will discuss this subject in any detail, we are forced to report in generalities and merely say that the U.S. was successfully decoding some Japanese radio messages prior to the Battle of Midway.

assumption on Yamamoto's part had the Americans not been reading his mail. However, Yamamoto had no reason to suspect U.S. Navy cryptographers were decoding many of his fleet orders. He considered himself the hunter, the U.S. Navy the hunted. Since Pearl Harbor, the American Navy had been too weak to do much except hit and run; and although it had fought fiercely in the Coral Sea, the loss of the *Lexington* had undoubtedly weakened it further. Besides, Yamamoto was counting on his submarines to intercept, or at least locate and track, hostile ships charging out of Pearl Harbor in response to the Japanese attacks on Midway and/or the Aleutians. The Japanese commander had no way of knowing that the U.S. Fleet was already at Point Luck when his submarines took up their stations north of Hawaii, and therefore the Nipponese pickets were watching an empty stable.

Early on the morning of June 3, Yamamoto's attack force in Aleutian waters leveled Dutch Harbor with a two-stage strike of carrier-based planes; and a few days later Attu and Kiska fell (though both islands were re-taken a year later with the help of the U.S. 11th Air Force).

Also, on June 3, at about 9 A.M., Yamamoto's Midway Invasion Force, approaching Midway from slightly south of east (260 degrees), was spotted by a Midway-based PBY *Catalina* patrol plane approximately 700 miles from the atoll. The Midway air commander dispatched a flight of Army B-17's for an afternoon attack, and late that evening sent off a squadron of *Vindicator* torpedo planes. But neither the *Fortresses,* attempting to hit their elusive targets from level, high-altitude bomb runs, nor the SB2U *Vindicators,* boring in low in semi-darkness, achieved meaningful hits. Back at Point Luck, Admiral Fletcher gleaned what he could from the terse radio messages (the American fleet was maintaining total radio silence therefore he could ask no questions), concluded that the enemy force involved wasn't the prize he was after, so he signaled Spruance to sit tight and prepare for action early the next morning. With the enemy invasion force nearing its objective, the powerful strike force was certain to come bulling out of the fog and rain to the northwest about daylight. During the night, Fletcher (in overall command of Task Forces 16 and 17) and Spruance moved to a point about 200 miles north and slightly east of Midway and then settled down to wait with about 10 miles separating the two commands.

At 4:30 A.M. on June 4, Fletcher sent ten SBD *Dauntlesses* from his flagship *Yorktown* to search his northern flank as a precautionary measure, while *Catalinas* from Midway were already fanning out to look for Admiral Nagumo's Strike Force One along the edge of the storm front some 200 miles to the northwest. At approximately the same time, Nagumo was launching bombers and fighters from his four carriers for the attack on Midway. And just an hour later —at 5:36 A.M.—a pair of *Catalinas* spotted Nagumo's Strike Force One through broken clouds and immediately radioed the enemy's position, course, and speed. At that moment, the advantage passed to the American fleet, for Nagumo was totally unaware of its presence. Yamamoto, hundreds of miles to the northwest with his main reserve force, was too far away to aid his doomed Strike Force One.

Nagumo's agony was exquisite. At first, victory appeared to be his. His shipboard gunners and combat air patrols repeatedly beat off attacks—between 7 A.M. and 10 A.M.—by Midway-based planes, which included Army B-26's carrying torpedos and Navy TBF *Avengers;* plus torpedo assaults by TBD *Devastators* from the three American carriers. Out of 41 *Devastators*—15 from *Hornet,* 14 from *Enterprise* and 12 from *Yorktown*—four returned to the *Enterprise,* two to *Yorktown* and none to *Hornet.* And not one Japanese ship was hit.

The failure of the torpedo planes was not due to lack of skill or resoluteness on the part of their crews. All pressed their attacks until blasted out of the sky during their torpedo runs. Spruance and Fletcher had sent these slow, vulnerable craft into the heart of the enemy's battle fleet with 26 *Wildcat* fighters for protection (36 *Wildcats* were held back to protect the U.S. ships). However, the *Enterprise's* ten fighters, led by Ensign James S. Gray, remained above the clouds and never went down to aid the sorely beset torpedo craft.* The *Hornet's* ten fighters (along with its 35 *Dauntlesses*) also missed the action because Nagumo had swung his fleet around to the northeast, and when the *Hornet* fighters and dive bombers reached the place where the enemy should have been and didn't find him, turned south toward Midway. It was a logical guess; but a wrong one. Therefore, only the *Yorktown's* six F4F *Wildcats,* led by Lt. Cmdr. John

---

* Gray probably should not be blamed. The torpedo planes far below were supposed to call for help when needed, and Gray never received such a message. Clouds blocked his own view of the action; and since his F4F *Wildcats* could neither climb nor maneuver with the *Zeros,* altitude advantage was of supreme importance when F4F's attacked the nimble Japanese fighters. Later in the war, Gray was decorated for heroism several times.

Consolidated PBY-5 *Catalina* amphibian was the Navy's principal long-range patrol plane during WW-II. PBY above has just dropped a depth charge on enemy submarine. Admiral Nagumo's Midway Strike Force was spotted by PBY patrol craft. (Photo courtesy U.S. Navy)

S. Thach, were on the spot to try and ward off Nagumo's *Zero* fighters as they swarmed down upon the lumbering torpedo planes. Thach's flight did the best it could; but outnumbered at least 6-to-1, it could not save the *Devastators*.

Nevertheless, the *Devastator* crews had not died in vain. Their stubborn attacks against impossible odds had, like the charge of a defensive end in football, stripped the opponent's interference and left his ball carrier at the mercy of defensive line backers. The torpedo planes had drawn Nagumo's air cover down near the surface and left the *Zeros* short of fuel and ammunition—while, at that moment, unmolested at 20,000 feet, *Yorktown's* 17 *Dauntless* dive bombers, led by Lt. Cmdr. Maxwell F. Leslie, were peeling off and taking dead aim on the 26,900-ton Japanese

carrier *Kaga.* It was 10:22 A.M., and time had run out for Nagumo.

Between one and two minutes after Leslie's 17 planes began their dives, Lt. Cmdr. Clarence W. Mc-Clusky, leading 37 *Dauntlesses* from the *Enterprise,* arrived to choose two more fat targets: Nagumo's own flagship, the carrier *Akagi,* and the smaller carrier *Soryu.* And two minutes after *that,* Leslie, McClusky & Company were heading back for their ships, leaving behind three enemy carriers aflame and sinking. Nagumo's fourth carrier, the *Hiryu,* hidden by clouds some distance away, escaped attack for the time being.

Meanwhile, a Japanese scout plane had found the *Yorktown* (Spruance's and Fletcher's commands were still separated by perhaps 10 miles or so), and while Admiral Nagumo was abandoning his flagship, the

Among first U.S. aircraft to attack the Japanese strike force on June 4, 1942, were Midway-based Army Air Force Martin B-26 *Marauder* medium bombers carrying torpedos. The *Marauder* had a high wing-loading and early versions had bad reputations among aircrews. Top speed was 315 mph; normal bomb load 4,000 lbs, and range 1,000 miles. (Photo courtesy Martin Marietta Corp.)

Rear Admiral Chester W. Nimitz, Commander in Chief of the U.S. Pacific Fleet, bore responsibility for the daring American ambush of greatly superior enemy force at Midway. (Photo courtesy U.S. Navy)

Too often forgotten by air historians are the Navy's "Slingshot Flyers" of WW-II who lived aboard cruisers and battleships and were catapulted into the air for reconnaissance missions. Theirs was a dangerous but unglamorous job. Their floatplanes were returned to mother ships by crane after they landed in the water alongside. Pictured is a Curtiss SC-1 *Seahawk*. (Photo courtesy Curtiss Wright Corp.)

commander of his remaining carrier ordered a strike against the U.S. carrier. Although three-fourths of Strike Force One's air power was gone, perhaps victory of a sort was yet possible if the Americans had but a single carrier to reckon with.

Hiryu's planes severely damaged the *Yorktown* in two attacks before 40 *Dauntlesses* from the *Enterprise* and *Hornet* (and some refugees from *Yorktown*) sank Nagumo's fourth carrier at 5 P.M. By then, the Japanese knew that other U.S. carriers were in the area, but it was too late. Yamamoto cancelled the invasion of Midway and ordered his battered Strike

Force One and the Midway Invasion Force to withdraw.

For the next two days, Spruance pursued the fleeing Japanese and on the 6th launched two final air strikes against them, sinking the heavy cruiser *Mikuma* and heavily damaging the cruiser *Mogami*. Then, with some of his escort vessels running low on fuel, Spruance reluctantly turned back.

Still, the enemy struck a final blow when, early the next morning (June 7, 1942), Japanese submarine I-168, commanded by Lt. Cmdr. Yahachi Tanabe, put two torpedos into the crewless *Yorktown* and sent her to the bottom while she was being towed to Pearl Harbor for repairs by the minesweeper *Vireo*. The destroyer *Hammann* went down to the same attacker. Thus, alone among Yamamoto's entire sea armada, submarine I-168 could return to Japan claiming victory over an American ship at Midway.

After the battle of Midway, strategic initiative in the Pacific belonged to the U.S. Navy. The enemy had lost two heavy carriers and two light carriers, along with 258 aircraft and many of his best pilots (U.S. losses were 40 planes from Midway; 92 carrier aircraft, plus the *Yorktown* and *Hammann*), and this significantly altered the relative sea power of the two nations. At the time of Pearl Harbor, the United States had 7 large carriers and 1 small carrier: *Lexington, Saratoga, Ranger, Enterprise, Wasp, Yorktown, Hornet* and the escort carrier *Long Island*. Of these, *Lexington, Saratoga* and *Enterprise* were assigned to the Pacific Fleet when hostilities began. Then, although the newly commissioned *Hornet* was sent to the Pacific, the *Saratoga* took a torpedo from a Japanese submarine in January, 1942, and went into port for extensive repair, and the *Lexington* was lost in the Coral Sea in May. Therefore,

One of the handful of Douglas SBD *Dauntless* dive bombers that sank three enemy carriers during the Battle of Midway, awaits its turn to take-off from the *Yorktown* on June 4, 1942. *Yorktown* was attacked a few hours afterwards and later went down. (Photo courtesy U.S. Navy)

Nimitz had the *Yorktown, Enterprise* and *Hornet* left to him for the Battle of Midway, while the *Wasp, Ranger* and *Long Island* were in the Atlantic, Mediterranean or ferrying planes to Australia. Immediately after Midway, the U.S. could count six carriers, including the *Saratoga* which soon returned to service; while Japan also had six carriers remaining. Considering the vastness of Japan's sea frontiers, and the newly established truth that carrier-based air power ruled the oceans, the sudden weakness of Japan's navy was apparent. And since Japan was an island nation, its very life now depended upon an impregnable sea defense. Clearly, Japan lost *that* at the instant U.S. Naval Aviator Maxwell Leslie peeled off in his *Dauntless* and centered his gunsight on the broad deck of the Japanese carrier *Kaga.*

The Douglas SBD-3 *Dauntless* was the Navy's aerial workhorse during the early, critical months of the Pacific War. Supposedly an unremarkable craft—it was neither fast, heavily armed, nor particularly maneuverable—but it was rugged and it was there. Fifty-four *Dauntlesses* from *Yorktown* and *Enterprise* turned the tide of the war during a frantic four minutes at Midway. (Photo courtesy U.S. Navy)

Lt. Cmdr. John S. Thach in his *Wildcat* fighter with three victory symbols beneath cockpit canopy shortly after the Battle of Midway. Thach's flight of six *Wildcats* engaged 38 *Zero* fighters during the disastrous low-level attacks by Navy torpedo planes before the *Dauntlesses* arrived that historic morning. *Wildcat* in background piloted by another Navy Ace, Lt. Edward H. "Butch" O'Hare. (Photo courtesy U.S. Navy)

Rear Admiral Raymond A. Spruance commanded Task Force 16 at Midway, which consisted of the carriers *Enterprise* and *Hornet,* six cruisers, and nine destroyers. The presence of Task Force 16 was not suspected by the enemy until three of his carriers were aflame and sinking. (Photo courtesy U.S. Navy)

So, Midway set the pattern for the sea battles (actually, air/sea battles, because opposing surface ships were seldom within gun range of one another) that followed during World War II in the Pacific; and with America's mighty industrial complexes at last operating at capacity, the U.S. Navy found itself stronger at each encounter. Between December 7, 1941, and September 2, 1945 (the day Japan formally surrendered), no less than 26 new fleet aircraft carriers and 75 new escort ("Jeep") carriers were placed in service. In July, 1941, the U.S. Navy and Marine Corps had 1,774 combat planes out of a total of 3,437 heavier-than-air craft. In July, 1945, this inventory had grown to 29,125 and 40,912 respectively. By that time, the Japanese Navy and Japanese naval air power had practically ceased to exist.

Yorktown, though grievously damaged during the Battle of Midway, managed to recover and re-arm her aircraft. Crew was taken off later when heavy list made flight deck unusable while her planes carried on the fight from *Enterprise* and *Hornet.* *Yorktown* finally went down to an enemy submarine attack on June 7, while being towed toward Pearl Harbor. (Photo courtesy U.S. Navy)

Rear Admiral Frank J. Fletcher, whose Task Force 17 had recently fought the Battle of the Coral Sea, had left to him only the carrier *Yorktown,* two cruisers, and five destroyers for action at Midway. In overall command at Midway, Fletcher allowed Spruance to fight the ships of Task Force 16 as Spruance saw fit after the *Yorktown* was put out of action. (Photo courtesy U.S. Navy)

Landing signal officer directs approach of F4F *Wildcat* to a carrier landing from a murky sky. (Photo courtesy U.S. Navy)

Grumman TBF *Avengers* return to ship with landing arrester hooks down after a mission. *Avengers* reached the fleet in February 1941 and fought from the Coral Sea throughout every campaign. Grumman built 2,291; General Motors built another 6,545 that were designated TBM. TBF/TBM torpedo was carried internally, and the craft could do 275 mph. (Photo courtesy U.S. Navy)

5. Festung Europa

N. R. "Bart" Bartimus of Columbia, S.C., remembers very clearly how it was to bail out of a crippled B-17 over Germany during Hitler's last days. "If any man flew in that war over 'Fortress Europe' and says he wasn't scared, he's lying in his teeth. And, God, we were uncomfortable! It's cold in an unheated *Fortress* at 30,000 feet. We wore long underwear, heavy socks, fleece-lined trousers, boots, gloves, jackets and caps—and still froze. The twenty-pound flak suit was on top of all that. It took about eight and a half hours from our base, just north of London, to Berlin and back. It made for a long day. From 30,000 feet, though, it's not a personal war. You're just scared and miserable and, part of the time, bored.

"We were on stand-by on April 24, 1945. We figured the war was nearly over, and we honestly thought no more missions would go. For many weeks we had mounted 1,000-plane raids against the enemy. The *Luftwaffe* had practically ceased to exist, and there weren't many targets left worth bombing. Supposedly, our assigned target for the 25th was Pilsen, Czechoslovakia—the Skoda Works. Even our radio, I mean the standard broadcast radio, had announced it. In fact, we wanted to be sure the people in Pilsen knew of the scheduled attack. Our radio suggested the citizens of Pilsen leave, for tomorrow the Eighth Air Force was going to bomb the Skoda plants. Nevertheless, we were surprised when the call came at 5 A.M. The trip was not scrubbed despite an announcement by General Spaatz that the strategic air war was over in the ETO. We were briefed, lifted off at our usual 100 mph, and headed, 500 airplanes strong, for Pilsen.

"The Czechs had left, I guess, but some top German gunners had moved in. Level, at 32,000 feet, the flak burst close all around us. The only thing to do about flak was try to ignore it; but all major industrial targets had from 500 to 700 anti-aircraft guns, mostly 88mm, protecting them. Usually, they'd begin by shooting a flare through our formation to judge our altitude. At the sight of that flare our guts would churn.

"On this mission I was both bombardier and navigator. It wasn't unusual late in the war for one man to do two jobs. We aimed for our target and I kept thinking how ridiculous it would be if we were shot down and then found the war was over. Suddenly, the old girl lurched, struggled and seemed to sigh. We were hit!

"I could see the formation leaving us and we were burning on the right side. Number three engine was burning and pieces of the airplane broke off in our wake. Our pilot, Paul Coville, punched the bell to leave.

"My assigned exit was up near the front, just aft of the props. I jettisoned the escape hatch and got down on the floor the way we had been taught. I sat there, looking down at my feet hanging out into space, and at the ground so far below. I was wearing

"At the sight of that flare, our guts would churn," said Bart Bartimus, describing how German anti-aircraft gunners sometimes fired small rockets into U.S. bomber formations to determine exact altitude of attacking force. B-17's above have been into Germany and suffered for miles under intense flak barrages. They are about to receive a final pounding. In the distance lies the French Coast and English Channel. Beyond is England and sanctuary. (Photo courtesy USAF)

Bart Bartimus, as a 2nd Lieutenant and navigator, was shot down in the last bombing mission of World War II. After 2 years as a civilian and a lieutenant in the Reserves, he re-entered the service as a cadet. He was in the first group of pilots sent to Korea, this time as a 2nd Lieutenant and pilot of F-51s.

those huge fleece-lined flight boots, and I watched, strangely amused, as the slipstream tore them from my feet. Then, I glanced back at the altimeter on my desk. It read 22,000 feet, and was unwinding slowly. I felt a little .sad leaving that scarred old bird that I'd ridden on 17 previous missions, and I noticed my yellow pencil rolling to and fro on my navigator's desk. That old Fort was pretty stable even with one engine afire and a couple of big holes in her sides. That's a pretty yellow pencil, I thought, one of those mechanical ones somebody had sent us guys overseas. I really liked it. I pulled my feet back in the plane, stood up, and managed to get back to the desk. I got my yellow pencil, unzipped my jacket and stuck it inside my shirt. I didn't think the airplane was ready to explode. I didn't know; I just didn't think it would. Then, I remembered my Colt .45 and shoulder holster and picked that up too. Everything was unreal, like slow

German fighter plane Focke-Wulf FW-190 attacks an 8th Air Force B-17 during mission to Bremen, Germany, November 29, 1943. Not until February 1944, when long-range P-51's appeared, were American bombers escorted by friendly fighters all the way deep into Germany and back. Use of external drop-tanks eventually made all Allied fighters longer-legged. (Photo Courtesy USAF)

An 8th Air Force B-17F of 332nd Sqdn., 94th Bomb Group, overtaken by B-17 above just as bombs are released over Berlin, has part of its horizontal stabilizer smashed away by 500-lb bomb (deflected at lower left). Crippled Fortress was part of a 1000-plane raid on the German Capitol, March 6, 1944. It crashed out of control into the city below. Scattered clouds obscured its final plunge, and companions in other Forts were unable to count parachutes leaving it. B-17's normally carried 10-man crew. (Photo courtesy USAF)

motion. I put on the shoulder holster, went back to the hatch, and sat on the floor again with my feet dangling outside. I didn't see anyone else; just me and my dying airplane. So, I thought, 'Guess it's about time to go.' I looked at my watch. It was ten minutes past eleven. For some crazy reason, I drew my .45, then grabbed the rip cord and rolled out.

"The white 'chute burst open just as it was supposed to, and suddenly there was the strangest quiet I've ever experienced. Not a sound. Really, a strange quiet. And there I hung, with that ridiculous pistol in my hand, floating along sightseeing. Off to my left, I saw another chute, and up above me two more chutes popped open. The old B-17 seemed to be still flying, though a lot of smoke and flame trailed behind. Then the right wing broke away in one huge splash of fire and the fuselage went into a flat spin and disappeared.

"The anti-aircraft fire around the target wasn't far away and I could still see that. Then my peaceful descent was interrupted by machine gun fire! I snapped forward and looked down. I was going to land between the lines, on rocky ground that separated enemy ground troops from our own, and this bloody machine-gun nest had opened up on me, I thought. A couple of big pieces of the plane lazed by me and struck the ground. The coughing of that damned machine gun was too loud and I started cursing and waving my pistol.

"By then, I was low enough to see they weren't firing at me, but at the parachute to my left. How-

To mechanics in a combat zone, war means work under primitive conditions. Crew here is changing an engine on an African field unmindful of sun, sand, and determined insects. (Photo courtesy USAF)

German Focke Wulf 190 fighter was a dangerous adversary for best Allied fighters. *Luftwaffe's* fatal weakness was extremely poor leadership at the top. (Photo courtesy USAF)

ever, I figured I'd be next. You can see very clearly from a chute. Too well, under those circumstances, and you feel like a pig in a barrel. I saw a couple of vehicles bounce over a little hill heading, hell for leather, for where I was going to land. My God! Not only are they trying to machine-gun us, now they're bringing in reinforcements. I flicked the safety off my pistol and aimed at them with about as much logic as the western movie hero who drops the bad guy from clear across town. Still about a thousand feet up, the whole scene was before me, and then I realized those vehicles were *our* Jeeps. Some of our wonderful G.I.'s had seen the Fort's trouble, watched us jump, then came piling to the rescue; and before I hit the ground, damn' if they didn't just erase that machine-gun nest! About then, I hit. Landed on a rock and

broke my right leg. That didn't matter then. I was down and alive. All but one of our crew made it. Our ball-gunner never left the airplane.

"Our troops loaded us into trucks, and fifteen minutes after leaving the Fort—at twenty-five past eleven —I was receiving medical aid in a nearby village."

We asked Bart what ever happened to his yellow pencil. He said he didn't recall.

"Two things I do remember, and will never forget," he said. "First, was the stench in that little village. A concentration camp nearby caused it, they said. You can't imagine how it was—people treated that way. I understood then what I was doing there. And when we drove to the nearest air base for evacuation, I saw for the first time the total destruction wrought by men like me in our bombers. Nothing was left standing along that road; everything was blasted down and burned. The bomber is a terrible weapon."

On May 7, 1945, thirteen days after Bart's plane went down, the war in Europe ended. And top enemy generals agreed that Allied bombers were indeed terrible weapons. General Feldmarschall Hugo Sperrle, commander-in-chief of *Luftflotte* 3 until Paris was re-taken, said, "Allied air power was the chief factor in Germany's defeat." And Generalmajor Herhudt von Rohden of the *Luftwaffe* General Staff: "The invasion of Europe would have been impossible without strategic bombing. It was the decisive factor in the long run."

This theme was repeated by almost every German commander after the fall of the Third Reich—and it would be reiterated in other accents following the defeat of Japan.

Still, despite air power's decisive role in WW-II, America had no air strategy. Objectives, yes. Policies (several), yes. But no air strategy. U.S. planners never considered that we could force surrender upon our enemies through the proper use of air power alone. Invasion and occupation of Germany, Japan, and Italy by massive ground forces were taken for granted by men who believed we should fight this war as we had the last; this was implicit in our unshakable demands for "unconditional surrender." But Project Control, a postwar study by the Air War College, concluded that the war with Japan could have ended six months sooner (without the atomic bomb), and the war with Germany ended as much as twelve months earlier had the Anglo-American powers embraced an air strategy calculated to bring our enemies to the peace table by total destruction of their electric power sources, industries, transportation and communications systems. No industrial nation, so grievously wounded at home, can long sustain its military or even feed its people.

In retrospect, U.S. Air Force General Carl Spaatz declared, "Had the revolutionary potentialities of the strategic air offensive been fully grasped by the men running the war, some of the fateful political concessions made to hold the Russians in the European war and to draw them into the Japanese war might never have been made."

The implications in that statement are boundless.

And General Hap Arnold later wrote: "Without attempting to minimize the appalling and far-reaching results of the atomic bomb, we have good reason to believe that its actual use provided a way out for the Japanese Government. The fact is that the Japanese could not have held out long, because they lost control of the air. They could not offer effective opposition to our bombardment, and so could not prevent the destruction of their cities and industries."

It should be remembered that when Japan surrendered its army was virtually intact.

All this naturally raises the intriguing question as to whether or not the Allied invasion of Europe was really essential to ultimate victory. From D-Day onward, we controlled the air above *Festung Europa*. How long could Germany have lived under constant air bombardment even assuming her army was not engaged in combat with Allied ground forces? Significantly, the question seems not to be whether the Third Reich could have survived under such conditions; but merely—for how long?

That such a question was not asked in the beginning is at least understandable when one considers that strategic air bombardment had never been tried on such a scale, and only our own experience, much later, would reveal that the best example then available to us—the failure of *Luftwaffe* bombers to force Britain to her knees during the fall of 1940—was a very poor example because a limited number of German aircraft were employed, none of which were actually heavy bombers, and all of which were mis-used. However, from the beginning, America did commit herself to a maximum air effort, even if we weren't too sure what the results would be or exactly how we would achieve them.

Almost as ill-prepared for this war as the last, the United States' build-up of a heavy bomber force was slow, and our strategic bombing offensive in Europe did not reach its peak until long after the Normandy landings (D-Day) on June 6, 1944. Only about 28 per cent of all bomb tonnage loosed against Hitler's Europe by the RAF and the AAF fell before July 1, 1944. And the fact that the U.S. Army Air Forces possessed B-17's and B-24's at all was largely owed to the perseverence of General Hap Arnold and a relative handful of other veteran air officers, most of whom had suffered earlier career set-backs for supporting General Billy Mitchell's crusade for a strategic bomber command.

On May 5, 1942, as the nucleus of America's Eighth Air Force was moving to England, Major General Carl A. Spaatz became its commander, with Brigadier General Ira C. Eaker taking over as bomber commander. Then, on July 4, the first American bombing mission in the European Theater of Operations

(ETO) was mounted when six U.S. aircrews borrowed half-a-dozen Douglas A-20's from the RAF and, led by six experienced British crews, attacked *Luftwaffe* bases in Holland. Two of the American-crewed planes were lost; a third came back damaged. On that same day, the first USAAF B-17 Flying Fortress landed in England.

Following routes blazed across the North Atlantic by British and Canadian ferry pilots early in the war, youthful American crews—most of whom had never been beyond sight of land before—had begun ferrying B-17's and C-47's (and even some fighter planes) to Britain. Almost 900 planes for the Eighth Air Force thus reached the British Isles during 1942. Losses were about 5 per cent; more than we could afford but less than anticipated.

After the token July 4 raid, the first true American mission over Europe came on August 17, 1942, when 18 *Fortresses,* led by Col. Frank A. Armstrong, Jr., and with General Eaker in the lead plane of the second flight, formed upon their own kind above England for a strike against railyards at Rouen, France. With an RAF fighter escort, that mission was successful, as were ten other small raids during the following three weeks. Only two B-17's went down to enemy action in the eleven missions.

But scarcely had the Eighth's build-up begun before much of this strength was drained away to form the Twelfth Air Force under Brigadier General Jimmy Doolittle. The Twelfth was needed to support "Operation Torch," the planned invasion of North Africa.

Meanwhile, the Ninth Air Force was born in Egypt as the German and Italian Armies threatened to take the Suez Canal. At first pieced together from whatever was at hand—it started with 23 *Liberator* bombers halted at an Egyptian fuel stop while enroute to the China-Burma-India Theater (CBI)—the 9th, initially commanded by Lieutenant General Lewis H. Brereton, teamed with Sir Arthur Coningham's RAF Desert Air Force to make possible the British Eighth Army's ascendency over Rommel's Afrika Korps in a series of great battles between October 24 and November 5, 1942.

North Africa was invaded November 8. In a multi-pronged attack, British and American troops came ashore at many points, surprising the Vichy French forces (portions of the French Army and Navy half-heartedly allied with their Nazi conquerors), and captured Algiers and Oran. Most of the Vichy French in Morocco were reluctant to fight against Americans and all threw down their arms within two days. Supporting the landings was U.S. Navy Task Force 34 Air Group consisting of four small aircraft carriers with 108 *Wildcat* fighters, 3 SBD's and 27 TBF's, plus the AAF's 33rd Fighter Group of some 70 P-40's which were launched from the *Chenango* and flew on to land at an Allied strip in Algeria. But the *Luftwaffe* did not appear, and the French offered almost no air resistance. Doolittle's 12th Air Force came from Gibraltar to occupy fields at Oran on the first day of the invasion.

However, the Allied drive eastward to take Tunisia was halted 15 miles short of Tunis by determined German forces and Allied failure to maintain control of the air. Responsibility for this mistake belonged to the Allied commander, Lieutenant General Dwight D. Eisenhower (later named supreme commander of the ETO). Eisenhower, with the foot-soldier's usual lack of understanding for the proper application of air power, had Doolittle's 12th, and RAF units at his disposal, scattered over 600 miles of North Africa to serve the presumed needs of local ground commanders —the classic and highly erroneous concept that aircraft should be tied to ground units to aid and protect them.*

General Eisenhower, evidently blaming his air officers for his aerial fumble, sent to England for General Spaatz to straighten things out. Spaatz was, of course, one of America's ablest air commanders; but bogged in the mud of primitive airstrips by winter rains, faced with a nightmare in logistics, penalized by inferior fighter planes (the P-40 was no match for the German ME-109) and having inherited a collection of air units that possessed no unified chain of command, Spaatz required several months to overcome these problems.

Spaatz was aided by the British who, despite opposition from top army commanders, helped him sell the idea of a unified North African air force run by air

---

* Today, helicopters *are* properly used in just this role by U.S. Army commanders, particularly in guerilla warfare situations. The U.S. had no combat helicopters in WW-II. The above statement applies to tactical aircraft—then and now. Such a force must not be broken up into small units, each assigned purely local objectives. Tactical air most effectively helps an advancing ground army by ranging ahead of it to knock out enemy airfields, choke off enemy supplies and disrupt his transportation and communications. Tactical air should be striking at the enemy's jugular vein, far over the horizon, while ground forces prepare to engage the enemy's extremities. This does not diminish the need for close air support during the ground battle, but such support is dependent upon *control of the air,* which cannot be achieved if air strength is frittered away piecemeal.

Republic P-47 *Thunderbolt,* commonly called the "Jug," was a 2,000-hp U.S. fighter that weighed 13,500 lbs loaded and seemed almost indestructible. Even the first ones, pictured here, were capable of 430 mph at 30,000 feet. Armament was eight .50-caliber machine guns. Jug's only weakness was short range. (Photo courtesy USAF)

officers. General Montgomery, whose British 8th Army was pushing Rommel's Afrika Korps north-westward across Libya, had delegated complete autonomy to Lord Tedder, his air commander. "Airpower is indivisible," Montgomery had said. "If you split it up into compartments, you merely pull it to pieces and destroy its greatest asset—its flexibility."

Tedder's force included General Brereton's 9th USAAF which, at the time of the North African invasion, consisted of 165 planes—B-17's, B-24's, P-40's and B-25's—plus the 1,100 aircraft of the RAF Desert Air Force. Opposing Tedder in Egypt and Libya were 2,000 first-line *Luftwaffe* craft. Then, during the winter of 1942–1943, all Allied aircraft in the theater were placed in the Mediterranean Air Command under Air Chief Marshal Tedder, and an effective chain of command, of air officers, was established by organizing, under General Spaatz, the Northwest African Air Forces (NAAF). Spaatz's deputies were Doolittle, whose strategic force would strike at Rommel's rear from Algeria, and Air Vice Marshal Coningham, whose tactical air force faced Rommel in

The Casablanca Conference of January 1943 was called by Allied leaders to plan grand strategy for Germany's defeat. Here it was decided to initiate 'round the clock bombing of Germany, USAAF by day, RAF by night. Seated are President Franklin Roosevelt and Prime Minister Winston Churchill. Standing left-to-right: Gen. Hap Arnold, Adm. Ernest J. King, Gen. George Marshall, Adm. Sir Dudley Pound, Gen. Sir Alan Brooke, and Air Chief Marshal Sir Charles Portal. (Photo courtesy USAF)

Lockheed P-38 *Lightning,* though designed before the war, encountered compressibility shock waves in high-speed dives resulting in structural failures. It took engineers some time to overcome the problems of this new phenomenon. *Lightnings* therefore did not see action until 1942. Pictured is the 1944 Model P-38L powered with twin Allisons of 1,600-hp each that gave this craft a top speed of 414 mph at 25,000 feet. Armament was a 20-mm cannon and four .50-caliber machine guns in nose, plus ten 5-inch rockets on wing mounts. (Photo courtesy USAF)

The British *Lancaster* heavy bomber, of which more than 7,000 were built during WW-II, continued in RAF service until 1956. All *Lancasters* could take 4,000-lb bombs for the RAF air offensive against Germany, and late in the war a few were modified to drop the 22,000-lb "Tallboy" super blockbuster. Maximum speed was 280 mph; engines were Rolls Royce *Merlins* of 1,460-hp. Craft was an AVRO design. (Photo courtesy USAF)

On August 1, 1943, 165 B-24 Liberators took-off from bases near Bengazi, Libya for an attack on the oil refining complex at Ploesti, Rumania, from whence came half of Germany's oil. The target was heavily defended and 44 Liberators did not return. Ten others, including the one above, crash landed back in friendly territory with battle damage. Production at Ploesti was not permanently affected, and American bombers were forced to go back, in far greater numbers, before that vital industry was destroyed. (Photo courtesy USAF)

General George C. Marshall, U.S. Army Chief of Staff (1), and General Henry H. "Hap" Arnold, Chief of the Army Air Forces during WW-II. Gen. Arnold is wearing on blouse pocket his original Army Aviator wings that he earned at the Wright brothers' school in Dayton in 1911 as a young, second lieutenant. (Photo courtesy USAF)

Libya. Whip-sawed in this crossfire, *Luftwaffe* elements in North Africa could not long survive. The Mediterranean Air Command, strengthened with American P-38 fighter units, gained control of the air in March, 1943, and, with Allied ground forces then free to move in a great pincer maneuver—the British 8th Army from the east, the North African invasion force from the west—Tunis and Bizerte fell on May 7. On May 18, 1943, the enemy gave up. Backed against the sea on Tunisia's north coast, denied supplies or reinforcements by Allied airpower, 270,-000 German and Italian soldiers surrendered. At the end, the Allies had 3,800 aircraft in North Africa: 2,630 American, 1,076 RAF and 94 Free French.

The enemy was allowed no respite. The combined Mediterranean Air Command immediately turned its attention to the heavily fortified Italian island of Pantelleria, about 50 miles off the Tunisian coast and which, with neighboring Sicily, would provide convenient stepping-stone air bases across the Mediterranean to Italy.

Pantelleria surrendered on June 11, after three weeks of concentrated air attack, and Sicily fell a month later. Then, just three miles across the Straits of Messina lay the tip of Italy, and beyond—the soft underbelly of Hitler's Europe.

With the end of the North African campaign, the 8th Air Force in England (under Brigadier General

Twelfth Air Force B-25 Mitchells of the 310th Bomb
Group on their way to strike at a German supply route
through the Brenner Pass. The 12th AF, operating
from captured airfields around Salerno, flew 5,000
sorties between March 19 and May 11, 1944, to almost
completely choke-off enemy supply lines in Italy.
Called "Operation Strangle," it allowed Allied ground
forces to take Rome on June 4, 1944, just two days
before the invasion of France. (Photo courtesy USAF)

Bridge-busting Martin B-26 Marauders of the 15th Air Force contributed significantly to the tactical air war in the Italian campaign. Craft above are returning to their base near Foggia after hitting targets in Northern Italy on August 30, 1944. (Photo courtesy USAF)

Ira C. Eaker) again received aircraft priority, and by June, 1943, the 8th could count 12 heavy bomb groups on paper with perhaps 9 groups actually operational.

Throughout the previous winter and spring, the 8th AF, though never able to assemble much more than 100 planes at a time, had sporadically struck at targets on the continent. But the chief return for these attacks was experience. The U.S. Strategic Bombing Survey made after hostilities ended, revealed that USAAF raids prior to the summer of 1943 had "no appreciable effect" on Germany's ability to continue the conflict.

Seeking first-hand impressions on this phase of the war, your authors contacted several air commanders of the period, including the late Major General Orvil A. Anderson who was, in 1943, a brigadier general and chairman of the Combined Operational Planning Committee, ETO. "We were in trouble," General Anderson recalled. "Our heavies, contrary to our beliefs, could not defend themselves. We needed long-range fighter escorts. Our losses, mostly to fighters, averaged ten per cent each raid which only gave a crewman a fair gamble of living for ten missions. He had a tour of twenty-five."

Another, and unnecessary problem was our own anti-aircraft artillery. General Anderson spoke bitterly about that: "The ratio of British and American anti-aircraft kills was seven friendlies for each foe. By '44 the enemy only used fighters and he never had

Troop-carrying gliders that were undamaged after landing in France on D-day were "air-snatched" and returned to England, some with wounded aboard. Here, a Douglas C-47 of the 9th Troop Carrier Command is about to engage glider's tow-line which is strung between two poles. Nylon rope stretches and absorbs shock after hook-up is made, and reel in plane allows additional play in tow-line until Waco-designed CG-4 glider accelerates to speed of tow craft. More than 13,000 Waco CG-4 gliders were built during WW-II. Note "invasion stripes" painted on aircraft above. (Photo courtesy USAF)

a four-engined bomber, yet our anti-aircraft gunners constantly shot down our four-engine heavies because of mistaken identification. Finally, we were in Luxembourg and two FW-190's flew overhead. Obviously, they were lost and when they found out where they were, they headed the hell out. The sirens and whistles blew, and anti-aircraft headquarters called General Quesada to get those damned fighters off their backs. Pete (Gen. Quesada) was fast on that one, and in less than five minutes two P-47's came rolling up.

They started looking around. Then the damned fools on the ground opened up so much artillery on those two P-47's they literally disintegrated. Two more scores for the American anti-aircraft gunners—on us! I had to say something. The guys on the ends of the lanyards were not guilty, but a higher-up was. The man responsible was guilty as hell. That had to be General Omar Bradley. You see, the Army controlled anti-aircraft and it had no right to those weapons. In less than a week, Vandenberg (AAF Gen. Hoyt Vandenberg) was in charge of all anti-aircraft in the theater. Bradley lost it; the score was getting too damned high."

In January, 1943, Roosevelt and Churchill agreed upon a combined bomber offensive against Europe as a principal decision at their Casablanca Conference. American heavy bombers, with the highly accurate Norden bombsight, would mount massive daylight attacks on strategic targets, priority going to oil refineries and German aircraft production. The Royal Air Force heavies would strike at night, relying less on accuracy than on saturation bombing. Thus were planned two significant though costly missions at the beginning of the strategic air war: the Ploesti oil complex in Rumania on August 1, 1943, and the Regensburg and Schweinfurt raids of August 17 which aimed at Messerschmitt aircraft plants and ball bearing factories.

The first Ploesti raid (actually, the second—a small raid by elements of the 9th AF hit Ploesti from North Africa in June, 1942, but inflicted little damage), launched from bases around Bengazi, Libya, set a standard for courage and determination by American aircrews. The attacking force consisted of two 9th

On the morning of March 24, 1945, two Allied airborne divisions—14,000 men—were airlifted across the Rhine River to establish bridgeheads for Allied forces advancing upon the Ruhr. This view, framed by the radio antenna atop its fuselage, is from a C-47 of the 439th Troop Carrier Group towing a pair of Waco CG-4 gliders, each with 15 combat-equipped soldiers aboard. (Photo courtesy USAF)

More than 9,000 American airborne troops, plus 5,300 British, landed in France during "Overlord," the invasion of the European Fortress. These, jumping from C-47's of the 12th Troop Carrier Command, landed near beachheads between Nice and Marseilles. More than 800 Douglas C-47's carried troops to France on D-day. Protected by Allied fighters above, not a single troop-plane was lost to enemy air action. (Photo courtesy USAF)

AF B-24 groups and three 8th AF B-17 groups for a total of 165 planes, after maintenance drop-outs had cut the figure from 179. Due to cloud cover, two formations took a wrong turn over Targoviste and alerted enemy defenses. Then, slashed by fighters and pounded by flak, the scattered *Liberators* stubbornly roared in at low altitude to loose their bombs on target. Ten went down to enemy fighters and 23 were lost to anti-aircraft fire. Others, badly mauled with wounded and dying crewmen aboard, somehow made it to friendly territory. Well over one-fourth of the strike force was lost, and, although 40 per cent of Ploesti's cracking and refining capacity was wiped out (Ploesti produced one-half of all German oil), the Germans had the plants back in operation within 90 days. Lacking planes and crews for a quick follow-up raid, the August, '43 Ploesti mission became a doubtful victory won at high cost.

Badly shot-up P-47 *Thunderbolt,* painted with "invasion stripes," nosed-up on landing as wounded pilot lost consciousness. Fire fighters control blaze from belly tank while crew chief struggles with cannon-damaged canopy, and medics, one with hands in pockets, remain at safe distance. (Photo courtesy USAF)

Martin B-26 Marauder of the 9th Air Force is hit in port engine and falls in flames during Battle of the Bulge, December 23, 1944. More than 500 of the 9th's tactical aircraft ranged ahead of the First and Ninth U.S. Armies to strike at enemy supply lines behind the lines between Melmedy and Marche. By mid-January, 1945, the German commander, von Rundstedt, pulled back the remnants of his 5th and 6th Panzers and German 7th Army, and the Allied advance continued. (Photo courtesy USAF)

General Dwight D. Eisenhower, Supreme Commander
of Allied Forces in Europe, inspects cockpit of 60-mis-
sion Martin B-26 *Marauder,* "Son of Satan," piloted
by Lt. Col. Sherman R. Beatty of Hoquiam, Washington. Although General Ike had soloed in the Philippines many years before, there is little evidence that
he ever really grasped the true potential of air power.
(Photo courtesy USAF)

The Regensburg-Schweinfurt mission on August 17, 1943, was a double-pronged attack, by 8th AF B-17's, with 146 *Fortresses,* led by Colonel Curtis LeMay against the Messerschmitt plants at Regensburg, and 230 *Fortresses,* led by General Robert Williams, against the ball bearing factories at Schweinfurt. LeMay's force met German fighter opposition—*Luftwaffe* elite, the yellow-nosed ME-109's and FW-190's of the "Abbeville Kids"—over the coast of Holland and the Forts had to fight their way 300 miles to the target. Twenty-four of them were shot down, but the remainder refused to be denied (the proud fact is, not one American bomber formation was ever turned

back by enemy action during WW-II). LeMay's Forts damaged every building of the Regensburg Messerschmitt works and managed to escape over the Alps to land in North Africa after eleven hours in the air.

The Schweinfurt-bound Forts, delayed three hours by weather, found the German fighter defense rested, refueled, and waiting, rather than on the ground with empty tanks or diverted by LeMay's force as had been hoped. Savagely attacked, Williams' Forts tightened-up to fill gaps in their box formations as their companions fell away mortally stricken—and stubbornly continued to their objective. Of the 230 bombers that struck Schweinfurt that day, 36 failed to return to

Douglas A-26's of the 386th Bomb Group, 12th AF, on low-level attack mission to Austria's Attnang-pucheim marshalling yards, April 1945, from their field in Belgium. These tactical craft were armed with 14 forward-firing fixed .50 caliber machine guns. The A-26 became the B-26 in 1947 after the "attack" designation was discontinued and all Martin B-26's were retired. (Photo courtesy USAF)

their bases in England. For this sacrifice, they achieved 80 direct hits on the vital ball bearing plants.

If the first Schweinfurt raid was costly to the 8th AF, the follow-up strike two months later was a near-disaster. It climaxed a week of maximum effort missions—and maximum losses. On October 8, 9 and 10, strikes against Bremen, Danzig and Münster claimed almost 100 American bombers, or 9.5 per cent of the attacking forces. Then, on the 14th, the Schweinfurt raid cost 60 of the 291 attacking planes when the Forts were set upon near the German border by an estimated 400 *Luftwaffe* fighters. The Americans fought 20 miles to the target and 200 miles back again until met by friendly fighter planes which

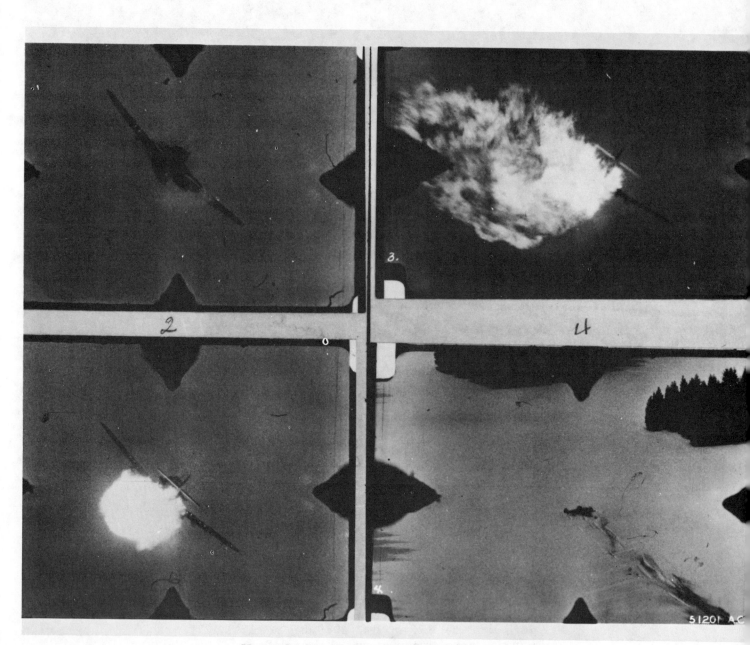

How a German Me-109 pilot cheated death is revealed in this series of photos taken by the gun camera of U.S. fighter pilot, Lt. Lee Mendenhall of Anahuac, Texas. Frames should be viewed top-to-bottom left, then top-to-bottom right. Mendenhall's guns exploded Messerschmitt's belly tank, but enemy had apparently already tripped tank's release and it fell away (threatening Mendenhall's plane). At lower right the Me-109 rests in snow after clipping tree tops and slewing to a stop in wheels-up crash landing. (Photo courtesy USAF)

General Ira C. Eaker, a famous Army Air Corps pilot of the 20s, commanded the U.S. Eighth Air Force in Europe during WW-II. (Photo courtesy USAF)

B-24 Liberator of General Nathan Twining's 15th Air Force breaks up in flames, its bombs tumbling from its bays, after receiving a direct hit in a heavy flak belt near Blechhammer, Germany. Records do not indicate fate of its crew. Sister B-24 of the 465th Bomb Group continues to target. (Photo courtesy USAF)

Retreating Germans smashed fuselages of this pair of ME-110 twin-engined fighters before allowing the craft to fall into Allied hands. These planes, along with hundreds more, were useless to the Luftwaffe because of empty fuel tanks. Allied strategic bombers had reduced Germany's oil industry to a mere 7 per cent of its normal capacity by the spring of 1945. (Photo courtesy USAF)

North American P-51 *Mustang* was designed and built in 117 days. The first ones, with 1,150-hp Allison engines, had a speed of 370 mph. The P-51D of 1944 (pictured) was fitted with the excellent Rolls Royce *Merlin* V-1650-7 engine of 1,790-hp and had a top speed of 443 mph at 25,000 feet. Normal armament was six .50-caliber machine guns. This one is landing at Ober Olm Airfield in Germany, April 17, 1945. In background is Cessna UC-78 *Bobcat* utility plane. (Photo courtesy USAF)

Capt. Dominic Salvatore Gentile of Piqua, Ohio is officially credited with 23 aerial victories as a fighter pilot flying *Spitfires, Thunderbolts*, and *Mustangs* in the ETO. An "airport kid" before WW-II, Gentile enlisted in the RAF in 1940, transferred to the USAAF when America entered the war. He was killed during a routine training flight in a T-33 jet in 1951. (Photo courtesy USAF)

The Northrop P-61 *Black Widow* night fighter went into service in mid-1944. Big, powerful, and heavily-armed, the *Black Widow* carried a pilot, radar operator, and gunner. Early models were fitted with four 20-mm cannon in nose and four .50-caliber machine guns in a remotely controlled barbette atop the fuselage, though the machine guns were soon eliminated. Speed was 362 mph at 20,000 ft.; engines were P&W R-2800's. (Photo courtesy USAF)

103

lacked fuel capacity to stay with the "Big Friends" that final, hellish 200 miles into enemy territory. It was the last mission attempted deep into Germany, in daylight, until new, long-range P-51 escort fighters became available in February, 1944.

Meanwhile, the Allied invasion of Italy had begun on September 3, 1943, a few hours after Italy's King Victor Emmanuel III, backed by a disillusioned Italian Army, approved Italy's secret surrender to the Allies (the King had deposed Dictator Benito Mussolini on July 25). But when, on September 8, the Italian surrender was announced, German forces in Italy under Rommel and Kesselring occupied Rome and dug-in north of a strong defensive line that roughly divided the country in half, with Allied ground forces in possession of the southern half. The ground war in Italy was thus stalemated throughout the winter, although Allied air power gained a tenuous control of the air by October 1.

At the end of 1943, General Spaatz was named overall commander of the U.S. Strategic Air Forces in Europe, and General Doolittle took over the 8th AF from General Ira Eaker who in turn was promoted to boss of the (renamed) Mediterranean Allied Air

German Messerschmitt 262 *Stormbird* jet fighter as found by advancing U.S. ground troops near war's end. Far ahead of anything possessed by the Allies, the 600-mph Me-262 could have greatly altered the air war in Europe had Hitler allowed its production sooner. About 1,300 were built late in the war, but lack of fuel and critical parts, because of the Allied strategic bombing offensive, kept all but about 150 out of action. (Photo courtesy USAF)

Forces. The Mediterranean command contained, in addition to RAF units, General Cannon's 12th AF and General Twining's 15th AF. The 12th, which, under Doolittle, had fought in Africa, given air support to the Sicilian conquest and invasion of Italy, relinquished bomber groups to General Nathan Twinings' new 15th AF which was formed in Italy on November 1, 1943. The 9th AF, by then under command of General Hoyt Vandenberg and which had fought beside the 12th from Africa to Italy, was moved to England in October, 1943, in anticipation of the invasion of Europe, then planned for May 1, 1944.

The coordinated strategic air offensive against Ger-

The world's first true strategic missiles were Adolf Hitler's "Wonder weapons," or "Vengeance weapons," the V-1 and V-2. The V-1 Buzz Bomb was a small, unmanned aircraft powered with a pulse-jet engine and carrying a ton of explosives. The V-2 was the forerunner of today's ballistics missiles. It delivered slightly less than a ton of explosives up to 220 miles. Both weapons appeared too late and in insufficient quantities to affect the course of the war in Europe, although they did kill 10,000 British civilians. V-1 pictured was found in France almost intact after it glided to a freakish, near-perfect landing and failed to explode. (Photo courtesy USAF)

many began early in 1944, with the first order of business elimination of the *Luftwaffe*, both the force in being and its industrial base. On January 11, 800 bombers with fighter escort struck at Nazi aircraft factories in Oschersleben, Brunswick and Halberstadt. Fifty-three heavies went down, along with 5 escorting fighters; but returning American crews claimed nearly 300 enemy fighters in exchange.

"Big Week" came during a period of good weather in February (20th to 25th) when more than 1,000 heavy bombers of the 8th AF and 500 from the 15th AF, shepherded by fighters, blasted mercilessly at German aircraft plants. On March 4, American bombers for the first time were escorted all the way to Berlin by P-51's, and twice more, within the next four days, formations of 1,000 heavies, accompanied by P-51's, made daylight raids on the German capital. By the end of March the *Luftwaffe* had lost more than 800 first-line fighters in air battles with American bombers and fighters. This, coupled with nightly Royal Air Force strikes of fantastic bomb-tonnage and low-level attacks on German airfields by B-25's, B-26's and A-20's, achieved Allied air superiority over Europe by April 1, 1944. From that day on, Hitler's Third Reich was doomed.

As previously mentioned, many air commanders today believe the Allies forfeited to old prejudices and WW-I thinking a chance at a relatively cheap victory in Europe during the spring of 1944. Allied air power, it is pointed out, was free to systematically destroy the enemy after defeat of the *Luftwaffe*. The costly invasion of the continent by massive ground armies was unnecessary, they maintain. And Japan's surrender, without invasion (and the estimated one million lives it would have cost), appears to endorse this view.*

Operation "Overlord," the invasion of *Festung Europa* by the Allies, began before dawn on June 6, 1944. "D-day" was a Tuesday. Eleven thousand Allied airplanes—painted with special black and white "invasion stripes" which would, hopefully, positively identify them to friendly anti-aircraft gunners—flew more than 14,000 sorties over the Normandy beachheads and beyond in support of the landings. Amer-

ica's air strength in the ETO had by this time grown to 7,500 first-line combat planes of which 2,900 were heavy bombers, 3,000 fighters and 400 twin-engined bombers. Equally important, though less glamorous, were more than a thousand C-47 transports, the airplane that General Eisenhower later called one of America's five most important "weapons" in WW-II. On D-day, a single flight of troop-laden C-47's, nine abreast, formed an unbroken line 150 miles long from southern England to the Cherbourg Peninsula. Protected above by an impregnable canopy of Allied fighters, not one troop plane was lost to enemy aircraft.

A handful of enemy planes did manage to filter through the Allied fighter screen to strike at the 4,000-ship invasion fleet crossing the English Channel, but these were futile, if brave, attempts on the part of the decimated *Luftwaffe* and resulted in little damage.

After D-day, most Allied tactical aircraft and many strategic bombers were diverted from the pure air offensive against Germany to supply close air support for ground troops. And although some air strategists felt that the resulting switch in target priorities diluted the effectiveness of our air supremacy by this comparatively "inefficient" use of our planes, there can be no doubt that this course was necessary once Allied ground forces were committed to battle on the continent. The invasion forces were able to gain a foothold in Normandy and advance across Europe almost directly in proportion to the efficacy of their air support.

The U.S. ground commander who perhaps best understood the proper use of tactical aircraft was Lieutenant General George S. ("Blood and Guts") Patton. On July 25, he sent his Third Army racing through a five-mile breach blasted in enemy defenses along the Saint-Lo-Periers Road by 8th and 9th AF planes, and dashed toward Germany depending entirely upon American fighters and fighter-bombers to protect his exposed southern flank. To many veteran ground soldiers, such a move seemed to border upon madness; but the American pilots—mostly from Brigadier General O. P. Weyland's 19th Tactical Air Command—deeply aware of their responsibility, bombed and strafed like demons at altitudes that should have entitled them to Combat Infantryman Badges. In fact, so well did these airmen do their job 20,000 German soldiers, attempting to turn Patton's flank, surrendered *directly* to the Air Force—without

* Your authors belabor this point because, clearly, America's security should be entrusted only to those aware of history's lessons. The above premise, if valid, would seem to assume importance today vis a vis the so-called "limited wars" that recurrently confront us. (Also in this connection, we will, in a later chapter, examine some of the known and evident results of the Kennedy-Johnson-McNamara defense theories.)

ever engaging the Third Army. Not surprisingly, General Patton, later speaking of tactical air support for his armored divisions, characterized it as "a matter of love at first sight."

A week after D-day, Hitler began sending his *Vergeltungswaffe,* or "vengeance weapons" against London. The first of these was the V-1 Buzz Bomb, or "Doodler," a small, un-manned and gyro-stabilized aircraft powered with a pulse-jet engine and carrying a ton of explosives. The Buzz Bombs had a range of 150 miles at a speed of 400 mph. Eight thousand of them were fired, first at London, then at Antwerp, Belgium, from bases in France and Holland. About 4,000 of the V-1's were intercepted—1,847 by fighter planes, 1,866 by anti-aircraft artillery, and 244 snarled themselves in barrage balloon cables around London before Allied bombers snuffed out V-1 production and destroyed the flying bombs' launching sites. By September, 1944, the V-1 was no longer a serious threat. However, Hitler had another and more terrible vengeance weapon, the V-2.

The V-2 was first fired against London and Paris on September 8, 1944. It was a short-range ballistic missile, fueled with liquid oxygen and alcohol, that reached a speed of 3,600 mph and a peak altitude of 60 miles. It carried slightly less than a ton of explosive in its warhead and had a maximum range of 220 miles. Fortunately for the Allies, Hitler failed to appreciate the V-2's potential early in the war and it—like the jet fighters that could have been available to him in significant numbers had he given the order in time—appeared too late to change the course of the war in Europe. Nevertheless, the 2,500 Buzz Bombs and perhaps 100 V-2's that struck England, killed almost 10,000 civilians and leveled more than 200,-000 buildings, mostly homes.

Meanwhile, Allied strategic bombers systematically eliminated the enemy's oil industry. By the spring of 1945, gasoline production in Germany and in German-occupied territory had dropped to 7 per cent of normal capacity and the Nazi war machine became almost immobile. The mechanized German Army was afoot; Panzer units were crippled, and new fighter planes for the *Luftwaffe,* produced with supreme effort in underground plants, were grounded with empty tanks—and there destroyed by low-flying Allied fighters.

Allied ground forces, moving swiftly beneath skies totally controlled by their own aircraft, swept over the Reich to meet Russian forces at the Elbe River on April 25, 1945—the day Bart Bartimus bailed out of his crippled Fort (with his yellow pencil) near Pilsen on the final Allied bombing mission of the European war. Five days later, Adolf Hitler committed suicide amid the rubble of Berlin. A week after that, a prostrate Germany, her cities in ruin, surrendered.

When the end came in the ETO, America had about 13,000 combat airplanes in that theater. The Western Allies had dropped 2,770,540 tons of bombs on the Continent during five years of war. Of that total, U.S. bombers were responsible for 1,500,000 tons, mostly during the final ten months of that conflict.

Aircraft losses are more difficult to pin down because official records do not agree. *Luftwaffe* figures are hard to reconcile with Allied tallies in some cases. Perhaps the most reliable summation is the scholarly and surprisingly unbiased U.S. Strategic Bombing Survey ordered by President Roosevelt. This source lists 18,000 American and 22,000 British planes lost or damaged beyond repair; 79,265 American and 79,281 British airmen lost in action. German aircraft losses are placed at 57,000, including those destroyed on the ground. The total dollar-cost of the American air effort in Europe during WW-II is given in this Survey as something over $43 billion.* The price of freedom, in both lives and treasure, has always been high. This generation of Americans was willing to pay that price.

---

* This figure obviously includes great sums that were spent in support of the air effort in the ETO but not chargeable to AAF appropriations, because the AAF's total direct expenditures from appropriations, world-wide, for the years 1941-1945 inclusive, were but 36.9 billion dollars out of an authorized 61.7 billion dollars.

The U.S. aircraft industry produced almost 300,000 airplanes during these years including planes for our Allies. Of this figure, about 175,000 units were combat aircraft of 18 principal types used by the USAAF, Navy and Marines. Total value of U.S. military aircraft production during WW-II was $45 billion.

6. Victory — and Distant Drums

Two days after the fall of Corregidor and the end of organized resistance to the Japanese invasion of the Philippines, a pair of self-appointed guerillas, USAAF Sgts. Al Fernandez and Jim McIntyre, fleeing from Japanese troops that had over-run their airfield on Mindanao, came upon a tiny village in the mountains and were greeted by a group of young Filipino patriots who had been discussing ways and means to continue their fight against the Nipponese conqueror. The Filipinos were armed with 1903 Springfield rifles, some ancient Enfields, a few M-1's, and a fair supply of hand grenades ("liberated" from a U.S. armory). They were leaderless and most lacked military training; but they were eager to fight. The U.S. had promised independence to the Philippines,* and these young idealists knew that under Japanese rule that dream would be forever dead.

"Those fellows were cautious at first," Fernandez remembers. "But they knew all about Mac and me; their jungle intelligence system was very good. We drank coffee and talked awhile and they asked Mac and me to lead them. We told them we would.

"Mac and I organized our new troops—there were more than 200 by the time they all arrived from the surrounding mountains—into platoons and companies; appointed non-coms, established a headquarters unit and promoted ourselves to 'acting first lieutenants.' It wasn't very legal, but it worked okay. In fact, we did a lot of things that weren't covered in the Articles of War, but our government later backed us up in every case. For instance, I refused to allow my men to confiscate anything from civilians. I printed by hand a lot of guerilla money, stating on each note that the U.S. Government would redeem it at face value in American money when we had won the war. We bought food and other things we needed with it and the civilians always seemed satisfied to accept this homemade currency. After MacArthur came back and retook the Philippines, every cent of that guerilla money was redeemed just as I promised. In fact, the dern' finance officers deducted almost $3,000 from my back pay for guerilla money I had spent on myself.

"Anyway, our guerilla units were forced into action almost immediately. The enemy had set up a large base at Cagayan and began sending patrols into the mountains. But my men knew those mountains like I knew the systems of a B-17, and since the Japs did not, we literally massacred them. We used the same tactic for a long time; rows of grenades tied to stakes about ten feet apart in the deep grass on both sides of a trail. We strung long lengths of wire through the grenade pins, fastened securely to each pin, and one of us would hide some distance up the trail holding

* The Philippines became a U.S. possession as a result of the Spanish-American War in 1898. America granted the emerging nation commonwealth status in 1935, with total independence planned 10 years later. The war interfered some, and the Philippines became an independent nation on July 4, 1946.

Allied forces returned to the Philippines Oct. 20, 1944, and Manila was liberated four months later. By early March 1945, Manila Bay was open to Allied shipping and at that time General Douglas MacArthur and Philippine Statesman/General Carlos Romulo (standing) made a symbolic return to Corregidor aboard a PT boat. (Photo courtesy USAF)

the ends of these wires like a pair of reins. Then, we'd wait for a signal from a companion positioned above who commanded a good view of the trail. When he waved, we'd pull the wires and, in a few seconds, all the grenades would explode at once in a corridor of death that usually left us with only some 'clean-up' work to do. We stripped the bodies of arms and ammo, buried them, and tidied up the scene to prevent the enemy from learning what had happened. It worked many times, although the Japs eventually wised-up and began sending much bigger patrols—as many as 300 men—in two sections.

"However, by that time we were a lot stronger and

began shooting it out with them at river crossings and other places carefully selected to our advantage. Also by that time, Mac had taken over another force on my west flank, and I had made contact with still a third bunch of guerillas on my east flank led by Col. Fertig and a Major Underwood. These men were artillery-men, I think, and had been on Mindanao with General Sharp when the Philippines fell. Fertig had saved a shortwave radio transceiver and made contact with MacArthur's headquarters in Australia. Soon after that American submarines began slipping in on dark nights to bring us supplies. I asked for Browning Auto-matic Rifles, Thompson Sub-machine guns and med-

Japanese Army heavy bomber, Nakajima Ki-49 Type 100 *Helen* served throughout the war. (Photo courtesy USAF)

icines, because all our fighting was at very close range.

"I received a field commission to make my 'lieutenacy' legal, and my guerillas were put on the books in MacArthur's headquarters as 'U.S. Army Irregulars.' Soon after that, Tokyo Radio, our chief source of entertainment, announced that the Japanese Imperial Government would pay a reward of $10,000 for me dead or alive. Tokyo Rose called me a bandit; but the Filipinos there in the mountains knew better. And the fact that I'm here and telling you this should give you an idea of the kind of people those Filipinos were. There were probably 2,000 people in those mountains who could have claimed that reward; instead, they were proud to know we were hurting the enemy so badly, and they made jokes about it to me, and were more than a little insulted to think the enemy believed their allegiance could be bought.

"After the subs began supplying us, we had a great edge in firepower. Fifty men, armed with BAR's and Tommy guns, suddenly raising up together from concealment to ambush a force less than a hundred feet away, can do a tremendous amount of damage in a very few seconds. Once, after a fire-fight at a river crossing, we pulled 151 enemy bodies from the water

out of a force of about 300. Our casualties were 2 men wounded.

"Finally, on October 12, 1944, after I'd been in the mountains 2 years and 5 months, Fertig sent word that MacArthur had ordered all of us to find strategic positions along the north coast from which we could assist downed flyers. This was what we'd waited for so long; it could only mean that the Americans were coming back to the Philippines!

"Three days later, I stood on high ground near a village called Balangisag and looked out across Macajalar Bay and cheered like a schoolboy as the sky filled with American planes and the enemy base at Cagayan was methodically leveled. A week later, a Navy PBY came and took me to MacArthur's headquarters near Tacloban Airstrip on the Island of Leyte where intelligence people picked my brain and I tried to get used to shoes again.

"Then they put me aboard a C-54 and sent me back to the United States. Lillian was waiting for me. They gave me some medals and another promotion and all my back pay. The adjutant general cut a special order authorizing me to wear the Combat Infantryman's Badge along with my Air Force wings,

110

and they gave me a staff car with a driver and 30 days leave and asked me to speak at war bond rallies. But I felt ridiculous riding around in that sedan, and shoes hurt my feet and I couldn't make a speech for sour apples. I just wanted to lounge around the house with Lillian, and go out to the field and talk airplanes with guys who spoke my language and maybe drink a few beers. And that's what I did."*

MacArthur's return to the Philippines climaxed a year-long combined offensive by Admiral Nimitz' Central Pacific forces that had moved 3,000 miles and captured bases from Tarawa through the Gilberts and Marshalls to the Marianas, and by General MacArthur's South Pacific forces that had fought 1,300 miles from Port Moresby to Hollandia on New Guinea's north coast and beyond to the island bases of Wakde and Biak. As these two great forces came together southeast of Mindanao, with MacArthur poised on the island of Morotai 250 miles from Mindanao and four large Navy Task Groups operating from the Palaus, Yap and Ulithi, their power was merged for the invasion of the Philippines at Leyte on October 20, 1944.

Throughout the twin campaigns Nimitz' forces had been spearheaded at sea by carrier-based aircraft, while General Nathan Twining's 13th Air Force and General Thomas White's 7th Air Force, along with shore-based Marine air units, took control of the air over "one damned island after another." MacArthur's ground forces in the meantime were able to move beneath General George Kenny's 5th Air Force, which had been put together from bits and pieces in Australia.

As U.S. Army, Marines and Australian troops secured ground after bitter fighting on Leyte, the 13th and 5th Air Forces were combined as the re-born U.S. Far East Air Force, and these flyers quickly took control of the air over the Philippines and paved the way for the Allied invasion of Luzon at Lingayen Gulf on January 9, 1945. Manila was liberated a month later.

Meanwhile, the Japanese Navy was finally and decisively beaten attempting to repulse the Allied invasion of Leyte. In three separate but related actions the Battle of Leyte Gulf cost the Japanese 26 major ships including 4 aircraft carriers (some historians

put this at 6 Japanese carriers; however, the U.S. Navy in its summary, "United States Naval Aviation 1910–60," NAVWEPS 00–80P–1, Govt. Pntg. Off. 0–568901, claims only the *Zuikaku, Chiyoda, Zuiho* and *Chitose*). The U.S. 7th Fleet under Vice Admiral Thomas Kinkaid lost the escort carrier *Gambier Bay* in the Battle of Leyte Gulf, and Vice Admiral W. F. Halsey's Fast Carrier Force from the 3rd Fleet lost the fleet carrier *Princeton* and the escort carrier *St. Lo*, the latter to the first enemy *kamikaze* attack when a Japanese pilot deliberately dove his bomb-laden plane into the U.S. warship. After the Battle of Leyte Gulf the Japanese were reduced almost exclusively to this desperation tactic in opposing American Naval forces (they also used *kamikazes* against some important shore installations); and although these suicide planes took a fearsome toll during the last ten months of the war—accounting for at least half of all Navy ships damaged and one-fifth of those sunk throughout the war—America's air/sea power had grown to such overwhelming proportions it could not be deterred.

While Allied troops were mopping up in the Philippines, Admiral Nimitz was ordered to take Iwo Jima, a volcanic island in the Bonins about 750 miles from Tokyo. Rear Admiral C. T. Durgin's Task Group 52, put together around 12 aircraft carriers, conducted pre-assault air strikes against Iwo Jima beginning on February 16, 1945. Then, on the 19th, two Marine divisions, assisted by minor Army units and later by a third Marine division, went ashore to face approximately 23,000 Japanese troops manning perhaps the strongest defensive positions in the Pacific. After bitter fighting, the island was at last secured on March 16, at the price of 4,590 Marine dead and the Navy's escort carrier *Bismark Sea*, which was sunk by *kamikaze* attack. The *Saratoga* was severely damaged and the *Lunga Point* lightly damaged by *kamikazes*.

The high cost of the Iwo Jima campaign was more or less justified during ensuing months since possession of this base cut in half the distance to Tokyo from U.S. air bases in the Marianas, allowing P-51 fighter escorts for the B-29 *Superfortresses* pummeling Japan, and also provided a much-needed emergency airfield for damaged or fuel-starved B-29's returning to the Marianas from missions over the enemy's home islands. (It was officially claimed that no less than 2,400 *Superforts* made emergency landings on Iwo Jima, and therefore 25,000 U.S. airmen were saved from ditching in the ocean as a result of the Marines' sac-

* As this is written, Major and Mrs. (Lillian) Fernandez live in a modern rancher atop a hill within the traffic pattern of Ft. Sill's Henry Post Army Airfield. Al served at Henry Post Field as an Air Corps sergeant before WW-II.

Air Force Major Richard I. Bong was top American ace in WW-II with 40 official victories. Bong, who flew with the 49th Fighter Group of General Kenney's Fifth Air Force in the Southwest Pacific, probably had twice that number of kills, but since they went down in the ocean, unseen by anyone but Bong, they could not be officially recognized. He is shown here in his P-38 *Lightning* in New Guinea, March 6, 1943. Bong was killed after returning to the U.S. in a P-80 accident on August 7, 1945. (Photo courtesy USAF)

rifice in securing this base. But this seems unlikely since only 3,763 *Superforts* were delivered to the Air Force before war's end, and less than 1,200 saw action in the Pacific.)

The B-29 air offensive against Japan began in mid-June, 1944, when the 58th Bomb Wing of the newly created 20th Bomber Command began operations from Chengtu in west-central China about 125 miles northwest of Chungking. But logistics problems (everything had to be flown over the Hump, and about 12 such supply trips were required for each mission

flown) and an airplane rushed into combat with insufficient testing, plus the fact that tactics learned in the ETO seemed less effective in Asia, marked the *Superforts'* China-based effort as relatively unsatisfactory. By October, however, bases taken from the enemy in the Marianas were ready to handle B-29's and *Superfort* strength was concentrated there on five big airfields, two each on Guam and Tinian and one on Saipan.

The 20th and 21st Bomber Commands, operating as the Twentieth Air Force directly under the Joint

Chiefs of Staff as a global Air Force, resumed the air assault against Japan on November 24, 1944, when 111 *Superfortresses* struck Tokyo. Still, this raid, and those that followed through the winter, failed to significantly affect Japan's industrial output. Clearly, high-level precision bombing could not get to the thousands of small shops that fed component parts and sub-assemblies to the enemy's war machine. Meanwhile, too many B-29's were being lost to defending Japanese fighters and to the long 3,000-mile round trip to Tokyo from the Marianas. The prevailing westerly winds—which at times included the

Major Gregory "Pappy" Boyington, maverick Marine ace and ex-Flying Tiger, reads orders to pilots of his Black Sheep Squadron (VFM-214) at Guadalcanal. Pappy later spent 20 months in a Japanese prison camp after being shot down during a dogfight in which he scored his 28th victory. (Photo courtesy U.S. Navy)

then-mysterious jet stream—drained away precious fuel and forced many B-29's to ditch in the ocean short of their home bases (wind always takes more than it gives back to an airplane in flight because, on a round trip, your plane is subjected to the headwind for a longer period of time than to the tailwind. For example, if you normally cruise at 300 mph, then a 3,000-mile round trip, in a no-wind condition, will require 10 hours. But if you have a 100-mph headwind for half the trip, or 1,500 miles, and a 100-mph tailwind on the return journey, the round trip will require 11 hours and 15 minutes. Outbound, the headwind cut your ground speed to 200 mph, and therefore that half of the trip took 7 hours and 30 minutes. Returning, your ground speed was 400 mph; therefore this half of the journey required 3 hours and 45 minutes. So, figures do "lie," don't they?).

In January, 1945, Major General Curtis E. LeMay was ordered to take command of the B-29 wings in the Marianas and to produce some results. General Arnold picked the right man. LeMay had been a flyer since 1929; had gone to war in 1942 as boss of the 305th Bombardment Group in England. As a colonel, he led many air strikes against Germany, including the first Regensburg raid which cost 24 of his 146 *Fortresses*. At the end of the European war, LeMay was a general, commanded a bombardment division, and had gained the nickname of "Iron Pants,"

Grumman F6F *Hellcat* escorting TBF's and SBD's from new carrier *Yorktown,* October 1943. The *Hellcat* replaced *Wildcats* aboard carriers begining in September '43. The F6F-3N was night fighter version with radar scanner mounted on starboard wing. Engine was the P&W R-2800 of 2,000 hp; speed was 375 mph at 18,000 ft; guns were six wing-mounted .50-calibers. (Photo courtesy U.S. Navy)

Japanese transport ship explodes after dive-bombing attack by Curtiss SB2C *Helldiver* south of Luzon near Marinduque Island during battle for the Philippines, November 1944. *Helldiver* at lower right. (Photo courtesy U.S. Navy)

although this assessment of his character seemed not to bother him: "Hell, I'm not here to win friends; I'm here to win a war." And an awful lot of Air Force people today will tell you that Iron Pants LeMay came as close to winning the war as any other one man they can think of.

He did so with a single command decision; a decision that brought Japan to her knees, beaten and helpless before delivery of the A-bombs which "ended" the war.

By early March, 1945, it was clear to LeMay that his B-29's simply weren't punishing the enemy as his B-17's had done in Europe. Iron bombs, dropped from 30,000 feet on selected targets, were not doing sufficient damage, and the B-29's superior bomb capacity was largely nullified by the heavy fuel loads

TBM *Avenger* takes-off from deck of *USS Bunker Hill* to attack Japanese Fleet during the Battle of the Philippine Sea, June 19, 1944. TBM was General Motors version of Grumman TBF. (Photo courtesy U.S. Navy)

required for the long haul to Tokyo and back. It was then that LeMay made the decision that turned his B-29's into the most awesome engines of war so far devised by man: he ordered them loaded with incendiary bombs, stripped of guns, and said they would raid Tokyo, at night, from a mere 7,000 feet of altitude.

Most of LeMay's air crews received this briefing with shock. Some vehemently declared that Iron Pants had finally popped his cork. To go over Tokyo, unarmed, unescorted and at 7,000 feet, was tantamount to mass suicide. The pressurized B-29 was designed as a high-altitude precision bomber. Equipped with the famed Norden bombsight and remote-control guns, it was the finest strategic bomber in the world; yet LeMay

was throwing out all the *Superfort's* superior features and was asking them to hot-rod it over Tokyo unarmed! But gradually, as the more experienced crews examined the idea, the plan became less fantastic, at least in theory. The Japanese certainly would not expect B-29's at that altitude and the heavy flak would be set up to fire high above them. Intelligence reports held that the target was defended by relatively few automatic weapons that could hit them down low; the enemy was known to possess few night fighters, and if no defensive guns were carried aboard the B-29's that certainly eliminated the danger of firing upon one another in the darkness, while the weight saved would lower their fuel consumption for the trip home. So, shock had turned into cautious optimism by take-

The *USS Franklin* was severely damaged by *kamikaze* attack on March 19, 1945, during the Okinawan Campaign. Four other U.S. ships were also damaged. (Photo courtesy U.S. Navy)

off time. All things considered, this bold plan just might work.

It did. Fifteen and eight-tenths square miles of Tokyo were destroyed by fire that night—one-fourth of all the buildings in the world's largest city. Eighty thousand people died in that conflagration, which was caused by 323 Superforts, each carrying 68 incendiary bombs dropped squarely on target from low altitude.

During the next ten days, similar fire-bomb raids on Nagoya, Osaka and Kobe added another 15 square miles of desolation to Japan's principal cities. In these five attacks (Nagoya was hit twice), between March 9 and March 19, a total of 1,489 *Superfort*-loads of bombs were dropped and only 21 planes lost.

A week later, March 26, 1945, the B-29's were temporarily diverted from their primary mission to aid the Allied invasion of the Ryukyu Islands and Okinawa. Here again they performed unusual duties for strategic bombers by blasting enemy airfields and sowing mines in Korean and western Honshu ports and in the Shimonoseki Straits.

The invasion of the Ryukyus began with seizure of the Keramas, just 15 miles west of Okinawa and about 400 miles southwest of Japan itself, when troops of the U.S. Tenth Army went ashore supported by Admiral Durgin's Task Group 52. Then, Okinawa was invaded on April 1 by four Army divisions and two Marine divisions. But despite American air superiority, many *kamikazes* slipped through to hit U.S. war-

Japanese *kamikaze,* although burning from hits by anti-aircraft fire, holds determinedly to its final attack. An instant later it smashed into the deck of the *USS Essex;* November 25, 1944, Philippine Campaign. (Photo courtesy U.S. Navy)

Mitsubishi Ki-21 Army Type 97 *Sally* was almost identical to Japanese Navy *Nell.* Main difference was *Sally's* shorter range. This medium bomber, which entered service in 1937, was powered with a pair of Nakajima Ha-5 Kai engines of 950-hp each. Top speed was about 270 mph at 13,000 ft., and normal bomb load 8,000 pounds. About 1,800 were built. (Photo courtesy USAF)

Fires rage on forward deck of *USS Saratoga* after she
was hit by three *kamikazes* off Iwo Jima, February 21,
1945. (Photo courtesy U.S. Navy)

ships. Both Durgin's 18-carrier Task Group, operating south of Okinawa, and Vice Admiral Marc
Mitscher's Fast Carrier Task Group 58, standing between Okinawa and Japan, were subjected to repeated
mass kamikaze assaults, sometimes as many as 400
suicide planes at once. During the 83 days of the
Okinawan Campaign, *kamikazes* sank 35 U.S. ships
and damaged 288.

Altogether, 176,000 Army and 88,500 Marine
troops were needed to slowly ferret out enemy soldiers
solidly entrenched in "Shuri positions" (a maze of
tunnels and caves) that American air power seemed
unable to breach. The island was at last secured on
June 21, at a cost of 12,500 dead or missing Americans; 110,071 of the enemy. The U.S. lost 763 airplanes in this three-month climactic battle, while Japan

lost 1,733 (several previously published books inexplicably put Japanese plane losses at 7,000-plus for
this period; but official Japanese records list a total
of 4,200 planes lost, 2,467 to operational accidents).

An unusual operation for Navy and Marine pilots
during this time was a series of carrier strikes launched
against enemy airfields and other tactical ground
targets deep in Japan. The Air Force wasn't particularly happy at this encroachment upon its responsibility; but the Navy, at last rich with carriers, undisputed master of the oceans, and still fighting mad over
the insult and injury done to it at Pearl Harbor, wasn't
easily slowed once it got to slugging with both fists.
Besides, the *kamikazes* were concentrating on aircraft
carriers, and the Navy had a personal stake in destroying Japanese air power as quickly as possible.

"Valencia's Flying Circus," four Navy fighter pilots who, between them, accounted for 50 enemy airplanes. Left-to-right: Lt. Harris E. Mitchell, Lt. (j.g.) Clinton L. Smith, Lt. James B. French, and Lt. Eugene A. Valencia. (Photo courtesy U.S. Navy)

With Okinawa secured, LeMay's *Superforts* resumed their firebomb raids, and by the end of July, 1945, more than 100 square miles were desolated in Japan's six largest cities while sixty lesser cities were badly damaged. All told, 2,333,000 Japanese buildings were leveled and about 241,000 people killed. Near the end, enemy resistance was so feeble that

General LeMay announced in advance where he would strike in order to cut civilian casualties.

So, by August 1, 1945, the enemy was exhausted, his ability to make war or even to defend his own cities totally destroyed. His Navy was gone, along with most of his merchant marine. Millions of Japanese were homeless and 313,000 suffering from injuries

Navy's top ace in WW-II was Cmdr. David McCampbell with 34 aerial victories, pictured here in cockpit of his F6F *Hellcat,* October 30, 1944. (Photo courtesy U.S. Navy)

Consolidated B-24 *Liberator* approaches for landing at Midway above nesting gooney birds. The goonies, named by U.S. servicemen, are actually members of the albatross family. (Photo courtesy USAF)

as a result of air attacks. Japan was desperate for peace (except for a tiny clique of militarists who preferred national suicide to surrender), and General LeMay, who did not then know America possessed an atomic device, urged his superiors in Washington to delay the planned invasion of Japan's home islands, because LeMay knew that it could cost a million American lives and he was convinced the enemy would, without invasion, soon be forced to accept the unconditional surrender ultimatum issued by Truman and Churchill at the July 26 Potsdam Conference.

We can only guess at how long Japan might have held out, her leaders arguing among themselves, had America not used the A-bomb. But it is true that the Japanese had already made an attempt to get peace talks started with the Allies. Unfortunately, they chose to send the message through the Russians (who had remained at peace with Japan throughout the war), and the Soviets sat on the proposal.

The Soviet leader, Josef Stalin, had promised the Allies that Russia would declare war on Japan the instant Hitler was defeated, but Communist promises have never been noted for their substance, and this one was no exception. In fact, Prime Minister Churchill noted that the Russians had been "acting in an astonishing manner" ever since the Yalta Conference in February, 1945 (by which time Germany's defeat was certain). Stalin had completely taken in President

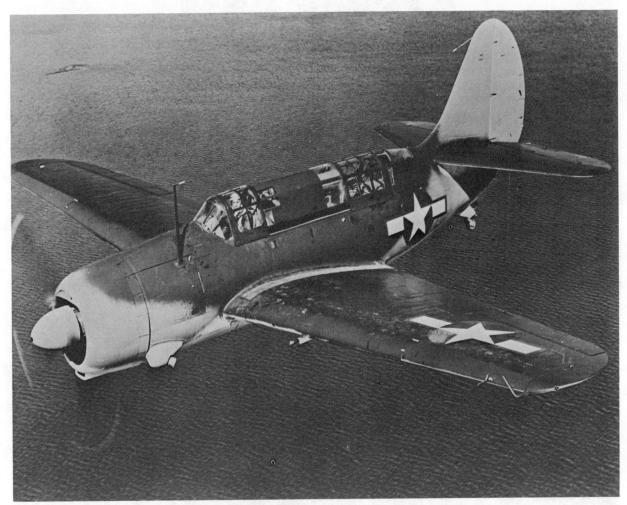

The Curtiss-Wright SB2C *Helldiver* replaced many of the SBD *Dauntlesses* during latter half of the war. Its top speed of 280-mph made it about 30 mph faster than the *Dauntless* and it had several hundred miles more range. *Helldiver*'s engine was a 1,700-hp Wright. (Photo courtesy Curtiss-Wright Corp.)

Flight deck scene aboard *USS Randolph* after night *kamikaze* attack, March 12, 1945, Iwo Jima Campaign. *Kamikazes,* operating during last ten months of the war, accounted for at least half of all U.S. ships damaged and one-fifth of those sunk during the entire Pacific conflict. (Courtesy U.S. Navy)

General Curtis E. LeMay, an Army Air Corps flyer since 1929, led bombers over Europe during first part of WW-II, then took over the B-29 offensive against Japan. His unorthodox but highly-effective tactics devastated Japan's principal cities and destroyed the enemy's ability to make war. Most historians today agree that America's use of the A-bomb shortened the war by a few weeks at most; Japan was already defeated. (Courtesy USAF)

Roosevelt at Yalta, although Roosevelt never knew it (he died suddenly, April 12, 1945) and it remained for future generations of Americans—and Germans and Poles, etc.—to pay for it.

Anyway, after the U.S. dropped its first atomic bomb on Hiroshima, August 6, 1945, the Soviets decided the time had come for them to share in the spoils of the Pacific victory, to which they had contributed nothing, as well as the booty they had won in Europe (plus European territory they were then in the process of stealing). Therefore, Russia, in one of Communism's proud moments, declared war on defeated Japan August 8, 1945. The Reds then wasted no time in occupying Manchuria and North Korea, and stepping up delivery of supplies to Mao Tse-tung, the Red

guerilla who had been fighting Chiang Kai-shek in China with increasing effectiveness since 1934. These and other signs revealing Russia's future international political posture were not lost on most U.S. military leaders. And when a Soviet fighter plane shot down an unarmed American B-29 flying into North Korea to drop emergency food supplies to Allied prisoners of war just a week after the war had ended, still other Americans could hear the distant Soviet drums that disturbed the world's newly won peace.

Whether or not the use of atomic weapons was justified in the Pacific War—and many people, especially in the Air Force, say today that, at best, A-bombs shortened the war by no more than a few weeks—

The B-29 *Superfortress* was fitted with the R-3350 Wright Cyclone engine of 2,430-hp; It had maximum speed of 358 mph, bomb capacity of 20-30,000 lbs, and a range of 3,250 miles at 230 mph and 25,000 feet. Less than 1,200 Superfortresses saw action in the Pacific. (Photo courtesy USAF)

Superforts pass Mt. Fujiyama enroute to Japanese targets. (Photo courtesy USAF)

President Truman did order their use because, to shorten the war by a few weeks, or even a single day, would save American lives. Therefore, at 2:45 A.M. on August 6, 1945, the *Enola Gay,* a B-29 from the 509th Composite Group, 20th Air Force, took off from Tinian in the Marianas accompanied by two sister ships (one to photograph and one to take special instrument readings) and headed for Hiroshima with an atomic bomb in its bays. The *Enola Gay* (named for the mother of the aircraft commander, Colonel Paul Tibbets) loosed her weapon above the Japanese city at 8:16 A.M. Four square miles of Hiro-

shima were obliterated; and eventually, casualties were put at 78,150 dead, 13,083 missing and 37,425 injured. Three days later, the B-29 *Bock's Car,* dropped the second A-bomb on Nagasaki, killing 73,884 people. That ended the haggling among Japanese militarists and Japan sued for peace on August 14, 1945. Formal surrender documents were signed aboard the battleship *Missouri* September 2, 1945, in Tokyo Bay, while 462 *Superforts* circled above.

It had been a long and bloody journey from the carnage at Pearl Harbor. From a few hundred combat planes in the Pacific in January, 1942, American

125

Corsair F4U fighter smashes into island on deck of the Escort Carrier *Prince William* after returning from strike in the Bonins, February 24, 1945. (Photo courtesy U.S. Navy)

combat aircraft strength in the Pacific grew to more than 12,000 in January, 1944, and a year after that approached 19,000. Total U.S. aircraft production soared from an output of 6,500 units in 1940 to a peak of 96,000 in 1944. Between July 1, 1940 and August 31, 1945, America produced almost 300,000 airplanes, 174,768 of which were combat aircraft. Total cost to the U.S. for military planes during WW-II was about $45 billion.

The Japanese had about 3,500 first-line combat planes at the time of Pearl Harbor; but so great were their losses (50,955 total, both combat and operational) during the ensuing 44 months of the Pacific War that at no time did Japan have more than 8,000

aircraft committed to combat duty. When the end came, Japan did have approximately 9,000 airplanes (including trainers) held in reserve for *kamikaze* missions against the expected invasion by Allied fleets.

Throughout the war Japanese aircraft production totaled 69,888 units, of which 52,242 were combat airplanes. Japan's peak production year was 1944, during which she turned out 28,180 planes, 21,055 of which were combat types. After the B-29 offensive against Japanese industry began in the spring of 1945, Nippon's aircraft production rate steadily declined until, by July, it had practically stopped altogether.

The U.S. Army Air Forces destroyed a total of 10,-343 Japanese aircraft in all theaters of the Pacific

Atomic bomb explodes over Hiroshima on the morning of August 6, 1945, dropped from the B-29 *Superfortress, Enola Gay,* piloted by Col. Paul Tibbets. Japanese casualties were later placed at 78,150 dead, 13,083 missing, and 37,425 injured. (Photo courtesy USAF)

War. Navy and Marine aircraft accounted for slightly over 15,000 Japanese planes.* Navy and Marine pilots sank 161 Japanese warships and 447 Japanese merchant ships. American submarines, however, accounted for 63 per cent of all Japanese merchant shipping sent to the bottom.

Clearly, no one service won WW-II in the Pacific. But none can dispute that air power was the decisive force.

* These are official Air Force and Navy figures. Japanese official figures (quoted in the United States Strategic Bombing Survey, Pacific) list 23,835 Japanese Army planes expended, of which 16,255 were lost in combat. Japanese Navy planes expended totaled 27,120, of which 10,370 were lost in combat. In other words, the Japanese lost a total of 26,625 airplanes in combat in WW-II. Since total claims of the U.S. Air Force and U.S. Navy pilots were 25,343 Japanese planes, that leaves but 1,252 kills for Army and Navy anti-aircraft gunners, British and Australian fighter pilots and *kamikaze* action. It's possible that both Air Force and Navy pilots' claims were a little high. Nevertheless, U.S. claims and official Japanese loss figures seem remarkably close together; much more so than Allied vs. *Lutfwaffe* figures for WW-II.

NEW HORIZONS

7. The Cocked Fist

The year was 1945 and, inevitably, the day would approach when the guns of World War II would be silenced. Early in February, the Big Three allied powers met at Yalta to map plans for world peace. From the Conference came two identifications which were to become watchwords in the days to come: the general structure of the United Nations was formed, and American and English leaders learned of the distrust and suspicion festering in the third member of the triumvirate, the Soviet Union. Time after time, suggestions for peaceful settlements were shrugged off by a Russian cold shoulder.

After much cajoling, the Soviets did agree to free elections of "liberated people," yet, only 2 weeks later, they threw out the peasant government of Rumania and, backed by troops, converted the country to a Communist dictatorship. By the end of another two weeks, USSR, with similar tactics, put a government in control of Poland.

This should have been sufficient warning that an end of World War II was not, necessarily, peace. But the brilliance of stilled weapons would not be tarnished.

As General Doolittle described the Army Air Force's demobilization from 243 groups to only 2, "destructively and explosively," millions of men returned to civilian life. The American military might dropped to a small force whose major job simply was to get the last of the soldiers, seamen, and airmen back home.

Germany and Japan had crumbled, yet the Russian Army remained intact and month by month overturned one government after another. Not all of our military leaders were blind to this, for, on September 20, 1945, General Ira C. Eaker, then Army Air Forces Chief of Staff, recommended the formation of a "Strategic Striking Force" to be based in the United States but constantly ready and capable of attacking anywhere on the globe. Its weapon, he explained, should be the atomic bomb, which, by its very power, weakened the defenses of post-war America. We were too complacent in holding that secret.

Meanwhile, on the Soviets rolled. They took over Eastern Europe and in the Far East, the Kurile Islands, Outer Mongolia, and Sakhalin Island. The Communist influence and doctrine spread throughout North Korea, North Vietnam, Manchuria, and China.

Anticipating a complete reorganization of the U.S. Defense Forces, Headquarters, Army Air Forces split their major operational command, the Continental Air Forces, into three: the Strategic Air Command, Tactical Air Command, and Air Defense Command. Most of the people and resources of the old CAF went to SAC which, formed on the Eighth and Fifteenth Air Forces, came to life on March 21, 1946 at Bolling Field just outside of Washington, D.C.

The U.S. and her allies faced a cold war with the Soviet Union whose forces were stronger than ever. On our side was the demand to "bring the boys home" no matter what the cost. To hold the atomic bomb

131

The Boeing B-52, in the foreground, eventually replaced the B-36 *Peacemaker* in the background. The B-52 *Stratofortress,* a sweptwing with 8 Pratt and Whitney turbojet engines, cruised at more than 650 mph, 200 mph more than the *Peacemaker.* Moving into SAC operations in 1955, the *Stratofortress* cost eight million as compared to $315,000 for SAC's first major bomber, the B-29; 744 B-52s were produced. The *Peacemaker,* fondly called "Big Bertha," came to SAC in 1948. Built by Convair, she bridged the gap between World War II aircraft and post-war airpower. Four J-47 GE turbojet engines were added to her original six Pratt and Whitney piston engines, and she was the world's largest airplane with wings reaching 230 feet and a fuselage length of 162 feet. Her bomb load alone, 84,000 pounds, tipped the scales higher than a B-24 fully loaded. From her fuel supply of 21,000 gallons, she burned 1000 an hour. She flew 12 years worth of SAC missions, and she never fired a single shot in anger. (Photo courtesy USAF)

and our leadership in that technology, and to build airpower to deliver it was the near impossible mission of baby SAC. With inherited B-29's, B-17's, and B-25's formed into 9 bombardment groups and 2 fighter groups, which could count only 3 jets, (Lockheed *Shooting Stars*) in the entire inventory, SAC could deliver a few "weapons," as the A-bomb was called.

From 1946 until the Berlin blockade of 1948, political and economic forces in the United States and in Europe made building a large military power a hopeless dream. Not only were we faced with defense order cutbacks and tight money at home, but we were faced with the necessity of rebuilding Europe so that she could protect herself. And politics? Who dared talk money or men for the services now? The voters were demanding civilians—now. Inflation began and with that added burden, the cost of supporting so much of the rest of the world skyrocketed.

The National Security Act of July, 1947, united

Boeing's B-47 *Stratojet* set speed records when delivered to SAC starting in 1951. A three-man crew manned the plane to speeds above 600 mph. This medium bomber, powered by six J-47s, also was equipped with high altitude cameras, starting the work of SAC's other big-league mission—reconnaissance. Over 1,300 models were in service including the uncomfortable area of the Western Pacific. The last B-47 left Guam on January 10, 1967, and by then, had cocked the fist in that part of the world for 11 long years. (Photo courtesy USAF)

Army, Navy, and the new separate service, the U.S. Air Force, under control of a single secretary of defense coordinated by the joint chiefs of staff. For the Air Force, this meant rebuild. The new service was hard hit since many of its trained support people were left with the Army; volunteers for the "blue suit" were mostly operations and maintenance specialists. With outdated equipment and only a handful of trained men, the morale of the fledgling Air Force was amazingly high. At long last, they were a service—individual and not tied down by any connecting strings.

The first commanding officer of SAC, General George C. Kenney, an early student of strategic bombing and a wartime commander of bomber forces, set forth to build some order out of post-war confusion. SAC's rolls counted 36,000 men and 600 airplanes, less than half of those bombers. The first operational

SAC activated the USAF's first guided missile combat unit—the 556th Strategic Missile Squadron, Presque Isle, Maine—in December 1957. Equipped with Northrop *Snarks,* an air-breathing "cruise" missile that flies at about the same altitude and speed as an aircraft, the 556th has manned various generations of later missiles. The *Snark* was phased out in 1961 due, primarily, to the vulnerability of its above-ground, "soft" launching system. Capable of carrying a nuclear warhead, the *Snark* was 69' long, with detachable wings of 42' span, and was 15' high. (Photo courtesy Northrop Aircraft, Inc.)

SAC's B-58 *Hustler* is a Mach 2 delta-wing. Capable of flights above 60,000 feet, the *Hustler* also excels on low-level operations. Nuclear bombs and some fuel can be carried in the slim disposable pod mounted beneath the fuselage. (Photo courtesy USAF)

consideration had to be building a strike force.

Only the next year, General Kenney's SAC came into the headlines with the famous "Mock raid" on New York City. One hundred and one bombers, mostly B-29's, slashed across our biggest city to prove how unprotected we are. It looked a mighty force to American civilians who had been spared the roar of thousands over Europe. In actuality, it was puny, yet it consisted of every possible bomber SAC could get into the air.

Early hard-driving leaders in SAC slowly shaped a core of professionals. Without a highly trained man-power heart, even with modern equipment, the Command was nothing. In the early stages, they had neither men nor equipment. They pioneered tech-niques as they grew, even making goodwill flights and training flights to Europe and to South America. These flights were not as they looked on the surface; basi-cally, they were proving a capability of American might.

By 1948, SAC's base structure began to stabilize. And this was the year of the Berlin blockade when the Kremlin pondered just how far the Allies would be pushed before committing themselves to another all-out war. Among the many and the immediate actions of American military arms, 3 SAC bomber groups descended on Europe. These planes were based so every major Soviet target was within range of the B-29's. They displayed their capability of reaching those tar-gets day in and day out. World circling, endurance

General Dynamics' Atlas, America's first intercontinental ballistic missile, first flew in June 1957, and went operational with SAC in September 1959. It had a range of 9,000 miles. (Photo courtesy General Dynamics)

records, the B-29's blasted aloft, 24 hours a day, from the German bases. With this show of strength came the common use of the word "deterrence." The aggressor, then, being faced with power and capability, must balance the odds. If he continues pushing, what is the amount of retaliation? Will the profits of war end up on his side? This is what SAC asked the Soviet Union while the Communists were deciding just how far they could go in Berlin.

The Kremlin didn't like what it saw, and after the Berlin blockade, SAC was formally recognized as the primary deterrent to Communist aggression. "Peacetime" as a way of living was over for the SACmen. From this date, they were a strategic bombing force, a cocked fist demanding that any aggressor assay the odds before stepping on toes.

Two major changes came to SAC later in 1948: the arrival of new equipment, the B-50 and the 10-engine magnesium monster, the B-36 *Peacemaker,* and General Curtis LeMay as commander. General LeMay, the man who initiated the Berlin airlift countering the Soviet blockade, and his deputy, General Thomas S. Powers, together molded the shape of SAC for 16 years.

An unusual and remarkably powerful force, it's said, is built by one man. If this is so, the one man who built SAC into the cocked fist the world respects is General LeMay. Only 5'10½" tall, the stocky cigar-smoking general is indeed formidable. Many men consider him too tough. Called "Old Ironpants" (not to his face) in World War II, LeMay, to put it politely, is unpredictable. As commander of the 305th Bom-

In operation since 1963, SAC's heavy-weight *Titan II* is launched directly from an underground silo. It's 103 feet tall and has a reaction time of one minute from orders to "go." Liquid propellants power this Martin-built nuclear warhead carrier. (Photo courtesy USAF)

Equipped with two *Hound Dog* supersonic guided missiles and several 13' long decoy ADM-20 *Quail* missiles, the B-52s can fly faster than 650 mph and either "on the deck" or at altitudes above 50,000 feet. The heavy bomber can cover 12,000 miles and hit several targets hundreds of miles apart on one mission, without refueling. The Air Force continues studies on SRAM (short range attack missiles) for the B-52's to hit targets such as airfields. (Photo courtesy USAF)

bardment Group, one of the first to enter combat, he insisted his bombers "put the weapons on the targets." The way to do this, he said, was to forget the anti-aircraft fire, no matter how deadly, and keep each bomber on a straight line for the target. He said that one man lost early in the war would save thousands later.

Never one to issue orders, then sit back and wait, LeMay flew the lead plane straight to targets, without dodging flak, time after time. And it worked.

Modified to the "Big Belly" version to carry more tons of conventional weapons in Vietnam, the B-52's are also America's first guided missile carriers. One *Hound Dog* missile is shown in the racks. Fifty percent of SAC's bomber and tanker force is on continuous ground alert, ready to go within the warning time provided by the Ballistic Missile Early Warning System (BMEWS). (Photo courtesy USAF)

After 27 months of hard fighting in Europe, LeMay was placed in command of the Mariana-based B-29's. Later proven one of the major decisions of World War II, his orders to stop high-level bombing of Japan came as a shock. Instead, his B-29's were to fly low-level, at night, with incendiaries against the wood and plaster buildings in the Emperor's homeland. By the time Japan surrendered, the low flying B-29's had destroyed 105 square miles of her 6 major cities and with that, her capability of waging war, even before the A-bomb hit Hiroshima and Nagasaki.

In his lonely early life, he had trained himself to be a perfectionist, and when he took over command of SAC, he "kicked out the gold bricks and promoted the tigers." He trained and maintained the force to a "certain urgency," and his men worked harder and longer than in any other command. Seventy-two hour duty weeks were not unusual, and General LeMay started bombing competitions. The winners were awarded—not trophies, but promotions. From the early pressure by LeMay SACmen have attained higher rank than equal service-time airmen in any other part of the Air Force.

He fought the battle of better housing for his men, and lost, but they knew he had tried. From his personal dedication and his willingness to lead the way down a hard road, there has come a spirit in SAC unsurpassed in any other branch of service anywhere.

SAC Headquarters moved to Offutt Air Force Base, near Omaha, Nebraska, on November 8, 1948. From this small start has evolved a tight, security-conscious building with as many floors below ground as above. In the control room, 3 floors and 46 feet below ground, is the heart of SAC's cocked fist "go-code." Two telephones, one red giving coverage to launch the aircraft against predetermined targets, and the other gold connects directly with the joint chiefs of staff in Washington. A radio net "short order" is in contact with all SAC planes in flight. The control room is filled with screens of needed globe-wide information ranging from weather to location of all aircraft. The walls are 24″ of steel reinforced concrete with a roof slab 36″ thick; it would be sealed off in time of war. Enough rations are stored to feed 800 people for 2 weeks.

The actual need for SAC came from the experience

In 1961, SAC became the single manager of the USAF tanker fleet. Retiring piston engine KC-97s, SAC's fleet turned to the jet KC-135s in 1957. These Boeing-built *Stratotankers* have a take-off weight of 300,000 pounds and of that, 175,000 pounds is fuel. They can transfer this at the rate of 1000 gallons per minute. They average moving 2.37 billion pounds of jet fuel each year, enough to fill 64,500 rail tank cars—a line that would reach from New York to Pittsburgh. The Tactical Air Command F-4C *Phantoms* are being refueled in Southeast Asia.

gained from World War II which proved strategic bombing's contribution in defeating both Germany and Japan. The World War II B-17 grew to the B-29 for such missions, and both came to SAC. The ETO Strategic Bombing Survey stated that "the best way to win a war is to prevent it from occurring." The Pacific's Survey said, "The U.S. must have the will and the strength to be a force for peace."

That added up to SAC, and soon industry sent the B-36's and B-50's. The B-36 *Peacemaker* built by Convair for a 16-man crew, permitted massive retaliation to become a fact. She was America's first and major weapons system for deterrent missions, and she was so huge that crewmen rode a 4-wheeled scooter from her nose to her tail section. Each *Peacemaker* cost $3,500,000. She even had cat-walks inside her wings so mechanics could work on her engines in flight.

Several *Peacemakers* were modified for various experimental studies including launching and catching,

The B-52 *Stratofortresses,* with J-57 jets creating 100,-000 HP, are wider and longer than the width of a football field. The top of the rudder stands nearly as tall as a five-story building, yet it can turn inside of any known fighter at altitude. The B-52s carry 35,000 gallons of fuel plus 1000 more in tip tanks. Modified to carry either two North American built supersonic GAM-77 *Hound Dog* missiles or the decoy missiles, the *Quail,* the *Stratofortress,* updated to various models, has been a SAC backbone since 1955. The *Hound Dog,* shown air launched, is a stand-off missile that can be guided to attack in front of, or to the sides of the mother-ship. (Photo courtesy USAF)

SAC's airborne command post is aboard a *Stratotanker,* EC-135C. Twenty-four hours a day this flying command post is ready to assume control over SAC's bombers and missiles if both the underground and alternate command posts are knocked out by the enemy. Laden with communications equipment, the *Stratotankers* fly eight-hour missions each. The general officer and his team of experts remain on station until the replacement craft arrives. (Photo courtesy USAF)

in flight, F-84's. She was the world's first airplane to fly with an operating atomic reactor aboard.

She was not inexpensive to operate, this magnesium monster. In 1950 dollars, the costs, less crew, came to $1,024.17 per hour and her missions often lasted 24 hours or more.

With General LeMay sitting at the head of the two-pronged phone, to Continental Air Defense Command Headquarters and to the Pentagon Command Post, SAC started day and night practice sessions. Each

of his intercontinental bombers could drop more firepower than all allied aircraft loosed on Germany and Japan in World War II. He directed 3 numbered air forces and 2 overseas divisions, each with a composite array of aircraft, a complete fighting package. Each aircraft, he insisted, must have complete mobility. A fly-away kit stowed, untouched, in each plane enough critical parts to support a plane for 30 days in a war military leaders figured would last only one-half that time.

Lockheed-built, for SAC, the SR-71 flies more than three times the speed of sound. Powered by two Pratt & Whitney J-58 turbojets, the SR-71 has a wing span of 55' and a length of 107'. The total engine thrust equals the power of 45 diesel locomotives. This advanced reconnaissance craft grew out of Lockheed's secret A-11 program, the follow-on to the U-2, all from Clarence "Kelly" Johnson's notorious "Skunk Works." (Photo courtesy USAF)

In 1949, the U.S. signed the North Atlantic Treaty, a show of allied common resolve which, in fact, set the stage for a many-nation NATO military force. At nearly the same time, again to prove SAC capability, the "Lucky Lady," a B-50, flew around the world, non-stop, with 4 air-to-air refuelings for an average speed of 249 MPH. SAC was getting ready.

The need came the next year when on June 25, the North Koreans marched across the 38th parallel into South Korea. Within 4 days, the Communists captured Seoul. Nine days after the alert, the 92nd and 22nd Bomb Wings of SAC launched major air strikes in North Korea. Within the first 4 months, SAC planes flew 6,500 sorties, dropped 42,000 tons of outmoded TNT bombs, and forced the North Korean industries to a virtual standstill.

Both SAC and the Far East Air Forces bomber commands were limited by so few actual strategic targets. North Korean industry simply was not widespread as in Germany or Japan. The presidential order prohibiting attacks beyond the Yalu River, where the supply sources were, hamstrung the might of the heavy bombers. Yet, when the "agreement" was reached in Korea (for it is no lasting peace even

The solid-fueled *Minuteman* ICBM is silo-stored and virtually immune to enemy attack. Boeing is the prime contractor and 1000 *Minutemen* are programmed for SAC's arsenal. Traveling over 15,000 mph, this 60,000 to 70,000 pound ICBM will be on the way only 32 seconds after orders to launch. The typical "Smoke Ring," present everytime a *Minuteman* is fired, is at the top of this picture. (Photo courtesy USAF)

after the loss of 33,629 American lives), SAC's B-29's had shot down 33 fighters (including 16 Russian-made jet Migs), 17 more probables, 11 damaged. They had paid with the loss of 16 B-29's to enemy fighters, 4 to flak, and 14 to operational accidents. Combined with FEAF, SAC's bombers had destroyed 75 per cent of North Korea's rail facilities and 50 per cent of the hydroelectric plant system.

SAC's force, both in Korea and in Germany, had to be divided with one-half of the men and equipment upholding the deterrent cocked fist. Only this ready power had prevented the outbreak of an all-out war, yet it could not stop the Soviet progress toward world domination. "Small" issue after "small" issue, such as the French defeat in Indo-China and the crushing of the Hungarian rebellion, ended as a battle of talk and appeals through the United Nations.

SAC, which at one time was bigger business than General Motors in assets and personnel, must be counted as the power which contained Soviet military expansion in the 1950's.

When the von Neumann Committee, in 1954, reported that the technological problems of an intercontinental ballistics missile could be licked, President

Headquarters, Strategic Air Command is at Offut Air Force Base, near Omaha, Nebraska. There are as many floors below ground as showing above—three. The lowest floor is the command post or control room and from here would be issued the "go code" to SAC's bombers and missiles. In case of direct hit on this headquarters, SAC has alternate commands in various places on the ground and an airborne command post flying 24 hours per day. The *Minuteman* missile shell is symbolic of SAC's missile force. (Photo courtesy USAF)

Eisenhower gave his go-decision, and he stuck by the program despite impressive arguments from famous scientists and engineers.

Industry turned to as did all the services, the Army, the Navy, the USAF, and NACA, the forerunner of NASA. SAC fired its first successful missile in August of 1957. Our tests of the mighty hydrogen bomb assured us the Russians could never catch our technology lead. Then, only short months later, the Soviets demonstrated their own hydrogen bomb and 2 long-range strategic-delivery-system airplanes. For a climax, on October 4, the USSR fired into space Sputnik I, the world's first man-made earth satellite. This rapid advance in space technology couldn't be slurred as a fluke for only the next month the Soviets launched Sputnik II with a passenger, a dog named Laika, aboard. Our technological lead no longer existed.

Stalin's death left uncertainty as to direction of the Communists. The necessity of an ever stronger nuclear deterrent force grew daily. With Soviet build-up of *Badger* and *Bison* big bombers, SAC's cocked fist shrunk.

Of SAC's 197,000 men, 15,000 were combat airmen by the end of 1957. They made up the most security-conscious outfit in the free world. The flying generals wore pistols, the patrolling privates carried loaded guns, and sass from any rank led to the guardhouse.

The 3,000 SAC planes included 1,200 speedy B-47's, and SAC's aerial refuelings were stepped up to act as flying service stations on the average of every 15 minutes, 24 hours a day.

General LeMay, to keep the Command in front of the Soviets, flew a SAC tanker KC-135 6,350 miles, nonstop, in 13 hours to set a new world's record for nonrefueling jet flight on November 11, 1957.

SAC was assigned the responsibility for U.S. Operational ICBM capability and the 672nd Strategic Missile Squadron was activated on January 1, 1958.

Three days later, Sputnik I reentered the atmosphere.

Northrop's *Snarks* came to SAC first. These air-breathing "cruise" missiles, so called because they flew at about the same speed and altitude as jet aircraft, were soon considered obsolete. Simply, their above-ground launch system was too vulnerable. In September of 1959, the Command fired the first operational *Atlas* ICBM, a 15,000 MPH powerhouse.

That this was impressive is best shown in the fact that a *smiling* Mr. Khrushchev, then the Soviet leader, came to visit President Eisenhower and the United States only a week later.

The smile didn't last long, for the following May, the Soviets rattled their new missiles at the Paris Conference. To show his own confidence, Mr. Khrushchev shouted and hit his desk with a shoe that summer at the United Nations.

Russia had decided to stress missiles in their long range strategic forces, and they apparently felt they

General Bruce K. Holloway became Commander in Chief, Strategic Air Command in August 1968. He commands SAC's three numbered Air Forces, the 2nd, 8th, and 15th, and the First Strategic Aerospace Division (missiles) at Vandenberg AFB, California. Besides bases in the United States, SAC's planes are in Labrador, Puerto Rico, Madrid, Spain, and Guam. The Command has an authorized strength of 200,000 personnel.

held an upper hand in this field. By then, SAC had a leader who understood the Soviet ICBM threat, General Powers, who, prior to becoming LeMay's deputy, had been commander of the Air Research and Development Command. He took over command of SAC in July, 1957, and the missile build-up started.

SAC's mission, however, could not be suspended while missiles were developed, generation on generation of improvements. First problems must come first, and under General Powers, the bomber force was streamlined to fit in "the mix" with deterrent missiles. SAC retired the B-50's and B-36's. The Command ended all fighter operations, and hundreds of 8-jet, long-range B-52 *Stratofortresses* rolled into the bases.

Primarily, SAC's bombers and tankers had to be protected from the threatened no-warning attack made by Premier Khrushchev as long as Russia led in the missile race. Secondly, SAC had to pioneer operational concepts for the new ICBM, train men, and prepare missile facilities.

As fast as possible, SAC moved to these needs. The Command went on a "reflex" concept, meaning a small number of aircraft were based in various locations near their targets—on 24-hour-a-day alert. They could take off in less time than the few minutes of warning expected before a missile attack.

With the retirement of the KC-97 tanker, SAC was all jet. The General Dynamics-built B-58 *Hustler,* the fastest bomber yet designed for SAC, became operational in 1960. This delta-wing reached speeds of over 1300 MPH. The *Hound Dog* missile, an air-to-surface nuclear warhead carrier, came into the inventory. It boasted a guidance system that could not be jammed.

Americans, in the good days of the early 60s, were made aware of the acute danger of nuclear war in the campaign speeches of John F. Kennedy. Communist missiles went to sea in submarines in 1961, and the Soviets fired the biggest nuclear device built so far in October of that year. In the fall of 1962, the Soviets started using their new satellite, Cuba, as a missile base.

From her birth, SAC stressed strategic reconnaissance. Special models of the B-29, B-50 and B-47 were developed for this specialized and non-publicized function. Early in the 60s, special high-performance recce aircraft, not modified bombers, were widely operational for the first time, Lockheed's black, super-secret WU-2, for instance. Two U-2s of the 4080th Strategic Reconnaissance Wing and piloted by Major

Richard S. Heyser and Major Rudolf Anderson, Jr., found the missile build-up looming only 90 miles from the United States.

President Kennedy demanded that the USSR immediately dismantle the sites and remove the missiles.

The entire world was sitting on a powder keg. The U.S. action was the strongest ever in a time of peace. Ninety per cent of SAC's 1600 bombers were on a 15 minute ground alert; their first airborne alert was launched. Tactical Air Force planes deployed to Florida bases, and the U.S. Navy sailed to enforce a quarantine on Atlantic shipping. A huge emergency airlift went into operation; Air Force Reserves, communications, and logistics systems moved into the breach. All the while, SAC and TAC recce planes kept the Cuban bases under constant aerial surveillance.

In 30 days, the missiles were on their way back to Russia, and Nikita Khrushchev's sabre-rattling days were nearly ended.

President Kennedy presented the Presidential Unit Citation to SAC's 4080th Wing on November 26, and he said, "The 4080th contributed as much to the security of the United States as any unit in our history and any group of men in our history."

Major Anderson wasn't there to hear plaudits; he was killed October 27, the only casualty suffered in the American air surveillance over Cuba.

Mao Tse Tung and his fanatical Chinese Communists had grown tired of Russia's slow progress and of the apparent fear of the Soviets for U.S. retaliation. Mao brazenly challenged Soviet Communist leadership first in Asia, then Africa and Latin America. When the Soviets backed down in Cuba, the Red Chinese started moving on their own. They encouraged uprisings in Korea, Malaya, Indonesia, the Philippines, Thailand, Burma, Vietnam—even in Laos and Cambodia.

Political action halted the moves in many countries and gave SAC time to fit the mix of all jet bombers and tankers with ICBM. Ballistic missiles were proving a short useful life; technology made first generation designs obsolete faster than any other major weapons system. In February, 1958, the Department of Defense approved the Air Force development of solid-fueled ICBM, the silo-sheathed 3-stage *Minuteman.* Boeing was the test contractor, and later the systems integrator with other major contractors—TRW, Thiokol, Aerojet-General, Hercules, North American, AVCO, and General Electric. During one period, early in the 60s, missiles were being added to SAC's force at the rate of one each day. From the "cruise" *Snark*, SAC switched first to early liquid-fueled *Atlas* missiles. The second liquid-fueled ICBM, *Titan I*, became operational April 18, 1962. The first *Minuteman* solid-fuel ICBM was combat ready that December.

By 1963, SAC had ready more than 600 *Atlas, Titan* and *Minuteman* ICBM's even a second-generation *Titan*, the heavy-weight II. During those busy days of the early 60's, SAC continued training crews for all three types of missiles and was launching all three types in complicated tests.

At the start of 1965, SAC counted over 850 operational missiles, and their tests had proven that the less efficient liquid-fueled ICBM should be retired. They were. All of the *Atlas* and *Titan* I's were phased out during 1965. By March of 1966, SAC could look back on development and retirement of the *Snark, Rascal, Thor, Jupiter, Atlas* and *Titan* I.

In the late 60s, the missile combat crews had duties that were as difficult and as responsible as flight crews. The silo operational sites are widely dispersed over extremely remote areas; the missilemen work 30 consecutive hours, 24 of those underground on alert.

SAC's missiles grew to 1,000 "instant ICBM" *Minutemen* and *Titan* IIs, on constant alert, fitting powerfully in the "mix" of a deterrent manned and unmanned weapon system. The ICBM gives the United States an option in response to attack providing a complete defense against one type of weapon. Missiles are faster than aircraft and can take over many strategic duties of the manned bomber. Once fired, however, a missile cannot be recalled, and for this, SAC has an elaborate system to prevent inadvertent firing. Two keys must turn in two consoles, 15 feet apart, at the same time. This firing sequence must be duplicated in another location, too, prior to launch. Stored in silos, the ICBMs are nearly invulnerable to any except a direct hit.

As the missile strength grew, SAC's bombers again were modernized. By the middle of the 1960's, the B-47's and KC-97's had been retired after millions of hours of flight, and the B-58 *Hustler,* powered by 4 GE J-79-5's became operational. Breaking supersonic speed records, the *Hustler* needs a 3 man crew and is only about one-third the size of the B-52 *Stratofort.* Improved models of the B-52 give greater range and make possible the airborne alert. This simply means that the B-52's stay aloft 24 hours a day, protected from a surprise missile attack.

In June, 1965 SAC took on the additional mission of bombing the Viet Cong while, at the same time, maintaining its combat aircraft on a 50 per cent ground alert, continual alert of the ICBM, and re-fueling not only its own sorties but those of the Tactical Air Command as well.

During the last half of 1965, SAC's B-52's flew more than 1,500 conventional bomb sorties against the Viet Cong and dropped more than 63 million pounds of "iron" bombs. Their tankers off-loaded over 314 million pounds of fuel.

In April, 1967, the bombing operations moved to base at U-Tapao in Thailand, and the B-52's 12 hour run from Guam was cut to 3 to 5 hours. By the start of 1968, 16,600 B-52 sorties had been flown against the Viet Cong. By April, 1968, SAC tankers had refueled 240,300 aircraft in Southeast Asia alone. Over 80 per cent of the total USAF support missions were flown by SAC, and by the middle of 1968, the B-52's had dropped 120,000 tons more bombs than dropped on Japan during World War 2.

In July, 1968, General Bruce K. Holloway became SAC's Commander-in-Chief. Under his leadership were 190,000 men and women. His command had $16 billion in assets and on the one hand was in a hot-war environment, the other remained the cocked fist of deterrence. Into his inventory came the Lockheed SR-71, a 2,000 MPH reconnaissance jet which utilizes systems from simple surveillance for interdiction to multiple-sensor systems for strategic missions over large areas of the world. From 80,000 feet, the SR-71, with its 45-degree viewing angle from each side, can survey 60,000 square miles of land and ocean each hour.

Closing out the 60s, new communications systems were added to SAC's command post. In case of enemy attack, SAC's "go-code" would be activated from the control room 46 feet below ground at Offutt. Should that post be inactivated by the enemy, control automatically moves to alternate posts in various other locations; if those are hit, then control of SAC moves to "Looking Glass," the flying command post which has been continually in the air, 24 hours per day, since 1961.

The direct command to "go" is called, simultaneously, to about 70 subordinate posts. This alerts missile combat crews to ready their "birds" for immediate launch. At the same time, SAC's bombers head for predetermined points barely short of enemy targets. In the length of flight time, the U.S. Government would be given the time to determine national action.

If it's "go," the bombers continue their lethal route and the missiles are loosed with their nuclear warheads of destruction. This order can come only from the President. If, instead, the order is to hold, or if the bombers receive no coded instructions, they automatically return to their bases, and the last key is not turned on the missile start.

A single and complicated operational plan for retaliatory strikes comes not from one man, or one command, but is instead a development of the Joint Strategic Target Planning Staff consisting of 175 men from the Army, Navy, Marines and Air Force.

SAC's prime responsibility then is nothing less than the physical security of the United States (and therefore the rest of the Free World). SAC's crest appropriately contains a mailed fist holding both a lightning bolt of destruction and an olive branch, thus implying that it is up to our enemies to decide which they prefer. The choice is theirs.

So, as long as freedom must co-exist on this small planet alongside a Communist conspiracy to destroy it, America's Strategic Air Command must possess the unquestioned strength to deter those who would start World War III. Whether or not that strength was seriously eroded by the Kennedy-Johnson-McNamara policies during the sixties, we'll try to discover in a later chapter.

8. Sound Barrier

The two broken ribs knifed into his chest. Bending nearly double to slide across the X-1's floor to his seat, Chuck Yeager grimaced from pain. How silly he had been, he thought, to horserace with Glennis last night. That damn gate at Pancho's "dude ranch for thirsty pilots" had banged shut, and his horse was no jumper. He had landed flat on his back in the dust.

Ah well, nobody seemed to notice how gingerly he had dropped, feet first, into that hanging and close-fitting orange bullet. His wife Glennis hadn't missed it earlier this morning, though, and said, "You're getting old, Pop." The heck he was! And, anyway, this flight would be over in a few minutes.

"Battery switch on," he snapped the check list back to Dick Frost.

"Rocket chamber switches off," he fingered each to be sure.

His earphones crackled as he hung there below the B-29 Mother Ship, "Muroc Air Force Base to all aircraft. Stay clear of Muroc Dry Lake area. Test in progress."

That's me, he thought. Even through the pain, he could feel the fear break out in sweat—as it always did. The sweep second hand on his watch started for the top, and the earphones came alive again, "Yeager? This is Ridley. You all set?"

"Hell, yes, let's get it over with." He hoped his voice didn't shake. He was worried that the orange bullet will drop before everything is set. It would be a disaster. At 20,000 feet, with an indicated airspeed of 250 MPH, he and the X-1 just rode with the big plane.

There's the time, 26 minutes past 10 this Monday morning, October 14, 1947. And the splitting CRACK! He and the bullet were free. He shoved all four rockets to full power and the seat slammed against his back. The plane's needle nose pointed nearly straight up, and the altimeter registered 35,000 feet in only seconds. No time to think about the ribs, now, move man—MOVE. There's so much to do and everything happens so fast.

He cut back on the power of 2 rockets and watched the shove of reaction send the plane's Mach Meter needle up to .92. Clumsy with those heavy gloves, he wrote on his knee pad, "Elevator effectiveness greatly decreased at .94 Mach," for the stick fell slack in his other hand. "Then, effectiveness regained above .97 Mach."

Strange, he thought, there's no jolt. After those elevators came back to life, there's nothing particularly unusual about this flight. Where's the buffet? The wings must still be there, too. When is it going to happen? Nothing does, it's just like any old ordinarily busy test flight, he thought. And the mach meter's needle fluctuated right off the scale! He had broken the invisible sound barrier! "Without the speed indicator," he wrote, "I would never have known I was smashing what we had thought was a solid brick wall in the sky."

Out of fuel now, the bullet was strangely quiet. He

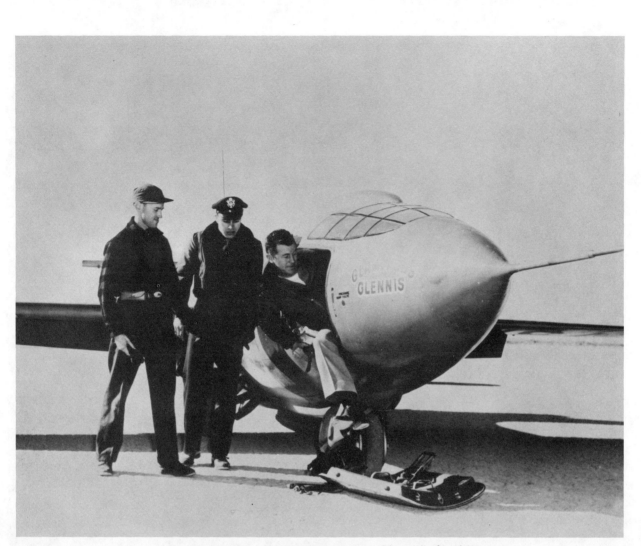

The Bell X-1, named "Glamorous Glennis" for his wife, was a tight fit at best for AF Captain Charles Yeager. The bright orange bullet-shaped craft was powered by a Reaction Motors, Inc. rocket assembly of four 1,500 pound thrust rockets, the equivalent, in power, of 25 diesel railroad engines. The fuel of liquid oxygen and alcohol surrounded the plane with smoke-like fog. It sat on fat tires flattened by its empty weight of 6500 pounds. Weird looking, "It growled with more power than I expected," says Yeager, now a Colonel. Left is Richard Frost, Bell Aircraft X-1 Project Officer; Captain Keith Garrison, Army Air Force; and Yeager, folding up to get into his craft. (Photo courtesy Bell Aerosystems Co.)

was stiff with cold, and suddenly, he was more fatigued than he had ever been. Only a scant few seconds had passed yet he had proven that sound was no barrier to speed. The sky didn't shroud an impenetrable line through which no aircraft could pass. Somehow, right then, he didn't care. All he wanted to do was get the bullet back on the ground and get out of his cramped position.

He aimed the shrill-whistling X-1 towards the 65 square miles of emergency landing field called Muroc. The chase planes had him in sight, now, as he glided— if you could call a near vertical descent a glide— towards home.

Stooped with fatigue, he stopped in the control building only long enough to call Larry Bell in his office in Buffalo. Laughing and swearing, Bell re-

The X-1, just under 31 feet long with a 28 foot wing span, was built to withstand 18 times the weight of gravity. Its four rockets burned 4000 pounds of fuel per minute and for 2⅓ minutes, the X-1 carried more than its own weight in fuel. Dropped from a B-29 "Mother Ship," Chuck Yeager and his "bullet" crashed through the speed of sound to become the fastest man alive on October 14, 1947. Yeager exceeded the speed of sound a dozen or more times in his 30 flights aboard the X-1. For 13 months he worked with the strange craft and logged a total of only four hours of flight time. The X-1 now is at the Smithsonian Institution, the veteran of more than 100 dangerous flights. (Photo courtesy USAF)

peated, "Achieved a speed in excess of Mach I in a climb—did you say a CLIMB?"

Yeager's chest throbbed, and as he walked slowly to the car where Glennis was waiting, he heard a loudspeaker announce it: "Today an American Air Force pilot became the first man to fly faster than the speed of sound."

All of a sudden, he wasn't tired at all.

Of course, this wasn't the first X-1 flight. Chuck Yeager had flown the research vehicle nine times with power since August 29. He dropped away from the "Mother Ship" that first time and did a slow roll—just because the plane felt so good! What a ride! Then, on the schedule went, calling for new data each day, nibbling away at speed. Chuck remembers it as an exhausting project. Remaining always alert with so many mechanical things to do each minute, and, always, there was the fear. He had been shot down by the Germans in World War II, and he had shot down Germans. He held the Purple Heart, the Bronze Star and the Air Medal with 6 Oakleaf clusters, the Distinguished Flying Cross, and the Silver Star. In World

The world's second successful jet aircraft, the English Gloster E 28/39 was designed by W. G. Carter of Gloster Aircraft Company with Air Commodore Sir Frank Whittle's jet engine. The E 28/39, flown by P. E. G. (Jerry) Sayer, took to the air from Cranwell, Lincolnshire on May 15, 1941. It was 25'3" long and had a wing span of 29' with a kerosene fuel capacity of 82 gallons. The Whittle was started with a small automotive gasoline engine and created 1150 pounds of thrust. The second British jet, the Gloster *Meteor*, first flew on March 3, 1943. The *Meteors* were the only Allied jets to enter combat in World War II. (Photo: Stuart Collection, National Air Museum, The Smithsonian Institution)

War II, he flew 64 combat missions for a total of 270 combat hours. He destroyed 11½ enemy planes and damaged 3 more. But the pressure of time and his own determination for success made the X-1 the most gruelling test of his whole life.

The landings were on the Mojave "Sandlot," not quite 100 miles northeast of Los Angeles. Even as early as 1924, when Sir Hubert Wilkins landed his Lockheed Vega on Muroc Dry Lake (now, Rogers Dry Lake), the open and flat space seemed perfect for testing. Both Northrop and Lockheed made use of the borax and alkali desert, and during World War II, Muroc was, indeed, a busy spot.

The name "Muroc" came from Ralph Corum's last name spelled backwards. He and his brother, Clifford, homesteaded the area but found the land impossible. It is—for homesteading.*

* Muroc was renamed Edwards in 1951 honoring Captain Glen W. Edwards who, in 1948, was killed test flying the XB-49 "Flying Wing."

America's first twin-jet aircraft, the Bell P-59, was built as a closely guarded secret in Buffalo, New York. The two GE Type I-A jet engines, based on the Whittle design, developed 1250 pounds of thrust each. The large plane had a wing span of 49' and a high curved tail to ensure clearing of the jet wake. Moved with a dummy prop to hide its true identity, the XP-59A reached 350 mph at the Material Command Test Base at Muroc. It was first flown by Robert M. Stanley on October 1, 1942. A total of 66 P-59 types were built but none reached combat.

154

Americans finally had something of the jet age they could brag about after Yeager broke the sound barrier. We had lagged, miserably, in jet engine development.

Props were losing effectiveness as their tips reached sonic speed in the late 30's. Engineers the world over realized the end had come for the speed race in prop driven planes. A propless engine had to be built.

As early as 1908, Dr. Henri Coanda, a Rumanian, built and flew a model of a jet plane near Bucharest. He continued successful experiments for several years and even took out a United States patent, in 1914, for a jet engine. Several others worked on the design, but fuel consumption of such engines discouraged development.

In 1928, an Englishman, Frank Whittle, wrote an exam thesis on the possibilities of gas turbines as airplane engines. In 1930, when he was twenty-three years old, he took out his first patents. Simultaneously, Hans von Ohain was doing similar research in Germany, and he applied for his patents in 1935.

The British government officials showed enough interest in Whittle's ideas for him to form a company, Power Jets, Ltd., to develop his ideas as early as 1936. In 1939, the Air Ministry awarded Power Jets a con-

Lockheed P-80 *Shooting Star* ("F-80" after 1947 when the old "pursuit" prefix was changed to "fighter") appeared in 1945. Its engine was the General Electric J-33 of 4,000-lbs thrust, which gave the P-80 a maximum speed of 558 mph at sea level, 533 mph at 20,000 feet. Model F-80C delivered in 1948 had a J-33A engine of 5,400 lbs thrust. (Photo courtesy Lockheed Aircraft Corp.)

Bell's X-1A flew 1,650 mph on December 12, 1953 and 6 months later attained a height of 90,000 feet. The X-1A measured 5 feet longer than the X-1 and was flown to the speed record by Chuck Yeager, the Air Force officer who is a "Triple Ace" and the first man to fly faster than sound, 967 mph in the X-1. (Photo courtesy Bell Aerosystems Co.)

tract for an engine and, at the same time, commissioned Gloster Aircraft Company, under the direction of George Carter, to build a special airframe for flight testing the device .

Across the Channel, Dr. Ernst Heinkel added a gas turbine engine division to his airframe plant. In collaboration with von Ohain, he produced the first turbojet aircraft suitable for flight. The He-178 flew August 27, 1939 near Rostock, Germany. Clothed in secrecy, the door opened to the jet age. Five days later, Hitler moved into Poland.

Nearly 2 years later, on May 15, 1941, RAF Major Phillip E. G. (Jerry) Sayer lifted the world's second successful gas turbine jet into the air, the Gloster E28/39.

Because of the secrecy, the Italians did not know of either aircraft. They, in turn, thought their Campini Caproni N-1 was earth-shaking news. Designed by Ing. Secondo Campini in 1939, the N-1 did fly in August of 1940. This "ducted fan" plane was powered by an Isotta Fraschini 900 HP piston engine driving a 3-stage compressor. With disappointing performance, such as a cruise of only 110 MPH, the N-1 was abandoned in 1942.

After Heinkel's success, the jet principle spread to the Junkers and B.M.W. engine factories in Germany. Professor Alexander Lippisch, when he moved to Messerchmitt in 1939, brought along plans for a rocket powered flying wing, the DFS 194. From his experiments grew the Me-163 which, in 1941, clocked 570 MPH from a standing start and 623.85 from an airdrop.

By June of 1944, the Me-163B *Komets,* with Walter rocket motors of 3750 pounds of thrust, flew 600 MPH and achieved a climb rate of 16,000 feet per minute. They became operational in August of 1944. Over 300 *Komets* were built, but, fortunately, for the Allies, the limited endurance of the rocket en-

gines—only 5 minutes—and the highly explosive fuel kept the use of the planes low.

While producing the *Komets,* Messerchmitt developed a twin turbojet fighter, the Me-262 which, with the Jumo 004 engines, flew in July of 1942. Blocked by Milch, yet still promoted by other more advanced thinkers, the Me-262's finally caught up with the He-280's.

The AAF's strategic bombing raids on Regensburg, again fortunately for the Allies, caused heavy damage to the 262's fuselage jigs. Hitting the production lines at Augsburg, the bombers successfully delayed pro-

Larry Bell, left, congratulates Chuck Yeager for the new speed record, Mach 2.42 in the X-1A. Major Kit Murray flew the craft to set the altitude record of 94,000 feet on May 5, 1954. (Photo courtesy Bell Aerosystems Co.)

Two X-2s were built for the Air Force. The first one, completed in December 1949, was destroyed in May 1953 before it had flown with its Curtiss-Wright rocket engine. The second X-2 was completed in July of 1954. On July 23, 1956, dropped from a "Mother Ship" B-50, Lt. Col. Frank Everest set a new speed record of 1900 mph. The following September, Captain Ivan Kincheloe climbed to 126,200 feet, an altitude record, in the X-2. The X-2's last flight came 20 days later, 27th of September, when Captain Milburn Apt reached 2094 mph only to crash to his death. (Photo courtesy USAF)

duction of the fighters. Me-262 assembly was moved to Leipheim, and the 8th Air Force hit there on April 24, 1944, again seriously disrupting output.

An RAF Spitfire met the first German rocket plane, a 163, in June, 1944. The next month, the shocking speed of this type plane jolted bomber crews of the USAAF, and, after that, encounters came more often. Me-262s were produced to a total of 1,294 during late 1944 and early 1945, in spite of

the bombing. Imagine the overwhelming competition of these fighters had the heavy bombers let up for an instant!

The British Gloster *Meteor* was the only allied jet to see combat in the war, and it established a successful record.*

* The Japanese flew their first jet, the Nakajima *Kikka*, a Naval attack fighter which looked much like the Me-262, on July 7, 1945.

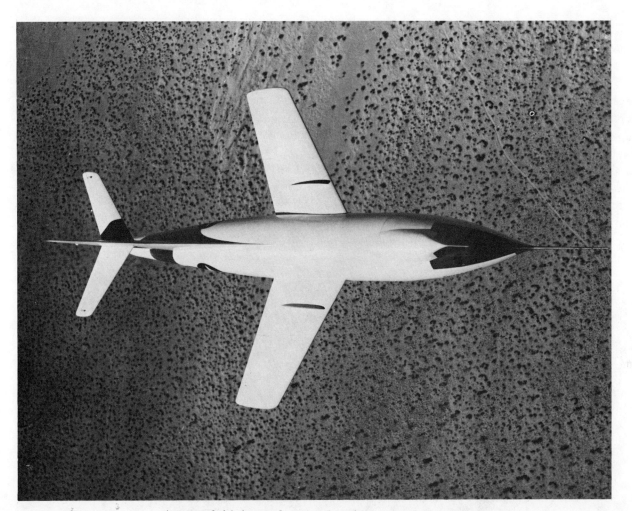

A second high-speed research vehicle was the Navy-sponsored Douglas D-558 *Skystreak,* a turbo-jet that eased close to the speed of sound. Modified to the D-558-2 *Skyrocket,* with both jet and rocket engines, it became the first plane to fly twice the speed of sound. (Photo courtesy McDonnell Douglas Corp.)

What about the Americans? General Hap Arnold was shown the Gloster jet and quickly realized its value. He called the first American meeting on jet propulsion September 4, 1941. He announced that he wanted 15 jet engines and 3 planes—*fast.* The English had promised to lend us a Whittle engine for design study, and General Electric, due to extensive research on turbo supercharging, was chosen for the engine work.

Larry Bell's unorthodox approach to research, as proven by his company's *Airacuda* and *Airacobra,* was the top contender for the airframe. Also, Bell's isolated facility was excellent for the top secret project. R. C. Muir, GE vice-president, promised delivery

of a jet engine, providing his company could make use of the Whittle's data in 6 months. Larry Bell's contract, signed September 30, 1941, called for three XP-59A jet aircraft, data, and a wind tunnel—for $1,644,431. Big money to the still small company! Bell's time limit was 8 months.

On October 1, a B-24 delivered the Whittle W-1X engine to GE. It had ridden from England beneath the floor boards of the plane's bomb bay for security. By March of 1942, GE was testing the new Type 1-A engine.

At Bell, the top secret project started in the old Pierce-Arrow plant but soon had to be moved to Ford's Main Street plant. The airframe grew and grew until finally, one wall of the building had to be knocked down in order to roll out the XP-59.

Exactly one year to the day after the B-24 arrived with the borrowed Whittle engine (October 1, 1942), Robert M. Stanley of Bell flew America's first jet aircraft off the desert at Muroc. The engine ran so smoothly that the instrument needles stuck. A vibrator had to be added to the panel. Counting experimental models, a total of 66 P-59's were built, but they, according to General Arnold, "were not long-legged enough" for combat. Though designed from the beginning as a fighter with armament space in the nose, the P-59's went into training squadrons.

Certainly, our first jet was not a successful and active fighter, but finally, we had built a jet aircraft. The GE engine grew to the I-16 of 1650 pounds of thrust which became the J-31, the first quantity produced American jet engine. It is interesting to note the J-31 had a maximum time-between-overhauls of 50 hours.

More promising as a jet fighter was Lockheed's XP-80, our second jet, powered with a British Halford engine. The P-80 first flew on January 9, 1944, but too late for an American-built jet to reach combat lines.

By the spring of 1943, planes in power dives had

Bell's X-5 was the first airplane with wings that could be changed in degree of sweep in flight. Enameled white, the X-5 was jet-propelled by an Allison J-35 of 4900 pounds of thrust. With capability of taking off from the ground, the X-5 helped the Air Force men defend against the Navy's description of the X-1 as nothing more "than a rocket-powered glider." (Photo courtesy USAF)

160

In 1918 Larry Bell (r) was factory manager for the Wright-Martin company. With Bell in photo above are Eric Springer; Martin, test pilot (center); and Donald Douglas, Sr., designer of the 1918 G.M.B. Martin Bomber behind them. This plane, powered with a pair of Liberty engines of 400-hp, appeared too late to see service in WW-I, but was the prototype for the MB-2 bombers that were purchased in some numbers by the Air Service during the early 20s. (Photo courtesy USAF)

approached the speed of sound. Several aircraft and their pilots were lost due to the serious vibrations, called buffeting, at that speed. Often, a plane nosed over and the pilot could not bring it level again. Stick forces reversed and pilots blacked out. Few people thought Mach 1* would ever be reached by a pilot-operated aircraft. Planes, simply, could not be built that strong.

* Speed of sound's "Mach" was named in honor of Ernst Mach (1838–1916), an Austrian physicist and psychologist, who did much with studies on behavior of sound. A Mach number is the ratio of the speed of an airplane to the speed of sound in the surrounding atmosphere. Speed of sound varies with temperature, and temperature varies with altitude; therefore, at sea level, with 59 degrees F, sound travels at roughly 750 MPH. At 40,000 feet, where the temperature may drop as low as 70 degrees below zero, the speed of sound will drop to about 660 MPH.

Flying near the speed of sound piles up air into shock waves and creates turbulence. In this transonic range, 600 to 800 MPH, airflow is partly faster and partly slower around the plane—a dangerous situation.

When the jet engines had become a reality in America, NACA (National Advisory Committee on Aeronautics), the military services, and industry were all taking a hard look at the sound barrier. At a meeting in December of 1943 called by NACA's director, Dr. George Lewis, a young engineer, Robert Wolf of Bell Aircraft Corporation, voiced the opinion that a high speed research vehicle should be built to study that transonic speed range. This was the time, he said, to find out what caused the buffeting.

Bell's first helicopter, the Model 30—ship #1—was a single-place, open cockpit craft powered with 165hp Franklin engine. Cruising at about 100 mph, the inventor, Art Young, is at the controls.

Others at the meeting agreed, and Bell delivered a preliminary design of an experimental craft to NACA in April of 1944. Meantime, at Wright Field, Captain Ezra Kotcher independently reached the same decision. This led to the Air Force and Bell getting together. Bell's Woods and Stanley signed with the Air Technical Services Command that they would design and Bell would build the X-1 specifically for the study of transonic speeds but hopefully for supersonic flight.

Within a year, the X-1 was finished and civilian test pilots had pushed the bullet-shaped craft to .8 Mach. The civilians demanded much higher pay before they'd try the sound barrier, and the Air Force couldn't agree. The program slowed to a stop.

The Air Force policy, at that time, was to hire civilian pilots for particularly hazardous duties. These men could be paid a large bonus; military pilots could not. With the X-1, the amount of money was getting out of line.

The post-war slump in the services and our delay

One end of the speed range was being studied by Bell's X series of research vehicles in California and production started, in Buffalo, on the first commercially licensed helicopter, the Bell model 47. Number one helicopter, shown here, was changed only slightly for the first sales to the military, which started in 1947. The Model 47 types proved their value and utility in the Korean conflict which started three years later. (Photo: Bell Aerospace Systems)

Lawrence Dale Bell's theory that the "primary value of an airplane was its use as a weapon of war" was made clear in his long life in the aviation industry. When he was 16 years old, he went to work for the Glenn L. Martin Company, and three years later was shop foreman. By the time he was 31, in 1925, he was vice-president and general manager. Three years later he became sales manager and vice-president of Consolidated Aircraft Corporation in Buffalo. With Robert J. Woods and Ray P. Whitman, he founded his own company, Bell Aircraft, on July 10, 1935. With only 60 employees, Bell produced the XFM-1 *Airacuda,* which, far ahead of its time, first flew on September 1, 1937. The Army purchased 13 and in 1939 Bell won the heavily armed pursuit competition with his P-39 *Airacobra.*

163

producing a jet combined for poor morale and a loss of prestige for the Air Force. It was essential that Americans once again take the lead in the air and particularly important that an Air Force pilot show the way. Almost every pilot in the Fighter Test Section at Wright Field volunteered.

Colonel Albert Boyd had to decide which volunteer, and this was no easy task. A failure now would be a heartbreaking discredit. Of the 125 test pilots, he picked Charles Yeager saying, "Yeager is one of the greatest flyers I've ever known." He chose Captain Bob Hoover as alternate and Captain Jack Ridley for the engineering pilot.

The three men flew to Muroc and found the X-1, a small protuberance beneath a B-29. Even the tail section of the 29 was larger than the tiny craft. The B-29's bomb bay doors had been removed and the whole mid-section loomed open. The X-1 was suspended in the center maw by standard D-4 bomb shackles.

The civilians briefed the new crew and said that earlier flights had proven that anything could happen. On "routine" days, the X-1 had suffered from a mid-air fire and from a stuck landing gear.

After three trips, Chuck Yeager said of the X-1, "It's the best damn airplane I ever flew."

In the X-1A, he explained, outside visibility had improved. "I saw things in the 1A I'd rather not have seen, like the wings buffeting with shock waves on them."

Approaching 1700 MPH in the X-1A, he and the craft were hit by violent shock waves. At twice the speed of sound, Yeager suddenly lost control of the ship at an altitude of 70,000 feet. He knew, without a doubt, and he yelled it, "This is the end. It's over. The whole damn thing is over." The X-1A twisted and screamed straight down. It fell 10 miles with the unconscious pilot no longer in control. Somehow, Yeager fought off the blackness. He remembers now that he thought, "I'm dead. There's something terrible about that kind of helplessness."

But, he didn't die. Battered and bruised, he led the screaming X-1A back to Muroc and a careening landing.

"I sat in that stifling cockpit with the dust settling around me and I thought—whatever I've done with the X-1 project, is it really worth it?"

Larry Bell answered—part of that: "Chuck, I think the records will show that this airplane—all the X-1's, I should say—is probably the most valuable research

airplane the government ever had. In terms of its performance, the X-1 would easily be painted as the most dangerous airplane in the world. Yet, it never killed anyone."

The X-2's did kill. First, Skip Ziegler and a crewman on the mothering B-29 died and Bell built another X-2. Eventually, that one ended in disaster, and soon afterwards, Chuck Yeager returned to his fighters. For that's his trade, really. He's a triple-Ace, now, and he's seen the jungles and the enemy in Korea and in Vietnam.

"Other pilots and other planes shared the sound barrier with me and with the X-1," he says, "But, the most important thing about that 1947 flight was— we got the job done. Even more important to me was that we got prestige for Air Force test pilots that they had never had before. They deserve that much."

The U.S. Navy's interest in jets started as early as 1942. The Navy planning desk was well aware of the English and German developments. The Navy, though, felt a jet's high-speed landing would necessitate long runways. Tricycle landing gears had never been used on carriers, and with the feeling that the Navy's small escort carriers then in use could not be utilized, the Navy looked elsewhere. An alternate composite craft combining a jet engine for speed in combat and a reciprocating engine for the operational capacity of the carriers might be the answer.

BuAer, under Admiral John S. McCain, submitted this idea to 9 manufacturers in December of 1942. Ryan Aeronautical Corporation, San Diego, California answered the call. Engineering vice-president B. A. "Bud" Gillies and engineer Ben T. Salmon were handed the contract in January, 1943 for what became the Ryan Model 2 *Fireball*.

The single-place first *Fireball* flew by power of the piston engine on June 25, 1944. During July, the craft ran qualification tests on the *USS Ranger* with the jet engine, too. The *Fireball* was the first airplane with laminar flow airfoil intended for carrier use. In the nose, a Wright *Cyclone* R-1820 radial engine of 1350 HP powered take-offs and landings. GE's J-31 was in the fuselage, aft of the pilot, for high speed cruise. The U.S. Navy ordered 600, but only 66 *Fireballs* were delivered. The contract was cancelled by VJ Day.

Gene May became the second human to go supersonic when he flew the Navy sponsored Douglas D558-2 *Skyrocket*. This jet-and-rocket engine-equipped swept-wing vehicle weighed in at a hefty

15,000 pounds and was designed for ground take-off rather than for air-drop.

Meanwhile Larry Bell had one eye on speed and the sound barrier, and, at the same time, he diversified in an entirely different direction. From the 15th century, men had made dozens of tries at achieving vertical flight. Russian-born Igor Sikorsky flew America's first free-flight helicopter in 1939, and Larry Bell watched with fascination.

In 1941, he hired a young inventor, Arthur Young, who, for 13 years, had been assembling his own helicopter designs. Young and about 30 other Bell employees moved into a small rented garage in Buffalo just to see if they really could build a helicopter. By 1943, Young's concept became a reality. He had a one-piece, open cockpit copter flying from a cable tether.

By 1946, this Model 30 had been refined and enclosed. In March, it was certified by the U.S. government as the world's first commercially approved helicopter. With Larry Bell's confidence in yet another unorthodox design, the company started production of the Model 47. The next year he was rewarded with contracts and deliveries of the first military copters.

Bell could produce in large numbers by the time the United States became involved in Korea. There, for once and all, the helicopter proved its merit and that it was not simply a toy. In the thick of battle, Bells rescued an estimated 25,000 wounded troops from battlefront areas.

By 1957, rotary wing industries had begun experiments with turbine engines. Could it be, that only 15 years earlier Bell and GE had combined for the very first American jet airplane?

Initially, the turbine copters were built as weapons of war; quickly, they moved into utility, construction and petroleum industries. The smaller reciprocating engine models continue vital work as air ambulances, with law enforcement, in charter, aerial agricultural, pipeline patrol, executive transportation and dozens of other chores.

As the needs for rotor-craft grew, Bell produced the UH-1 series for the Army as part of their new airmobility concept. When the U.S. became committed to Vietnam, the Army was ready—with copters.

9. One Little Airline and How It Grew

Let's face it; most of us in aviation are romantics at heart. That's why we were attracted to flying machines and space vehicles in the first place. It's nothing to be ashamed of; romantics have done most of the world's exploring. Dreamers have always been in the vanguard of technology. The sound barrier was not conquered by a businessman. But the problem has always been that romantics often adjust poorly to the hard realities of economics, which is why so many die broke, though perhaps famous. And this probably explains why aerospace writers—as romantical a bunch as you'll find—usually regard captains-of-industry with suspicion. In the clean, hard-blue above Earth, the selfless good guys should always win, and our idealism is easily outraged by a shrewd master of sound and tough business practices who invades this pure air and reaps fabulous rewards for his cold efficiency. Therefore, it is hardly surprising that Juan Terry Trippe has suffered greatly at the hands of some writers. "Robber baron" is just one of the less offensive sobriquets that have been used to describe him.

Juan Trippe built Pan American World Airways. With influence and ability and plenty of cash and yes, ruthlessness, he put together the world's single most important airline; an airline that, in 1968, grossed a billion dollars flying to 86 countries on 6 continents. Had Mr. Trippe had his way, Pan Am would be, today, America's only overseas airline (he has always regarded competition as wasteful). In-deed, Juan did have his way until WW-II spoiled everything.

Trippe was twenty-eight years old when he started Pan Am in 1927. That was the year Charles Lindbergh flew to Paris and touched off the boom in aviation that had been building since 1921. Significant risk capital had been coming into aviation as fledgling airlines spread across the nation in the wake of the 1925 Kelly Bill (which promised profits via air mail contracts); Gen. Billy Mitchell's crusade for a strong air force (and his resulting court-martial) had helped make the public airplane-conscious, and introduction of the Wright *Whirlwind* engine had at last given airplanes true reliability. Therefore, when Lindbergh —the very personification of the All American Boy— alone in a small single-engined plane, presented to the world a dramatic preview of aviation's boundless future, aerial ventures of all kinds, both sound and silly, suddenly found a plethora of eager investors.

Into this auspicious atmosphere stepped Juan Trippe; and his ideas were anything but silly. Frighteningly ambitious, perhaps, but not silly. Trippe viewed Latin America as railroad magnate Commodore Vanderbilt had viewed the American Midwest a half-century before. Here, in Mexico and Central America and South America and the Caribbean, a transportation empire awaited.

Trippe was not unprepared for empire-building. Born to wealth, educated in the best schools and pos-

Pan Am's first planes were three Fokker Trimotors, two F-7 Models, and a C-2. Pictured here is one of the F-7's that began regular mail service between Key West and Havana on October 28th, 1927. Actually, a token flight was made over the route on the 19th by aviation editor Cy Caldwell, flying a privately-owned Fairchild FC-2, because the new Fokkers were not delivered in time to meet Pan Am's contract deadline for beginning of operations. Scheduled passenger service was added to the route during the following January. (Photo courtesy Pan American World Airways)

Charles Lindbergh (r) and Juan Trippe at Miami, January 9, 1929. A month later, Lindbergh flew one of Pan Am's two new S-38's on the company's inaugural flight to the Canal Zone. Lindbergh surveyed many of Pan Am's international air routes. Plane in background above is a Fokker F-10, a larger, improved version of the F-7. (Photo courtesy Pan American World Airways)

The Sikorsky S-38 amphibian carried eight passengers
(as did the Fokker F-7), was placed in service late in
1928, and was Pan Am's standard airplane in the
Caribbean for several years. Engines were 420-hp P&W
Wasps, which gave the S-38 a cruising speed of 110
mph. Top wing span was 71' 8"; length was 39' 8".
Useful load was 3,000 lbs. Price at factory about $50,-
000. (Photo courtesy Pan American World Airways)

sessing as friends all the right people (i.e. other
wealthy young men of influential families), Juan had
no trouble gathering capital for his proposed airline;
and he also had some aeronautical background to insure that he knew what he was about. He had learned
to fly during WW-I as a Naval aviation cadet and,
between 1923 and 1925, gained "airline" experience
operating, with surplus Navy planes, Long Island
Airways, which actually amounted to a local charter
service. When Long Island Airways expired of mal-
nutrition, Juan joined newly formed Colonial Airways as a minor executive for a time. Colonial meanwhile won the first Contract Air Mail Route, between
Boston and New York, and began scheduled service
in June, 1926. It was later absorbed by the Aviation
Corporation (AVCO), and ended up as part of Amer-

ican Airlines. Trippe, however, left Colonial late in
1926, worked briefly for the banking firm of Lee Hig-
ginson & Company while toying with the idea of
entering his family's business, Trippe & Company,
Brokers & Investment Bankers, then quit to form his
own airline company in March, 1927.

Trippe at first called his new company the Aviation
Corporation of the Americas,* and he sought a route
only from Key West to Havana. This 90-mile stretch
held little actual value in itself; but as a primary gate-
way to the Caribbean and all Latin America its potential was tremendous.

* Not to be confused with AVCO, the Aviation Corporation,
organized in March, 1929, by C. M. Keys, who had earlier put
together the Curtiss-Wright complex as well as North American
Aviation.

Now, a scheduled air service between Key West and Havana had been tried before by Mr. Inglis Uppercu, who operated WW-I-vintage flying boats over the route from 1919 to 1923 with the aid of a small mail contract. Uppercu's Aeromarine West Indies Airways went under when this modest subsidy was stopped. But this failure proved nothing to Trippe except that AWIA had been premature. Uppercu's money had run out long before the Foreign Air Mail Act of 1928 guaranteed meaningful government support to overseas air carriers, as the Kelly Bill had done to domestic airlines.

Trippe, of course, was counting upon passage of the Foreign Air Mail Act—which was pending in Congress when he decided to bid on the Key West-Havana route—and he was also counting upon the same kind of route protection enjoyed by airlines at home. Postmaster General Harry S. New—the man who held the air mail purse strings and therefore, in effect, decided which airline got which route, since none could long survive at that time without mail pay—had established a policy of dealing only with "responsible" (i.e. well-heeled) bidders, because Mr. New (as well as Walter Folger Brown who succeeded him in 1929) viewed his power as a mandate to build a strong and healthy air carrier network. Small,

The 13-passenger Ford Trimotor Model 5-AT-B went into service in March 1929, and flew Pan Am's Mexican and Central American routes until 1936. This craft sold for $55,000; cruising speed with three P&W *Wasps* of 420-hp each was 122 mph.; range was 500 miles; gross weight 12,650 lbs., and empty weight 7,650 lbs. (Photo courtesy Pan American World Airways)

poorly financed operators were ignored; and competition was carefully controlled by means of the postmaster general's mail-pay whip. He wasn't interested in the lowest bidder, but rather a fat one, with plenty of expansion capital. These policies would lead to the "air mail scandals" of 1934, after the Democrats returned to office,* but meanwhile the foundations of mass air transportation were to be built. Justice—if that's what it was—could wait.

* See Chapter 21, Command the Horizon, Volume I of this two-volume series.

As was to be expected, in this roseate climate Trippe was not the only one to appreciate the possibilities of the Key West-Havana air route. Florida Airways, organized by John Harding and war aces Eddie Rickenbacker and Reed Chambers, wanted to extend its Atlanta-Jacksonville run (Contract Air Mail Route 10) through Miami and thence to Havana. Another contender was Pan American, Inc., which was the creature of J. K. Montgomery and Grant Mason. Pan American, Inc., seemed in a favored position in that Mason had obtained exclusive landing rights in Cuba from Dictator Gerardo Machado. But while Mason was

Pan Am acquired 14 Consolidated *Commodore* flying boats in September 1930, when it absorbed James Rand's New York, Rio, Buenos Aires Airline. During this period, Juan Trippe had little to fear from U.S. competitors, because Pan Am, as the U.S. Government's "chosen instrument" for international airline development, received all overseas air mail contracts—without which no airline could survive at that time. The *Commodore* was powered with a pair of 575-hp P&W *Hornets,* cruised at 105 mph, and cost $125,000. (Photo courtesy General Dynamics)

smugly strolling the grounds of Cuba's national palace, Juan Trippe was in Washington, with *his* feet planted comfortably on the desk of the postmaster general.

Apparently, Postmaster General New gave Trippe something more than simple encouragement, because Juan then traveled to Cuba and, for some reason, seemed to have not the slightest difficulty in persuading Machado to tear up his agreement with Pan American, Inc., in favor of an identical one with Trippe's company. Thus armed, Trippe found it an easy matter to buy out—at bargain prices—both Florida Airways and Pan American, Inc. And having eliminated the competition, Trippe won the air mail contract, with maximum pay, for the first small chunk of his empire. He re-named his company "Pan American Airways," and began scheduled operations on October 28, 1927, when Capt. Hugh Wells took off from Key West with a handful of mail in the Fokker Trimotor NC-53. Passenger service began the following January.

From this modest beginning, Trippe reached out to the Dominican Republic, and, in July, 1928, gobbled up West Indian Aerial Express, which had started flying between Haiti and Puerto Rico seven months earlier. WIAE was acquired at a fraction of its assessed value because the U.S. postmaster general ig-

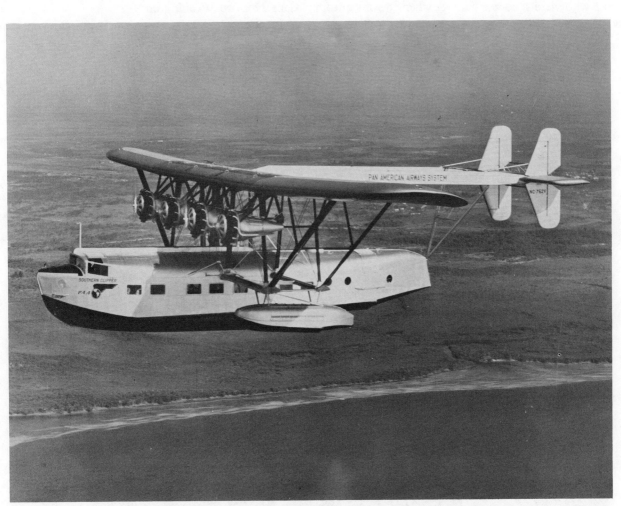

The 40-passenger Sikorsky S-40, first of the famed "Clippers," was essentially an enlarged S-38. Pan Am has owned more than 600 airliners between 1927 and 1968: about 80 pre-1935 landplanes; 150 twin-engined craft of the DC-3 class; 200 four-engined piston planes; 100 flying boats/amphibians/float planes, and 120 jets. (Photo courtesy Pan American World Airways)

nored its "pioneer equity" (the fact that it was there first and in operation), and awarded the mail contract for the route to Pan Am instead.

Now, some have claimed that Trippe's purchase of West Indian Aerial Express was a magnanimous act; that Pan Am's inside track on obtaining mail contracts made WAIE worthless, and therefore Trippe didn't have to pay *anything* for his competitor's equipment if he didn't want to. But the truth is, it wasn't Trippe's conscience that allowed WIAE's investors to salvage something from their effort; it was the postmaster general who was conscience-stricken. The postmaster general, from the beginning, saw to it that the government's "chosen instrument" in the overseas airline business should have some consideration for those who were squeezed out. So, when the office from which flowed all things good suggested a "merger,"

Pan Am merged—if that's the proper term for it. And it is important to remember this fact if one must judge Pan Am and its creator. Pan Am itself (and/or Juan Trippe) did not establish its monopoly. The "chosen instrument" concept was U.S. Government policy. At home, domestic airlines were being put together the same way. United, TWA, and American were formed with the postmaster general's heavy hand on the shoulder of each, directing similar mergers with conflicting and weaker lines, and filling-in route gaps with mail contracts to establish a trio of great transcontinental carriers. Of course, Juan Trippe never protested this federal philosophy. Indeed, whenever other airlines looked covetously upon Mr. Trippe's growing fiefdom, his indignation was felt all the way from Cape Horn to Washington.

In January, 1929, Pan Am acquired Compania

The Sikorsky S-42 went into service for Pan Am in August 1934. It accommodated 32 passengers in unparalleled luxury, had a gross weight of 40,000 lbs., and cruised at 140 mph. Range was about 750 miles. (Photo courtesy Pan American World Airways)

Pan Am began regular service across the Pacific—via
Hawaii, Midway, Wake, Guam, and the Philippines
—on November 22, 1935, with a trio of Martin M-130
flying boats built to Pan Am specifications. The M-130,
capable of carrying 48 passengers, was powered with
four P&W R-1830 *Twin Wasps* of 800-hp each. The
sponsons, located on either side of the fuselage for
stability in the water, were a new feature on American-
built flying boats, but had been employed by German-
made Dornier aircraft since 1918. (Photo courtesy Pan
American World Airways)

Mexicana de Aviacion, the Mexican airline that had
been in operation since 1924, and this gave Trippe a
route from Brownsville, at the southern tip of Texas,
along the Gulf of Mexico through Guatemala to
Nicaragua; and, in September of that year, service was
extended through the Canal Zone to Barranquilla,
Columbia, then continued eastward via Caracas to Port
of Spain, Trinidad, where the route turned back north-
ward to complete its circle of the Caribbean at San
Juan Puerto Rico. This locked-up for Pan Am the two
primary air routes to South America from the U.S.,

with one approach through Texas and Central America, the other by way of Florida and the Antilles.
Meanwhile, Miami replaced Key West as the Florida
terminus, and America's overseas flag carrier began
measuring the distances to Buenos Aires and Santiago
—where some very formidable competition was well
entrenched.

Anticipating continued and rapid expansion, Trippe
had sent Pan Am representatives throughout Latin
America to obtain landing and operating rights, and
to gauge the established competition. This former

The DC-6 was a beefed-up, speeded-up, pressurized version of the DC-4. It began airline service Nov. 24, 1946, when American and United Air Lines received the first two. DC-6 engines were P&W R-2800's providing a total of 8,400 horsepower and a speed of 300 mph (as opposed to the DC-4's 240-mph). Stretched further, the DC-4/6 family added the DC-7 in 1953, and the Dash Seven, fitted with the Curtiss-Wright turbo-compound 3350 engine, could do 400 mph. Improvements in the R-2800 engine eventually raised speed of DC-6B to 370 mph. These craft, along with Lockheed's *Super Constellation,* were the last of America's big, piston-engined transports.

duty involved U.S. Department of State people, because, in some cases, a simple unilateral agreement wasn't enough. In fact, Colombia, which already had a pretty good German-operated airline (and hadn't forgotten Teddy Roosevelt's perfidy in wresting away Colombian territory for the Panama Canal), bargained so stubbornly that she ended up with a bilateral agreement which gave that nation aerial access to the entire U.S. coastline—Atlantic, Pacific and Gulf

of Mexico. This was considered a mere formality at the time, because Colombia was in no position to start a big international airline. But years later—after WW-II—times had changed; and when Colombia then began to eye the lucrative U.S. air-travel market, with its carte blanche agreement in hand, that occasioned some diplomatic back-sliding of truly magnificent form.

Trippe's toughest early antagonist was W. R. Grace

Following the DC-4's and early Connies, Pan Am added to its inventory the Boeing *Stratocruiser,* Douglas DC-6B, DC-7B—then the DC-7C Model (above), a pressurized, stretched and more powerful version of the basic DC-4 design. The DC-7C had a total of 13,600 hp and a cruise speed of 355 mph with 104 passengers. Pan Am bought 26 of these craft, the last prop-driven planes in the company's fleet. (Photo courtesy Pan American World Airways)

Lockheed *Constellation,* Model L.49, also served Pan Am during the immediate post-war years, with a total of 28 registered to the company. This early "Connie" was fitted with Wright R-3350 engines of 2,200-hp each; cruising speed was 250 mph with 45 passengers. Pan Am introduced the first pressurized trans-Atlantic service with this craft on January 20, 1946. (Photo courtesy Pan American World Airways)

175

& Company, a shipping/banking/trading monopoly that had for years been a mighty power on South America's West Coast. Pan Am and Grace warily circled each other, growling menacingly for a time, then each decided the other's teeth were too sharp for a nose-to-nose showdown. So, they formed a holding company in Peru, each taking exactly 50 per cent of the stock, and the airline that resulted was called Pan American Grace Airways (Panagra), which flew the route from Buenos Aires up the South American West Coast to Panama. This product of artificial in-

semination grew up unloved, and at last, in 1965, Panagra's name was dropped from the list of international air carriers when the parent Pan American World Airways took over all international routes and its surviving subsidiaries were restricted to domestic operations.

Trippe also had a fighter to contend with on South America's East Coast. That was the New York, Rio & Buenos Aires Line, a company organized in 1929 by James Rand of Remington-Rand (now Sperry-Rand), and Louis Pierson of the Irving Trust Com-

Although Pan Am was prepared to start jet service as early as 1955 (in 1952 it ordered three British-built DeHavilland *Comets* that were never delivered because of metal fatigue problems in this earliest commercial jet), the company actually began jet operations over the Atlantic with the Boeing 707-121 in October 1958. The Boeing 720B is a short-fuselage version of the 707, and began flying Pan Am's Latin American routes in 1963. (Photo courtesy Pan American World Airways)

Juan Terry Trippe built the world's most important airline and directed its operation for 40 years. He retired early in 1968 after half of a century in aviation. Among industry captains, he was a general—admired, respected, feared. In international air transportation, he set the standards. (Photo courtesy Pan American World Airways)

Boeing 727-21, added to Pan Am's fleet in December 1965, cruises at 35,000 feet with 128 passengers averaging 575 mph. Gross weight is 169,000 lbs. Pan Am's "Jumbo Jets," seating 250–300 passengers, were programmed in the late 60s for operational status in 1971. (Photo courtesy Pan American World Airways)

pany. NYRB was quite as rich as Pan Am at the time—in fact, its fleet of 14 Consolidated *Commodore* flying boats was superior to Pan Am's assortment of Sikorsky's, Ford and Fokker Trimotors, and Fairchild 71's. But NYRB never really had a chance once Trippe was ready to muscle in, because James Rand lacked the state department backing that Grace's steamship lines commanded. The mail contract went to Pan Am and that was that. On September 15, 1930, Trippe bought NYRB, including its excellent *Commodores,* for about half its book value, thus adding the entire east coast of South America to his routes. This closed the big circle, from Miami all the way around the South American Continent and back to Brownsville. In order to facilitate the take-over of NYRB's Brazilian agreements, Trippe formed Panair do Brasil, and this subsidiary flew the route south of Belem to Buenos Aires. It, too, disappeared as an international carrier in the mid-sixties.

During the early thirties, Pan American Airways and its subsidiaries developed domestic extensions of the Latin American routes, and, foreseeing the need for future Pacific terminals, Trippe purchased a couple of small Alaskan lines and bought into Chiang Kai-shek's China National Aviation Corp. He also obtained a mail contract from the obliging postmaster general for a Boston-Halifax route, anticipating future Atlantic service.

As it turned out, the Alaska base wasn't needed for the inauguration of trans-Pacific flights, because a new, long-range Martin flying boat made possible a route to the Orient from California via Hawaii, Midway, Wake, Guam, and the Philippines—a route that mightily pleased the U.S. Navy (which lent Pan Am all possible assistance in establishing these bases), for the Navy had long been looking for an excuse to get such facilities on the stepping-stone islands of Midway, Wake, and Guam without upsetting the Department of State's delicate relations with Japan. Therefore, with help from the United States Navy, Post Office Department, Department of State, Department of Commerce (and, surely, all things considered, God Himself), Juan Trippe began scheduled flights across the vast Pacific to Hong Kong on November 22, 1935. Capt. Ed Musick was in command of the Martin M-130 *China Clipper* for the initial flight.

Regularly scheduled Atlantic flights didn't follow until July 8, 1939, when Capt. Arthur LaPorte lifted the Boeing-built *Yankee Clipper* from the channel at Port Washington, Long Island, and headed northeast on a Great Circle course for Southhampton, England. Actually, Trippe had been prepared to start the Atlantic run long before; but the British had stalled negotiations on a reciprocal agreement until they possessed transport airplanes capable of flying the route. By that time, Pan Am faced trouble from another quarter as Hitler's aggressions in Europe finally awakened America to the deficiencies of her air power, and some people in Washington began to suggest that the U.S. needed additional overseas air carriers to strengthen its aerial fleet in case of war and an attendant submarine menace in the Atlantic.

Now, the last thing on earth (or above it) Juan Trippe wanted to do was share one of his oceans with another airline. He offered to schedule extra flights at little extra cost to the post office (Pan Am was already being paid nearly six times as much per mile for carrying the mail as any domestic airline*), and even buy more airplanes, if necessary. There was no point in wasting taxpayers' money by giving a mail contract to a competitor.

But a potential competitor had quietly been preparing to challenge Pan Am's Atlantic monopoly for more than two years. This was American Export Airlines, Inc. (AMEX), which was headed by John E. Slater and James M. Eaton. AMEX was conceived as a subsidiary of American Export Lines, a successful U.S. steamship company operating principally in the Mediterranean; though the aerial offspring had separated itself from its parent when, on May 9, 1939, it filed application with the Civil Aeronautics Board for a route certificate to fly the Atlantic.

Trippe bitterly fought the AMEX application, with the help of Sen. Pat McCarran who had co-authored the Civil Aeronautics Act of 1938. And although that bill specifically provided for "competition to the extent necessary to assure sound development of an air transportation system properly adapted to the needs of foreign and domestic commerce," Sen. McCarran said, in defending Pan Am's monopoly, that what he had really meant by that provision was *foreign* competition; and that, clearly, such competition was assured as a result of the necessary reciprocal landing agreements made with European nations served by Pan Am. This didn't sound too convincing, since the

---

* The postmaster general's annual report for 1940 revealed that, since 1929, Pan Am received almost 80 per cent as much mail pay as all other U.S. airlines combined ($47.2 million vs. $59.8 million).

CAB obviously had no control over such agreements, that being the business of the Department of State. Anyway, on July 12, 1940, President Roosevelt endorsed the CAB's recommendation that AMEX be granted a route certificate to fly the Atlantic. That should have ended the matter; but it didn't.

There remained the question of mail pay for AMEX; and though Postmaster General Jim Farley was ready, as always, to carry out the President's wishes, the Post Office Department, like everyone else, had to look to Congress for its money. And that's where Sen. McCarran and Pan Am lobbyists almost won the ball game. They simply stole the mail-subsidy football in Congress and ran it back through the entire executive branch of government for a Pan Am touchdown: the Senate repudiated the CAB decision, and the House refused to vote money for AMEX's air mail contract.

But the game wasn't over. Events in Europe were changing the (economic) rules. AMEX found so much business waiting, it didn't *need* an air mail contract to survive. Then, when the Army and Navy took over all U.S. airlines upon America's entry into the war a year later, the Pan Am-AMEX battle ended.

So, the precedent was established; and when peace returned Juan Trippe knew he'd be confronted with scores of AMEX's. However, neither Trippe nor his future competition intended to wait for peace to do their planning. The State Department, too, was anticipating the problems of post-war global air travel.

Assuming Allied victory, it was plain as early as 1942 that the United States alone would be in position to establish international civil air routes when peace returned; or, at least, in a highly favored position to do so, because America's only serious rival— the British—had earlier been forced to abandon transport-airplane development in favor of desperately needed fighting planes. The U.S., with its own desperate hour two years delayed, meanwhile produced such excellent transport craft as the Lockheed *Constellation* and Douglas DC-4. Both airplanes had been thoroughly proven in war service by 1942, and both were being built in large numbers. In sum, at war's end, the U.S. would have superior planes, plenty of ocean-flying experience and, as a partner in an Allied victory, a solid diplomatic posture from which to deal for foreign landing rights.

The British, of course, were well aware of this, and had no intention of allowing America to completely take over post-war international air transportation. Al-

though Britain would not be ready to fly world air routes immediately upon cessation of hostilities, she did control within her (then) far-flung empire many of the overseas bases and terminals essential to such operations. Therefore, our English cousins were not without effective bargaining power in the matter.

Another factor in Britain's favor was a real determination on the part of both governments (including a verbal agreement between President Roosevelt and Prime Minister Churchill) to maintain, when peace came, the close bonds of friendship being case-hardened in the fires of war. Both governments foresaw that a peace so dearly won could be drained of much of its significance if the U.S. and Britain should split over post-war economic issues. Thus, with agreement on international air commerce looming as the first critical test of future British-American relations, a conference was called in Chicago, during November of 1944, to divvy-up world air traffic.

Now, if the assumption that the world's airways would primarily belong to England and America seems presumptuous, perhaps it was in a way. Still, it was realistic. No other country, except Australia and Canada, could hope to have overseas airlines soon after the war. In defeat, Germany, Japan, and Italy would be out of the running. Liberated France, its economy and industry ruined, would not be an immediate factor. The Soviets had not responded to U.S.-British queries on the subject.

Agreement between the U.S. and British didn't come easily, because under Roosevelt, the U.S. Government had totally abandoned the chosen instrument approach and now favored the encouragement of as many U.S. overseas airlines as the traffic would support. The English looked with horror upon this wasteful Yankee concept because their flag carrier, British Overseas Airways Corporation (BOAC), which had temporarily disappeared into war service, was a state-owned enterprise that Parliament regarded as a prestigious symbol of Britain's global influence. Really, old boy, one could hardly expect such an instrument of the government to make money, now could one?*

However, after much haggling, British-American differences were settled when the airlines themselves organized the International Air Transport Association, offered membership to all nations possessing or

---

* Protected by international passenger fare agreements, BOAC became profitable after all. For example, despite a pilots' strike that cost an estimated $19.2 million, BOAC registered profits of $19.68 million for the first half of 1968.

expecting to possess an overseas airline (including Russia, who again ignored the decadent West), and proclaiming that IATA would establish international air fares. This allayed British fear of cut-throat competition from the Americans and promoted a friendly and optimistic setting for a new conference, at Bermuda, in January and February of 1946, from which delegates—not only of the U.S. and Britain, but most of the Free World—emerged in happy agreement.

A single dissenter was Pan American Airways. Ever since the 1944 Chicago conference, Juan Trippe, aided by his old ally Sen. Pat McCarran, along with new recruit Sen. Owen Brewster, had been fighting in Congress for re-establishing of his cherished chosen instrument principle. Sen. McCarran repeatedly introduced bills (S. 1790, S.326 and S. 1814) that would, in effect, return America to its air policies of the early thirties. When the McCarran bills failed to win much support, they were slicked-up with fresh goodies to attract other interests and tried again. It was a good fight (your reporters should refrain from commenting upon its morality—or lack of it); but about all it engendered in the end was a lot of resentment for Pan Am, especially in the executive branch of government. And since Harry S. Truman had become President in April, 1945, resentment in the executive branch could result in a fearsome response.

There is plenty of evidence that President Truman was ready to slap Pan Am around pretty substantially. He ignored the recommendations of his own CAB and arbitrarily awarded to Braniff Air Lines a route from the U.S. via Mexico City and Rio to Buenos Aires—right through the heart of Pan Am's hitherto private preserve. The President also announced that Eastern Air Lines would be granted a route from Miami to San Juan, Puerto Rico (although Eastern hadn't even asked for it!), again, a raid on exclusive Trippe territory. But it now appears that cool hands in the CAB, particularly those of CAB Chairman L. Welch Pogue, calmed-down the spirited Mr. Truman, and the CAB then proceded with its rather thankless task of parceling out America's portion of the world air routes to the eighteen U.S. airlines that wanted to share Mr. Trippe's air.

On June 1, 1945, the CAB ruled that three U.S. carriers should fly the Atlantic to European terminals. These would be TWA, Pan Am, and American Air Lines. United Air Lines, alone among the major U.S. domestic air carriers, sought no international routes at the time. United's president, William Patterson, believed that not more than two dozen airplanes could handle all the post-war Atlantic air traffic. Actually, no one knew then just how much traffic there would be; but none of the others was as pessimistic as Patterson.

Late in 1945, American Air Lines bought 60 per cent of AMEX and renamed that company American Overseas Airlines. Four and a-half years later (May, 1950), when American offered to sell AOA to Pan Am, an American Airlines stockholder filed suit in the Federal District Court in Chicago charging that the $17.5 million sale price was far too low. The CAB denied the merger and President Truman concurred. But a few days later the President reversed himself, again ignored the CAB and approved the sale of AOA to Pan Am. Most observers felt they knew from whence had come the obvious political pressure; but that, of course, was academic.

The CAB's route decisions on Latin America were handed down in May, 1946: in addition to the routes given to Braniff and Eastern by the President, National Air Lines, American Air Lines and Chicago & Southern were awarded certificates to operate south of the border.

In August, 1946, the CAB decreed that Pan Am's competitor in the Pacific would be Northwest Air Lines (later, Northwest Orient Airlines), which would fly the northern Great Circle route to the Orient where it would connect with TWA to effect round-the-world service. Pan Am, retaining its pre-war Pacific run, would be the other round-the-world airline. And United was at last edged into commercial ocean flying with a San Francisco-Hawaii route, duplicating Pan Am service to the islands.

These decisions, all carefully watched over by President Truman, resulted in the basic structure from which present-day international air routes evolved. There have been many additions—particularly, foreign flag carriers which have the right to serve the U.S. in return for U.S. airline service to and across their countries—and there have been many route extensions and duplications as traffic increased. Introduction of the jets brought most of this increase. Pan Am placed its first jet in service in October, 1958, when its new Boeing 707 began flying from New York to Paris.

But despite the tremendous competition, Pan American World Airways has continued to grow—and to lead. Clearly, there just isn't any way to stop a man like Juan Terry Trippe.

Succeeding Juan Trippe as Chairman and Chief Executive Officer at Pan Am in 1968 was Harold E. Gray, who joined the company in 1929 as a pilot. Gray captained Pan Am's first Atlantic flight in 1939. Stepping into Pan Am presidency vacated by Gray was Najeeb E. Halaby, a WW-II Navy pilot who served as FAA Administrator for five years before joining Pan Am in 1965. (Photo courtesy Pan American World Airways)

Mr. Trippe at last stepped down, as Pan Am's board chairman and chief executive officer, early in 1968. His successor, however, is a Trippe protege, Mr. Harold E. Gray, whom Trippe hired as a pilot in 1929. It therefore seems unlikely that Pan Am's character is about to change. When commercial space travel begins, that first great machine will probably bear the emblem of the "Blue Ball Express" (as aviation people refer to Pan Am), and, surely, a latter-day Sen. McCarran will dust off S. 326 and declare in Congress that outer space just isn't big enough to justify competition with Pan Am.

10. For Business and Pleasure

Walter Herschel Beech probably should be considered the Father of General Aviation in the United States ("gen-av" includes all civil aircraft except airliners). As early as 1922, while working as a salesman for Wichita's first airplane manufacturer, Beech was trying to promote the Laird *Swallow,* an open-cockpit biplane, as a business and utility machine. Total aircraft production in the U.S. was 35 units that year; there were no more than a dozen non-military airfields in the nation, and permanent, scheduled airline service was still several years in the future. But Walter Beech saw a potential in wood-and-fabric wings that had not occurred to most.

To the average American of that day, airplanes were dangerous vehicles operated by carefree daredevils who lived hard and died young. Such men and machines had fought gloriously in the skies of France in 1918, shooting down heartless Huns in their black-crossed Fokkers; but airplanes really weren't much good for anything else, except perhaps as thrill-producers at county fairs.

And Mr. Average American wasn't too far off with this assessment at that time. Most private plane owners in 1922 were barnstormers (Beech himself was not above a week-end of barnstorming to help meet the Laird company's 18-man payroll); still, Walter believed that privately owned airplanes would inevitably prove to be valuable business tools. Commerce had always depended upon communication and

transportation. Time and distance had been of primary importance to businessmen since the days of sailing ships and camel caravans; and the airplane was a compressor of each of these dimensions. In short, Beech was thinking in terms of a corporate airplane market before that market existed—or rather, before a practical aerial vehicle existed to serve that market. Perhaps the Laird *Swallow* he sold to the Nourse Tractor Oil Company of Kansas City would not greatly expand that company's territory—it cruised at 75 mph and had a range of 255 miles—but the theory which prompted its purchase was sound.

Of course, Beech was not the only aviation pioneer to foresee the private airplane's promise as a business machine; many pilots and would-be plane makers of that day held similar beliefs, as did almost anyone who understood the nature of the flying machine and the manner in which it must evolve. But Beech was more than a dreamer or prophesier, and his visions for the future were accompanied by present action.

Walter Beech was born on a farm near Pulaski, Tennessee, January 30, 1891, the son of Cornelius and Tommie (Hay) Beech. In 1905 he reportedly built a crude glider, and as a teenager worked in a sawmill and the municipal power plant. After attending Giles College, Walter was employed by a Minneapolis automobile builder for whom he traveled in Europe, apparently as a mechanic. In the meantime, Walter and a companion purchased a wrecked

Walter H. Beech left the U. S. Air Service in 1920 and began his career of promoting business airplanes. Along with Clyde Cessna and Lloyd Stearman, Beech formed the Travel Air company late in 1924, and built Travel Air into the world's largest producer of commercial aircraft by 1929. He and his wife, Olive Ann, founded today's Beech Aircraft Corporation in 1932. A visionary, pilot/builder/businessman Beech nevertheless believed that airplanes should support themselves economically as well as aerodynamically. (Photo courtesy Beech Aircraft Corp.)

In 1922 Walter Beech, while employed as a salesman and test pilot for the E. M. Laird Company of Wichita, sold a Laird *Swallow* to the Nourse Tractor Oil Company of Kansas City. Though the *Swallow* was used by Nourse for executive transportation, its advertising benefits were probably of greater value to that company. (Photo courtesy E. M. Laird)

Curtiss pusher of 1911 vintage which they rebuilt and, on January 11, 1914, Beech soloed the craft.

Beech joined the Aviation Section of the Signal Corps soon after America entered WW-I, and spent most of the war at Rich Field, Waco, Texas, first as a sergeant in charge of the engine overhaul shops and later as a pilot and flight instructor. Discharged in June, 1920, Walter took a job with Errett Williams and Pete Hill, operators of a "flying service" (barnstorming) based at Arkansas City, Kansas, and this experience may or may not have been particularly significant because one of the planes Beech flew for Williams and Hill was a WW-I surplus deHavilland DH-5 which was a negative stagger biplane (its lower wings positioned ahead of its upper ones), a configuration later made famous with the Beechcraft "Staggerwing," Model 17. Following a year of barnstorming, Beech joined the E. M. Laird Company of Wichita, which had been formed early in 1920 by Jacob M. Moellendick, Emil Matthew "Matty" Laird and William A. "Billy" Burke to produce the 3-place open-cockpit OX-5-powered Laird-designed *Swallow*. Lloyd Carlton Stearman, a former Naval Aviation cadet and architectural student, was also employed at the *Swallow* works, at first in the rigging department, later as a draftsman.

Walter tested and sold *Swallows* until mid-1924, then he and Stearman quit because boss Jake Moellendick refused to convert from wood to steel tubing in the *Swallow's* fuselage. At least, that's the way the story has always been told around Wichita. Perhaps it was mere coincidence that Lloyd Stearman happened to have just completed drawings of a clean and handsome new biplane (featuring, it must be admitted, a tubular steel fuselage frame). Anyway, Beech and Stearman recruited as a partner barnstormer Clyde V. Cessna (to whom Beech had sold a *Swallow* in 1923), and formed the Travel Air Manufacturing Company to build and sell Stearman's design. The first few Travel Air Model 2000's, powered with the OX-5 engine, were built in a 30-foot-square rented workshop in downtown

Travel Air Model R racer, called the "Mystery Ship" by news reporters, won first Thompson-sponsored race in 1929 and proved far faster than America's first-line military biplane fighters. Most racers that followed were of similar configuration, and the military switched to "low-wingers" soon afterwards. Model R could do 230 mph; it was powered with 420-hp Wright engine. (Photo courtesy Beech Aircraft Corp.)

Travel Air production line, May 29, 1929. Model 6000 cabin monoplanes in foreground, biplane fuselages in background. Travel Air produced almost 1,000 of the 5,357 civil aircraft reported built by 95 companies that year. There were 10,287 licensed pilots in the U.S. in 1929. (Photo courtesy Beech Aircraft Corp.)

Wichita, and a total of 19 were sold during the company's first year in business. More than 300 new planes were produced in the United States that year (1925), up from a total of 60 in 1924. Also during that year, Travel Air became a public corporation, bought land on Wichita's East Central Avenue and

began construction of a factory building on what is today the site of Beech's Plant No. 1.

An early Travel Air employee was Miss Olive Ann Mellor, officially hired as secretary-bookkeeper, though she was in fact "girl of all work." For example, one of Miss Mellor's duties on week-ends and holidays was to don a carpenter's apron containing silver currency and small bills for change-making, and station herself along the east fence to sell tickets for airplane rides while Walter did the flying. Blonde Olive Ann, born September 25, 1903, at Waverly, Kansas, joined Travel Air with a business college background and three year's office experience at the Staley Electric Company in Augusta, Kansas. She and Walter were married February 24, 1930, and had two daughters: Suzane, born in 1937 (now Mrs. Thomas N. Warner), and Mary Lynn, born in 1940 (now Mrs. John E. H. Pitt).

In 1926, Travel Air sold 46 of the 650 planes built in the U.S. that year. In the fall, Lloyd Stearman pulled out to form his own company (which he merged with the Boeing Division of United Aircraft in 1929); and then Clyde Cessna left in April, 1927, to found his own company (taken over in 1936 by Clyde's nephew Dwane Wallace, still Cessna's board chairman as this is written).

In addition to Stearman and Cessna, other plane makers had entered the market. The 1925 Kelly Bill, which provided for substantial federal subsidies for flying the mail, resulted in the appearance of significant risk capital, particularly for the production of new airplanes. At first, most of these civilian contractors were not interested in carrying passengers for they saw no profit in that tenuous market; therefore most bought converted open-cockpit biplanes. This brought Harold Pitcairn of the Pittsburgh Plate Glass Company into the field with his Pitcairn *Mailwing,* and Matty Laird, who had left Swallow and returned to Chicago, sold the first of his famed *Laird Commercials* to the forerunner of today's Northwest Orient Airlines. T. Claude Ryan who, aided by Hawley Bowlus, modified some WW-I Standards into four-passenger cabin biplanes and started scheduled flights between Los Angeles and San Diego in 1925, entered the market with his Ryan M-1 monoplane the following year. Swallow was selling its share of biplanes to the air mail operators, as was WACO, a company actually formed back in 1919 by George "Buck" Weaver, Elwood "Sam" Junkin and Clayton Bruckner, and which had somehow hung on selling but a handful of airplanes until its WACO 9 appeared late in 1924 just in time to satisfy the immediate needs of several air mail operators.

Still another was the Eaglerock Aircraft Company of Denver, formed by J. D. Alexander of the Alexander Film Company, makers of short motion picture commercials. The Eaglerock, a 3-place open biplane powered by the ubiquitous OX-5, was designed by Dan Noonan and Al Mooney and priced at $2,475. Mooney, in partnership with Charles Yankey, would start his own company after WW-II.

Tony Fokker also entered the U.S. aviation scene during the early twenties. He put his foot in the door in 1921 with establishment of the Netherlands Aircraft Manufacturing Company at Amsterdam, N.Y., a sales and information office run by Bob Noorduyn. In 1924, Fokker landed a contract to convert the fuselages of 100 Army DH-4's from wood to steel tubing, and this resulted in formation of the Atlantic Aircraft Company, the first Fokker factory in the U.S. at Hasbrouck Heights, N.J. Fokker then introduced his first, hastily built trimotor in the 1925 Ford Reliability Tour. Fokker was purchased by General Motors in 1930.

Fokker's chief competitor for the transport-plane market was Henry Ford. Shorty Schroeder test-flew the prototype Ford Trimotor Model 4-AT in June, 1926. This classic craft succeeded the earlier Ford-Stout 2-AT *Air Pullman* which saw service on the original Ford mail runs as well as with Florida Airways.

Three other plane makers of significance began operations in 1926. These were Sherman Fairchild, in Farmingdale, N.Y., with an OX-5 cabin monoplane; E. E. Porterfield of Kansas City, offering his 3-place open biplane the *American Eagle;* and Eddie Stinson, who built the first of his famous *Detroiters* in a Congress Street loft in Detroit that year. Stinson was later financed by auto magnate E. L. Cord who at one time controlled American Airways (later American Air Lines) and AVCO. Eddie was killed in a plane crash in 1932, and Piper Aircraft Corporation absorbed the Stinson Company after WW-II.

And then there was Grover Loening's company, established in 1917, and which in the mid-twenties, concentrated on amphibious aircraft; and Glenn Martin, who began in Los Angeles before WW-I, had his factory in Cleveland during the twenties when he catered mostly to the military, and moved to Baltimore in 1928. On the West Coast were Boeing, Douglas, and Lockheed. Ex-lumberman William E. Boeing and Conrad Westervelt formed the Pacific Aero Products Company in 1916 to build twin-float open biplanes, and this enterprise developed into the Boeing Airplane and Transport Corporation from which United Air Lines grew as well as the present-day Boeing Company. During the twenties, the company built transport planes for its airline affiliate, and military aircraft. Donald Douglas, who started his own company in 1920 in Santa Monica, sold only to the military during this period: torpedo planes for the Navy, and observation planes for the Army. Also totally oriented to military designs were the Thomas Morse Aircraft Corporation, founded in 1917, which had grown from the original Thomas Brothers Aeroplane Company started in 1912; and the big Curtiss plant at Buffalo, N.Y., although some hefty Curtiss biplanes—the *Carrier Pigeon* and the *Lark* are examples—were sold to air mail contractors.

Finally, there was the Lockheed Aircraft Company. Allen Lockheed (originally "Loughead") had started his aviation career in Chicago in 1910 as a mechanic on James Plew's Curtiss-type pusher, and built several planes before WW-I with the help of his brother Malcolm (who later perfected the first hydraulic brake system for automobiles). During WW-I they had a factory at Santa Barbara, California, and constructed two flying boats for the Navy. In 1919, they offered a single-place sportplane chiefly designed by Jack Northrop. It did not sell and the company went out of business and did not return until 1926—with a new design by Northrop called the Lockheed *Vega*.

These then were Travel Air's contemporaries and competitors in 1926. To help complete the picture, we should add that 1926 was the first full year of domestic airline operation in the U.S. Eleven airlines/air mail contractors flew a total of 4,318,087 miles, carried 5,782 adventuresome passengers, 3,555 pounds of air freight and 269,671 pounds of mail, receiving for the last mentioned item $710,042 from the Post Office Department. Airline passenger fares averaged 12¢ per mile. Also, the Bureau of Air Commerce was established within the Department of Commerce by the Air Commerce Act that year and the first air regulations and pilots' licenses issued— though a year later (1927) only 1,572 pilots held licenses. In 1927, the first year an official count was made, the Bureau of Air Commerce found a total of 2,612 civil aircraft, both licensed and unlicensed, plus 900 airliners and mailplanes.

By 1929 there were 10,287 licensed pilots in the U.S., and the civil aircraft fleet had grown to 9,315 plus 1,500 airliners and mailplanes. Travel Air produced almost 1,000 of the 5,357 commercial aircraft reported built by 95 companies (among the new airplanes appearing during the "Lindbergh Boom"

were Kreider-Reisner, Mohawk, Spartan, Hamilton, Great Lakes, Monocoupe, Bird, Fleet, and Bellanca, though a couple of these companies had been dabbling ineffectually in the market before that). Still, Travel Air managed to garner more than its share of the market despite this proliferation of new airframe makers, and despite the difficulties inherent in competing with the big aviation complexes such as United Aircraft, AVCO and Curtiss-Wright who were absorbing promising av-properties in great numbers as Wall Street poured huge sums of money into an industry intoxicated by the excellent financial brew resulting from the Kelly Bill and the Lindbergh flight to Paris.

Perhaps Walter Beech anticipated the economic crisis that was to come. Despite his streak of showmanship (which seems really a manifestation of his sales ability) and his flair for gathering newspaper headlines with altitude, distance, and racing records, Walter was clearly an astute businessman. But whatever the true reason—foresightedness, luck, or maybe just because he received a good offer—Beech and his board of directors accepted, in August, 1929, a proposal to merge with the (then) huge Curtiss-Wright combine. The 100,000 shares of Travel Air stock then outstanding were traded for 175,000 shares of Curtiss-Wright Corporation common, and Beech became president of the Airplane Division of C-W and vice-president in charge of sales of the Curtiss-Wright Corporation. The Great Depression began just two months later.

Meanwhile, Travel Air biplanes, by then mostly powered with the reliable new radial engines, still accounted for the bulk of the company's sales. The Travel Air Model R (called the "Mystery Ship" and later the "Mystery S" by newspapers), built as a pure racer, partly as a research project and partly for publicity purposes, won the first Thompson race at Cleveland in 1929. The Model R was a clean, low-wing design of advanced though not radical configuration that proved at least 30 mph faster than the best U.S. military fighters then flying. Almost every subsequent racing plane was of similar design, and two years later the Army switched to the Model R's configuration for its fighters with the Boeing P-26.

But it was the Travel Air cabin monoplanes, the Models 10, 5000 and 6000 being sold to the young airlines and finding some businessmen buyers that possessed the greatest significance in Beech's view. These four, five, and six-place working aircraft were

Walter Beech with 15th Model 17 *Staggerwing,* built
in August 1934. Engine in this B17L was a 225-hp
Jacobs, which gave a cruising speed of 150 mph.
(Photo courtesy Beech Aircraft Corp.)

justifying their existence economically; and that was
precisely what the airplane must do, Walter believed,
if it were to ever become a standard piece of business
equipment and thereby establish a stable and sizable
civil airplane market.

Predictably, Walter was unhappy as a Curtiss-
Wright executive. His plush office in New York
offered no substitute for the quiet excitement of a
drafting room, the noises and smells of a production
line, the easy lift of sturdy wings, and a contented
squint into the prairie's bright vastness through a
propeller's blur. Besides, he wanted to build a true
executive airplane; say, a five-place cabin biplane with
posh interior appointments and the comfort of a

limousine. It should have a range of nearly 1,000
miles, and above all it must be fast.

Walter stuck it out at Curtiss-Wright until early in
1932. Then, in the darkest year of the greatest
depression the world had seen, he and Olive Ann
moved back to Wichita and, in April, 1932, formed
the Beech Aircraft Company. Their associates, numbering less than 10, included engineers Ted Wells
and Herb Rawdon, Walter's brother, R. K. Beech,
and a half-dozen former Travel Air employees. In
rented space in the Depression-closed Cessna factory,
this group designed and produced the first Beechcraft, the prototype of the classic Model 17 *"Staggerwing."* The *Staggerwing* made its initial flight on

November 14, 1932, and was publicly demonstrated a week later at Wichita Municipal Airport. It was a luxury cabin-biplane with negatively staggered wings, streamlined fixed landing gear, and was powered by a 420-hp Wright engine. It had a top speed of 201 mph, cruised at 170, landed at 60 and climbed 1,600 feet per minute. Even today, these are impressive performance figures for single-engine prop-driven gen-av airplanes.

Still, the country *was* suffering from the Great Depression, and the truth is only one *Staggerwing* was sold during 1933. Then, in May, 1934, the first retractable-gear *Staggerwing* appeared and this, plus the plane's fast-growing reputation for speed and comfort and the fact that most U.S. businessmen believed they could see some light at the end of the financial tunnel, increased sales to 19 units that year. From then on production steadily climbed: 36 *Staggerwings* were sold in 1935 and 59 in 1936, by which time Walter's payroll had increased to 175 employees and Beech Aircraft had become a public corporation with a paid-in capitalization of $100,000.

Early in 1937 Beech purchased his old Travel Air factory from Curtiss-Wright for $150,000. And just 8 days later, on January 15, a new all-metal twin-engine monoplane, the Beechcraft Model 18, made its first flight. The famed "Twin Beech" met with instant acceptance. Beech sold 71 airplanes that year; and the Bureau of Air Commerce reported that there were 17,681 licensed pilots in the U.S., 10,446 general aviation airplanes and 2,299 airports.

The 7-place Beechcraft Model 18 outwardly re-

Beechcraft D17S, powered with 450-hp P&W R-985 engine was the GB-1 and GB-2 in Navy service during WW-II. Top speed was 205 mph. USAAF also used the *Staggerwing* and called it the UC-43 and YC-43. (Photo courtesy Beech Aircraft Corporation)

189

Beechcraft Model 18, which first flew in 1937 (and in 1969 reached its 32nd year of continuous production; a record equalled by no other airplane in history), was the JRB in the Navy during WW-II, and the AT-7, AT-11, and C-45 in the USAAF. (Photo courtesy Beech Aircraft Corporation)

sembled the first Lockheed *Electra* and the Barkley-Grow T8P1 of the same period, but the three craft were not in fact "sisters under the skin," because the Twin Beech incorporated a number of unique construction features which paid homage to simplicity and made it easy to repair and maintain by the average mechanic. This as much as anything else accounts for the fact that the Model 18 survived in production while the other two did not. Indeed, as this is written (April, 1969), the Model 18 is still in production— 32 years after its introduction—a record of course unequalled by any other airplane in history. Almost 10,000 have been built.

In 1938, Beech sales exceeded a million dollars

for the first time, and in 1939 when war came to Europe Beech sales of $1.3 million produced a profit for the third year in a row while the corporation's payroll rose to 660. Then, on the eve of the Battle of Britain early in the summer of 1940, Beech suspended commercial production in order to fill frantic orders from the U.S. military.

During WW-II, Beech employment reached a peak of 14,000 while the company delivered 7,400 airplanes to the Navy and USAAF, in addition to great quantities of components for the Douglas A-26 *Invader*. In uniform, the Model 17 *Staggerwing* was called UC-43 and YC-43 by the Army; GB-1 and GB-2 by the Navy. The Model 18 was the AT-7,

Meanest Beechcraft was the XA-38 *Grizzly*, a twin-engined attack craft built late in WW-II but never produced. Engines were Wright R-3350's; armament one 75-mm cannon and six .50-caliber machine guns. Company sources say it could outrun a P-51. (Photo courtesy Beech Aircraft Corporation)

AT-11 and C-45 in the Army; JRB and SNB in Navy dress. Also built in some numbers was the all-wood Beechcraft AT-10, which had no civilian counterpart; and two prototypes of the XA-38 *Grizzly*, a twin-engine attack bomber which the AAF asked for then decided it didn't need. The *Grizzly*, powered with a pair of Wright R-3350's, had a gross weight of 36,300 pounds, was armed with a 75-mm cannon, two forward-firing fixed machine guns and four .50 caliber guns in remotely-controlled turrets. According to Beech Aircraft, the *Grizzly* could out-run a P-51.

Four months after Japan's surender, Beech rolled out the prototype of another pace-setter, the Beech-

craft *Bonanza*, Model 35. Certified in November, 1946, *Bonanza* deliveries began the following February, and the first ones—with 165 hp, 172-mph cruise, and payload of 730 lbs.—were priced, unrealistically, at $7,975, a price settled upon in expectation of a new boom in civil flying that failed to develop.

Actually, there was some justification for believing a new av-boom was imminent because 35,000 civil aircraft were sold in 1946; but this figure dropped to 7,302 by 1948, and hit a low of 2,477 units in 1951. *Bonanza* sales dropped correspondingly from an initial 1,000 units in 1947 to less than 350 in 1949. Contributing to this rollback was the fact that the *Bonanza* was underpriced to start with, and its

191

The prototype Beechcraft Model 35 *Bonanza* first flew December 22, 1945, and has since claimed its place beside the *Staggerwing* and the Model 18 as a true classic. Early production *Bonanzas* were powered with a 165-hp Continental E-165-1 engine and had a top speed of 184 mph. Almost 24 years later, in the spring of 1969, Beech delivered its 9,000th *Bonanza,* which should be proof enough that the V-tailed darter from Wichita "serves as a standard of excellence," to quote Webster's definition of the term "classic." (Photo courtesy Beech Aircraft Corporation)

Beechcraft T-34 *Mentor* (Model 45) was developed as a military primary trainer. Appearing in 1948, it remained in production until 1959. In service with both the Navy and Air Force, the T-34 was also sold to 12 foreign nations. (Photo courtesy Beech Aircraft Corporation)

192

Beechcraft Super 18 built in 1968 was, of course, much improved over the Model 18 of 1937, though basic configuration remains the same. The Super 18 has tricycle landing gear, low-drag wing-tips, picture windows, and a purty pointy nose; but in the main it's the same airplane Walter flew to Miami before WW-II to establish a cross-country record. (Photo courtesy Beech Aircraft Corporation)

price adjustments upwards (multiplied by customer demands for more power and more frills and spiraling production costs) paralleled the decline in civil aircraft sales. In 1948, the *Bonanza* sold for $10,875; in 1951, $15,990. By 1963, in a once again healthy market, the 17th generation *Bonanza* had a basic list of $28,750; and in 1967 the V35 Model was priced at $32,500. This 400 per cent increase in price over the first *Bonanza* paid for an additional 35 mph in speed, a few hundred pounds of extra pay load and a whole lot of inflation.

Meanwhile, in 1948, the Beechcraft Model 45

Mentor (T-34) was developed as a military trainer. Produced for the Air Force and Navy, it remained in production until 1959. It was built under license in Argentina, Canada, and Japan, and was chosen by 12 foreign nations as a primary trainer.

Late in 1950, despite the depressed civil aircraft market, Beech Aircraft, along with the rest of the industry, suddenly found itself with plenty of business following the outbreak of the Korean War. America, as usual, was unprepared for war (WW-II surplus C-47's that had been going begging at $5,000 each two years earlier were, overnight, worth $40-50,000);

and though Beech was not primarily a builder of military aircraft, the company quickly collected a $50 million backlog for military production.

Then, in the midst of this expansion—on the evening of November 29, 1950—Walter Beech was stricken with a heart attack and died suddenly. He was fifty-nine. Active to his last day, Walter left behind a viable company and a proud heritage. He had 10,000 hours in the air. He was a true pioneer in aviation with the vision and talent to bridge the chasm between barnstormer and businessman. Gen-av would have grown up without him; but it wouldn't have been the same.

Of course, Walter didn't build Beech Aircraft alone. In common with all successful industrial leaders he possessed a knack for hiring the proper people and inspiring them to produce their best. And since 1925 he had had Olive Ann. At Travel Air she sold tickets while he barnstormed, ran the office, kept the books, stalled creditors, and arbitrated employee gripes. At Beech Aircraft she was secretary-treasurer and a corporate director. She knew the business and had a capacity for work equal to her husband's. So upon Walter's death, Olive Ann Beech took over as president and chief executive officer and Beech Aircraft Corporation continued to grow.

By the end of 1952, Beech Aircraft had a backlog of $210 million in military contracts and $20 million in civilian orders. An Air Force contract to design, develop, and test a pressurized twin-engine jet trainer —designated the T-36A—accounted for $100 million of this. But the T-36 contract proved a traumatic experience. On June 10, 1953, after Beech had added 110,000 square feet of new factory space and hired 6,000 additional employees for production of the T-36, the Air Force cancelled the contract. There was not to be another dollar spent or another rivet driven. The T-36 prototype was just hours away from its first flight; but the Air Force would not even allow that. The plane was ordered destroyed.

This was a serious blow; and few would have blamed Olive Ann if she had retreated to the simpler and more constant civil airplane market altogether telling the military to please take future orders elsewhere. Instead, she and her officers profited from the experience and concentrated upon military subcontract work as an extra-income source. Perhaps this approach is not quite as profitable, but it has proved a sound concept for Beech, and the prospect of a sudden government cancellation holds less terror

with military and space contracts averaging but 30 per cent of Beech's total sales ($54.4 million out of $184.3 million in 1968) and spread over a number of projects, from airframe components for the F-4 fighter to cryogenic tanks for Apollo command and LEM modules.

Therefore, it has primarily been expansion of the Beech line of civil aircraft that has accounted for the company's growth under Olive Ann's leadership. From three airplanes in 1950, Beech has steadily added new craft until, in 1969, the Beechcraft line contained twenty business and utility airplanes from the two-place Musketeer *Sport* to the 17-place Model 99 airliner.

And Olive Ann Beech, like her husband before her, would be the first to tell you that her success has been backed by one of the sharpest and most cohesive managerial teams in the business. When Olive Ann vacated the presidency of Beech Aircraft in 1968 (she remains, as this is written, board chairman and chief executive officer) in favor of Frank E. Hedrick, the leader of that team, she could do so knowing that Hedrick's influence on the company had long since been established and his decisions proven. He had, after all, been a Beech executive since 1940.

Others in top management could boast similar constancy. Among Beech vice-presidents, for example, were L. L. Pechin who had joined the company in 1934, James N. Lew and E. C. Burns, 1940, and L. E. Bowery and Leddy Greever, 1941, while Secretary-Treasurer John A. Elliot went to Beech in 1942. Vice-President M. G. Neuburger became a Beechcrafter in 1946, and presumably feels like a rookie among this bunch. Indeed, the balance of the Beech management group averaged 22 years' service in 1969—and 1/3 of *all* Beech employees had more than 10 years with the company. Employment early in 1969 totalled 11,600 in six plants, three in Wichita, one each in Liberal and Salina, Kansas, plus the Beech space facility at Boulder, Colorado.

So, this is a brief look at a corporation that is representative of private airplane manufacturers in the United States. Of course, Beech's competition— Piper, Cessna, Mooney, Aero Commander, and others —builds good airplanes too; but lack of space precludes an account of each. We chose Beech to represent this segment of the industry because the Beechcrafter's dedication comes through so clearly. It's unmistakable; these people build airplanes because

Air launched from Air Force *Phantom* jet fighter, the
Beech rocket-powered target missile AQM-37A flies at
near Mach 2 speeds at altitudes above 50,000 feet for
air combat training and as a target in new weapons
evaluation. Military contracts constitute about 30 percent of Beech's total business. (Photo courtesy Beech
Aircraft Corporation)

they'd rather do it than anything else. They're proud,
real proud of their creations, and you somehow get
the impression, down on the production lines, that
the only reason they accept pay for this labor of love
is because their wives (or maybe the union) insist
upon it.

The modern promise of general aviation, which
the industry saw bloom and quickly fade in the
late forties, now appears on its way to fulfillment.
Early in 1969, the number of gen-av aircraft passed
the 125,000 mark (compared to some 2,500 airliners
using the nation's airways). What is not generally
realized by those who still think of gen-av in terms

of a single pilot boring holes in the sky for his own
amusement is that more than 66,000 of these planes
were capable of carrying four or more passengers.
Some 15,000 were multi-engine craft, and about
40 per cent of the total were business aircraft, including 600 pure jets. A study made in 1968 would
certainly have warmed Walter Beech's heart, for it
concluded that there were 390,000 U.S. businesses
that profitably could make use of and could afford
a business airplane.

The reason was a simple one: there were more
than 9,000 airports in the nation; but the big airlines served only 515 of them (nearly 70 per cent

Mrs. O. A. Beech, board chairman and chief executive officer of Beech Aircraft, and Frank E. Hedrick, President, greet Air Force Colonels Malcom Frazee (1) and Earnest Tripplett as the air officers take delivery of a Beechcraft *King Air* for service with the Special Air Missions Fleet. (Photo courtesy Beech Aircraft Corporation)

of all airline passengers were enplaned at only 22 hub areas). So, the businessman, eager to go where he wanted when he wanted was finding the corporate-owned airplane a time and money saver, especially when seeking contacts outside the 22 or so principal metropolitan areas of the country.

An important new factor has been the rapid growth of the air taxi business, which includes the mushrooming "third level" airlines, regularly scheduled service in planes like the 17-place Beechcraft 99 prop-jet, linking communities too small to interest the big air carriers. In 1968, air taxis flew 3.5 million passengers, many of them into and out of airports not served by commercial airlines. Third level air carriers, many with air mail contracts, increased tenfold during the late sixties.

General aviation also includes agricultural flying (crop spraying, seeding, etc.), student instruction, forest fire control, and sport flying. The 13,698 new civil aircraft built in the U.S. in 1968 had a manufacturer's net billing value of $425.8 million; and the 600,000-plus civilian flyers, logging more than 25 million hours in the air, performed countless essential services while contributing substantially to the nation's economy.

Significantly, the median age of civilian flight students in 1968 was 32; and the average buyer of a civil aircraft was 44 years old. Clearly, the day of the youngster circling the airport on Sunday afternoon in his Piper Cub is past. The private airplane today is basically a utility machine, and in most cases must earn its keep.

196

Beechcraft turbo-prop Model 99 Airliner is a 17-passenger 254-mph short-haul transport designed for service with the fast-growing "third level" air carrier fleet. (Photo courtesy Beech Aircraft Corporation)

Beechcraft Model D55 *Baron* is a four-to-six-place business and personal plane fitted with a pair of 285-hp Continental engines. *Baron's* top speed is 242 mph, and its range is 1,143 miles. (Photo courtesy Beech Aircraft Corporation)

Beechcraft Model 23 *Musketeer Sport* is offered in two or four-place with choice of engines beginning at $13,300 for the training and personal fun-plane market. The *Musketeers,* smallest and least expensive of the Beech product line, cruise at about 135 mph. (Photo courtesy Beech Aircraft Corporation)

Beech's *Queen Airliner* is an 11-place, 248-mph, light transport powered with two 380-hp supercharged Lycoming engines. It has a range of 1,560 miles with reserves and is in service with several third level air carriers. (Photo courtesy Beech Aircraft Corporation)

Modern Beechcraft *Bonanza,* Model V35A, is powered with a 285-hp Continental engine and carries four to six people at speeds up to 210 mph. Range, with reserves, is 1,111 miles. (Photo courtesy Beech Aircraft Corporation)

Beechcraft *Bonanza* Model E33 was originally marketed as the *Debonair,* but the airframe was all *Bonanza* from the beginning—that is, a *Bonanza* with a "conventional" tail. The conventional tail is obviously a concession to tenuous pilot preference ("If a vertical rudder was good enough for Orville and Wilbur and Charles Lindbergh, it's good enough for me!"). Anyway, the *Bonanza* has two tails; you pay your money and take your choice. (Photo courtesy Beech Aircraft Corporation)

199

11. Retread Tigers

Korea, immediately following WW-II, seemed of small importance to most Americans. Above the 38th Parallel Korea was occupied by the Soviets when the war with Japan ended (Russia declared war on Japan only after the U.S. dropped the A-bomb). Below the 38th Parallel, American troops landed to direct withdrawal of the Nipponese invader. The Reds installed a Communist government in North Korea and the U.S. backed free elections and the return of Korean Statesman Syngman Rhee in the southern part of the Korean peninsula.

By 1948, the People's Democratic Republic of Korea in the north, under Premier Kim Il Sung (who had been a major in the Soviet Army) was producing goods for Russia in return for arms while U.S. troops were being withdrawn from the south, their job supposedly done after the Republic of Korea was established and functioning under Rhee.

The Russians began their withdrawal that same year, leaving behind their Aviation Mission and a number of WW-II combat aircraft for use of the Korean People's Army Air Force (KPAAF). This fleet included PO-2 trainers and YAK-18's; Ilyushin IL-2M3's, IL-10's, Lavochkin LA-5FN's, -7's, -9's; some YAK-3's, -7B's and -9's plus a few Lend-Lease P-63 *Kingcobras*.

Meanwhile, the United Nations organization of world governments had been formed (June, 1945), and in May, 1947, the U.S. Congress had approved

President Truman's request for $400 million to prevent a Russian take-over of Greece and Turkey. Truman expanded that concept into the "Truman Doctrine" which promised aid to any country threatened by Soviet aggression (an entirely credible stance at the time since America was the sole possessor of the A-bomb, and had plenty of B-29's to deliver it).

In Asia, the Far East Air Forces, activated in Brisbane, Australia on June 15, 1944, under command of General George C. Kenney, came under the leadership of General George C. Stratemeyer in April of 1949. Specifically a defense force, FEAF (pronounced, rhymes with "leaf") consisted of five wings, two in Japan and one each in Guam, the Philippines, and Okinawa. The largest segment of this occupational force was the 5th AF with fingers of tactical units to defend the Japanese home islands from bases on Kyushu, the southernmost of the main Japanese Islands, to Misawa Air Base on the northeastern shore of Honshu, across the Sea of Japan from the peninsula of Korea.

The stage was set. At 4 o'clock in the morning of June 25, a Sunday in 1950, the North Koreans, under cover of bad weather, launched an all-out aggression into South Korea. As General MacArthur was to later say, "They struck like a cobra."

Apparently, the KPAAF had an air arm of 70 YAK-3 and YAK-7B fighters, 62 IL-10 bombers, 22 YAK-18 transports, and 8 PO-2 trainers. The FEAF

B-26 *Invaders,* changed from the World War II designation of Douglas A-26s in 1947, had a range of 1,527 miles with 6,000 pounds of bombs. The *Invaders* served in Korea from the start of the war and often worked in pairs at night. The "Hunter," equipped with flares, found Red supplies forced by air attacks to move by night, and the "Killer" B-26 came in for the kill. (Photo courtesy USAF)

had a grand total of 1,172 aircraft of all description, some in storage or salvage. This left 553 operational aircraft; of those, the largest number were F-80 *Shooting Stars* jets (365) and 32 F-82 *Twin Mustangs.*

Though inadequately trained, pilots of the KPAAF were eager. They anticipated a fast fight, for neither the North Korean leaders nor their Russian advisors expected the United States or the far-off United Nations to stand up and give battle. They were wrong.

Spearheaded by Russian built tanks, the Reds moved with deadly speed. Over-running the lightly defended separation line, the troops slashed south.

Small boats landed more of their soldiers below Kangnung, and the two bands of fighters threatened to wipe out everything in their way as they joined forces.

In the beginning, the FEAF was given one pressing and primary mission—move all Americans out of South Korea. The 374th Troop Carrier Wing took off for Seoul, the South Korean capital, on the 26th of June, with the Red advance perilously close.

Due to American economic cutbacks in the years of peace following World War II, only 4 Japanese airfields could handle combat-loaded F-80's. And to this oldest of American operational jets fell the duty of protecting the unarmed transports, but the distance

A soft-nosed Invader, so called because of the bombardier's glass cubicle instead of optionally mounted nose cannons, bellied in for an emergency landing in Korea. Enemy small-arms fire, particularly hostile in North Korea, damaged the plane's hydraulic system and the landing gear could not be lowered. With the canopy open for immediate evacuation, the Invader crashed seconds later. No one was hurt. (Photo courtesy USAF)

(350 miles) from their nearest base limited their use. The F-80's, on internally carried fuel, had the barest radius of action of 100 miles. Even if external tanks replaced bombs, the *Shooting Stars* could reach out to a maximum of 225 miles—and return. These limits left much of the earliest "little friend" protector role to the piston-engined long-range fighters, the F-82's, from their base in Itazuke, Japan.

On the 27th of June in an emergency meeting of the Security Council of Secretary-General Trygve Lie's United Nations, a resolution was passed to "furnish such assistance to the Republic of Korea as may be necessary to repel the armed attack and to restore international peace."*

That same afternoon, President Harry Truman announced he had ordered the USAF and the 7th Fleet to aid South Korea.

North Korean pilots, in 5 YAKs, launched an attack against the American base and transports on Seoul's Kimpo Airport. The YAKs were met by 5

* Likely this resolution would not have passed, 7 to 1, except the Soviet delegation had walked out of the UN after the refusal to grant a U.N. seat to Red China. Doubtless, Russia would have used her veto power had her delegation been present.

Twin-Mustangs. American pilots Lt. William G. Hudson, Major James W. Little and Lt. Charles B. Moran each downed a YAK. Lt. Hudson, with S/Sgt. Nyle S. Mickley, officially are credited with the "kill" of the first Communist aircraft over Korea.

Later that same day, KPAAF, with more optimism than logic, headed to Kimpo for another go at destroying the American transports. Eight IL-10s (improved versions of the dread Stormovik planes of WW-II) met 4 *Shooting Stars* which had refueled at Kimpo before the attack. The jets quickly flamed down 4 IL-10s before the group could turn tail and run. These were the first victims of American jet fighters, which, by all standards, then obsolete, were persuasive in their ability to out-maneuver top conventional prop planes of the day.

As early as the 27th, it was quite evident that though the ROK (South Korea) forces fought valiantly, they would be crushed without active and immediate military aid.

We were back in war.

The USAF, which had been forged into the mightiest air force in the world by the end of WW-II, again was ill-prepared. From 218 groups on V-J Day, the USAAF was stripped down to 52 groups—on the books—only two being operational to any degree. Not one USAF group could be counted as on alert to the nation's defense when the Korean conflict started. From the war-time peak of 2,253,000 men in the USAAF, the USAF was down to 303,000 by the end of May, 1947. Only 24,000 aircrewmen were in uniform when it entered into its first war without ties to the Army.

Military plane production, with peace cut-backs,

Four Navy F4Us returning from a combat mission pass over the USS *Boxer,* CV-21. (Photo Navy Dept., The National Archives)

had dropped to less than 150 planes per month.

Emergency orders exploded, and a total of 29 Air Reserve Wings were called to active service.

FEAF moved to attack and the mission was first to Pyongyang, the oldest and most active airfield in North Korea. A quite creditable tally of 25 KPAAF planes destroyed (air and ground) was racked up for the first UN offensive; however, more help was des-

The F-80 *Shooting Stars* proved the value of fighter-bomber conversions as these "old" jets carried the defense and offense in the early days of Korea. This particular *Shooting Star's* landing gear was shot off by tank cannon fire. More cannon holes can be seen in the fuselage below the letters FT. Rather than risk a belly landing on the hardsurfaced runway, this pilot walked away from the emergency after landing in a rice paddy. (Photo Official Dept. of Defense Photo)

The Navy's first fighter with a tri-cycle landing gear to operate successfully from carriers, the F7F *Tigercat* was kept busy by the First Marine Air Wing over Korea. This one is seeking a target for the napalm (jellied gasoline) bomb hanging underneath. (Photo courtesy Defense Dept., Marine Corps)

perately needed. The North Koreans had captured Seoul in only 3 days and streamed south with no halts. Top UN and military officials received reports that the ROK Army suffered as high as 50 per cent casualties.

On the first of July, carrier-based F9F *Panther* jets and Douglas AD *Skyraiders* went into action. On this day, the Navy was credited with their first victories in Korean air-to-air combat when Lt. (JG) L. H. Plog and Ensign E. W. Brown each shot down a YAK-9.

A month later, Marine fighters entered the fray. The controversy between the new Air Force and the Navy, started in 1946, continued heatedly into 1949 and, of course, sucked in the Marines. Despite spec-

tacular hard-won battles in WW-II, the Marine Corps seemed doomed in the peace-time service structure. Secretary of the Army Kenneth C. Royall, when asked by a Senate Committee in April, 1949, if he suggested that the Secretary of Defense "Abolish the Marine Corps and make it part of the Army," answered, "That's exactly what I am proposing."

Secretary of Defense Louis A. Johnson ordered a 48 per cent drop in Marine Aviation's combat strength for fiscal year 1950 (beginning in mid-49). Eleven aircraft squadrons were decommissioned leaving the Marines with only 12. In spite of the repeated protests by politically powerful General Clifton B. Cates,

The *USS Boxer* raced across the Pacific with pilots, crewmen, and airplanes recalled from the Reserves, Air National Guard, and mothballs. "I had flown several of those same Mustangs in training," says Bartimus. "And here we were, going to war together, aboard a ship." (Photo courtesy Bart Bartimus)

the Marine Commandant, Secretary Johnson did, in fact, seem determined to wipe out Marine Aviation on the grounds the US had "too many air forces." Only because Chairman Carl Vinson of the House Armed Service Committee stepped in (late April, 1949) was even this small part of Marine Aviation saved.

By the 30th of June, while the Reds marched roughshod over the ROK Army, the Marine Corps, which had been so pitifully cut down to 78,715 men the year before, again was to be slashed, this time to 67,025. This never happened, for 6 days earlier, Secretary of State Acheson had called President Truman in Independence, Missouri, to say that the Communists were invading South Korea.

That day, the Korean "incident" became the Korean War. Would it be fought without Marines? General Cates, through Admiral Sherman, asked General MacArthur* if he wanted a Marine Brigade complete with a supporting air wing. Backed only by ill-equipped and inexperienced occupational troops in

* The commander in the theatre until July 7th when the Security Council established a united command under President Truman with the US as agent for dealing with Korea. Truman named MacArthur as commander of the UN military forces which numbered, at the start, Great Britain, Australia, Turkey and the US. More nations later sent forces, a total of 16 besides the South Koreans.

Japan, MacArthur answered with a resounding yes—and added, "Immediately!"

The First Provisional Marine Brigade, 6,534 Marines and 3 fighting squadrons including a helicopter detachment, sailed from San Diego on July 14.

On August 3, only hours after the Brigade debarked at Pusan, Marine F4U's of The Black Sheep Squadron (Pappy Boyington's old VMF-214), from the USS *Sicily* scored in an air strike over Inchon. By the 11th, the North Koreans knew they now faced tough and powerful "plugging" ground troops on the Pusan Perimeter. VMF-323, from the jeep carrier *Badoeng Strait* (called, by the Marines, "The Bing-Ding") raked North Korean troops and supplies as the Brigade moved forward toward Sachow.

Marine Aviation, according to General Richard C. Mangrum, retired in the late 60s from the post of Assistant Commandant, Marine Corps, "doesn't duplicate anybody else's aviation. We have dive bombers, fighters, and helicopters but no large aircraft since all of our 'craft must be transportable by ship. Our mission is to propel Marines on a foreign shore and to keep them there. Marine Air, then, primarily, is to support that Marine with a rifle on that piece of real estate, wherever it is."

Five days after the Marine Brigade sailed, President Truman ordered mobilization of the Organized Marine Reserve, mostly experienced hard-core professionals from World War II. During that war, Marine Reserve units, like the other service's, were called to

Bartimus and his fellow pilots land back in Japan, after becoming a part of the Pohang K-3 evacuation, via LSTs. Their new base was "Sun Valley" on the Japanese Island Kyushu, 350 miles from Seoul, the capital of South Korea. (Photo courtesy Bart Bartimus)

"The C-47 shut down only one engine when it landed at Pohang K-3 after bringing us in from Japan," explains Bart Bartimus. "When we asked these guys where we checked in, they answered, "hell, we're evacuating." Under that American flag, in Korea, they were watching North Koreans fighting barely on the other side of the airfield. So, we came in by air, and we left again, the same day—by ship." (Photo courtesy Bart Bartimus)

duty leaving their reserve ranks sadly depleted. "When the Korean War flashed to life, we did not have a force cruising in the Pacific mainly because of the cuts in our manpower. We did have Marines on the West Coast, who, because of our tradition of mobility and readiness, could go fast, when ordered. And thank God, we had our Reserves back to strength. They were needed badly—and quickly."*

* After tours of duty which ranged from squadron leader at Ewa Field during the attack of Pearl Harbor to fighting in the air over Guadacanal, General Mangrum had been assigned the duty of rebuilding the Marine Reserve structure, which he did with thoroughness. The 74,000 Marines active in June, 1950 doubled within a few months. By 1952, the Marines could count a quarter-of-a-million active men. 32,000 of those came from the Reserves.

On July 11, President Truman signed the bill for appropriations for a 70 group Air Force, and their Reserves came back into active service. All major units of the Army were at greatly reduced strength having a total operating force of only 325,000.

The National Guard joined the Organized Reserve Corps units in the calls to active service on August 1, 1950. By the following June, National Guards from nearly every state were in. Assigned to the Army were 135,658 officers and 204,922 enlisted men from the active reserves. This was a war of "retread tigers."

The Navy, in the pre-Korean days, could count only 238 ships. By 1953, 572 ships sailed under Navy colors. Only 10 of those were new, the others came out of mothballs as did 3300 of their 13,000 aircraft.

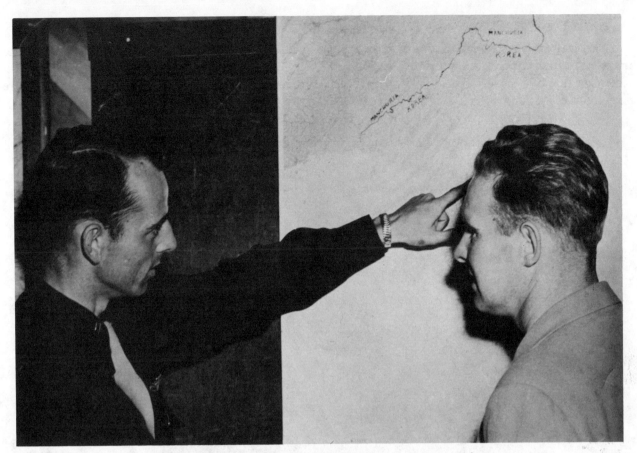

Bart Bartimus, right, and Cliff Winters were two of the first pilots to fly 100 missions in Korea. Before this was considered an "official duty tour," Bart had flown one more—a total of 101. (Photo courtesy Bart Bartimus)

Four planes serving in Korea are the F-82 Twin *Mustang,* the only prop plane shown: an F-80 is to the left, F-94 on the right, and the F-86 *Sabre* in the slot position. (Photo courtesy USAF)

Emergency mobilization found our friend Bart Bartimus practicing gunnery off the coast of Texas. You'll remember that as a navigator in WW-II, he was shot down on the last bombing mission over Europe. As a civilian, he lasted only a year-and-a-half in Parks College studying aeronautical engineering. He was too restless for the student life, and he flew, with the reserves, on week-ends.

Marine F4U-4s, loaded with rockets and napalm, were launched in support of Marines at Inchon, September 19, 1950. General Field Harris's Corsairs of the First Marine Wing from the USS *Sicily* and the jeep carrier, the USS *Badoeng Strait,* raked enemy positions barely in front of "that Marine, with that rifle, on that piece of real estate." (Photo courtesy Navy Department, The National Archives)

The Marines also used their Sikorsky helicopters in "Operation Rocket." On August 21, 1952, HMR-161's copters moved 4.5 rocket launchers dircetly to the firing site in Korea. (Photo courtesy Defense Dept. Marine Corps)

He reenlisted in the USAF, this time as a flying cadet. As a no-rank trainee, he flew week-days from Randolph Field. On week-ends, he changed to his reserve lieutenant uniform and continued flying at Brooks AFB. He graduated from Williams (Willie) Field as qualified to fly F-51's, a full-time lieutenant this time, and a fighter pilot assigned to the 524th Squadron, SAC.

With less than 2 days warning, on July 14, Bart and 20 other *Mustang* pilots were flown out of Bergstrom AFB for the west coast, and eventually—Korea. He left the States on the USS *Boxer* with aircrewmen and 145 National Guard reclaimed *Mustangs.**

* The US had a total of 1558 F-51's when the Korean War started. With the advent of jet fighters, these *Mustangs* were considered obsolete and 794 had been consigned to storage. The remaining 764 were in Air National Guard units, quickly recalled to active service.

The *Boxer* raced across the Pacific disgorging its passengers and machines at Johnson AFB in Japan. After 10 hours of refresher flying, Bart's group was loaded aboard a C-47 for transportation to the south Korean port and base of Pohang.

"We saw this bunch of guys sitting up on a hill looking towards the other end of the runway, and we asked directions to operations," Bart tells. " 'Hell, they said, 'we're evacuating. You shouldn't have come.' They were watching the skirmishes just off the end of the runway when we landed. Small arms fire made it pretty uncomfortable for planes coming in and out, too. They were that close. On our first day in Korea, we were all loaded on Korean Navy LSTs and sent back to Japan. This time, we ended up at Tsuiki on Kyushu, and I flew my missions from there for the next 3 months.

"As far as I know, we were the first Air Force men

Fourth Fighter Interceptor Wing's F-86 *Sabres* proved exceedingly durable in combat, Lt. William A. Todd's *Sabre* had horizontal stabilizer blasted away by 37-mm cannon of enemy MiG fighter. A second cannon shell shattered cockpit canopy, though Lt. Todd received only minor hand injuries. This October 1951 air battle gave two MiG victories to the *Sabres* without loss to themselves. (Photo courtesy USAF)

to arrive on the scene. The only earlier ones were already there when it started. Things were plenty bad in Korea. That August, our 24th Infantry and the ROKs had been shoved all the way down the peninsula. By sheer guts, they were holding on to the country only by one small corner, around Pusan. That was all. The Commies were beating the hell out of us.

"I flew my first mission on August 3. Our orders sent us out of Japan and we strafed every possible enemy encampment we could find, then we'd land at Taegu-K3, refuel, fly another mission then return to Tsuiki. We couldn't afford to leave any airplanes on Korean land overnight. It was that touch-and-go.

"I found hitting tunnels was the most fruitful target. Think about it. What are tunnels good for besides running trains through? The Commies knew and used them for storing supplies and hiding troops during the day. If there was any evidence of activity near a tunnel, we'd drop those *Mustangs* down to not 50 feet above the ground, but 5 feet and throw in napalm. Those tunnels were cut into sheer cliffs, and you had to really know your airplane to get out of there. The *Mustang,* though, was the very best airplane I have ever flown, before or after Korea.

"Even as late as September of 1950, we didn't have enough supplies. Things like flashlights and cockpit

Major James Jabara, who as a Captain, was the world's first jet Ace. On his second tour of duty, he raised his total kills to 15, to become the world's second triple jet ace, following only Joe McConnell whose MiG kills came to 16. (Photo courtesy USAF)

By September 1951, British Gloster *Meteor* jets were at Kimpo Airfield in Korea. The FF (Friendly Foreigns) were credited with destroying 152 enemy aircraft in air-to-air combat. (Photo courtesy USAF)

Watching the take-off of the veteran 49th Fighter Bomber Wing, bound for a rail cutting mission in North Korea, are: Standing on left are, Lt. Gen. O. P. Weyland, who replaced General George Stratemeyer in June 1951 as Commanding General, FEAF, and Major Gen. Emmett (Rosie) O'Donnell, former head of FEAF Bomber Command. Behind the jeep steering wheel is Col. Joe L. Mason, 49th Wing Commander. Maj. Gen. Frank F. Everest, 5th AF Commander sits in the rear. The 49th FB Wing was the first unit to strike back with jet fighter bombers when the Communist forces invaded South Korea. (Photo courtesy USAF)

light bulbs were so scarce. We made pre-dawn take-offs in order to be on target by first light. Trying to find your airplane on that dark ramp with no flashlight was something else. You could only home in on your plane by yelling back and forth to your crew chief. The occasional ship with lights automatically became the flight leader. We could make no instrument or engine checks on the ground because we couldn't see the needles. We flew in 4-ship formations so we could follow the exhaust stacks, then broke down to 2-ship formations at daylight.

"All of my targets were on the ground. I never saw an enemy aircraft in the air that I could definitely identify as an enemy.*

"We strafed supplies, rail marshalling yards, troops, roads, trucks, anything we could find. None of us ever flew higher than 1000 feet over the terrain unless we had to top weather.

"Even after the tide of war improved, we suffered

* In July and August UN bombers nearly had the air to themselves. They flew freely over the north and destroyed KPAAF planes on the ground and in the air. By August 10, FEAF intelligence reported that 110 KPAAF planes had been destroyed. By the end of August, the reports stated that only 18 planes were left in the KPAAF.

Bell H-13s joined the job started by the Sikorsky H-5s in medical evacuations in Korea. Copters completed 8,598 medical evacuations, mostly front-line casualties. If a serious casualty, the man would be in a hospital's surgery within hours. Fully one-half of these wounded would have died without the copter hospital technique perfected in Korea. (Photo courtesy USAF)

from short supplies. If, for instance, we dropped an external fuel tank, we had to explain the reason in writing. We didn't drop many. This was not a shortage of fuel tanks but too few fuel tank fittings. Really, it was an old-fashioned kind of war, the one we fought in *Mustangs*."

General MacArthur believed this type of war called for "full utilization of the Army-Navy-Air team," and he placed command of all aircraft under FEAF's General Stratemeyer, a decision which became more unpopular with all the services as the war progressed.

Two B-29 groups were organized on July 8, 1950, from SAC's 15th AF as FEAF Bomber Command under General Emmett (Rosie) O'Donnell. Right from the start, the politico-military restrictions stressing that all bombers stay clear of Manchuria and the Soviet Union frontiers limited the value of full-scale strategic bombing. The strict adherence to only specified military targets and the restricted use of incendiaries made the Korean War a vastly different effort for the bombers, some of which were over 5 years old. Add to that, this war was managed by coordinating orders from England, the United States, France, and other friendly powers. Korea, at best, was the center of a difficult war to fight.

SAC's B-29's started interdiction, which, as used in Air Force parlance, means air action to prevent, delay, and destroy movements by the enemy of men and supplies to a battle area. Admiral C. Turner Joy and his Navy Task Force 77 found command of his aircraft by FEAF impossible to live with. Often, targets assigned the Navy pilots would be wiped out the day before. Frustrated, the Task Force received orders, August 12, to move up Korea's west coast. The carriers *Philippine Sea, Valley Forge,* and Bart's transport, the *Boxer* steamed off for their own targets.

Korea, whose name means "high and lovely land," looks, in shape, much like Florida. It is about 575 miles long with the narrowest point, the "neck of Korea," only 95 miles wide. The South Korean capital, Seoul, about midway down the peninsula, is 340 miles from Kyushu and 730 miles from Tokyo. Filled with mountains, ravines, and mud flats, the country has few landmarks to help navigating pilots. Very few good roads criss-cross the country, and maps, particularly of North Korea, are extremely inaccurate. Many towns have several, even the same, names. The UN forces designated airfields with K-site numbers for identification. The most modern airfield was Kimpo, K-14. That one and Suwon with its 4900 foot runway were

Lt. Joseph McConnell, Jr., the top jet ace in Korea, downed a total of 16 MiGs before he was relieved of duty, after 106 missions, in May of 1953. The world's first triple-jet ace, Lt. McConnell flew *Sabres* with the 51st Fighter Interceptor Wing. Third *Sabre* ace in number of MiGs downed was Captain Manuel J. Fernandez, Jr., with 14½ verified count in 125 missions. (Photo courtesy USAF)

the only two airports in South Korea suited for high performance aircraft. Later, Pusan's field was used, of necessity, but that had only 4" of concrete hurriedly poured on top of rubble.

While America was rushing to put the WW-II tigers back in uniform and move them thousands of miles, General Walker's 8th Army faced a grave challenge on the Chinju during August and September. FEAF airmen flew over 238 sorties for close support each day. The North Koreans threw a strong force against the U.S. 1st Cavalry and the ROK 1st Division on a new front, near Taegu. Navy, Marines, and FEAF answered with rocket firing fighters, night bombers and day strafers, like the *Mustangs*. General Walker was high in his praise of the air support and said, "If it had not been for the air support that we received from the 5th AF, we would not have been able to stay in Korea."

On September 15, General MacArthur's strategy formed on Inchon, even against serious opposition by

Out of mothballs came 3,300 of the Navy's planes used in carrier-based attacks in Korea. The F9F, on the deck edge elevator of the USS *Princeton* (CVA-37), shows a remarkable marriage of parts. The blue forward half of the plane is original equipment. Riddled by flak, the fighter landed on an emergency fighter strip in Korea. Finding an intact section of another damaged *Panther,* mechanics fitted the two halves together. (Photo courtesy Navy Department, The National Archives)

the joint chiefs of staff. Inchon, 20 miles from Seoul, was on the coast with tides permitting landings on only rare days. September 15 was one of the days. Planes from the 7th Fleet worked over the area first, then a Naval barrage was followed by part of the Marines landing with the dawn tide. More Marines hit the beach with the dusk tide, and General MacArthur's dispatch to President Truman read, "The Navy and the Marines have never shone more brightly than this morning."

Combined with the Army X Corps, the Marines took Kimpo Airfield. Marine copters and planes moved in for shore-based air support. On September 29, the slugging UN foot soldiers liberated Seoul

finally stepping back on the cocky North Koreans. With this boost, the 8th Army broke out of the Pusan Perimeter and headed north. For the first time, the news from Korea was good. The ROKs, U.S. Army and Marines pushed farther north and prepared to advance all the way to the Yalu River, the Manchurian border. On October 19, ROK troops took the North Korean capital of Pyongyang with support from paratroops and air. In fact, between July and October, that first year, UN airpower destroyed 39,000 enemy troops, about one-third of the original 10 divisions starting the assault.

With close-support from their *Corsairs* the Marines see-sawed back and forth in the snow and cold. From

Combat operational helicopters could move troops to the front lines—fast. The Marines, in Korea, were the first to use copters in actual warfare. (Photo: Defense Dept., Marine Corps)

October 26 until December 11, 3,703 sorties were flown on request of troops. The VMO-6 Marine copters made aviation history by flying 837 missions in combat zones, a first for helicopters. In addition to evacuation of wounded (the trade for which they were best known until this date), the copters delivered rocket launchers and battle-equipped troops directly to the front lines. They picked up, from the battle lines, reconnaissance troops and delivered them to vital mountain spotting sites.

The *Mustangs,* both Bart's group and RAAF Squadron 77, moved back to Pohang in October bringing the force up to 3 full squadrons. Bart says, "We flew seek-and-destroy missions and for targets-of-opportunity along all the roads and routes to the Yalu and

back. The 51 needs only 2,500 feet of runway, loaded, and with internal fuel, we had a range of 4½ hours. We had 6 guns, 3 in each wing, and could carry either 6 rockets on external racks or change that around to fit the need. In other words, we carried a mixture of rockets, bombs and napalm depending on the target. Napalm is best for tanks. Russian T-34 tanks are hefty, and you were only lucky to stop one with .50 calibres. Run napalm up the back end of any tank, and you'll burn it out in a hurry.

"We followed rivers, roads, anything at a normal cruise of 220 to 250 MPH, the lower and faster, the better. We flew around trees, not over, for the higher you were, the more opportunity for that guy on the ground to see—and shoot at you. Most of our losses

Mustangs over Korea show the ROK insignia, an ancient emblem—the monad—painted over the U.S. star. (Photo: USAF)

The Piper *Cub,* likely the best traveled aircraft in the world, served in the ROK Air Force during 1953. (Photo: USAF)

came from small arms, the North Koreans had no heavy stuff early in the war.

"Close to Thanksgiving, we moved up to Hamburg, north of Wonsan, and we thought this war was nearly over. I was given the duty of tactical controller about then and rode around in a jeep, from Pyongyang, co-ordinating air strikes with our ground troops. That's when the Chinese started down. . . ."

The Red Chinese could not stand the potential of a free Korea, and on November 26, they marched in force—for what was, in fact, another war.

"We got slaughtered. There's no other word for it. Our situation was grim, and, in my opinion, was completely because President Truman said General MacArthur didn't know what he was doing. Right across from our base at Sunny Joe (Sinviju) was

Antung, a major base for Red supplies and men. It was a court martial offense to even spit across the Yalu at them. Those Reds came sneaking across at night and hid out during the day. Then, we had to go and try to find each one individually. How much easier it would have been to hit them over the river where they grouped. General MacArthur, in spite of President Truman's announcements, didn't want to invade China. Hell, all he wanted to do was fight the war. So did we. We started getting the hell beat out of us and had to retreat again. Nobody likes to get shot at, but we were there to do a job, and when we were forced to stop doing that job at a river, it was plenty hard. It was so tempting to go across and really hit those Reds, particularly after you saw what they did to some of your friends. "Wo" Womach, for in-

YAK-3 (Yakovlev) built and supplied by the Russians to the KPAAF (Korean People's Army Air Force). (Photo: USAF)

The second F-82 model was a night interceptor with a huge radar dome between the two fuselages. The pilot sat in the left side; the radar oprator in the right, and the plane could be flown from either side. Looking much like the Northrop *Black Widow,* the *Twin Mustang* was controlled, according to Bart Bartimus, "As if your one side was the total plane. You never looked at the tail, though," he adds, "That waved up and down at you and would make you nervous." (Photo: USAF)

General Omar N. Bradley, left., Chairman of the U.S. Joint Chiefs of Staff, and General Matthew B. Ridgeway, right, Commander-in-Chief, Far East were special guests of General Frank F. Everest (center), 5th AF Commander, at a briefing in Korea on October 2, 1951. (Photo courtesy USAF)

stance, an old friend who came across with me, was shot 16 times in the back, with his hands tied, after he had to bail out.

"My last mission was January 6, 1951, number 101, and I even flew Christmas Day. We really didn't have an official tour of duty, then. Simply, you flew 100 missions and went back to Japan for test flights of repaired equipment. I flew 101 before any of us counted too carefully.

"Korea's terrain was such, without the air, we would've lost. The only way the ground troops could move was along the path of destruction cleared by airplanes.

"When I came home, I knew this war wouldn't be won. Politicians can't fight wars, and in this particular case, politics prevented the maximum use of our weapons."*

When the Red Chinese took up the battle, FEAF, Marine and Navy air continued close air support which permitted an "orderly" retreat, but retreat it was.

The new air war started on November 1 when 3 YAKs jumped a Mosquito controller† and a B-26 near Yangsi, south of Sunny Joe. The B-26 crew destroyed 1 YAK and called-in *Mustangs* took care of the other two. Later that same afternoon, 6 sweptwing Russian MiG-15 jets‡ opened fire on another Mosquito and a flight of *Mustangs*. The Communist Chinese were not starting a little war; they were coming by the thousands and with equipment much more modern than our's.

The MiG fighters didn't come as a complete surprise to the UN forces. As early as July, 1950, intelligence reports stated that Russian jets were in Canton and Shanghai. The US quietly shipped in the 4th Interceptor Group, under Colonel John C. Meyers, with F-86A *Sabrejets* which then held the speed record of 670.98 MPH.

---

* Bart Bartimus came back to the States in the spring of 1951. He remained in the AF as a 1st. Lieutenant for three more years, returning to civilian life with 1605 USAF pilot-time hours. For 7 years he flew as a technical representative on Lear auto-pilots both in military and civilian jet aircraft. In the late 60's, he joined VIP of Columbia (South Carolina) as chief instructor, charter pilot, and designer of teaching aids.

† Mosquito controllers were AT-6 trainers or light observation planes which flew, unarmed, as the "eyes" and directors for fire from the combat planes.

‡ Designed by Artem Mikoyan who used design data captured from the Germans for the sweptback wings. The MiGs, with a low wing loading and a 5,000 pound thrust engine, had a level speed of about 660 MPH. Extremely maneuverable, the MiGs flown by early, highly experienced pilots were tremendous threats to UN air superiority.

A week after the advent of the sweptwings, the first aerial jet battle took place when our obsolete F-80s tangled with the MiGs. Though the sweptwing jets were clearly superior, their pilots were less combat-trained. Lt. Russell J. Brown machined-gunned down a Red and goes into the record as the first UN pilot to claim a victory over a Communist jet.

The *Sabres* arrived in mid-December, and on December 22, a flight of these F-86As downed 6 MiGs. The jet war was on, and the battle lines of MiG Alley, the area between the Yalu and Chongchon Rivers, were drawn.

Early in 1951, the RCAF was supplied with F-86E *Sabres;* the F-86F, the first model Sabres to close the gap in competition with the MiGs in performance, didn't arrive on the scene until 1952. The 12,000-pound MiGs, as compared with the heavier *Sabres* (16,000 pounds), could outclimb, outspeed, and out maneuver our jets above 30,000 feet. The later *Sabres,* however, with larger fuel capacity, though still unable to climb as high did have more range, superior gunsights, and better armament—and equipment—for pilot safety.

As the jet fighters primed for battle, FEAF Bomber Command's B-29's, for the first time in Korea, employed incendiaries against the arsenal and communications center of Kanggye. Sixty-five per cent of the city's industrial area was destroyed. Then, both the bombers and the carrier-based planes from Task Force 77 were given the mission of destroying the bridges across the Yalu. These were vital targets for across them streamed "Men and material in large force," explained General MacArthur. They were also dangerous targets. The Manchurian border lay at one end of the bridges and a single mis-directed bomb could violate the stressed orders of the Joint Chiefs and would, in their opinion, escalate the war.

The international bridges were deadly in another way, too. Red pilots, from their base at Antung, played a cat-and-mouse havoc game against UN planes. They would gain altitude on their side of the river, scream down on our planes, then race back to the sanctuary across the Yalu before our fighters had an opportunity to reply in fire. UN pilots, even with the collapse of our ground troops in front of the Reds, were never given permission for "hot-pursuit," that is, to chase the enemy back into his territory.

With heavy losses, FEAF bombers and Navy planes finally succeeded in cutting about half the bridge spans only to find the expensive targets practically worth-

Lt. Iven C. Kincheloe became a jet ace April 6, 1952, the 10th jet ace of the Korean War. He flew *Sabres* of the 51st Fighter Interceptor Wing. (Photo courtesy USAF)

The Marine Douglas F3D *Skyknight* jet, all-weather night fighter, was used, with much success, throughout the Korean War. (Photo: Defense Dept., Marine Corps)

223

less. The Yalu froze and heavy equipment moved directly across the ice.

Medium bombers continued attacks on industrial and communication centers in North Korea, and General Rosie O'Donnell's heavies ran out of targets. UN ground forces dug in, then were forced back, then dug in again as the Reds advanced.

With the fighters, Lt. Commander W. T. Amen destroyed a MiG in the first Navy encounter with the sweptwings. On May 20 two flights of Sabres closed in on some Red pilots who were willing to fight. MiG Alley became the battleground of 36 Sabres vs. 50 MiGs. Captain James Jabara, even though his wing tank would not jettison, smashed into the fray and knocked down two MiGs, his 5th and 6th, to become the world's first jet ace.

In June, 1951, the Soviet delegate at the United Nations suggested that cease-fire talks start, but the fighting continued for 2 long years. General Matthew Ridgway, who had replaced General Walker in December of 1950, took over UN Command in September, 1951. It was mainly an air war by then, and the Communist's offensive arm was estimated at 1250 aircraft with over 500 of those MiG-15s, far superior to anything the UN had except the F-86s, and they could only count 105 of those.

The Red's spring offensive failed and they started retreating before the 8th Army. The vitality, power and success of the Chinese Communist's operations in North Korea turned to defeat in South Korea. The ever-lengthening supply lines, constantly harassed by bombers, the destructive winter weather, and the Red shortage of air support simply because their airfields were regularly "cratered" by bombers added up to more expense than Red China would pay.

That spring, Operation "Strangle," the policy for overall interdiction, day and night, sent attacking bomber forces to Pyongyang, Wonsan, Hungman. Though the bomber raids were small in comparison with those of WW-II, the sorties and tons delivered per plane broke all records.

The Marines consider Strangle disappointing if not a complete failure. Their history states that "While we bombed, the enemy rebuilt." General Mangrum, who, at that time, was a group commander midway up the Korean peninsula, says of Strangle, "The North Koreans could haul 400 pounds of supplies on a bicycle, and they had thousands of those. Too, we'd bomb out a rail line and they would have it back in business by daylight. Hundreds of extra rails were hidden all along the tracks. Those Koreans simply would rush

out and build a by-pass for the segment we had removed. Granted, they were hard put to haul tanks or bulldozers on those bicycles, but they could and did move about everything else. For transportation of heavy equipment, interdiction was important. It could not eliminate the problem of the enemy's ability to attack, however. Reduce the problem, yes; eliminate it, no."

Navy leaders agree with the Marines. Vice-Admiral J. J. Clark, who commanded the 7th Fleet, said, "The interdiction program was a failure, it did not *interdict*."

Even FEAF's final analysis noted: "Operation Strangle was not successful . . . due to Communist logistic systems."

This old-fashioned kind of war had to be fought one bloody footstep after another, on the ground, and in the air.

When General Stratemeyer suffered a heart attack in May, 1951 General Earle Partridge assumed the duty of acting commander, FEAF, until the arrival of General O. P. Weyland in June. General Frank E. Everest took command of the 5th AF about the same time.

President Truman was convinced that General MacArthur did not agree with the US military objective in Korea, the objective "to repel the attack and to avoid the spread of the conflict." General MacArthur's policy statement of his beliefs which basically said, "There is no substitute for victory," was interpreted to mean the Commandant planned to destroy the enemy's source of supply even above the Yalu. When the President relieved General MacArthur of all commands, General Ridgway was given control.

Replacement parts were in short supply for the Sabres in early 1952. An average of 45 per cent of the jets were carried as out of commission, 16.6 per cent for want of parts and 25.9 per cent for want of maintenance. Pilots could only fly 10 combat missions, not enough to keep current, and overhead, MiGs, often between 100 and 200 strong, formed in combat training gaggles. The Red sweptwings grouped over Manchuria and came in at .99 Mach, often as high as 50,-000 feet, not looking for a fight. Sabre pilots called these "jackpot flights," knowing that if the Reds could be lured to a lower level, the F-86E's would mount scores of kills. The 51st Wing, for instance, counted 25 MiGs destroyed by the middle of January.

In February, Intelligence reports said that 540 MiGs were based at Antung airfields. This was the month the MiGs decided to come down and fight. On the 23rd, Major W. T. Whisner flamed his 5th MiG and became the 7th Korean jet Ace. He was followed, on April 1, by Colonel Francis S. "Gabby" Gabreski, who ended the war as the top living Ace with a total of 37½ kills, 6½ of those in air-to-air combat in Korea, and the others over Europe in World War II. He's one of 7 Americans listed as an Ace in 2 wars.

For the records, Captain Robert H. Moore became the 9th Korean Ace on April 3, followed, 3 days later, by Captain Iven C. Kincheloe.

The *Sabres,* built by North American Aviation who, by 1953, had built more airplanes than any company in the world, claimed and verified 36 MiGs during that March, and 44 in April, losing only 6 of their own in the same 2 months.

Armistice talks had started a year earlier with no results. The see-sawing war continued and in June of 1952, Communist night defenses came alive. Searchlights locked on old B-29's and B-26's and MiGs knocked them out of the skies.

The Marines did not get their planes back from centralized control for their "primary mission" of close support until the last few months of the war. The *Corsairs, Panthers,* and AD *Maulers,* directed by Mosquito control planes and ground troop identification of targets with white phosphorous, threw tons of munitions in front of the 8th Army. On June 28, 1952, General Lemuel C. Shepherd, Jr., Commandant of the Marines, by passage of legislation, became the first Marine leader to sit, as a co-equal, with the Joint Chiefs of Staff. The First Marine Aviation Wing, during Korea, flew 127,496 combat missions, more than *all* Marine air flew during World War II.

Hoping to speed up the peace talks, a new campaign of "air pressure" went into orders. Utilizing every possible fighter-bomber of the FEAF, Navy, and Marines, major targets were smashed day after day. These included the North Korean power stations and the generating plant at Suiho on the Yalu. Combined, the AF, Navy, and Marine pilots flew 1200 sorties against this target, the largest single attack since World War II. This station supplied electricity to war plants in Manchuria and its destruction cost northeast China 23 per cent of her total power.

That September, the F-86s destroyed 63 MiGs while losing only 6. *Sabre* pilots identified each MiG either as "honcho" or "recruit." The Honchos were flown by the more experienced Russian pilots, and the Recruits by Chinese Communists or North Korean pilots. Red China had 22 air divisions for her use by

the fall of 1952, which amounted to 1800 aircraft with at least 1000 of those jets.

Still the peace talks at Panmunjom bogged down. For a whole year, UN negotiators had made compromise after compromise, and they could no longer afford to yield particularly to the Communist demand of forcible repatriation of Chinese and North Korean prisoners.

General Mark W. Clark relieved General Ridgway as commander of UN forces, and in March, 1953, Joseph Stalin died. Soviet Premier Georgi Malenkov spoke in favor of peaceful coexistence, and doubtlessly, this influenced the peace negotiators.

During that spring, fighter-bombers of the 5th AF made 2 attacks which history may decide were decisive in this war. The overall rice economy of North Korea depended on controlled irrigation from reservoirs. On May 13, 59 *Thunderjets* damaged the massive irrigation dam at Toksan. Flooding waters wiped out rail lines and highways. Three days later, 90 F-84s broke the dam at Chosan causing another destructive flood.

In May and June, the jet fighter battles were reminiscent of the WW-II Marianas "Turkey Shoot" when Japanese planes were blasted out of the sky in fantastic numbers. That May of 1953, *Sabres* downed 56 MiGs losing only 1 plane, its pilot rescued. In June, the MiG kills jumped to 77 verified and 11 probables with no UN planes lost.

Also, in June, *Panthers* and *Skyraiders* from the *Boxer, Princeton* and *Philippine Sea* again hit Suiho's generating plant. That afternoon, 5th AF *Mustangs* and the 1st Marine Air Wing attacked the reservoirs. The final tally for the 4-day assault showed the air attacks had destroyed fully 90 per cent of the hydroelectric system in North Korea and Manchuria.

The combat-ready MiGs were becoming scarce. Captain Ralph Parr, a double Ace, shot down a Red transport on July 27, the last kill of the War. Red negotiators at Panmunjom modified their demands, and, at long last, an armistice was signed. This is no total victory* but the United Nations did achieve two

* In January 1968, the American Navy ship, the *Pueblo,* was boarded and captured by North Koreans, who held the *Pueblo's* captain and crew as prisoners for a year before releases could be negotiated. During the late 60's, increased numbers of fire fights and ambushes broke out between the Communists and the South Koreans with 4000 American troops still guarding the 151-mile Demilitarized Zone separating North from South Korea. By 1969, a gigantic line of fortified concrete positions was started about 15 miles behind the DMZ. A new war, military leaders knew then, could start any day. Premier Kim Il Sung's KPAAF, again considered one of the strongest in the Far East by the late 60's, was poised to strike again.

major objectives. The aggression was halted, and South Korea's independence was secured. General Harrison and General Nam Il signed the armistice of this unpopular and technically old-fashioned war on July 27, 1953.

Army Aviation had flown 86,000 forward missions, 103,000 administrative missions and had made over 7,000 front line evacuation flights. From 325,000 men in 1950, the Army's strength grew to 1,600,000 by January 1, 1953. Of the casualties in Korea, the Army suffered more than 80 per cent.

The U.S. Navy ferried men and equipment and landed supplies in addition to protecting troops. The Chinese and Red Korean Navy was nearly non-existent, so the American Navy could move at will. The carriers steamed close into shore making flights shorter for their planes. Battleships, cruisers, and destroyers sailed in close for needed bombardments. The Navy delivered 13,000 Marines to Inchon and threw her aircraft into every kind of battle fought in Korea.

FEAF controlled 1,536 aircraft at the end of the war, three times as many as in the beginning. These included 7 squadrons of Marines and 3 squadrons of "Friendly Foreign Forces"—FFF. Personnel strength in FEAF more than tripled from 33,625 in 1950 to 112,188 in 1953. Twenty-two Wings of Air National Guard and Air Force Reserve were called into active service. FEAF flew a total of 720,980 sorties and dropped 476,000 tons of explosives. Marine units flew 107,303 sorties under centralized control of FEAF and dropped 82,000 tons of munitions. Land-based FFF flew an additional 44,873 sorties while dropping 20,000 tons of munitions. The USN flew 167,552 sorties adding to the damage 120,000 tons of rockets, napalm, and bombs.

From June 26, 1950 through July 27, 1953, USAF, Marines and FFF claimed as destroyed (likely high figures) 976 aircraft, 1327 tanks, 82,920 vehicles, 963 locomotives, 10,407 railway cars, 1153 bridges, 118,231 buildings, 65 tunnels, numerous barges, boats, gun positions and 184,808 enemy troops.

FEAF lost 1466 aircraft (139 in air-to-air combat), Marines 436 aircraft, and FFF—152. In aerial combat, FEAF downed 900 aircraft with 168 more probables; the Marine Air Wing downed 35, including 15 MiGs, and the USN—16 (4 MiGs). FFF accounted for 3 aircraft in aerial combat.

FEAF suffered 1,841 casualties. 60 per cent of the entire Marine Corps fought in Korea and they lost 4262 men verified as killed with about 22,000 more wounded.

The *Sabrejets* were the biggest enemy aircraft killers over Korea. They downed a total of 810 enemy planes of which 792 were MiGs for a 10-to-1 kill ratio since only 78 *Sabres* were lost. The 38 jet Aces in Korea destroyed a total of 305 planes in air-to-air combat, and a check of pilots with MiG kills revealed that they had an average of 18 missions in WW-II.

If the United States gained anything from this war —besides preserving the freedom of South Korea— it was the knowledge that our nuclear deterrent force alone could not guarantee world peace, for the Communists were clearly prepared to subsidize and instigate limited wars anywhere the Sino-Soviet Reds detected weakness in Free World defenses. In Korea, America's "retread tigers"—men who had already fought other aggressors in the previous decade—carried the burden once again. And they did so despite a government—particularly the Congress—that, attempting to maintain a bargain-basement defense, once again short-changed its fighting men.

12. Sport Wings For the "Little Guy" (and Gal!)

Surely, nothing that flies—no proud machine that boldly challenges the limitless blue—should be called, *Pretty Purple Puddy Tat*. Good grief! But there is such an airplane, over in Highland Park, Illinois. It is owned by Mrs. Tracy Pilurs; and this just goes to show what can happen when you have a free country and anyone who wants to may build his own flying machine—even girls.

For that's exactly what Mrs. Pilurs did. She built *Puddy Tat* with her own itty bitty—er, with her own hands. She also tested it herself, and has since flown it all over the United States. And Tracy is typical of the thirty thousand young and not-so-young sport aviation enthusiasts who make up the Experimental Aircraft Association.

The EAA, a member-controlled, non-profit organization, exists to serve private individuals everywhere who build their own aircraft and fly for fun. To get the EAA story, the authors met with Tony Spezio, president of the Atlantic City EAA Chapter. Tony, and wife Dorothy, fly a Spezio *Tuholer,* a neat low-winger Tony designed and built himself.

Tony grew up during WW-2 and learned to fly in 1947 at the age of seventeen. Married in 1950, his wings were effectively clipped for several years while he and Dorothy acquired a home and four small Spezios. Any wage-earner will understand: insurance premiums and car payments and kids' tonsillectomies leave little extra cash for things like airplanes.

Then, in 1957, Tony heard about the EAA and immediately joined (it had just 4,000 members then). Soon he had sketched his dream plane on brown paper and the Spezio *Tuholer* was born.

At this point we interrupted to ask Tony if he knew who had built the first home-made airplane and how the whole movement started.

"Well," he grinned, "aviation began with an amateur-built craft, the Wright brothers' *Flyer*. And although a lot of planes have taken shape in this country's basements and barns and bedrooms since then, the Golden Age for homebuilt aircraft began fairly recently."

Tony went on to say that this "Golden Age" started in the early fifties, after the FAA (then CAA) set up sensible rules covering the construction and licensing of such machines, and the movement has snowballed because the amateurs themselves have proven remarkably responsible. Aviation's long-forgotten little guy has parlayed his common sense and eyeball engineering into finished products that may be parked with pride on any airport.

Of course, there are still those who believe that building an airplane in a bedroom indicates a marked deficiency of the aforementioned common sense; but a close examination of the do-it-yourself airplane set reveals nothing so much as a bunch of pretty solid citizens—or maybe we should say, "disciples," for it has required the faith of true believers to attain the

Tracy Pilurs of Highland Park, Illinois with *Pretty Purple Puddy Tat,* a single-place biplane of 65-hp she built herself during a four-year period. Tracy and *Puddy Tat*—and Tracy's four teenagers—miss few sport aviation events about the country. (Authors' photo)

status enjoyed by today's sportplane fans. Their battle has been a long one. So long, in fact, that a new generation has taken over.

Their predecessors, during the twenties, knocked together hundreds of barely flyable machines (it was not uncommon to find the leather tongue of an old shoe serving as a rudder hinge), and those craft surely established the existence of that legendary Guardian Angel who is supposed to look after the daring (and dim bulbs). The early stick-and-wire creations, with relatively few exceptions, were built to no particular standard of craftsmanship; and no discernable minimums were observed in selecting materials. Many an early homebuilt fuselage was framed from sugar pine then covered with unbleached muslin and four coats of dope. The fact that most of them actually flew, with motorcycle or Model A Ford engines, now seems a minor miracle.

Some early home-built designs were sound. The Pietenpol *Air Camper,* a two-place parasol monoplane made completely of wood and powered with a Model A Ford engine, was a homely but safe aerial flivver that was built in some numbers during the thirties. The Heath parasol, fitted with a converted motorcycle engine, was another popular design. Both were offered in kit form, less engine, for about $200.

A choice of engines was the small-plane builder's biggest problem in the twenties and thirties. He could choose between the two-cylinder V-type motorcycle mills (which vibrated excessively), the four-cylinder Henderson (which presented cooling problems), or, perhaps, scrounge a second-hand airplane powerplant such as a three-cylinder Lawrance, a small Anzani, the Cleone or Szekely (all of which were temperamental), or he could pay the weight handicap and chug along with a Model A Ford automobile engine—

We snapped this picture of Tony and Dorothy Spezio of Atlantic City at 4,000 feet above western Oklahoma. Despite the November chill, they were smiling happily, cruising at 130 mph in the Spezio *Tuholer* that Tony designed and built himself. Craft's engine is a Lycoming 0-290G of 125 hp, converted from its original function of powering a portable electric generator. *Tuholer's* wings fold back so plane may be towed home from the airport behind Spezio station wagon and parked in family garage. Materials for plane's construction cost "about $1,000, plus a lot of scrounging." (Authors' photo)

though even this simple and rugged bit of iron had its idiosyncrasies. Its $1.79 (exchange, Montgomery & Ward) carburetor sometimes gasped for breath when it was put into climb attitude on take-off.

Actually, a number of fairly good lightplane engines began appearing in the U.S. as early as 1927: the LeBlond with 3, 5, or 7 cylinders in 40, 60 and 90-hp; the 110-hp Warner radial; the Siemens-Halske radial in 60 or 90-hp, or the 40-hp French Salmson and 32-hp British-made *Cherub*. But even the cheapest of these was priced near $1000, and in the days of twenty-five-cent haircuts and nickel hamburgers, this was a preposterous sum for an amateur plane builder to consider.

Appearing about 1930, but not in real production until 1934, the Continental 40-hp opposed engine eventually found its way into the noses of some home-builts by way of salvage from wrecked factory-built planes.

This meant, of course, that factory-made planes in the air flivver class had begun to appear. The idea was not new. Manufacturers had dreamed of blackening the skies with personal planes ever since the end of WW-I. Matty Laird had tried it in 1919 with his Model S; Allan Lockheed tried it with a tiny single-placer in 1920, as did the founders of the WACO company, Buck Weaver, Sam Junkin and Clayt

Bruckner, with their ill-fated *Cootie*. There were others.

Among the first commercial sportplanes to finally achieve a measure of success was the Monocoupe (1927) which was priced at $2,675 and powered with a 60-hp Velie. Its designers were Don Luscombe and Clayton Folkerts. Others entering the market—a market largely created by Lindbergh's New York to Paris flight—were the Mohawk *Pinto,* Driggs *Dart,* Irwin CC-1, and the Elias EC-1 *Aircoupe* (no kin to today's Mooney *Aircoupe*). Later, the Buhl

Broomstick owned by Ruth Spencer (who isn't really an old witch, but a very fetching lady) was constructed in basement of Newark, Delaware home with help from pilot-husband Warren. *Broomstick* is a single-place parasol monoplane of wooden structure, powered with a Continental 65-hp engine that gives it a cruising speed of about 85 mph. (Photo courtesy Mrs. Warren E. Spencer)

Chevrolet Corvair engine of 95 hp is fitted to a Pietenpol *Air Camper,* a two-place open-cockpit parasol monoplane design that dates back to 1928. This all-wood craft is still being constructed by amateur plane builders because of its simplicity and honest—if slow—flight characteristics. Original Pietenpols were powered with Model A Ford engines. Designer Bernard Pietenpol still operated, as a hobby, the small airport at Cherry Grove, Minnesota in 1968. (Photo courtesy Bernard Pietenpol)

Pup came along, a single-seater, mid-wing, fitted with a three-cylinder Szekely. It was followed by the Curtiss-Wright *Junior,* the wonderful little Aeroncas, and then the Taylor *Cub,* pappy of the venerable J-3.

But it wasn't the marketing of these store-bought types that forced the amateur plane-builder underground for more than twenty years, Tony Spezio explained. The early sportplane buff's undoing was his lack of organization. The little guy had no one to speak for him in Washington. As a result, he was legislated out of the air.

The Air Commerce Act of 1926 set the stage. This law was written and re-written by various non-flying congressmen, and seasoned with recommendations from the Lampert Committee and the Morrow Board. Briefly, it was designed to eliminate, from inter-state flying, the barnstormer and the "irresponsible" little guys—the very men who had kept aviation alive in the U.S. since WW-I—because Big Money was coming into aviation upon the heels of the Kelly Bill (which provided for generous subsidies to the new airlines), and the bankers wanted things tidy and well regulated.

Now there was no question but that the barnstormer

Three-time Women's National Aerobatic Champion Joyce Case of Wichita (first woman in Kansas to earn an airline pilot's rating), is shown with her Pitts Special, *Black Jack*, built by her father Dean Case. This craft replaces Joyce's original Pitts, *Joy's Toy*, also built by "Casey." *Black Jack* is powered by a 180-hp Lycoming engine, has a 19½ ft. wingspan, a gross weight of 1,100 lbs., and is stressed for 12-G flight loads—both positive and negative. (Photo courtesy Dean Case)

and the homebuilt-plane enthusiast of the day needed some sensible regulation. Their planes were too often below any reasonable safety standard; and air traffic rules were needed to replace the every-man-for-himself approach. But this federal law was not written for the little guy. It simply wrote him off. It offered John Doe no way to license a homebuilt airplane. And without a federal license, he could not legally fly across a state line.

Despite this restriction, the homebuilts continued

to multiply until about 1934. Most complied with the law and flew only within the borders of their home states. Those that did not apparently felt that it was a matter of "catchin' before hangin' "—and few were hanged because few were caught.

By 1934, however, most of the states had adopted state laws that were rubber stamps of the Air Commerce Act, and this effectively grounded the homebuilts.

Then, in 1946, a solitary citizen, Mr. George Beau-

Another facet of the sport aviation scene is sailplane flying. Attached to a towplane by a 200-foot nylon rope, the sailplane pilot releases this line usually at about 2,000 feet altitude and then seeks thermals (rising currents of warm air) to take him higher. Under ideal summertime conditions, a sailplane may remain aloft for hours and travel many miles. Sailplane pilot's "crew" is usually an understanding wife who follows him cross country in family car pulling a trailer upon which dismantled sailplane is returned to home field. (Authors' photo)

gardus of Troutdale, Oregon, one of aviation's "little guys" who merely wanted the right to build and fly his own airplane, finally broke the subsonic legal barrier. Beaugardus, who had helped organize such homebuilt plane buffs as could be found into the American Airmen's Association, went to Washington, wrangled an audience with top CAA officials, and eloquently presented the case for fair play, freedom, and fun flying. Remarkably, the CAA not only listened to George, but cautiously agreed with him.

Thus, in 1948 a new "Amateur-Built" aircraft category was established which for the first time gave full official status to the homebuilt plane and its pilot; and rules were set up to govern this activity that were both equitable and workable—with the public safety paramount.

The boom did not develop at once, however. Many of the pre-WW-II amateur plane builders had become old or rich or for other reasons were no longer around, and it required some time for the new generation (like Tony) to come along. Other factors were that almost nothing was available in the way of plans, construction tips, or other basic information. Also, during the immediate post-war years great numbers of surplus training planes were in the market for as little as $250 each. Not until 1953 did the combination of circumstances come together that were needed to get the homebuilt sportplanes into the air in significant numbers.

By then the surplus bargains were gone. Spiraling production costs were eliminating planes of this class offered by the manufacturers by forcing prices beyond reach of the average man. The do-it-yourself philosophy was becoming popular. Aircraft-grade materials were available at reasonable prices. Homebuilt planes were legal and respectable. And, most important of all, according to Tony, were two additional factors that early amateur plane-builders lacked: suitable engines and Paul Poberezny.

Poberezny is the man who led the grass-roots flying fraternity out of the wilderness. He organized, and has deftly guided, the Experimental Aircraft Association ("Experimental" because homebuilt aircraft are licensed in this class), since its inception in 1953.

When Paul started the EAA, he and the seven original members (all from the Milwaukee area) considered it as a kind of "mutual aid society" for their homebuilt plane projects. However, they wisely did not limit membership to back yard designers alone, but welcomed all lightplane people, including fans who had no planes and no intention of building any, but at least shared the dream. Therefore, the EAA, while retaining its identity as the Amateur plane builders' official organization, has also become to a very large degree the spokesman and champion for sport flying in general. But the members who build their own airplanes are the hard core of it. And the Spezios, and Tracy Pilurs, are typical.

Tony had been doing all the talking, so we asked Dorothy how the *Tuholer* (two open cockpits; hence, "two holes," or "tuholer") had affected things at home.

She sighed. "After Tony drew his plans, he started bringing in the junk, or 'goodies,' as they were known around our house, like a squirrel storing nuts for the winter. Of course, I was against it at first. I didn't want *my* husband risking his neck in one of those things. And, selfishly, I suppose, I secretly resented him spending money on that collection of so-called goodies when we might have had a new car instead.

Founder and president of the Antique Airplane Association is Bob Taylor of Ottumwa, Iowa, whose affection for ancient planes and talent for organization—plus an effective junior chamber of commerce —has made Ottumwa world headquarters for historic airplane fans. We snapped above picture from our airplane as Bob wearily directed us to a parking spot during the 1968 Fly-in. (Authors' photo)

"But I learned to fix meals at all hours and to be prepared to add an extra plate on short notice—you know how EAAers help one another—and I finally became accustomed to finding Tony's bureau drawers stuffed with airplane fabric and pinked tape and second-hand airplane instruments." She rolled her eyes heavenward in mock exasperation. "The wing ribs were made on our kitchen table; tail surfaces were made upstairs, covered in our living room, doped in the garage, and hung in the bathroom to dry!"

"Well," Tony put in, "it didn't turn out so badly. We've only got about a thousand dollars cash in it, and I have a chance to sell it at a neat profit and—"

"Over my dead body!" Dorothy interrupted firmly. "Sell the car or something else, if you want to, but don't you dare sell our airplane!"

Tony winked smugly at us and made no reply.

Later, we stopped at the Ottumwa, Iowa, Industrial Airport to attend the annual Antique Airplane Association's Fly-In/Convention, held Thursday through Sunday preceding Labor Day.

The antiquers, another segment of the sport avia-

The Monocoupe 113, originally built in 1928, is fitted with a 60-hp Velie engine that gives it a cruising speed of 85 mph. This craft, designed by Clayton Folkerts and Don Luscombe, was America's first truly successful sport plane. It weighs 700 lbs. empty, seats two side-by-side, and sold for $2,675 in 1928. This example is owned by John Hatz of Merrill, Wisconsin, and was photographed at the 1966 fly-in/convention of the Antique Airplane Association. (Authors' photo)

tion scene, are dedicated to the preservation and restoration of historic aircraft. In 1969, the Antique Airplane Association had about 3,500 members; but this figure merely reflects the number of pre-WW-II airplanes still around, and falls far short of revealing the extent to which av-people in general revere the old birds. The antiquers' convention draws about 40,000 spectators each year.

At an earlier antique fly-in (which one doesn't matter; at these meets the time is always 1935), we met Bert Kieffer, a forty-one-year-old electronics engineer of Long Island, N.Y. Bert was flying a 1929 Curtiss Fledgling which had been restored by Joe Erale, also of Long Island.

"It only took us three days to get to Ottumwa from Brentwood, Long Island," Bert shouted, dividing his attention between us and Gene Thomas, who was bending into the crank of the plane's inertia starter. "Faster! Faster!" Bert yelled to Thomas. Then: "Contact!" Thomas stepped away as the Challenger engine barked to life at the peak of the inertia's whine. He leaned on a wingtip to catch his breath.

Bert motioned to the rear cockpit. "Get in, if you want to ride in a real airplane!"

It wasn't necessary to ask us twice. We eased onto the seatpack 'chute, buckled up and found the ancient Gosport inter-com (a simple tube plugged into the ear-pads of one another's helmets). Bert pulled down his goggles and spoke into his end of the tube. "You ready?"

We weren't sure whether or not a "Roger" was fitting, so we tried to recall a more appropriate term: "Rack 'er back, Jack!" And Bert's grin told us we were with it. He laced the acres of yellow fabric wings between the WACOs and Monocoupes on the apron and shoved the throttle forward. The *Fledgling's* tail was up as we swung onto the runway, and we broke ground a couple of hundred feet later—at 46-mph indicated.

You've never flown in a Curtiss *Fledgling?* Well, just subtract about 40 years from your thinking and have a ball. Maybe you won't figure out the reading of the green juice in the "inclinometer" on the instrument panel; and a 55-mph cruising speed is unsettling at first (84-mph in a long dive!) and stickforces are

heavy. But she's lovely. She sounds lovely and she smells lovely. Her smell, a mixture of gasoline, nitrate dope, leather and sweat, is the smell of adventure. Throttle-back and glide the Fledge at 50-mph and her wires produce a low, bass note. Then slip her and the pitch rises. It takes but a few minutes to understand how this old biplane's original pilots could fly her from the sound of her wires and with the wind on the side of their faces. Of course, you have to coordinate; no inter-connected controls. So, get on the rudder with authority when you put a wing down. But, like we said, she's a marvelous airplane, and as honest as an Iowa sunrise. Bert later told us that the only embarrassing thing about flying her from Long Island (following the turnpikes), was that Volkswagens below kept passing him.

Approximately 200 antique aircraft owners fly their

DeHavilland *Moth* of 1929, powered with a 95-hp 4-cylinder in-line *Gipsy* engine, is flown by Dudley Kelly, Versailles, Ky., at antiquers' gathering. The *Moth* may be described as the United Kingdom's Piper *Cub.* It was built in Britain, Canada and—under license—in the United States. (Authors' photo)

Enroute to Antique Airplane Association's annual fly-in/convention at Ottumwa, Iowa, airline pilot Herb Harkcom of Tulsa stops by Beech factory in Wichita where his beautifully restored Travel Air L-4000 was built nearly 40 years ago. (Photo courtesy Beech Aircraft Corporation)

planes to Ottumwa for the antiquers' convention each year, and, during the five-day meet, most are in the air each day giving rides to friends, demonstrating their skills or merely boring holes in the sky for the pure fun of it. Late each afternoon, the aerobatic pilots take over and provide the crowd with thrilling displays of precision flying. This pack is usually led by Frank Price of Waco, Texas.

Frank, founder and "Top Tiger" of the American Tiger Club—a non-profit organization dedicated to amateur aerobatics—ranks alongside Harold Krier and F. Don Pittman as a precision aerobatic pilot. Trailing a plume of white smoke, Price performs the most intricate and difficult maneuvers known—just off the

grass, and within a tiny block of airspace directly before his audience.

Crowding the male akro-flyers with precise routines of their own, girl champions Joyce Case, Mary Gaffney, and Mary Aikins add their aerial artistry to the spectacle, and their inverted Cuban-Eights, back-to-back rolls and outside loops are models of perfection.

It was after 10 P.M., Sunday, when about a dozen of us put some tables together at Molly's ("the Restaurant for Airplane Drivers") in downtown Ottumwa and ordered steaks. We were tired, quiet, reflective. Tomorrow would be Labor Day, and we'd all take off on separate headings for distant homes. Twelve year old Tom Bright, who had flown in with his parents

Bert Kieffer, a 41 year-old electronics engineer from Long Island, flew a 1929 Curtiss *Fledgling* to antiquers' convention in Iowa following the turnpikes and bravely bore the embarrassment of watching Volkswagens below zip past him at his 55 mph cruising speed. At the convention, however, Bert had plenty of interesting and decorative passengers for short hops. *Fledgling* is powered with its original 175-hp Curtiss *Challenger* engine. (Authors' photo)

in a 1929 Curtiss *Robin,* was seated about four inches off his chair because aerobatic great F. Don Pittman had treated Tom as an equal and squatted down to talk with him in the shadow of Don's famed Pitts Special, "Tiny Tiger." And a lady pilot across from us idly observed that she was sometimes mystified by the affection we all had for ancient airplanes. "Why should otherwise normal people become so worked up over the sight of an old biplane overhead, its wings golden in the morning sun?" she demanded rather ambiguously.

No one tried to answer; at least, not aloud. Some emotions are not easily described. Perhaps these feelings were born in another time, a time of adventure and freedom and legend. A time of fearless men and fabulous women and sturdy biplanes with wings of gold in the morning sun. . . .

So, perhaps this account reveals why sport aviation is important. One measure of our society is its ability to create giant, efficient airplanes—essentially, it seems, winged computers that carry hundreds of passengers at incredible speeds. But the fun airplanes are also a measure of our society. The super jets may reflect the state of our technology; but Bert's *Fledgling* and Tracy's *Puddy Tat* more accurately reflect our character.

Air racing during the 60s is typified by Bob Downey of Whittier, California, and his amateur-built Miller Special midget racer. This craft squeezes 230 mph out of a stock Continental 85-hp engine and has a wing-span of but 14 ft. In 1968, there were about 40 such aircraft in the U.S. participating in five to ten racing meets per year for purses that usually promised little more than expense money. Air racing is therefore a hobby, even for top race pilots like Downey—a paint manufacturer. (Photo courtesy Don Downie)

Sport parachuting, or "sky diving," exploded into a popular sport during the 60s. Although a handful of people had been parachuting for fun for years, thousands of others seemed to discover the airborne "rag bag" almost simultaneously. In 1956 there were 200 sport jumps in the U.S. By 1961, this figure had increased to an estimated 60,000; the projected figure for 1970 was set at 250,000 by the FAA. Sport para-chutists come from all walks of life and are not necessarily, in fact not usually, aviation people. (Authors' photo)

239

Three-time National Aerobatic Champion, Harold Krier of Wichita, Kansas, flies formation (inverted) with our camera plane. Krier's craft is a modified deHavilland *Chipmunk* powered with a 200-hp Ranger engine fitted with an Aeromatic propeller. Krier is paid about $40 per minute for a heart-stopping display of precision flying at air shows. He averages about 40 performances per year and his routine lasts about 15 minutes. If this seems like excellent pay for one hour per month; remember that there's no room for error performing aerobatics at tree-top height.

Homebuilt Bensen Gyrocopter is powered with a Volkswagen engine. The Benson is not a helicopter because its rotors, which provide lift, are driven by the machine's forward movement and have no direct power source. Gyrocopter builder/flyers are loosely organized as the Popular Rotorcraft Assoc., with 37 active chapters in the U.S. Headquarters is in Raleigh, N.C. (Photo courtesy Bensen Aircraft Corporation)

Arlo Schroeder of Newton, Kansas painted his homebuilt Mong Sport to resemble the Curtiss *Hawk* biplane pursuits of the twenties and calls his little plane *Hawk Pshaw*. It cruises at 120 mph, has a wingspan of 18 feet. (Photo courtesy Kathryn Schroeder)

A 1940 Dart Model GC arrives for antiquers' meet over Ottumwa Industrial Airport, flown by Chuck Hellinger of Mansfield, Ohio. This model is powered with an A100 Continental engine, though earlier ones were fitted with small radials such as the Warner Scarab Junior. The Dart was an Al Mooney design that first appeared about 1936, while Mooney worked for Monocoupe. In 1938 the Dart design was purchased by the Culver Aircraft Company of Columbus, Ohio, and Mooney—who had, as a 19 year-old, started with Eaglerock in 1926—went with Culver to design the popular *Cadet*. He later formed the post-WW-II Mooney Aircraft Company; therefore, modern Mooneys can trace their ancestry back to the pert little Darts. (Authors' photo)

FIRETAILS, FREIGHTERS
AND FLINGWINGS

13. Target: Mach 6

Scott Crossfield, guiding the 4,000-mph X-15 on its first, bellowing charge beyond the high places, could have been, it seemed to us, more considerate of those who were anticipating a dramatic report from this new frontier of flight. Scotty's radioed comments, as he rode a trail of thunder into the unknown and back, just didn't measure up to the histrionics of "Space Patrol." His first transmission, immediately after air-launch from beneath the wing of his B-52 mother-plane, was a calm, "Got eight of 'em going" (meaning all eight rocket barrels were firing). Then he recited some instrument readings, adding, as if it weren't particularly important, "Going uphill at forty-five thousand." And that's the way the whole historic flight was described for posterity.

Nor did the chase-plane pilots, who at last caught up with Crossfield upon his return to the lower atmosphere, add any exciting bits to the matter-of-fact reports. When Scotty blasted away the X-15's lower ventral fin prior to landing, its parachute opened to chase-pilot Bob White's uninspiring, "That's nice."

Finally, as the X-15 touched down at almost 200-mph, trailing a rooster-tail of dust from Rogers Dry Lake, White said, "Very nice."

"What did you expect from an old pro, daddy-O?" Crossfield replied. Historic words indeed! Clearly, modern test pilots would never make it in Hollywood.

Or, could it be that your reporters lacked perception? Maybe we simply failed to recognize true drama as presented by real-life professionals, these finely honed pilots with engineering degrees who are today's aerospace researchers, and who, like the seat-of-the-pants air pioneers that preceded them, make a handmaiden of Danger, regard Fear as a fraud, and believe the only worthwhile goals to be those which seem beyond Man's reach.

Therefore, it occurred to us that if we had lived with the X-15—as had Scotty Crossfield and his team—since this ominously beautiful craft first took shape on drawing boards in the North American factory almost four years before, we'd understand that her initial powered flight, while quietly exciting in its way, was actually but a single sub-drama, one of many dramas within the whole fantastic adventure of the X-15 Project.

It was a project born of necessity—in October, 1955—after it belatedly became clear to Eisenhower-era planners that the U.S. possessed no research airplanes capable of exploring speed and altitude ranges ahead of the up-coming Century-series fighters, the F-100 and its follow-ons. Civilian test pilots working for NACA (National Advisory Committee for Aeronautics, forerunner of NASA) and military test pilots had, by that time, exhausted the capabilities of existing research airplanes. They had, in fact, wrung every ounce of potential from our first generation of rocket planes long before that.

In the beginning, the "sound barrier" had been

The X-15 roll-out party on October 15, 1958, was attended by (then) Vice President Nixon and Pat Nixon. Mr. and Mrs. Dutch Kindelberger at left; Lee Atwood on right. (Photo courtesy North American Rockwell)

bridged by Air Force Capt. Chuck Yeager in the Bell X-1 on October 14, 1947. Following that breakthrough, it took six years to double Yeager's speed—which Scott Crossfield did on November 20, 1953, when he managed to push the Douglas D-558-II *Skyrocket* to Mach 2.04, and this stretched things to the limit in a plane originally conceived as a sub-sonic

fighter. Then, three weeks later, Yeager upped the ante to Mach 2.42 (principally because the Air Force wanted a headline-getting announcement for the Wright Memorial Dinner celebrating the airplane's fiftieth birthday). Yeager's mount that time was the Bell X-1A, a swept-wing version of the X-1, but it was barely sufficient unto the task and tumbled wildly

X-15 drops away from B-52 mother plane at 38,000 feet and its rocket engine of one million horsepower (60,000 lbs thrust) thunders to life with an echo heard over 400 square miles of desert. X-15's were 50 feet in length; wingspan was 22 feet, empty weight 14,500 lbs. Fuel was anhydrous ammonia (8,400 lbs.) and liquid oxygen (10,400 lbs) giving the craft a gross weight of 33,300 lbs at launch. (Photo courtesy North American Rockwell)

X-15's 22-foot wingspan seems ridiculously brief to those of us accustomed to more conventional airplanes. Lower portion of ventral fin was jettisoned prior to landing. Retractable landing gear consisted of a pair of metal skids beneath tail and two nose-wheels on a single strut. XLR-99 engine, designed by Reaction Motors, consumed fuel at a rate of 12,000 lbs per minute. (Photo courtesy North American Rockwell)

247

In 1967, the X-15 number two—redesignated X-15A-2 received a coating of white ablative material to protect its nickel alloy skin beyond the 1,200 degrees Fahrenheit it could normally withstand, and a pair of external fuel tanks were added, increasing its Lox and ammonia fuel capacity by 13,500 lbs, allowing longer engine burn. Thus equipped, the plane reached a speed of 4,534 mph (Mach 6.73) with Air Force Major Pete Knight at the controls. NASA test pilot Joe Walker established X-15 altitude record of 354,200 feet in 1963, flying X-15 number three. (Photo courtesy North American Rockwell)

248

WW-II advanced trainer, the AT-6 *Texan,* was developed from the pre-war North American BT-9 and BT-14. Powered with a Pratt & Whitney 600-hp engine, the AT-6 had a top speed of 215 mph. It was designated the SNJ in Navy service, and was known as the *Harvard* in Canada. Late in its Air Force career it became simply the T-6, and was used as a primary trainer by students preparing for jets. In the early 50s, T-6's were replaced by North American T-28's and Beech T-34's, which were in turn retired in favor of the Cessna T-41 Primary Trainer during the late 60s. (Photo courtesy USAF)

X-15 pilot Scott Crossfield (r) chats with Bill Lear. Scotty, forever looking for new worlds to conquer, learned to fly helicopters just in case that skill should ever be useful. (Photo courtesy Lear Jet)

for 51,000 feet in payment for the accomplishment.

Meanwhile, prototypes of both the North American F-100 fighter and the Lockheed F-104 had arrived at Edwards Air Force Base Flight Test Center and, in January, 1954, another "old pro," Lockheed test pilot Tony LeVier, cracked Mach 2 in the F-104 *Starfighter*. So, with new jet-powered fighters dogging the heels of the early rocket-powered research planes, even the most uninformed (and/or politically sensi-

tive) decision-makers in the Pentagon and on Capitol Hill (a complex sometimes known in aerospace circles as "Malfunction Junction") were forced to admit the urgent need for solid flight data in the Mach 3 range and beyond. This called for a bold new design, an airplane that would be stable up to Mach 6, if possible, and one that could be controlled in space where its aerodynamic surfaces would be useless.

The new plane's exact conception-date is impossible

The North American F-86 *Sabre* first flew in 1947 and was operational in time for the Korean War. It's maximum speed was over 670 mph, and its normal armament was six .50-caliber machine guns plus 16 five-inch rockets. Nearly 8,700 *Sabres* were built. (Photo courtesy Hudek Aeronautical Collection)

to determine. The X-15 idea was a series of developments, not a happening. Crossfield had drawn flight profiles for an imaginary Mach 6 airplane in mid-1952 while employed as a NACA pilot. NACA Director, Dr. Hugh Dryden*, had discussed such a craft with his engineers even before that. Such bits and pieces eventually coalesced into a formal NACA study which was completed in April, 1954.

This engineering study kicked around for six months. Then, in a stormy meeting attended by airframe makers, Air Force, Navy and Defense Department people, along with members of NACA's Aerodynamics Subcommittee, the "dreamers" managed to prevail and the Department of Defense okayed the project. The Air Force was to supply 90 per cent of the funds, the Navy 10 per cent. NACA would be in charge of initial flight testing.

Only Bell, North American, and Douglas submitted

bids; and each company should have been cited for "unusual devotion to duty," because they could have reasoned, as others did, that the chance for profit was uncertain at best since only three examples of this research tool were to be built and no production lines would follow. Besides, the contractor's best engineers would be diverted, unselfishly, to solve problems that would benefit the entire industry, for the X-15, as a federal agency program (NACA), would freely share with all whatever data it collected.

North American's proposal was the boldest, and since boldness was the name of the game, North American got the contract in October, 1955. This was to prove a fortunate choice; North American not only had the management, talent, and facilities, but a real desire to do the job.

Now, it's hard to get emotional over a company like North American, because it was born rich and has been fat and sassy all its corporate life. Still, any company, rich or not, has a character, and that quality is imparted by its management: decision-makers in

* Dr. Dryden was responsible to NACA Chairman Gen. Jimmy Doolittle, who in turn reported directly to the President.

Prototype of the F-100F *Supersabre,* a two-place version of the original F-100A, takes-off from Los Angeles International Airport (formerly Mines Field). Altogether, four models of this mainstay fighter-bomber were used by the Air Force's Tactical Air Command during the 60s. The *Supersabre's* speed of almost 900 mph, and long legs—because of its air-to-air refueling capability—kept it in production from September 1954 to October 1959. F-100's were widely used in Vietnam, although metal fatigue in the wing structure of the ageing craft limited their usefulness until corrected. (Photo courtesy North American Rockwell)

the front office, engineering and production. Thus, unusual men make unusual companies—and often history. Three such men at North American were C. M. Keys, J. H. "Dutch" Kindelberger, and Lee Atwood.

In the beginning, North American had been put together as a holding company by wheeler-dealer Clement Melville Keys (who had previously built the Curtiss-Wright empire). That was in 1928, and Keys' backers included General Motors, Hayden, Stone & Company, and Bankamerica-Blair. At that time, North American's *raison d'etre* was simply to acquire promising aviation properties, everything from instrument makers to airlines (Eastern Air Lines, known then as

Eastern Air Transport, was an early acquisition, as was Transcontinental Air Transport. TAT was then merged with Western Air Express to form TWA), because this was during the great aviation boom precipitated by Lindbergh's flight, when almost any aviation stock was viewed by investors as an airlift to affluence.

North American Aviation Company got into the airplane-making business as a result of its General Motors' ties. GM owned the American Fokker Company, which made a wooden-winged tri-motor used by TWA in the early thirties. Then, when President Roosevelt decreed (via the Air Mail Act of 1934) that the airlines separate themselves from manufac-

North American *Sabreliner* was conceived in 1956 as an Air Force twin-jet combat-readiness trainer with business jet potential. Production began October 29, 1958, and the first T-39A was delivered two years later. Speed is 560 mph; range 1,950 miles. About 300 were built during the 60s for both military and civil use. (Photo courtesy North American Rockwell)

The 2,000-mph North American XB-70 was conceived under Eisenhower's Secretary of Defense, Neil McElroy, during the fall of 1957. Originally intended as a Mach 3 Air Force bomber, it was reduced to a research role in October 1959, under McElroy's successor, Thomas Gates, Jr. (no kin to Lear Jet boss Charles Gates, Jr.). After John Kennedy became President in 1961, Congress attempted to revive the B-70 bomber program and twice voted funds for it—which the new Secretary of Defense, Robert McNamara, adamantly refused to spend. In the end, two XB-70's were built to gather data for possible future 2,000-mph heavy bombers and/or transport (SST) planes. One was lost in 1965 when NASA pilot Joe Walker, flying an F-104 chase plane, inexplicably collided with it at 45,000 feet. XB-70 is 189 feet in length; has wingspan of 105 ft., and a gross weight of 500,000 lbs. Its six General Electric YJ-93 jet engines each produce 30,000 pounds of thrust. (Photo courtesy North American Rockwell)

turing complexes following the "Air Mail Scandals" of that year*, North American traded its TWA stock to General Motors for Fokker, which, added to Berliner-Joyce, another North American property, made up North American's new industrial foundation. The original factory in Baltimore was the old Curtiss-Caproni facility, and its chief contribution was its roster of skilled aircraftsmen, largely Germans and Hollanders that had come to the U.S. with Anthony Fokker.

So, committed to airplane manufacturing, North American brass cast about for the proper man to get things rolling. They settled upon James Howard "Dutch" Kindelberger, chief engineer at Douglas Aircraft, which had just introduced the prototype of the world's most efficient transport plane, the DC-1.

Dutch Kindelberger, at thirty-nine, possessed an impressive aeronautical background. Born in Wheeling, W. Va., the son of an iron molder, he learned to fly in the Air Service during WW-I then joined the Wright-Martin Company as a draftsman in 1919. Martin's chief engineer at the time was Donald W. Douglas; Lawrence Bell was factory manager. Later, Dutch went with Douglas after Douglas started his own factory (on the second floor of a Santa Monica planing mill) with $600 capital. Therefore, when Dutch accepted North American's offer, in July, 1934, he had 15 years' experience of a kind few could match.

Upon leaving Douglas, Dutch took two top hands with him: Lee Atwood as his chief engineer, and Stan Smithson, project engineer. This trio found that the plant in Baltimore had no product to sell and nothing on the drawing boards, but decided this offered an advantage because, whatever happened, they'd answer for no one's mistakes but their own. Their first project, however, was anything but a mistake. Within nine weeks they designed and built the BT-9, a basic military trainer which won an Air Corps' contract and proved the viability of their organization. Then Dutch, spoiled by the California climate during his ten years with Douglas, went back to the Los Angeles area and leased—for $600 per year—twenty acres on Inglewood's Mines Field. A factory building went up on this site during 1935, and the first production BT-9 came off the Inglewood production line in February, 1936. Dutch had a payroll of 250, a substantial por-

tion of which represented former Fokker personnel that followed him to California.

The BT-9 was so well conceived that it was soon modified into the AT-6/SNJ series of advanced trainers for the Army and Navy, and was sold to the RAF as the *Harvard,* to Australia as the *Wirraway.* The 0-47 Army observation plane was next, then, in 1940, two North American designs appeared that would firmly establish Dutch Kindelberger and conferees as airplane fashioners of rare ability. Their B-25 *Mitchell* first flew in August of that year, and, a month later, the prototype P-51 *Mustang* was rolled out for tests.

By that time, Dutch's workforce had swelled to almost 5,000, and plant expansion became a frenzied and constant problem as warplane orders flooded in from the U.S. Air Corps and America's allies-to-be. At year's end, North American had 8,300 employees in the Inglewood factory and big new facilities ready for occupancy on Hensley Field in Dallas and Fairfax Field at Kansas City. The company delivered about 1,250 airplanes in 1940.

Less than five years later, at war's end, North American had produced 42,683 military aircraft including 16,000 trainers, 15,500 fighters and 10,000 medium bombers. Peak workforce reached 91,000.

When the Japanese surrendered in August, 1945, the U.S. Government cancelled all warplane contracts. Overnight, North American's backlog of orders dropped from 8,000 planes to 24; and mass lay-offs reduced its payroll to pre-WW-II levels at the Inglewood factory while the Dallas and Kansas City plants were closed.

But as jet engine development pointed to the inevitability of a new generation of military aircraft, Dutch's people tested the water with a subsonic Navy fighter, the FJ-1 *Fury,* and a twin-jet medium bomber, the B-45 *Tornado.* The B-45 was only moderately successful, though the *Fury* evolved—through models FJ-2, -3, and -4 for the Navy, and the F-86 *Sabrejet* series for the Air Force—into a classic design matching the fame of the WW-II *Mustang.* Meanwhile, the company dropped a reported $10 million on a *Puddy Tat* version of the *Mustang.* This was the *Navion,* a four-place lightplane meant for the boom in private flying immediately after WW-II that never developed. This same dream had, of course, dry-gulched optimistic plane makers a quarter-century earlier at the end of WW-I. Actually, the *Navion* was an excellent little plane and many are still around; but the market of 50,000 private planes per year

* See *Command the Horizon* (Chapter 21), Volume I of this two-volume series.

forecast for the late forties appears to have been merely a product of wishful thinking in the av-industry.

However, North American soon recovered both its demeanor and dividends with the transonic *Sabre-jet,* because it was, fortunately, available to the U.S. Air Force in time for the Korean War. American F-86 pilots above Korea scored a 10-to-1 kill ratio over the vaunted Soviet-built MIGS.

Meanwhile, in 1948, Dutch Kindelberger had stepped upstairs to become North American's board chairman, and Lee Atwood took over the day-to-day operation of the company as president. Atwood, a slim, soft-spoken type with a keen analytical mind, had been with Dutch since the beginning of manufacturing operations in 1934, and his natural conservatism seems to have provided just the right balance to Dutch's natural boldness.

During the following seven years, the company scored with several outstanding military craft—including the F-100 *Super Sabre* and the A3J *Vigilante*—and significantly broadened its industrial base with establishment of new divisions and subsidiaries to produce atomic reactors, military missile systems, a variety of space hardware including rocket boosters, and a passel of magical "black boxes." New facilities were opened at Columbus, Ohio, and in Downey, Fresno and Canoga Park, California, plus a rocket-engine testing installation in California's Santa Susana Mountains.

Thus, when the Department of Defense sought bids for the design and contruction of a slightly preposterous airplane (many engineers believed the X-15 should be planned for the Mach 3 or Mach 4 range of speed, rather than attempt a quantum jump to Mach 6), Kindelberger-Atwood & Company was uniquely prepared and even downright eager to accept the challenge.

And Albert Scott Crossfield, Jr., feeling that his own destiny was somehow entwined with that of the X-15, resigned from NACA, obtained an interview with North American's president, and asked to be the X-15's pilot. Although Lee Atwood had a number of excellent test pilots already on his payroll, he silently studied Crossfield for a few seconds, asked a couple of questions, then hired Scotty on the spot.

This swift *rapport* was hardly surprising, for Crossfield was the kind of professional the no-nonsense Atwood appreciated: an unflappable perfectionist combining unusual skill as a flyer with the detached curiosity of an engineer. Scotty was an ex-Navy fighter pilot who had been an "airport kid" during the thirties; had married a pretty blonde telephone operator during WW-II while serving as a flight instructor at Corpus Christi Naval Air Station, and had since acquired a home, five children, a master's degree in aeronautical engineering and the sedentary habits of a confirmed family man. After five years as NACA's chief test pilot, he possessed, at age thirty-three, more rocket-plane experience than any pilot in the world.

Crossfield also possessed, as a result of his NACA job, an awareness of the many pitfalls awaiting any new airplane design from overenthusiastic gadgeteers—the specialists and component-suppliers and others who could complicate already-complicated aircraft systems to the point of hopelessness. Therefore, Scotty determined that his main responsibility during the X-15's design and construction stages would be that of chief son-of-a-bitch. As the pilot, he was less vulnerable to pressure than others on the project; and he was the one who could effectively say "No" when the engineering team was confronted with a request to add, say, a wondrous whatchamacallit that only weighed seven pounds and would electronically monitor air pressure in the nose-wheel tires. Scotty had seen promising airplanes before rendered so overweight and complex by such refinements their true potentials were compromised to death (and we must observe here that there are those who believe one of the things the F-111 clearly lacked was an engineering son-of-a-bitch).

At North American, the X-15 team was selected from among top specialists in a number of fields, and Charles Feltz, a graying Texan who had so proved his ability that he could affect the air of an ignorant country boy and get away with it, was named to boss the group. Almost at once, the gadgeteers descended upon them, and Scotty was forced to marshal a task force of engineers which spent thousands of unnecessary man-hours shooting-down—with graphs, charts and persuasion—an Air Force general's directive that the X-15 be equipped with an escape capsule for the pilot—a refinement that would have added 9,000 pounds to total aircraft weight (including the fuel and beefed-up structure needed to haul it around), would have required an extra year or two for development, and cost at least one Mach number in speed. However, Crossfield, Feltz, and friends stood adamantly against this and other proposals and adhered strictly to the sound engineering axiom known as KISS ("keep it simple, stupid").

Of course, "simple" in this case was a relative term. The X-15 could not be simple in a normal sense because the airplane and all its systems were planned for flight regimes only imagined. Its XLR-99 rocket engine of one million horsepower (consuming a ton of fuel every 11 seconds) was expected to propel the X-15 to a speed of 6,600 feet per second and to altitudes of more than 50 miles above earth. Then, re-entry into earth's atmosphere at, say, 4,000 mph, would subject exterior surfaces to extreme frictional heat, and this called for a new kind of skin, Inconel X, a nickel alloy that retains its strength at temperatures up to 1,200 degrees F. And this in turn meant that North American production people must find a way to weld this exotic new metal.

The plane's operating systems, too, were far-out concepts at the time. In addition to conventional flight controls, the craft needed a set of small jets in nose and wingtips for attitude control in space (later copied for use in the Mercury and Gemini capsules), and small turbine engines as auxiliary power units to generate electricity for instrumentation and to heat the pilot's space suit. These jewel-like turbines, designed by General Electric, would turn at 50,000 rpms, use hydrogen peroxide for fuel, and function as well in airless space as in the lower atmosphere. A liquid nitrogen system, designed by Garrett Corporation's AiResearch Division, pressurized and cooled the cockpit. These and other innovations—almost all representing engineering breakthroughs—were slowly, agonizingly perfected after countless disappointments and failures during a four-year period.

Compromises were inevitable. When the XLR-99 engine fell far behind schedule (primarily due to the requirement that it be "throttleable"), the first two X-15s were temporarily equipped with pairs of 4-barrel rocket engines that, although possessing but 30 per cent of the thrust of the XLR-99, would allow preliminary flights in the Mach 3 area and provide useful data while awaiting completion of the big engine.

In truth, the projected XLR-99 engine was just a little unreasonable considering the state of the art in the late fifties. Nevertheless, everyone seemed to have faith in the ability of Thiokol's Reaction Motors Division to deliver as advertised, and perhaps this in itself furnished that small (then) engineering group with the spirit to overcome brain-numbing problems,

and, in the end, Reaction Motors came up with a dependable, throttleable, rocket engine—the YLR-99—capable of thrusting the X-15A-2 to the very edge of Mach 7 and more than 354,000 feet above earth.

The first of the three X-15s was rolled out October 15, 1958, with number two following a week later. Number three was held at North American to await its XLR-99 engine. Flight tests began at Edwards Air Force Base over the miles-long dry lakes on March 10, 1959, after much ground-testing of the planes' systems. The first air tests, too, were cautious, tentative probes. None of these precious birds would be lost if careful, hard-nosed planning could prevent it. America could ill afford such a loss; the Soviets had beaten us into space with their *Sputnik* eighteen months before (Oct. 5, 1957), and though President Eisenhower—whose total background was that of a professional foot soldier—apparently never really understood why the U.S. should go into space (he was quoted by newspapers as saying he couldn't see why Americans should be so impressed with Russia's basketball-sized satellite), this nation did, after *Sputnik,* massively increase its space effort.

Actually, at that time, we had large ballistic rockets—Atlas, Titan, Thor—under development, albeit at a leisurely pace due to lack of funds and a somnolent Congress; and the Vanguard Project was stumbling along, hoping, they said, to place our own basketball-sized satellite in orbit sometime between July, 1957 and December, 1958. But when the X-15 began flying, in mid-1959, it was by far America's most advanced piece of aerospace hardware. It was the world's first space airplane; and the prestige of this country rode precariously on its ridiculously-brief wings.

After a couple of glide tests in which the X-15 was dropped from its B-52 mother plane at 38,000 feet, without fuel, to circle down for a deadstick landing on Rogers Dry Lake, Scotty Crossfield made that first powered flight in the ship on September 17, 1959. And it seemed indeed an anti-climax to the X-15 team. Perhaps these men had little emotion remaining after four years of work—ten million engineering man-hours filled with crises and failures and triumphs and sweat. Of *course,* the airplane would perform as intended. It simply could not do otherwise.

Nor did it. Scotty alternately flew X-15s one and two for a total of fourteen flights, methodically investigating the crafts' flight characteristics and, in effect, writing an X-15 Pilot's Handbook. But he was never allowed to lay back her ears and let her ramble. As the contractor's engineering test pilot, his duty was to assume the initial risks, catalog the plane's habits and deliver to the customer a proven machine. The glory which would come later with new speed and altitude records, would belong to Air Force pilots because, after all, Air Force funds had made the project possible.

Crossfield's responsibility to that project ended late in 1960 when he completed check-out of the new XLR-99 engine in flight. He was under orders not to exceed Mach 3, and, officially his highest speed with the big engine is on record as Mach 2.97; but Scott Crossfield is only human and, well, there are a few guys around—some who should know—who'll merely grin at you when you remark upon how close Scotty came to fudging on his orders that day.

Anyway, the X-15's ultimate best speed of Mach 6.73 (4,534 mph; established Oct. 3, 1967), was attained with Air Force Major William J. Knight at the controls. Maximum altitude was reached early in the ten-year flight program by Joseph A. Walker who had taken Crossfield's old job at NACA— though NACA had since become NASA—when Walker topped 354,200 feet (more than sixty miles) on August 22, 1963.

A total of eleven Air Force and NASA test pilots flew the three X-15s during these ten years, and the reams of data they recorded provides much of the base for our next quantum advance into space and offers engineering ground rules for our hypersonic military and transport aircraft. Many of the X-15's systems or similar ones went into Mercury, Gemini, and Apollo capsules. And future space vehicles will necessarily draw heavily upon X-15 experience because they must possess aerodynamic qualities that will allow them to re-enter the earth's atmosphere and land, as an airplane, on a pre-selected runway. Plainly, we cannot employ the expensive and impractical capsule recovery system of Mercury and Gemini and Apollo beyond manned rocketry's infancy; and we need not because the X-15 demonstrated with its own re-entries and landings how it can be done.

By 1968, the X-15's had been souped up with the YLR-99 engine, stretched, coated with ablative material—had even suffered the addition of "saddle tanks"—as NASA and the Air Force sought to wring every possible ounce of hypersonic information from them. Late in 1967, one of the three planes had been lost in flight, and this, plus the fact the X-15 design had yielded about all data possible, presaged the project's end.

However, long before the X-15 faced retirement, NASA and North American engineers and test pilots were talking of a Mach 20 airplane. And if we know anything at all about this breed, we know they'll gladly pay the price in heartbreak and sweat and unwavering perserverance to build and fly it. As Scott Crossfield once pointed out, "There's always another dawn."*

* *Always Another Dawn,* by Scott Crossfield with Clay Blair, Jr., World Publishing Company, 1960.

14. Air Age Frontiersman

Aviation has progressed so far during its brief history that many young av-engineers today are prone to lament that there's practically nothing left to pioneer; no new frontiers, no un-explored concepts. Fortunately, however, there are men like Bill Lear around whose lives and works soundly refute this enervating charge.

William Powell Lear, Sr., born in Hannibal, Missouri in 1902, has been pioneering for almost five decades. His stubborn pursuit of new ideas has fostered everything from break-throughs in aviation radio and automatic pilots to revolutionary airplane designs—and, as this is written, Bill has tackled a new challenge: development of a practical steam-powered automobile.

Like the rest of us, Bill has known dark moments; but he's one of those who seems to perform best when the going is the toughest. Perhaps the lowest point of his several careers came near the end of March, 1934. He was broke. Worse, he was deeply in debt. His little company, Lear Developments, which had opened for business in New York less than four months previously, was bankrupt.

Bill sat glumly in his tiny office. Never had he so keenly felt his handicaps; never had he so bitterly hated his lack of education. Had he been fooling himself? Wasn't it just a bit ridiculous for a kid from the Chicago stockyards—who had never got past the eighth grade—to think he could design and build radios better than those offered by the country's biggest manufacturers? Wasn't it just downright presumptuous for a young man so obviously ill-equipped to challenge the products of the best engineers in the world?

But then, suddenly aware of the danger of such thoughts, Bill angrily got to his feet. He had two good hands and the will to work; that was enough. He'd *make* it enough. He headed for his workshop. The thing to do was decide upon something the world needed, then build it. Faith and determination were the keys, he firmly reminded himself.

Now, if this story so far has a cornpone ring to it, perhaps we'd all be well advised to temper our cynicisms with a large dose of such corn. It's pretty hard to argue with success; especially the kind of success one may measure in terms of a multimillion-dollar personal fortune—even more especially when that accomplishment springs from the humblest kind of beginning.

Bill's parents had separated when he was six, and he had gone with his mother to live in a tenement on Chicago's South Side. He attended Kershaw grade school and played in the streets and had a Negro friend by the name of Shargo who owned the most glamorous junk collection Bill had ever seen.

Shargo's basement was full of scrounged electrical equipment; mysterious things like Leyden jars and coils and telegraph keys. Enthralled, young Bill

Lear in his Monocoupe, 1931, in which he demonstrated his first aircraft radio receiver. Sales were infrequent because few private pilots of that day could imagine any use for a radio in flight.

spent countless hours there tinkering and experimenting.

Then, in his early teens, he earned money by riding nearby country roads on his bicycle and performing on-the-spot repairs for stalled motorists. Ignition troubles were common on the cars of 1915 and 1916, and Bill had taught himself enough in Shargo's basement to fix almost anything electrical. His standard charge was $2, which he learned to collect in advance after receiving nothing more than a pat on the head for a couple of jobs. He gave most of his earnings to his mother.

Today, Bill's mention of his mother is in a tone of affection tinged with sadness. He cared for her until her death in the mid-thirties; but there is some evidence that she—herself treated harshly by life— was often harsh with her son. After she remarried, Bill dropped out of school. His stepfather, a plasterer, earned enough for only the barest essentials.

Finally, at sixteen, Bill tied his few belongings in a shirt and quietly left home.

During the next four years, he went from job to job. He was never fired; he always quit. As soon as he had mastered a job, he'd ask for more responsibility or a different assignment. If he didn't get it, he'd quit. Bill wanted to learn and he wanted to advance. Salary was secondary. In 1919, he quit a forty-dollar-a-week job to work without pay as a mechanic at Grant Park Airport. As long as his meagre savings held out, he performed all the more unpleasant tasks at the airport in order to learn about airplanes.

Later, he took a job as office boy for Mr. C. R. Perry, Secretary of the Rotary International, simply because Bill admired the voluble Mr. Perry's precise grammar. Bill's own speech was the vernacular of the streets, and he was acutely aware of such a drawback. Thus, the unsuspecting Mr. Perry served as Lear's English instructor.

By 1922, Bill decided to go into business on his own, selling and repairing the primitive home radios of that day. His first shop, in Quincy, Illinois, was opened with $500 borrowed capital.

At his repair bench he got to tinkering and ex-

Not a still picture from an old Humphrey Bogart movie, but young Bill Lear, Sr. with the WACO he flew coast-to-coast in the thirties to demonstrate his early avionics offerings. Bill's two friends at left are unidentified. (Photo courtesy Lear Jet Industries)

Lear Jet production line. In mid-1968 a Gates Aviation executive (who should have been out playing golf) decreed that the name of these craft henceforth be spelled "Learjet." So, copy-editor and proofreaders please note: Lear Jet builds Learjets. Honest. (Photo courtesy Lear Jet)

Learjet 24 off California Coast. The first Learjet made its maiden flight Oct. 7, 1963; Model 24 appeared in 1966 and in May of that year it circled the earth in 65 hours, 40 minutes establishing 18 world's records for planes in its class. (Photo courtesy Lear Jet Industries)

Learjet 23's being serviced at Wichita factory prior to delivery. Follow-on Learjet 24—slightly heavier and more powerful than the 23—is unchanged externally; has a top speed of 564 mph (Mach .81), and cruises at 507 mph up to 45,000 feet. It sells for $649,000 including all avionics and operates for about 65¢ per mile total cost with average use of 400 hours per year. (Photo courtesy Lear Jet)

Instrument panel of Learjet Model 23. Large circular
tube at bottom center panel is weather radar scope.
Deep pile carpeting in cockpit is typical Lear touch.
(Photo courtesy Lear Jet Industries)

Lear Jet Model 24 joins the Friendly Skies of United
—to be used by the airline at its Flight Training
Center in Denver, Colorado. (Photo courtesy Lear Jet
Industries)

Prototype Learjet's successful test flights dispelled gloom of snowy days for Bill and Moya Lear. "First," Bill recalls, "they said I wouldn't come to Wichita. But if I did, I wouldn't get a factory. If I did, I wouldn't make a plane. And if I did, it wouldn't fly." Bill proved his critics wrong on all counts. (Photo courtesy Lear Jet Industries)

perimenting again. Clearly, those early sets held much room for improvement; and many of the newly established engineering laws, according to which radio sets were then designed, seemed not above suspicion to Bill. He accepted no theory until he had proven it to his own satisfaction, and this attitude led to some significant discoveries. He miniaturized coils (believed impossible at the time); eliminated the need for batteries and worked out other improvements that led to the development of the home radio in its present form.

This, of course, brought him to the attention of the big companies, and he was soon working with such leaders as Majestic and Motorola.

During these years—while Walter Beech was building Travel Air biplanes in Wichita; Frank Hawks was barnstorming in Mexico; Donald Douglas was producing his first planes on the second floor of a Santa Monica planing mill, and Charles Lindbergh was an unknown parachute jumper employed by pasture-pilot "Cupid" Lynch—Bill Lear gradually accumulated a few dollars he could call his own. This money was to be his stake in aviation; a future he had decided upon in 1919 when he worked as an apprentice grease monkey at Chicago's Grant Park Airport.

Finally, in 1931, Bill set up shop on Chicago's Curtiss-Reynolds Airport and began making an airplane radio receiver, the Lear Radioaire. He was well ahead of the market (a consistent Lear trait), and sales were infrequent. Most private pilots in those days could see little use for a radio. "I don't need to be entertained while flying," they would tell Lear. Most were unconvinced that they could profitably use the airway radio stations, as the airlines did, for navigational aids.

About that time, Lear soloed a Fleet biplane, then bought a Warner-powered Monocoupe with which to demonstrate his product. Later, in a deal with the Stinson company, Bill acquired a Stinson *Reliant* in exchange for 300 radio sets. If he couldn't sell for cash, he'd swap.

Later in 1933 he decided to start anew in New York City. And it was there, at 157 West Chambers Street, that he found himself bankrupt at the end of March, 1934.

In his workshop, Bill pondered "what the world needed," and, in his own words, it went like this: "I conceived the idea of designing the front end for a home radio, from the second detector back; and this front end would be common to all kinds of radio sets that you might want to make. By virtue of this

Roominess and plushness were sacrificed to speed in the Learjet 25's pressurized cabin. Lear believed that a business plane should be capable of taking a busy executive anywhere within the average company's operating radius within two hours. "After two hours, not even wall-to-wall girls substitute for getting there," Bill told his engineers. (Photo courtesy Lear Jet Industries)

fact, it would enable a manufacturer to make a better front end, and at the same time at lower cost. This became the *Magic Brain,* which RCA bought from me . . . I designed, built and demonstrated this concept within two weeks, and on the 13th of April, 1934, I had in my hand a contract for $250,000."

The way Bill tells it, it sounds easy; but more than twenty years of experimentation and experience preceded the two weeks that produced his new concept. The *Magic Brain* was begun in Shargo's basement.

Suddenly and soundly solvent, Bill Lear scarcely looked up from his workbench until he produced another, more important radio device. Reasoning that, if he had trouble navigating his plane across country —usually, by following railroad tracks—most other

pilots would have a similar problem. So, he developed the Learscope Direction Finder for aircraft. This logical piece of equipment, based upon well-known radio principles, enjoyed almost instant success and nudged aerial navigation a giant step closer to the electronic age.

Close upon the heels of his direction finder, Bill designed a 35-Watt aircraft radio transmitter. In 1935, he installed his new transmitter in a WACO cabin biplane and flew to the West Coast and back.

"It was the first time that many airway radio stations had heard a private pilot on the air," Bill recalls. "As a result, they would teletype to each other and say, 'There's a private airplane flying with a transmitter. Give him a call.' So I was sitting up there, listening to all the different stations calling me in an effort to get some communications. Now, you know how it is today, you can hardly get a word in edgwise; but on that trip I was the only private plane on the air and they were all calling me."

In 1939, to be near Wright Field and his best customer, the U.S. Air Corps, Lear moved to Dayton Municipal Airport at Vandalia, Ohio. In addition to his established products—the direction finder, transmitter and receiver—Bill introduced the first OMNI receiver, a radio receiver that, tuned to any ground station, would lead a pilot to its transmitter. This Learmatic Omninavigator was identical in principle to present-day OMNIs, except that it was necessarily low frequency, because all ground stations were LF at that time. But it represented another breakthrough in avionics (aviation radio) and won for Bill the Frank M. Hawks Award.

With the beginning of the war in Europe, and America's belated efforts to build an air force, Lear, Inc., moved into the electro-mechanical field and expanded rapidly. This began when an official of Con-

Learjet 25 is a ten-place craft, a stretched version of the 23/24 series, with a high-speed cruise of 528 mph at 41,000 feet. It is powered with two General Electric engines (Model CJ610-6) that produce 2,950 lbs. thrust each. Normal range with full load is 1,658 miles. Learjet 25 established official world's record for planes in its class by climbing to 40,000 feet in six minutes and 19 seconds on February 20, 1968. (Photo courtesy Lear Jet Industries)

Learjet 25

SPAN   35' 7"
LENGTH 47' 7"
HEIGHT 12' 7"

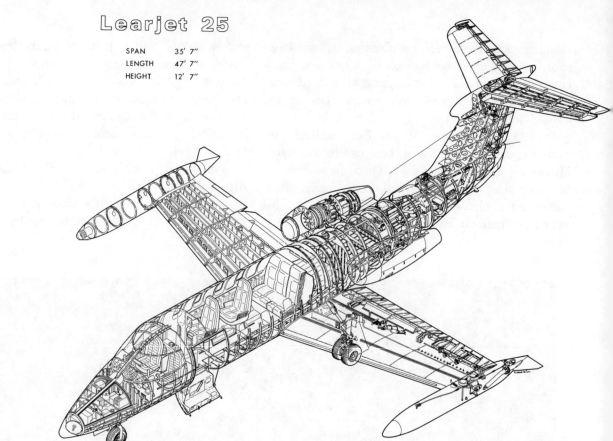

(Photo courtesy Lear Jet Industries)

Bill Lear's quick sense of humor, which includes fortunately the ability to laugh at himself, is undoubtedly one reason he has so many friends. Here, he gets a chuckle from President Nixon. (Photo courtesy Lear Jet Industries)

vair, enchanted by some of the experimental devices Bill had in his personal plane, asked Bill if he could design a light and simple mechanism to operate cowl flaps. Lear did so, in a single afternoon, on a borrowed drawing board.

Later, Bill entered the auto-pilot market with a 3-axis device that not only surpassed in performance existing automatic pilots, but was a whopping 75 per cent lighter in weight. It gained for him the Collier Trophy (civil aviation's highest award), presented by President Truman in 1950, and an honorary degree in engineering bestowed by the University of Michigan. Other awards, domestic and foreign, came to Lear during the fifties and early sixties as his restless imagination fathered newer and more sophisticated flight systems. These included a completely automatic blind landing system, demonstrated in Paris in 1962; a system that was then, and remains at this writing, somewhat in advance of equipment now in general use.

Thus it was that, by 1959, Bill Lear headed a company that was grossing a hundred million dollars per year. The boy who had left home with everything he owned tied in a shirt had become a very wealthy man. The self-educated kid from the stockyards had earned a place in aviation history beside Lawrence Sperry, Fred Rentschler and Eddie Stinson.

Still, retirement was not to be considered by Bill Lear ("I'd rather wear out than rust out"). While most of his pioneering contemporaries had either taken their fortunes and retired to a gentler life, or had been by-passed by aviation's supersonic progress, Bill not only remained in the thick of things, but a few steps ahead of the sixties' fast crowd. By this time, he had dreamed up a certain kind of airplane.

In Bill's view, the airplane makers were missing a bet with their new business jets. As he saw it, the world needed a *small* executive jet plane; a craft that could match the comfort and speed of the jet airliners, yet one that would operate from average airports— a simple aircraft ("You'll never have to repair, replace, maintain, or service anything you leave out") that would be easy to fly, and, above all, priced within sound economic range of corporations then flying medium-sized twin-engined craft.

A review of the "bizjets" in or entering the market made Lear's ideas on the subject seem radical indeed. All were much bigger, more complicated, and more expensive than the plane he envisioned. But this proved nothing to Bill except, perhaps, that such old

hands as Lockheed, DeHavilland, North American, etc., had simply failed to recognize (or were dubious of) a big economy-jet market. In Lear's judgment, they were scrambling for a high-priced 200-plane market when a potential 3,500 customers actually awaited—provided that someone offered a craft within the means of the middle-sized corporations, and one tailored to their needs.

But lucid though these facts seemed to Bill, he was unable to convert his board of directors. They wanted no part of a multi-million-dollar gamble that would pit them toe-to-toe against the biggest airframe makers in the world. No, thank you.

Bill didn't argue. Instead, he sold his share of a company he had spent twenty-five years building, took his personal fortune and went into the jet airplane business. And that was the act that forever rendered invalid such pale descriptions of him as "stormy" or "presumptuous" or " lucky." The special qualities from which courage and faith emerge are impossible to confuse when so tested.

Preliminary design studies of Bill's new craft were done in St. Gallen, Switzerland, because the Lear Jet Model 23 was to be patterned after the Swiss P-16, a rugged fighter-bomber. Then, in 1962, Bill moved the project to Wichita.

During the long months that followed, while a factory building went up in a Kansas cornfield and while the Model 23 design was firmed up, Bill walked alone (except for the encouragement of his wife, Moya. Her reaction: "Well, whatever happens, as long as Bill's alive we'll not go hungry"). Certainly Bill was aware that the money it had taken a lifetime to earn could vanish in a matter of months if he was wrong. But if he possessed a doubt during those hectic days of genesis, only Moya knew it. To those in the aviation industry, his self-confidence and ready wit appeared undiluted.

Most of the aviation industry was openly skeptical. "First," Bill recalled recently, "they said I wouldn't come to Wichita. But if I did, I wouldn't get a factory. If I did, I wouldn't make a plane. If I did, it wouldn't fly. And if it did, I wouldn't make any more of 'em."

Well, Bill went to Wichita. Construction of his factory began in August, 1962. Thirteen months later, he had built his first jet airplane. It flew. Man, how it flew! Nine months after that, his eight place "economy" jet—priced at $595,000—was certified by the FAA. More than a hundred were sold during its first year in production.

Meanwhile, in November, 1964, Lear Jet became a publicly owned corporation with an offering of 500,000 shares of common stock at $10 per share. This allowed Bill to open Lear Stereo Division in Detroit, making and selling Lear-designed 8-track stereo tape units for autos and airplanes. He also expanded Lear Jet Avionics Division which was headquartered in Grand Rapids, Michigan.

In March, 1966, an improved and slightly heavier jet plane, the Lear Jet Model 24, received FAA certification in the air transport category, and production was halted on the original Model 23. Two months later, Lear Jet purchased the Brantly Helicopter Corporation and began making Brantly two and five-place 'copters at the Wichita facility. However, in March, 1968, Lear Jet announced that the Brantly subsidiary was for sale because the company planned to offer a larger, Lear Jet-designed helicopter aimed at the developing shuttle and executive markets.

In August, 1966, the Lear Jet Model 25 was introduced. A stretched, 10-place version of the 23/24, the new plane gave the company a two-product line in business, small airline and air taxi fields.

During this period, three Lear Jets were lost in fatal accidents that had no immediate explanations and Lear Jet sales suddenly dropped to near zero. Representatives of at least one competitive company spread a rumor that the Lear Jet's windshield was blowing out at high altitude, a totally unfounded but particularly frightening prospect to contemplate at 540 mph. However, by the time Department of Transportation investigators fixed the "probable cause" of at least two of the crashes as failure of an electrical system that lacked a back-up, this fault had long since been corrected in all Lear Jets and the temporary dip in sales overcome. Exhaustive tests proved the craft's windshield to be structurally sound.

The company's quick recovery from the bad publicity the crashes occasioned should be primarily credited to Lear himself because of his gift for selecting the best people available to produce and sell his products. In this case, key men were James R. Greenwood, Director of Public Relations for Lear Jet Industries, and Allan K. Higdon, Press Relations Manager. Greenwood's department attempted no cover-up ("the worst thing you can do is lie about a thing like this"), but managed to build fresh confidence in Lear Jets from the whole dark episode by refuting rumor with factual evidence and by showing every reporter who appeared exactly how the Lear

Charles C. Gates, Jr., president of Gates Rubber Company, which was founded by his father in 1911 and now employs 15,000 workers on four continents, has, since the mid-50s, expanded into other fields including trucking, mutual-fund management, and metal products. Charles Gates, a pilot, also became president of Lear Jet when Gates Rubber purchased 57 per cent of the Lear Jet common stock in 1967. He then formed Gates Aviation Corporation as a Gates-owned subsidiary to function as exclusive sales organization for Lear Jet planes in the U.S. Lear Jet sales for fiscal 1968 were $34,582,898, a gain of 11 per cent over fiscal 1967. Sales volume for the year ending April 30, 1969 was forecast at $60,000,000. (Photo courtesy Lear Jet Industries)

Jet was built and tested. Greenwood also had some suggestions for his boss; one of them, which Bill quickly endorsed, was a dramatic 'round-the-world flight. Lear Jet 427L, a Model 24, carried four people around the earth in May, 1966, in 65 hours and 40 minutes elapsed time (50 hours, 20 minutes flying time), establishing 18 world records for planes in its class.

But more significant to Lear Jet's current position and future potential was the purchase, in May, 1967, by Gates Rubber Company of Denver, Colorado, of all of Bill's common stock in the company which amounted to 57 per cent of the total. Charles C. Gates, Jr., Gates Rubber president, became presi-

Announced at the Paris Air Show in June, 1969, was the Learjet Model 25 powered with Garrett AiResearch turbofan engines. Only change in outward appearance is larger engine nacelles, but new powerplants added to plane's efficiency increasing range to 3,000 miles with a 45-minute fuel reserve. As of June 1, 1969, 230 Learjets had been delivered to customers, making it the number one executive jet saleswise. (Photo courtesy Lear Jet Industries)

dent of Lear Jet Industries; and Bill, for the time being anyway, remained as board chairman—while announcing formation of a new company to be known as William Lear Enterprises, with offices in Santa Ana, California, and on Reno-Stead Airport, Reno, Nevada.

In the meantime, Charles Gates formed Gates Aviation Corporation, a wholly owned subsidiary of Gates Rubber, to provide a worldwide sales organization for Lear Jet Industries. G.H.B. Gould was elected president of Gates Aviation, and H. B. Combs, chairman of the board (Combs, long a major Beechcraft dealer located in Denver, sold his operation to Gates; but Beech immediately revoked this franchise and constructed its own Denver outlet). Lear Jet sales through 1968 proved the efficacy of the new Gates manufacturing/sales combination. A total of 47 were built.

But however well the Lear Jet may ultimately succeed, its greatest significance should be to other inquisitive minds in other basement workshops. This sleek-winged machine—this Mach .8 creature of the high places—surely reaffirms that imaginative men, able to "see what the world needs," and bold enough to bet on it, may still find challenges aplenty. The world of the pioneer hasn't really changed so much; only our vehicles are different, and the stars closer.

15. Black Magic and Gooney Birds

During the forties, fifties, and sixties, a slight, pleasant man named Jim McDonnell called forth some fearsome spirits from the nether world: Banshees, Goblins, Demons and Phantoms. His secret potions, however, were not concocted from powdered bats' wings and beetles' legs, but from simple elbow grease and black coffee. And his incantations, while highly mystical, came not from the *Book of the Dead,* but were conjured up with a slide rule. His black magic was practiced on a drawing board, and the creatures that resulted emitted their first, ominous wails from the depths of a wind tunnel. Jim McDonnell's deadly creations were fighter airplanes.

Jim (or, inevitably, "Mr. Mac"), and his assistant spectre designers, also produced America's first command modules for manned space vehicles—which marks McDonnell as one of the pioneers who began his career during aviation's open-cockpit days and lived to see his machines bound deep into space.

James Smith McDonnell, Jr., was born in Denver, Colorado, April 8, 1899, and grew up in Little Rock, Arkansas, where his father was a successful merchant and cotton buyer. Jim, a fourth child and third son, graduated from Princeton in 1921, then, having decided he'd be happier in the tiny and uncertain aircraft industry than as a research physicist, went on to Massachusetts Institute of Technology for an M.S. degree in aeronautical engineering—M.I.T. being the only school in the U.S. offering such a degree at the

time. In 1923, his work at M.I.T. completed, McDonnell entered the Air Service and learned to fly at Brooks and Kelly Fields. Released from active duty the following year, as a second lieutenant in the Army Air Service Reserve Corps, Jim spent several months seeking a job in an industry that supported no more than 200 aircraft engineers (total aircraft industry employment in 1924 was about 2,000), and at last counted himself lucky to be hired, at $108 per month, by the Huff-Daland Company of Ogdensburg, N.Y.* He stayed with Huff-Daland but a short time, however, moving on to Consolidated Aircraft Company in Buffalo, which had been organized by Major Reuben H. Fleet in the spring of 1923 from the bankrupt Gallaudet Engineering Company.

Still looking for wider experience (and a better job), Jim left Consolidated in 1925 to work for Bill Stout at Dearborn, Michigan, whose Stout Metal Airplane Company was at first backed, then bought, by Henry Ford. There, Jim helped with the design of

---

* Huff-Daland Airplanes, Inc., became Keystone Aircraft Corp. in March, 1927, when E. N. Gott, former president of Boeing Airplane Company, took over from Thomas Huff and moved the factory to Bristol, Penna. Keystone merged with Loening Aeronautical Engineering Corp. in 1929, and Keystone-Loening became a subsidiary of Curtiss-Wright soon after. Loening's general manager was LeRoy Grumman, later to found Grumman Aircraft Engineering Corp. An early (1921) Huff-Daland subsidiary, Huff-Dusters, Inc. of Monroe, La., was headed by pioneer duster-pilot C. E. Woolman, and this outfit survived independently throughout the twenties to eventually evolve into Delta Air Lines.

First McDonnell design was the Hamilton Metalplane of 1926, which seated 4 in enclosed cabin while pilot flew from open cockpit. Engine was Wright J-5 *Whirlwind*. Pilot Randy Page (above with trophy), placed second behind Eddie Stinson in the Ford Air Tour of 1927. Company founder Tom Hamilton (foreground), later merged with Bill Boeing's and Fred Rentschler's United Aircraft Corporation following success of Hamilton's new steel propeller. (Photo courtesy Charles W. Meyers Collection)

the first Ford Trimotor, Model 3-AT—which he, and everyone else involved, would surely like to forget, because this forerunner of the classic *Tin Goose* was a monstrosity and a failure. But McDonnell did gain practical experience working with all-metal airframes at Ford—the first produced in America—and when, in 1926, he was offered a job as chief engineer of the Hamilton Aero Manufacturing Company in Milwaukee, he quit Ford and joined the Wisconsin firm. Hamilton Aero was making wooden propellers and metal flying-boat hulls, and wanted Jim to design

an airplane to be constructed entirely of the new duraluminum alloy used in the Ford-Stout planes. The result was the Hamilton Metalplane, the first of a series of cantilever-winged, single-engined cabin monoplanes that saw service chiefly with newly formed Northwest Airways.

Jim McDonnell remained with Hamilton until 1930. Meanwhile, the success of Hamilton's new steel propeller insured that this comparatively small manufacturer would be gobbled up by one of the big holding companies that were founded to acquire promising aviation properties during the 1927-1929 aviation boom. That is exactly what happened. Bill Boeing and Fred Rentschler's United Aircraft and Transport Corporation got there first, or at least with the best deal. Therefore, late in 1928, Hamilton, along with Chance Vought, Sikorsky, Stearman and Standard Steel Propeller, was added to Rentschler's Pratt & Whitney and Boeing's Boeing Air Transport (which emerged as United Air Lines) to make up the powerful United Aircraft complex. After merging with United, Hamilton Metalplane was expected to move to Wichita and combine with Stearman; but this plan was dropped when the Great Depression struck in October, 1929, and the av-boom turned to av-bust overnight.

But the optimistic little Scotsman from Arkansas had been looking to wider horizons even before Hamilton plane production began to sag. Jim McDonnell had dreamed up a two-place sport plane design that he felt would be the safest airplane in the market. Its wing slots and flap arrangement would allow extremely short take-offs and landings at low speed, yet the craft would match the cruising speed of any with comparable horsepower. What he envisioned was, of course, an STOL—about thirty years before the term was coined. He recruited a pair of fellow engineers as partners in the venture, and went to work on the *Doodlebug,* intending to enter it in the $100,000 Guggenheim Safe Aircraft Competition scheduled for judging in November, 1929.

Second airplane designed by Jim McDonnell was the *Doodlebug,* intended for competition in the 1929 Guggenheim Safe Aircraft Contest. A 110-mph STOL with wing slots and long-span flaps, the *Doodlebug* lost its chance at the contest's $100,000 first prize when a connecting rod failed in its Warner *Scarab* engine. (Photo courtesy McDonnell Douglas Corporation)

McDonnell XP-67 was designed as a "bomber de-stroyer" during WW-II and first flown on January 6, 1944. Fitted with two counter-rotating Continental engines of 1,060-hp each and armed with six 37mm cannon, this 405-mph single-seater had a range of 2,380 miles and a gross weight of 20,000 lbs. It was not put into production and only two were built. (Photo courtesy McDonnell Douglas Corporation)

Unfortunately, the *Doodlebug* (honest; that's what Jim called it) was denied a chance at the Guggenheim prize money when a connecting rod failed in its Warner *Scarab* engine; but the plane did perform as advertised—often landing with a roll-out of less than 50 feet—in subsequent flights which McDonnell made about the country in search of financial backing for its production. However, as the Depression deepened, risk capital had become almost non-existant; so Jim sold his *Doodlebug* prototype to the National Advisory Committee for Aeronautics

(NACA), and accepted an engineering and test pilot's job recently vacated by Charles Meyers at Great Lakes Aircraft Corporation in Cleveland.

Great Lakes, however, was doomed to go down with many other plane makers during the lean and hungry years. Its excellent little 2T-1A Sport/Trainer, designed by Charles Meyers and Cliff Leisy, may have kept the company afloat had it not been for Great Lakes' affiliation with the American Cirrus Engine Company which dictated that the 2T-1A be penalized with a Cirrus engine installation; but that unhappy fact, plus the failure of Great Lakes' amphibian (not a McDonnell design), at last closed the Great Lakes factory.

By that time, Jim McDonnell was fairly nimble in the art of job-hopping, and his *Doodlebug,* though never marketed, had impressed the aviation community; so the Glenn Martin Company—the great incubator of design talent from which matriculated men like Donald Douglas and Lawrence Bell—found a place for Jim in its Baltimore plant. McDonnell stayed with Martin through 1938, during which time he acquired a wife—Mary Elizabeth Finney of Baltimore—two sons, the title of chief engineer of Martin's landplane division and a growing determination to form his own aircraft company. He talked over the "big gamble" with his wife, then resigned from Martin just before Christmas, 1938, and set out in search of capital to start the McDonnell Aircraft Corporation.

It required six months to scrape together $165,000 in stock sales from family, friends, and business acquaintances. With this money—partly in cash, partly in pledges—plus Jim's usual optimism, one typewriter and a secondhand filing cabinet, McDonnell Aircraft opened for business on July 6, 1939, on the rented second floor of a small building adjacent to the Lambert-St. Louis (Missouri) Municipal Airport. Actual operations began in September, when the engineering department was activated with 15 engineers working under McDonnell Vice-President Ivan H. Driggs (whose own company, in Lansing, Michigan, had succumbed during the Depression while offering the Driggs *Dart*).

The McDonnell Company's first annual report, dated Oct. 25, 1940, revealed that the company had done $3,000 worth of business during its first year and suffered a net loss of $3,892.17. That report also contains a terse summary, in Jim's own sparing prose, telling of that difficult year; but also of undiminished faith, and the fresh promise that justified that faith: "During the period of actual operations from September 15, 1939, to October 3, 1940, the Army held only one airplane paper competition, which we entered and obtained a cash award of $3,000. We have presented eleven other military designs to the U.S. Army, as a result of which we now have a small engineering contract on one of these designs.

"During the same period, the Navy held no airplane paper competitions. Our company has presented four designs to the Navy, and we have been invited to compete in a paper competition which is to start shortly.

"On July 23, 1940, our company moved into a factory of 36,000 square feet at Lambert-St. Louis Municipal Airport, and during the past three months we have been suitably equipping this plant with machinery.

"During the past month, 555 units of stock, each unit consisting of 1 share of preferred and 10 shares of common, have been sold at $120 per unit, thus completing the sale of 2,777 units of the 3,000 units registered with the Securities & Exchange Commission on August 30, 1939.

"As of October 25, 1940, personnel totals 57. Undelivered orders on hand total approximately $3,111,000, consisting of an engineering contract with the United States Government, and sub-contracts with Vultee Aircraft, Inc., the Boeing Aircraft Company, Douglas Aircraft Company and the Lockheed Aircraft Corporation."

So, after a year of uncertainty, the company at last possessed significant contracts, undoubtedly fostered by the threat of war. And though Jim McDonnell has never publicly said so, it seems probable that Hitler's aggressions in Europe influenced his decision to organize his company at that time. Just three months before Jim resigned from Martin, President Roosevelt had called a conference, attended by his secretaries of war and Navy, chief of staff and Gen. Hap Arnold, from which was issued the announcement that America must seek an annual production goal of 10,000 airplanes (this took place just 48 hours before Chamberlain's capitulation to Hitler at Munich). At that time (Sept. 1938), U.S. aircraft factories employed a total of 35,000 workers. A year later—when McDonnell's "undelivered orders" suddenly soared to more than $3 million, from almost nothing—total industry employment had leaped to 150,000. Clearly, McDonnell's timing was perfect.

For security reasons, that first annual report did not say so, but the "engineering contract with the United States Government" (amounting to $20,000), was for research in the application of jet propulsion to fighter aircraft; and that modest program led to a multi-million dollar contract, in 1943, to develop a jet fighter for the Navy, the McDonnell FH-1 *Phantom*. This craft was the first combat jet to operate from a U.S. carrier, and 60 were purchased by the Navy during the mid-forties.

Throughout WW-II, however, McDonnell was

Navy's first jet fighter, the FH-1 *Phantom I,* was developed concurrently with the Air Force's Bell P-59, Both were grossly underpowered with the first generation of U.S. jet engines (copied from the British Whittle jet). The FH-1 made its initial flight in October, 1944. Top speed was about 500 mph. Lt. Cmdr. James Davidson, flying an FH-1, made first U.S. carrier landing in a jet on July 21, 1946, when he touched down on the deck of the *Franklin Roosevelt.* Navy bought 60 FH-1's. (Photo courtesy McDonnell Douglas Corporation)

forced by the urgency of the situation to concentrate upon airframe components for war-plane designs of the big companies. Fifty-two hundred employees turned out 7,000,000 pounds of sub-assemblies; but no McDonnell-designed airplanes were made during those frantic war years—except a prototype "bomber destroyer," the XP-67, which, in the end, the Army Air Force decided it didn't need.

But the circumstances of war did work to McDonnell's ultimate advantage. Its wartime sub-contracts placed the company on a sound financial footing, and its early lead in jet fighter development insured a running start for production of the new generation of military aircraft. As soon as production started on the FH-1 *Phantom* in 1946, engineering work began on Jim's next spook, the F2H *Banshee.* It, too, was successful, and was ordered into production in May, 1947. *Banshees,* in three principal versions— day fighter, night fighter, and photo-reconnaissance— were operational in time to serve with the Navy and

James S. McDonnell with his Robert J. Collier Trophy which he received in 1966 for "significant achievement in aeronautics"—development of the F-4 *Phantom II* and the *Gemini* spacecraft. McDonnell began his career in the aerospace industry in 1924 when he took a job as engineer with the Huff-Daland Airplane Company after learning to fly at Kelly Field as an Air Service cadet. He founded the McDonnell Aircraft Company in 1939. (Photo courtesy McDonnell Douglas Corporation)

Marines during the Korean War. A total of 895 were built.

Concurrent with *Banshee* development, McDonnell engineers worked on the XF-88, a long-range penetration fighter for the Air Force. This plane eventually became the 1,200-mph F-101 *Voodoo*, which went operational in 1957. Among 807 *Voodoos* delivered, were the RF-101 photo-recon versions which made repeated low-level forays over missile sites to bring back solid evidence of the Soviet missile build-up in the 1962 Cuba crisis. In 1968, most *Voodoos* remaining in service were placed in storage by the Air Force.

Following the *Voodoo* was the F3H *Demon* for the Navy, an all-weather fighter and the first designed for all-missile armament in place of guns. The last of 519 *Demons* was delivered in November, 1959, and, late in 1968, many were still on duty with the Fleet.

But it has been the fabulous *Phantom II* that earned the McDonnell team a place in history beside the makers of the P-51 *Mustang* and F6F *Hellcat* of another time—and another war. Indeed, the F-4 series *Phantom II* of the late sixties could be called a composite *Mustang/Hellcat/Corsair/Lightning/Thunderbolt* of its day; because this 1,600-mph multi-mission craft, used by the Navy, Marines, Air Force (and some of our allies) performs all of the classical fighter and fighter-bomber tasks required of tactical aircraft. It first flew in May, 1958. Ten years later it was still in production (the first thousand were delivered by mid-1965), and at least 10 models were in service with varying armament, different engines and a variety of avionics packages. Proven in combat over Vietnam, the F-4 *Phantom II* was America's first-line interceptor as the sixties drew to a close.

In the meantime, McDonnell had expanded into space research and, early in 1959, was selected by NASA as prime contractor for Mercury, the Free World's first manned orbital spacecraft. A contract for Gemini command modules, the two-man spacecraft, followed in April, 1963, and the near-perfect performances of these vehicles enhanced the company's reputation in a field that has a low tolerance for error.

Also during this period, McDonnell established three divisional companies: McDonnell Aircraft Company of St. Louis, McDonnell Astronautics at Titusville, Florida, and McDonnell Automation Center of Houston, Denver and Columbia, Missouri. In addition, the parent company acquired a number of electronics and other aerospace-related manufacturers through a series of stock-swap deals which made McDonnell, by 1966, one of the largest aerospace companies in the world. But even that wasn't enough for the mild but canny little Scot given to calling his airplanes by scary names. Suppose, just suppose, he should merge the sprawling McDonnell complex with *another* giant; a thoroughly sound company, of course, but perhaps one that needed more operating capital and a broader market base. Say, for instance, Douglas Aircraft Company. Well, why not? Douglas was big in the civil air transport field, a market McDonnell had never cracked, except for the building of sub-assemblies.

As it happened, Donald Douglas was more than a little bit interested. After nearly half-a-century building airplanes, his company was short of money—due to a bad guess concerning the proximity of the jet

McDonnell F-101 *Voodoo* was developed from a 1948 prototype, the XF-88. Produced in long-range, fighter and photo-recon versions for the Strategic, Tactical and Air Defense Commands of the Air Force, the 1,200-mph *Voodoo* served until mid-1968 when most were moth-balled. A total of 807 were built. Parachute attached to rear of fuselage is deployed to act as a brake during landing roll-outs. (Photo courtesy McDonnell Douglas Corporation)

revolution and its size—and would certainly welcome back some of its former military business.

Donald Wills Douglas, the son of a Brooklyn bank cashier, resigned from the Naval Academy in 1911 after two years as a midshipman to enter M.I.T. and earn a B.S. degree in aeronautics. Graduating in 1914, he remained at the school for a year as an assistant instructor, then was hired as chief engineer by Glenn Martin whose factory was then in Los Angeles. He left Martin in November, 1916, to work for the Aviation Section of the Signal Corps in Washington, D.C., but after a few months' frustration in that seemingly directionless wonderland—where America's

military air effort was dominated by the automobile industry—Douglas returned to Martin (by then the Wright-Martin Company) where he designed the prototype of the Martin MB-1 bomber. He quit Martin in 1920, and, with $600 capital, rented office space in the back of a Santa Monica barbershop and went in business for himself. He was twenty-eight years old, with a wife and son to support.

Douglas' first order for an airplane came from a wealthy West Coast sportsman, David R. Davis, who wanted to be the first to fly non-stop across the U.S. Since Davis had to finance Douglas during construction of this machine, the firm was known as "Davis-

The McDonnell XF-85 *Goblin* was conceived as a "parasite" fighter to operate from the bomb bay of the B-36 intercontinental bomber and to protect the B-36 from enemy fighters. The *Goblin* appeared in 1948 but was never completely developed because the success of smaller, faster jet bombers—particularly the B-47—signalled the end of the B-36 era. (Photo courtesy McDonnell Douglas Corporation)

Preliminary design work on the 1,600-mph F-4 *Phantom II* began in 1953; the prototype first flew in May, 1958, and early models established a number of world records for speed and climbing ability. This two-place air-superiority and attack craft proved so versatile it was, during the 60s, adopted by the Air Force as its first-line fighter-interceptor, as well as by the Navy and Marines who had originally fostered its development. Unique feature of *Phantom II* is a pair of automatic intake-air deflectors that control volume of air entering engines' air scoops for maximum power efficiency at all altitudes and speeds. (Photo courtesy McDonnell Douglas Corporation)

Douglas O-38 Army observation plane, powered with P&W R-1690 *(Hornet)* engine of 525-hp, had top speed of 149 mph. Army bought 181 of this model between 1930 and 1934. Such craft were Douglas' bread-and-butter products until introduction of the DC-3 series. (Photo courtesy Boardman C. Reed)

Douglas Airplane Company." Its product, the Davis-Douglas *Cloudster,* built on the second floor of a planing mill, was a hefty biplane of 55-foot wingspan powered with a WW-I 400-hp Liberty engine. This plane had a gross weight of 9,500 pounds and an empty weight of about 4,500 pounds, making it the first airplane in history capable of lifting a load greater than its own weight.

But the Liberty engine—the only powerplant available of sufficient horsepower—was not exactly the most reliable mill ever built, and the *Cloudster* was forced down at El Paso with a stripped timing gear to spoil Davis' first transcontinental attempt. He returned the plane to March Field for a second try; but before he and pilot Eric Springer could take off again, Army Lts. Oakley Kelly and John Macready spanned the nation non-stop (May 2-3, 1923) from the opposite direction in a Fokker T-2—also Liberty-powered. The *Cloudster,* modified as a passenger and freight hauler by Claude Ryan, eventually ended up wrecked on a remote Mexican beach with a load of beer aboard.

The *Cloudster* did, however, serve as the basis for the Douglas DT Model Navy torpedo plane. The Navy bought more than 50 DT's between 1921 and

1924, and Douglas financed production of the initial batch by getting ten Los Angeles businessmen to co-sign his note at the bank for $15,000.

By 1925, Douglas had earned an excellent reputation, greatly aided by the first round-the-world flight, in 1924, completed by four Army pilots in a pair of Douglas *World Cruisers.* The *Cruisers* were specially built craft, remarkably similar to the original *Cloudster.* Douglas also had a factory by that time (an abandoned movie studio) at the eastern edge of Santa Monica on Wilshire Boulevard, a payroll of 112, and an order for six M-2 mailplanes from Western Air Express. Then, during the next four years, he delivered 260 observation planes to the Army Air Corps and sold 78 commercial aircraft, including 40 M-3 and M-4 mailplanes to the Post Office Department, Transcontinental & Western Air Lines (now Trans World Air Lines), and National Air Transport (later merged into United Air Lines). In 1930, the company was still small, but reasonably sound despite the Depression that began late the previous year, because Douglas had never depended upon that segment of aviation hardest hit by the money shortage, the private civilian buyer. Donald Douglas had been a "big airplane" man from the

The one, the only, the fabulous *Gooney Bird;* the Douglas DC-3. She was the last word in speed and comfort and reliability when she entered airline service in 1935. Late in life, she seemed slow and noisy, and a big electric fan over each seat, while quaint, was no substitute for air conditioning—but she'd still get you there. Late in 1968, more than 3,000 remained in service about the world.

start. And that simple fact conspired with circumstances to produce the single most significant airplane design of aviation's first 50 years; the venerable Douglas DC-3.

It's unlikely that there'll ever be another like her. Surely, no other single airplane can ever so markedly affect the affairs of Mankind. She had a unique character and a mind of her own. The pilots are legion who'll swear that she often ignored the laws of aerodynamics. She had many names. To the British she was the *Dakota;* to the U.S. Navy, R4D. Her official Air Force designations were C-47, C-49 and C-53. She was also the *Skytrain, Gooney Bird, Magic Dragon,* and *Spooky.* She had but one gait, and additional streamlining or more powerful engines had

little effect on her speed. Her wingtips flapped and her cockpit leaked and she even seemed to show favoritism, since pilots' reports on her flying habits often disagreed. But the DC-3 had in extreme measure that most endearing of all traits: she'd get you there. Once, during WW-II, a pilot decided to ditch in the ocean because his C-47 was so badly shot-up he believed it impossible to get back to base. The airplane struck the water with a mighty splash and bounced back into the air. The dazed pilot automatically applied power again, sat there for a few seconds, decided she was going to insist upon flying, so, with bent propellers added to the plane's other damage, he flew her home. Designed for 21 passengers in civilian use, a C-47 once carried 74 refugees out of Burma; and when the starboard wing of a China National Airways DC-3 was damaged beyond repair by strafing Japanese fighters, the much shorter wing panel from a DC-2 was attached to the right-hand side and the lopsided plane flown to safety. It was the only DC-2½ ever reported. Such stories could go on and on. Almost 11,000 of these craft were built (1935–1944 inclusive), and an estimated 3,300 were still flying in 1968. At one time, the DC-3 carried 95 per cent of all commercial air traffic; but in mid-1968 those remaining in scheduled U.S. airline service were all slated for retirement by year's end. Ozark, Trans-

Texas, North Central, and Frontier were the last to give up their *Gooney Birds*. North Central's #N21728 was perhaps the most "experienced" DC-3 when it was at last replaced, for it had almost 52,000 hours in the air and had flown more than 11 million miles. It had worn out 136 engines and 550 tires during its thirty-year career. As this is written, it is still flying as an executive plane. But it would be rash to predict that no other airplane will ever equal Seven-Two-Eight's record as long as three thousand other *Gooneys* are still scattered about the world.

In the beginning, the DC-3 owed its birth to a

The Douglas DC-4 was originally designed to United Air Lines' specifications and first flown in June, 1938. It seated 62 passengers and was powered with four P&W R-2000 engines of 1,450-hp each which gave it a cruise of 190 mph. Prototype DC-4 was triple-tailed like the *Constellation*. Pan Am owned a total of 76 DC-4's, the first of which was acquired in 1945. (Photo courtesy Pan American World Airways)

combination of circumstances. First, the McNary-Watres Act of 1930, fostered by Postmaster General Walter F. Brown, included the provision that air carriers' mail subsidies would be computed according to the payload space available in their airliners. This was frankly intended as a means to get larger, more efficient planes into service, because Congress had no intention of forever underwriting the airlines with unrealistic air mail subsidies. The airliners then in service—mostly 10 or 12-place trimotors—simply could not operate at a profit on passenger fares alone. Next, when famed Notre Dame football coach Knute Rockne died (March 31, 1931) in the crash of a wooden-winged Fokker Trimotor airliner, the resultant public furor shook the infant airline industry and increased pressure for an airline equipment revolution. These things prompted design of the first "modern" airliner, the Boeing 247. And it was the

Douglas AD-6 *Skyraider* attack craft (pictured) was from a batch of 713 delivered to Navy in 1953. The AD series began in 1946 with the AD-1, and 28 versions totalling 3,180 units were ultimately built. Last ones were AD-7's which entered Navy service in 1956. Engine was the Wright R-3350-24 and -26. A number of AD's were swapped to the Air Force for service in Vietnam and designated A-1E's. Though comparatively slow at 220 mph, the A-1E *Skyraiders* proved excellent close-support craft and carried an awesome ordnance load. (Photo courtesy McDonnell Douglas Corporation)

The Douglas A-4E carrier-based attack bomber was first flown in June 1954, and improved versions—A-4E and A-4F—remained in Navy service and production continued into the late 60s. Range is about 2,000 miles in the 600 to 700-mph regime; engine the P&W J-52P-8A. Wingspan is 27 ft. 6 in.; length 42 ft. 10 in. Empty weight 9,300 lbs., and loaded weight 24,500 lbs. (Photo courtesy McDonnell Douglas Corporation)

threat of the 247—a 180-mph all-metal, low-winged twin-engined craft—planned for service on Boeing's affiliate, United Air Lines, that sent TWA's Jack Frye into the marketplace searching for a competitive machine.

This looked like opportunity to Donald Douglas—provided he was willing to bet everything he had on it. He had never built an airliner; he knew development costs would be high and that his offering would have to be good enough to find buyers in sufficient number to pay-off those development costs. However,

both American and Eastern would also be in the market for better equipment, and that, plus the fact that two of the most brilliant engineers in the business—Dutch Kindelberger and Jack Northrop—were then under his roof, decided Douglas to go for broke.

Forty-eight days later, on September 20, 1932, TWA bought the Douglas design. It was called the DC-1. It first flew July 1, 1933, and it was the prototype for 191 DC-2's and the thousands of DC-3's that came after.

The short and medium-range DC-9-10 made its first flight Feb. 25, 1965, and entered scheduled airline service with Delta that same year. The Dash Ten was expanded into the DC-9-30, which is 15 feet longer and increases passenger capacity from 70 to 115, while the DC-9-40 ups this to 125 passengers. Cruising speed is 557 mph for the -10 and 590 mph for the -40. Also planned is a "mini" version of the DC-9 with 50-60 seats. "Short-haul" means simply that these craft can operate profitably on routes of a few hundred miles in length, whereas the larger jets cannot. (Photo courtesy McDonnell Douglas Corporation)

Today, we'd probably call the DC-2 and -3 "stretched versions" of the DC-1 (instead of "DC-3," it'd likely be called "DC-1-21") because the -2 and -3 were not new designs, but logical improvements of the original—bigger engines, greater wingspans and a fuselage one silly millimeter longer.

The DC-3's maiden flight came on December 17, 1935. Its total development cost was about $300,000 and it sold for $110,000 (development costs of the DC-8 jetliner were about $250 million; it sells for $6 to $8 million, depending upon model). Approximately 450 DC-3's were built as airliners prior to WW-II; something over 10,000 were delivered to the military during the war, and many of those—no one knows just how many—were bought as surplus at war's end and converted for airline and other civil duties.

The last few years before that war saw commercial air travel on the increase at the rate of about 20 per cent per year; and the three transcontinental lines

The McDonnell Douglas DC-10 trijet (which had not flown at this writing) is a 250–300 passenger transport designed to operate from short-runway airports like LaGuardia as well as larger terminals. The DC-10 has a cruising speed of 600 mph and is planned for routes up to 3,000 miles in length. It is 179 ft. 8 in. long; wingspan is 155 ft. 4 in. Its height is 57 ft. 3 in., and gross weight 386,500 lbs. (Photo courtesy McDonnell Douglas Corporation)

—TWA, United and American—began thinking of bigger airplanes. This time, it was William Patterson of United who came to Douglas for a new design. Following the Air Mail Act of 1934, all airlines had been divorced from manufacturing affiliates, and United no longer had to buy Boeing airplanes. The Douglas DC-4 emerged from this 1938 conference, and forty DC-4's were ordered by domestic airlines for delivery in 1942. But war came in the meantime and the armed forces commandeered these craft and added their own orders for a total of 1,162. The

DC-4 became the C-54 in the Air Force; the R5D in the Navy. After the war, this plane logically evolved into the DC-6 and DC-7, just as the DC-3 grew from the DC-1.

Douglas' wartime sales peak was reached in 1944 when it delivered more than a billion dollars' worth of aircraft to the fighting forces. Peak employment was 160,000 in six factories. Douglas-designed combat planes were the SBD *Dauntless* and the A-20 *Havoc*. The *Havoc* eventually developed into the A-26 and B-26 *Invader*. In all, Douglas built 29,385 aircraft during War Two, roughly 16% of the total American effort.

When the fighting stopped, Douglas, like all other airframe makers, was faced with wholesale cancellation of its military contracts; but, unlike the others, Douglas had the *Gooney Bird's* reputation going for the company, and the airlines badly needed new equipment—say, a pressurized version of the DC-4. In other words, a four-engined *Gooney Bird* with all the trimmings.

It proved a good market. Millions of first-time air travellers had been forced to fly by the exigencies of war, and even under those adverse conditions their fears of flying had been dispelled. Commercial air travel really grew up between 1946 and 1956. And 1,041 Douglas DC-6's and DC-7's left the production lines to equip a major portion of that new civil air fleet. At the same time, Douglas put a pair of military planes in the air that resulted in more black ink in company ledgers. These were the C-124 *Globemaster,* a champion cargo hauler procured by the Air Force to the tune of 450 units, and the AD series of Navy attack planes which went through 28 versions for an ultimate production run of 3,180 aircraft.

Also introduced, in June, 1954, was the jet-powered A-4 Navy attack (light bomber) which was due a long service life, and more than 1,500 A-4 *Skyhawks* were delivered by the end of 1966. The

Donald Douglas, Sr., (center) makes a point to Port of New York Authority's Herb Fisher. At left is Jackson R. McGowen, an Alabama native and engineer who joined Douglas in 1939 and worked up to boss of the Douglas Aircraft Division. (Photo courtesy Port of New York Authority)

twin-engined A-3D *Skywarrior* was produced between 1953 and 1959 as the Navy's heaviest carrier-borne strike craft, and the Air Force liked it so well a substantial number (294) were ordered as the Air Force B-66 *Destroyer*.

So, Douglas was in good financial condition through the early fifties. However, the transition to jet transports was painful; in fact, almost fatal. To begin with, Donald Douglas (and son Don Douglas, Jr., who by this time had advanced to share management responsibility with his father) failed to perceive the nearness of the jet revolution in airline travel and allowed Boeing to beat Douglas into the market with the Boeing 707. Boeing had a further advantage in that much of the 707's development cost was absorbed by the very similar and prior KC-135 jet tanker for the Air Force. The first Boeing 707 entered airline service with Pan Am in October, 1958; and though Douglas managed to follow with the first DC-8 delivery, to United Air Lines, in June, 1959, Boeing transports outsold Douglas DC-8's two to one during the next five years (General Dynamics, meanwhile, took an even worse licking with their jet transports, the Convair 880 and 990).

Douglas was $53 million in the red for 1959 and 1960. This was partly owed to the slow write-off of the DC-8's $250 million development costs, and partly due to a marked decline in military orders. During the early sixties, things indeed looked dark for the company. Then, in 1963, the Douglas homestead in California was saved when the decision was made to go ahead with a short-haul jet transport. This was the DC-9, an airplane that may well prove to be the *Gooney Bird* of the Jet Age. It joined the airlines late in 1965, and 200 were delivered during the next two years while a seemingly-endless back-log piled up.

Of course, Boeing determinedly if belatedly reacted with a short-haul jet of its own—the 737—to challenge the DC-9 (and the British BAC-111, which was really first in the field); but it appeared that the "Dash Nine" would dominate the big short-haul

passenger market. And the DC-9 kept Douglas optimistic until DC-8 development costs were at last written-off and stretched versions of the DC-8 began picking up some sales. That point was reached early in 1966, and the 250-passenger DC-8-61 and -62, selling for $6 to $8 million, began earning upwards of $900,000 on each unit sold.

Meanwhile, on June 17, 1966, when the nation's largest brokerage, Merrill, Lynch, Pierce, Fenner & Smith, Inc., was arranging public sale of $75 million in new Douglas securities, the brokers allegedly found that Douglas' profits' prospects were again turning downward after 5 months of good earnings. According to the Securities and Exchange Commission (SEC), who tries to police Wall Street, Merrill Lynch, etc., withheld this discovery from all but 15 favored clients, and Douglas stock remained at a healthy $90 per share while these favored ones dumped their stock. Then, on June 24, Douglas itself announced that its profit outlook for 1966 was less than encouraging and its stock fell to $61.75 per share. Douglas ended 1966 with a net loss of $27,600,000. Therefore, the SEC cracked down on the brokerage firm charging fraud and, late in November, 1968, Merrill Lynch and company "negotiated its penalty" with the U.S. Government while claiming innocence.

Nevertheless, the Douglas company was still a giant of the aerospace industry and its potential still tremendous. It was a valuable property, with a proud name and an unsurpassed reputation for building honest airplanes. Therefore, shortly after Jim McDonnell and Donald Douglas got together, the shareholders of Douglas and the shareholders of McDonnell voted to henceforth love, honor and share one another's dividends. The two were officially united April 28, 1967, and the resulting McDonnell Douglas Corporation became the 28th largest industrial firm and the second largest aerospace company in the nation. Jim McDonnell, as board chairman and chief executive officer of the combined complex, would surely tell you that a fellow can do a lot with a drawing board and a little black magic.

16. Straight Up and Away

When you're in a struggle against death, the sounds WHOOP, WHOOP, WHOOP, and above the sight of a funny looking box-like machine, may suddenly make you a believer. This noisy, clumsy-looking creation, born only in the early forties and already a legend, has made believers out of many thousands.

You don't have to be a pilot in a combat zone. The "Guardian Angels" are there, over water, jungle, over fires and sinking ships, over flood waters and mud slides. These machines, friends to every man (until a brush-fire war in Vietnam caught up with them), give back life. Call them and they'll save; fight them and they'll kill. A paradox, this whirlybird, this square-in-the air called a helicopter. But it wasn't always so.

The dreams of rotary wing aircraft date back centuries. Leonardo Da Vinci envisioned whirling wings and recorded his ideas in drawings as early as the 15th century. Experiments with this type of flight showed up in the 16th, 18th, and 19th centuries.

Even the Wright brothers, when they pondered flight, toyed with a rotary wing gadget. It took a Frenchman, Louis Breguet, to design the first helicopter* capable of lifting itself and a pilot. The

Breguet first flew on September 27, 1907 with four 4-bladed biplane rotors. Nearly uncontrollable, even on tethered flights, this machine didn't last long.

Only a month after Breguet, November 13, near Lisieus, France, Paul Cornu took off in his helicopter and ascended to about 1 foot above the ground. His 2-rotor machine, powered by a 24HP Antoinette, eventually reached 5 feet of altitude and a speed of 6 MPH to become one of the first successful mounted copters let loose in free flight.

The very next year, nineteen-year old Igor Sikorsky constructed a helicopter in his native Russia; however, he ran into the stone wall that plagued so many of the early flyers—no suitable engine—and gave up that project for 30 long years.

During World War I, about 1915, some military minds turned to a replacement for observation balloons which had proven dangerous due to the hydrogen gas. They needed some device to replace this eye-in-the-sky. The result was the Petroczy-Karman helicopter, a monster with two 19-foot counterrotating propellers located below the 2-man cockpit. This was a created device, all right, that would go up and down, but under no circumstances would it move forward! One flight, so it's reported, reached an altitude of 100 feet, but the machine crashed the next time up and the project came to a crumbled halt.

The Army Air Service still had the idea in mind after the armistice. The leading rotary wing figure in

---

* The word "helicopter" comes from the Greek *helix* for spiral and *pteron,* wing.

the United States was Dr. George de Bothezat, and, in 1921, he received an Army contract to build a helicopter. Two years later, his 2 ton, 4-rotor ship was test flown at McCook Field. Flights continued for several months before the project was abandoned; simply, the machine could not do any kind of a job for the Army.

Meantime, back across the Atlantic, a young Spanish aristocrat became obsessed with stall character-istics of airplanes. His first aerial venture, a 3-engine bomber built in 1919 for the Spanish Army, had crashed out of a stall. This Spaniard, Juan de la Cierva, conceived a craft which could be flown slowly, safely. On January 9, 1923, he and his 4th model rotary wing craft flew a 3 mile circuit at an altitude of nearly 1000 feet for the world's first successful autogyro. This machine, converted from a LeRhone powered World War I Hanriot Scout biplane, retained only 1 wing

Cierva Autogiro, 1929 Cleveland Air Races, shows the basic configuration of a normal airplane fuselage, engine, and propeller. The limited wings do have airplane control surfaces; Cierva's early machines re-tained rudder controls. The craft received support from the rotating vanes instead of full wings. These rotor blades were flexible and unrestrained and auto-gyros had no translational speed of minimum support. The man facing the camera, in dark suit, is Señor Juan de la Cierva. He's talking with the famous Ger-man lady pilot Thea Rasche. (Photo courtesy Charles Meyers)

along with its aileron for roll control. This C-4 had a free spinning rotor on top of an otherwise conventional aircraft fuselage.

Senor Don Juan found, in his first models, that autogyros had a nasty habit of turning over. To gain control of the machine as it reached velocity for take-off, he developed hinged rotor blades which freely pivoted at the inboard end.

By 1925, these machines, called by de la Cierva "Autogiros,"* because they could claim freedom from fatalities (unlike airplanes of the day) were hailed as much more creditable than they actually were.

By 1926, the Spaniard's later models connected rotors, by means of a shaft and clutch, to the engine. This started the rotors spinning and the clutch disengaged when the blades reached a velocity of 140 RPMs. The blades, then, continued windmilling due to the forward motion of the craft.

These machines could take off and land in a short distance; they could fly at slow speeds and maneuver quickly. If the conventional engine failed, which it was prone to do in the 20s, the rotor blades permitted a safe descent. Unfortunately, the standard aircraft controls which were used in autogyros still lost all use when the craft slowed below stall speed. So, the whirling rotors slowed the downward plunge of the machine to a safe velocity, yet the pilot had no directional control.

The Cierva Autogiro Co., Ltd., was established on March 24, 1926, in Aldwych, London. Experiments continued and production started on the C-8. This Cierva was built on an Avro 504N and had 2 sets of 4-bladed rotors which could be trimmed laterally. Two auxiliary planes, with ailerons at their tips, were attached to the bottom longerons of the fuselage. This model became the American prototype when Harold Pitcairn† became fascinated with the design.

In 1929, Pitcairn formed the Pitcairn-Cierva Autogiro Company and held all American rights to the Cierva patents. This company, in turn, licensed Pitcairn Aircraft, DBA Autogiro Co. of America, Kellett Autogiro Corp., Buhl Aircraft Co., and F. W. Steere.

Steere evidently did no manufacturing. Buhl built a pusher type Autogiro which, under the capable hands of Jimmy Johnson, flew in December, 1931, but it was never certificated.

The first Autogiro granted an Approved Type Certificate by the CAA (now FAA) was the Pitcairn PCA-2 with a Wright J-6-9 engine and a ground adjustable Hamilton Standard prop. About 28 of these were sold along with a few variants, one with a P & W, Jr. of 300 HP and another with 400HP.

In 1931, 46 Autogiros were sold and 2 other Pitcairns, the PA-18 and PA-19, were licensed. The latter was a 5-place cabin type designed by Bob Noorduyn, also responsible for the design of the famous Noorduyn *Norseman*.

The U.S. Navy accepted delivery of a Pitcairn XOP on June 1, 1931, the first military autogyro. Lt. A. M. Pride landed this craft with much fanfare aboard the USS *Langley;* then, the same machine was turned over to the Marines. They took it, in 1932, to Nicaragua and into active combat operations. But, not often since the Autogiro could only lift 50 pounds more than the weight of the pilot and fuel. As a combat aircraft, it lacked.

Between 1931 and 1935, the small fixed wings of the early models disappeared and control effectiveness came through tilting the rotor head. In the years 1935 and 1936, the Air Corps took delivery of 2 Kellett YG-14s and 1 Pitcairn YG-2, but all 3 were cracked up too soon for evaluations.

Another enthusiastic effort for military support came with the sale of 7 Pitcairns to Great Britain. Called PA-39s, but actually PA-18s, all 7 were lost when the ship was sunk on the way to England.

In 1941, the Pitcairn Company was sold to a group who renamed it A.G.A. (for Autogiros, Gliders, and Airplanes) then, as the G and A Aircraft Company, was acquired by Firestone Tire and Rubber Co. As a division of Firestone, but still located at Willow Grove, Pennsylvania, the last of a long line of Pitcairns, the YO-61, was started. Development of a small copter, the XR-9, was in progress when Firestone closed their aircraft division about 1946.

The other major autogyro producer in the United States, Kellett, was formed with Wallace Kellett as president, his brother, Roderick G., as vice-president, and with W. Lawrence LePage, chief engineer. They chose to use wider chord in their rotor blades and more fixed wing space than Pitcairn. The first practical Kellett, the K-2, was a side-by-side model pow-

---

* Autogiro is the specific Juan de la Cierva type of autogyro which is a term for a machine whose free spinning rotor creates lift.

† Harold Pitcairn's company had successfully built various fixed wing aircraft such as the *Orowing, Mailwing,* and some race planes, the *Fleetwing* and *Fleet Arrow.* When he put all of his energies and faith in the Autogiro, he gave up a successful air mail route which eventually became Eastern Airlines.

ered by a Continental 165HP engine and priced at $7885.

The K-2 was followed by the K-3 available with a "coupe" top as an option. In all, about 24 of these 2 types were sold with the most famous, a K-2 converted to a K-3, for Admiral Byrd. This machine made several flights at the South Pole.

Kellett built an open tandem cockpit model with blades that could be folded for a "roadable" Autogiro. 13 of these sold with a small rudder attached to the rear of the fuselage and a tilting rotor head.

Despite early disappointments, the War Department still believed in rotary wing craft and ordered 7 Kelletts which were delivered in 1938. These machines, designated YG-1Bs, cost the government between 40 and 50 thousand dollars each. They had a swiveling seat in the rear for an observer and a plastic enclosure covered both cockpits.

Another Kellett was purchased by Eastern Airlines for the shortest air mail route in the world. Five times a day, the Autogiro covered the distance from the top of the 30th Street Post Office in downtown Philadelphia to Camden Airport. It took 6 minutes.

The Pitcairn and Kellett machines gave the Cierva design light weight drives for pre-rotation and introduced pushers.* Several large American companies, such as Beechnut, Coca Cola, and Champion Sparkplugs, purchased these machines particularly for promotion and advertising.

A total of about 500 Autogiros built or licensed by Cierva flew during their life-span. The closest an autogyro ever came to the helicopter design and utility was during the "jump off" technique. In this, the pilot would speed up the rotors in non-lifting pitch as fast as possible, then he'd adjust them to an angle of incidence for flight. The momentum of the rotor then lifted the craft straight up to a maximum of 50 feet.

Due to the impending conflict in Europe and largely because the autogyros were not free of defects, the Air Corps reverted to light planes for duties they had hoped to give to autogyros. The Autogiro quite simply was too expensive to build, hard to fly, and could not carry sufficient payload.*

In Germany, the Focke-Achgelis FA-61, a true helicopter, first flew in 1937. This copter's 2 rotors were mounted, side-by-side, on outriggers extending from the fuselage. The FA-61 cruised at 75 MPH and to show off its qualities of control and hover, put on a demonstration inside the 100x300 foot exhibition hall in Berlin.

This successful machine proving the wide gap in rotary wing development between that country and ours forced through the Dorsey Bill in 1938. This authorized the expenditure of $2,000,000 for helicopter research and development.

The first USAAF copter was ordered in 1940, a Platt-LePage twin side-by-side rotor configuration. Free flown on June 23, 1941, as the XR-1, a second model designed by Havilland Platt and ex-Kellett engineer, Laurence LePage, was delivered in June, 1944. This was not a particularly successful machine and in the meantime, Igor Sikorsky finally had found engines to fit his helicopter dreams.

In Kiev, when Sikorsky temporarily gave up his helicopters, he pioneered manufacturing of multi-engine aircraft. He built the world's first 4-engine bomber in 1914. He came to America on the eve of Russia's Revolution and produced a series of amphibians and flying boats, eventually to hold 19 world's records, for the backbone of transoceanic air travel.

In 1929, his company, Sikorsky Aviation Corporation, became a subsidiary of United Aircraft Corporation, and later a division. The following year, Igor Sikorsky applied for a helicopter patent, and, in the late winter of 1939, United's management gave him the go-ahead. The Vought-Sikorsky (VS) 300 was built that summer and Sikorsky lifted its wheels on September 14. By November, flights were of 2 minutes duration though held close to the ground by

---

* A number of small companies and individuals built autogyros during this period. E. Burke Wilford signed an agreement with 2 Germans, Walter Kreiser and Walter Rieseler, to work on their design of "cyclic-pitch control" of rotors. His first gyroplane, with wings, flew in Paoli, Pennsylvania on August 5, 1931. Later, without wings, and with a rigid-rotor and cyclic-pitch control, his XOZ-1 made several successful flights. Gerard P. Harrick built a two-place convertaplane, the HV-2A, with a lower fixed wing and an upper wing which rotated. In 1937, this machine took off as an airplane at 50 feet, the rotor released for the first conversion in air of an American aircraft from fixed wing to rotary flight. With George Townson as pilot, many HV-2A flights were made throughout the 40s and until Herrick died in 1955.

* Juan de la Cierva died in an airplane crash in 1936, and his design didn't survive him long; however, Kellet rebuilt one of the YG-1Bs (also designated YO-60) in the early 60s to check the potential market. Harold Pitcairn committed suicide and his company disappeared after a long and fascinating history. In the mid-50s, homebuilders created a new demand for autogyro designs, and one of the earliest factories to produce free wheeling rotor machines is Bensen Aircraft, still going strong in the late 60s. Also in the 60s, the Umbaugh 18 pusher was developed and efforts made for certification. Canada had the Avian 2/180 and in France, the 60s saw the advent of Rotordyne's Girhel L-50.

Igor Sikorsky designed and learned to fly, at nearly
50 years of age, the first successful direct lift craft
in the western hemisphere. Tethered, the VS-300 lifted
off the ground the first time on September 14, 1939
from the grounds of the Vought-Sikorsky plant, Stratford, Connecticut. Powered by a four-cylinder Franklin engine of 75 hp, the VS-300's main rotor was a
three-blade design 28 feet in diameter. Originally, two
tail rotors aided control and the craft was constructed
of tubular steel welded into shape and, therefore,
easily changed as problems dictated. (Photo courtesy
Sikorsky Aircraft)

ropes. The first free flight was made in May of 1940.

The following May, Sikorsky and his VS-300 set a helicopter endurance record of 1 hour and 32 minutes. The United States was on the brink of the helicopter era.

In December of 1940, $50,000 of Public Act #61, for developing copters, was turned over to Sikorsky for a new model, the XR-4. By this time, United Aircraft had spent $100,000 and estimated an additional $100,000 would be needed for completion of a successful military helicopter. The government paid only one-fourth of the price for this first helicopter work.

The XR-4 was built with a 175HP Warner engine and with all controls, except directional, in the main tilting rotor. It first flew on January 14, 1942 and made the first official flight the following April. Production started in 1943 on the world's first military helicopter, the R-4 (R for rotary) first for the USAAF and then for USN deliveries.

Only Sikorsky could deliver machines in time for use in World War II, and those were used mainly as couriers and experimental platforms.* Only 20 years later, in 1964, Department of Defense estimates that more than 10,000 people have been rescued by Sikorsky-made copters alone.

Much was to happen to the baby-industry in those 20 years. The R-4 of Sikorsky grew to a larger R-5, then back to a smaller version, the R-6. Over 400 of these 3 models were delivered to the armed services during World War II.

The U.S. Coast Guard was extremely active as an early user of the machines. They developed the first pilot training program and the first rescue hoist. On January 3, 1944, their Commander Frank A. Erickson flew a R-4 through a snowstorm to complete the first copter mercy mission to deliver a desperately needed cargo of blood plasma to Sandy Hook, New Jersey, for victims of a ship explosion.

The first rescue by copter was in November of the next year; an Army R-4 flown by Jimmy Viner and hoist-man Captain Jackson E. Beighle snatched 2

* Members of an exclusive club called "The Twirly Birds," an association made up of pilots who soloed a helicopter prior to V. J. Day, August 14, 1945, did most of the testing of the new machines. They are credited with the few casualty evacuations, with radar calibration, sonar equipment tests and dozens of other pioneering efforts. The Twirly Birds numbered 150 by 1969 with another 150 eligible, a small number for the giant steps. The *Whirly Birds* are world-wide licensed female helicopter pilots and numbered 130 by 1969.

bargemen to safety from a reef in Long Island Sound.

Sikorsky produced 220 S-51's, starting in 1946, the first copter sold for commercial service. By the end of 1947, Los Angeles Airways flew 5 of these machines to cover the first officially recognized copter air mail lines. Both the model 51s and 52s saw extensive service in the Korean War.

By 1956, Sikorsky had 10,000 employees and by the end of that year had delivered 1000 additional S-55s from the plant in Stratford, Connecticut. The S-56, ordered by the Navy, Army, and Marines, was being built at the Bridgeport plant. The S-58, a 14 passenger heavyweight, went into extensive service both for the military needs and for commercial use. This model started the first international helicopter airline with Sabena Belgium World Airways and passenger travel with New York Airways in July, 1953. By July 1, 1968, Sikorsky had delivered 4,871 helicopters.

In the meantime, of course, other companies entered the business. Bell's basic design of the Model 47, as mentioned, was built by Arthur M. Young and chief engineer Bartram Kelley. In 1946, 10 Model 47's were built for certification tests and Type Certificate No. H-1 (Helicopter-1) was issued that spring. The

Igor I. Sikorsky, called "Mr. Helicopter," is a pioneer in three different phases of aviation: four-engine bombers, the Flying Clippers of transoceanic fame, and rotary wing aircraft. Russian, by birth, he came to the United States soon after World War I, (Photo courtesy Sikorsky Aircraft)

The VS-300, with enclosed cockpit and fuselage, in the final design with one small rotor on the tail to offset the torque of the main rotor and to provide directional control. This basic design is characteristic of all Sikorsky copters and, in fact, about 90 per cent of the helicopters operating in the world as late as the 1960s. The power transmission consisted of V-belts and bevel gears. (Photo courtesy Sikorsky Aircraft)

first commercial delivery was made by Bell that November to Arizona Helicopters.

And Bell was on the way with the whirly-birds! The development and later production of the AF YH-13* and Navy HTL-1 forced that company's copter branch to spread out and to move to the main Bell plant at Niagara Falls. By 1950, with the large production program for the Navy of the HSL and an experimental project for the Army XV-3

Convertiplane plus the increasing demand for commercial and military 47s, it became clear the helicopter division needed a separate facility. The next year, copter activity and 350 key employees transferred to the newly created Texas Division, under direction of Harvy Gaylord. First, production was concentrated in the former Globe Aircraft plant in north Ft. Worth, then in a specially built facility between Ft. Worth and Dallas.

The 47s grew from the original powerplants of 178HP Franklins to 200 HP in 1951, then 250HP Lycomings in 1955. Key feature of the basic Bell is

* USAAF designation changed from "R" for rotary to "H" for helicopter in 1947.

The third of the original Sikorsky R line, the R-6 lands on a dirt road in China in 1945. R-4s, the first copters built for U.S. military service, were utilized by the USAAF, USN, USCG, as well as the RAF and RNAF. A total of 131 were built. The second production Sikorsky, the R-5, went to the Army Air Forces and Navy, and this model, a count of 229 were put to use by the same two branches of the service during World War II. (Photo courtesy USAF)

Hiller's OH-23 "Ravens" served as light observation copters and, with two external litters, for medical evacuations in Korea and early in the Vietnam War. Over 1100 Ravens were built by Hiller in Palo Alto, California. (Photo courtesy U.S. Army)

Bell's 47J (HUL-1 designation for Navy and Coast Guard, H-13J for Army) was certificated August 23, 1956. This four-seat version of the 47G was purchased by the Air Force for use of the President. The Navy used the craft for general duty and ice-breaking patrols. Two were modified, for the Navy, with Allison shaft turbines. (Photo courtesy Bell Helicopter)

a stabilizing bar directly below the main rotor blades. This bar, weighed at both ends, combined with its control system linkage, is designed to utilize gyroscopic inertia to provide stability.

Then came the Korean War and copters proved their true value. The HTLs and H-13's (47's) were credited with saving 3000 UN lives in that far-away country. By the time the truce was signed, Bells evacuated 18,000 of the 25,000 wounded carried out by copters. Guardian Angels, indeed.

Again, war is credited with advancement of technology. Copters, in Korea, gained at least 10 years of service experience and public acceptance in less than 3 years.

After Korea, Bell developed a tandem-rotor Model 61 for Navy anti-submarine work. Called by the USN, the HSL-1, this machine was equipped with sonar-dipping type detection equipment and powered by 1,900HP P & W engine. Diversification entered the whirling field.

In 1955, Bell built 3 XH-40 high performance copters for experiments with turbines for the Army, and testing continued on the XV-3 tilting rotor convertiplane.

296

By 1956, it was said that the sun never set on Bells for the Model 47s were in service in 40 different countries on 4 of the 6 continents of the world.

Dwane L. Wallace, Cessna Aircraft's president, watched this progress in helicopters and became interested in the efforts of Charles M. Seibel and his associates who were operating in Wichita as the Seibel Helicopter Company. By 1949, Seibel had designed and built 4 models and 2 were certificated.

Cessna acquired the assets of Seibel in 1952, and under the leadership of Charles Seibel, Cessna built the CH-1. This copter, all metal and with a lightplane-type fuselage, and engine in the nose, was certificated on June 9, 1955. Called the "Skyhook," either a 2-place or 4-place model, Cessna's copter was offered to the commercial market in 1959. The Army had purchased 10 models, YH-41s and called "Senacas," but Cessna dropped the idea in 1962 due to disappointing sales. Only 20 machines were built.

Literally dozens of manufacturers and individuals jumped into the copter field when they saw the records being made by Sikorsky and Bell. Many fell by the wayside. One who seemed destined for failure was a twenty-four year old named Glidden S. Doman. He

Hughes Tool Company came into the helicopter field in 1948 with a flying crane. The second project was the 269, accepted both by the Army (as the YHO-2HU) and by commercial markets. The 269 is of simple construction as is this widely used OH-6A *Cayuse*. By the late 60s, the *Cayuse* was replacing the other Army observation copters, the OH-13 and OH-33. (Photo courtesy U.S. Army)

The Coast Guard was one of the earliest users of helicopters for rescue work. Two Sikorsky-built Coast Guard HH-52As flew to the site of a ship collision off Cape Cod. When the ships caught fire, the copters supplied rescue vessels and firefighters with foam, pumps, and other equipment as well as evacuated the injured. Together, the two copters made more than 130 hoists over the burning ships. (Photo courtesy Sikorsky Aircraft)

left his job with Sikorsky and with $800 of borrowed money and an idea for a radical type rotor blade founded Doman Helicopters, Incorporated in August of 1945.

He moved into a barn in Stratford, Connecticut and installed his rotor on a Sikorsky R-6. The results were highly successful, and Doman moved to Danbury, Connecticut. Financed by Curtiss-Wright, he designed and built the LZ-4, with a supercharged Lycoming engine. His next design, the LZ-5 (YH-31, Army designation) was started in 1952 with deliveries to the Army in 1956.

R. J. Enstrom Corporation, Menominee, Michigan,

after years of development, received certification, in the late 60's, for their F-28, a 3-bladed rotor machine with a Lycoming 180HP engine and V-belt drive. Designed specifically for the commercial market, the Enstrom has a cruise of 90 MPH.

Gyrodyne Corporation of America was formed by Peter Papadakos, in 1946, on Long Island and built 3 GCA-41A Rotorcycles for the Navy. By early in the 60's, Gyrodyne was building more refined Rotorcycles powered by either a 62HP Porsche or Solar turbine engine.

As early as 1940, young Stanley Hiller, Jr. drew his first copter sketches in Berkeley, California. His

The Army accepted the first Bell UH-1D in 1963. From that time, throughout the 60s, the "slicks," as the unarmed troopships are called, moved literally thousands of foot soldiers over the dangerous zone of attack in Vietnam. (Photo courtesy U.S. Army)

company, Hiller Aircraft Corp., formed in 1942 at Palo Alto, was busy making magnesium bombs for the government. He spent his week-ends in a garage working on the HX-44 Hiller-copter. This single-place co-axial copter was flown publicly in 1944.

Stanley Hiller and his associates became affiliated with Henry J. Kaiser and as the Hillercopter Division of Kaiser Cargo Company, built co-axial rotor systems under a Navy contract. Hiller's association with Kaiser ended after World War II when Kaiser turned to an ill-fated automobile venture.

In 1945, Hiller incorporated as United Helicopters, Inc., but the name Hiller Helicopters was adopted in 1951 in order to avoid confusion with United's Sikorsky Division.

Hiller built several experimental craft and finally switched to single rotors. In 1948, the Hiller 360 was certificated, the first production copter designed specifically for agricultural work.

In the years 1949 and 1950, Hiller sold more commercial copters through its distributorship system than all other manufacturers combined. Statistics can sound tremendous, but that was for a total of only 82 machines. The industry was yet a baby.

When Korea exploded, Hiller was ready to deliver in quantities. Maintenance had been a copter headache, and Hiller's UH-12A was the first helicopter designed to operate a minimum of 1000 hours between overhauls. The Navy received the first UH-12A in September, 1950, and deliveries then started to the Army, the same machine designated the YH-23 *Raven*. Hiller's number of employees jumped

Early in the Vietnam War, men of the 1st Cav Div (Airmobile) protected themselves and their UH-1Ds by manning M-60 machine guns out of the copter's open door. The UH-1D is a variant of the Model 205 and capable of carrying 12 troops. (Photo courtesy U.S. Army)

Boeing-Vertol's *Chinook* brings a load of 105-mm ammunition to Company B, 25th Infantry Division, near Phu My, Vietnam in February 1967. (Photo courtesy U.S. Army)

300

Textron, Inc. purchased the defense activities of Bell Helicopters in 1960. In 1963, the U.S. Army placed an order for over 2100 of these UH-1B *Iroquois* copters; they had served in Vietnam since late 1962. These *Huey* Gunships were equipped with a wide variety of weapons systems ranging from machine guns to rocket and grenade launchers. By the late 60s, it was said that the gunships could not only hit a specific building, but a particular window in that building. The Royal Australian Air Force ordered 16 UH-1Bs for that country's first two helicopter squadrons. (Photo courtesy Bell Helicopter)

UH-1Bs and UH-1Cs in Vietnam, in the middle 60s, were equipped with an Emerson Electric armament system that gave the capability of hitting ground targets with a large volume of machine gun fire and with rockets. (Photo courtesy U.S. Army)

301

Sikorsky-built CH-54 "Flying Crane" works for the 1st Cav Div (Airmobile) in Vietnam during 1967. The huge weight-lifter moved this 155mm howitzer during a search and destroy mission near Song Re. (Photo courtesy U.S. Army)

from 100 to 700, and 1100 of the UH series copters were delivered to the services.

The company merged with Electric Autolite and production of trainers continued. In 1956, Hiller's employees numbered 850 with projects ranging from a foldable one-man copter for the Marines to ramjet engines. Their ramjet engine was the first to be given CAA approval and was the first approved for tip mounting on rotor blades.

This company pioneered tilt-wings and the Flying Platform, which was controlled by body balance of the pilot. This design used a new principle of lift and propulsion called the ducted fan.

The Kaman Aircraft Corporation came into being when Charles H. Kaman and his chief engineer, Norman Stone, turned full-time to helicopters in 1945. With limited working capital, the Kaman machine grew slowly. It first flew, this K-125, from Bradley Field, near Hartford, Connecticut, in January, 1947. The Navy saw some possibilities in this develop-

Even before the Vietnam conflict, in fact, as early as 1960, statistics show that for each helicopter built, seven lives had been saved. Here, an Air Force *Huskie* hoists Captain Lee F. Dusard out of the South China Sea. He had been forced to punch out of his disabled jet fighter in May 1968. The Kaman-built machine was there in only a few minutes, and another life was saved. (Photo courtesy USAF)

ment and gave the small engineering company a contract that May. A larger Navy contract followed in 1948, and Kaman was on the way.

All Kaman copters utilize aerodynamic servo flap systems for blade pitch control; both collective and cyclic come from the twisting of the blades.

In April of 1949, the Kaman K-190 was certificated, and soon the K-225 followed. The first production contract came from the Navy in June, 1950, just before the Korean conflict. Kaman moved to a modern Navy-owned plant in Bloomfield, Connecticut and mushroomed to 1100 employees pre-

dominately building the Marine HOK and the HTK for the Navy. After the Korean hostilities subsided, Kaman had back-orders for some 20 projects in research and development for all branches of the military service.

Kaman numbers a list of firsts including the world's first turbine copter and the first twin-turbine.

From sales of $5 million in 1951, Kaman grew to $54½ million in 1960. Much of this backlog came from orders for the K-600-3 (USAF-H-43B *Huskie*) which first flew in December, 1958. This model became the standard AF rescue copter in 1960

A Sikorsky *Jolly Green Giant,* flown by the Air Force, is a comforting, life-saving sight to a downed pilot in the ocean off Vietnam. (Photo courtesy USAF)

Sikorsky's S-65, first flown on October 14, 1964, was in use by all the services in Vietnam. Called by the Marines, the *Sea Stallion,* this copter was the largest and fastest in production in the free world by the end of 1968. The Marines, using an unknown number of these crafts, averaged at least 35,000 copter missions each month of 1968 in support of their men. A classified number of Navy copters served in Vietnam. The Seventh Fleet used them for antisubmarine work, rescue, and light attack. Called by the USAF, the *Jolly Green BUFF*—for Big, Ugly, Friendly Fellow—this S-65 (also designated HH-53B and CH-53A) doubtless will topple records in the 70s. (Photo courtesy Sikorsky Aircraft)

and set altitude records the following year.

By 1961, Kaman had 4000 people on the payroll and besides full-scale production of the Huskie, started turning out the Seasprite for the Navy.

Our old friend Kellett, in 1943, turned to helicopters with the XR-8 "Flying Bean." With this design, Kellett introduced an unusual rotor, the intermeshing "egg beater" type called synchropter, originally developed by the German Flettner Helicopter organization. Kellett built 2 side-by-sides of this configuration with the first flying on August 7, 1944.

Sikorsky S-61s, commercial and miltiary versions, had space for 30 passengers plus crew by the start of 1969. In those eight years of production, S-61s rolled out of the Stratford, Connecticut plant for a total of over 600. Commercial models were flown on all seven of the world's scheduled helicopter airlines, including Los Angeles Airways, San Francisco and Oakland Airways, and New York Airways at the end of the 60s. The oil industry utilized the S-61s for changing crews on offshore rigs. The U.S. Military and eight foreign military services used the machines for a number of duties ranging from the USN's use here in anti-submarine warfare by dipping sonar gear to search and rescue, troop and cargo transport, and mine detection. By the start of 1969, the S-61s had flown a total of nearly 1,000,000 flight hours. (Photo courtesy Sikorsky Aircraft)

For Los Angeles Airways, the S-61 carries from 28 to 30 passengers on their suburban network in California. (Photo courtesy Sikorsky Aircraft)

This company moved to suburban Philadelphia for work on an Army Air Force 12-place in 1945. The following year, Kellett turned to the XH-17 Cargo-crane, with GE turbojets. Hughes Tool Company bought out this design in 1948, and Kellett went into sub-contracting work.

Hughes Aircraft, in Culver City, California, flew the Cargo-crane in 1952. In 1956, Hughes became an important part of the helicopter field with the certification of the 269A (Army YHO-2HU) ultra light machine; then, later built the OH-6A Cayuse, which, by the late 60's, was replacing all older observation helicopters in the Army inventory in Vietnam.

During Frank N. Piasecki's senior year at the Daniel Guggenheim School of Aeronautics at New York University, he started thinking of helicopters. With a group of young Philadelphia engineers, Piasecki built a model, the PV-2, in a vacant restaurant

for the purpose of testing theories on rotor blades. This machine, made up of various bits and pieces from a junk yard, even took advantage of a scrounged outboard motor for tail rotor gears. The 3 blades of the rotor balanced and for the first time, blade flapping restrainers were used. The rigid tail rotor blades were twisted for directional control. Frank Piasecki, with a total knowledge of flying gained from only 14 hours in a Piper Cub, test flew this PV-2 on April 11, 1943. Right from this first flight, Piasecki and his co-designers, Elliot Daland and Donald N. Meyers, knew they had something worthwhile.

From the PV-2 came a Navy study contract and the "Flying Banana" design. This, the first successful tandem copter, the XHRP-1, flew in May of 1945.

By 1946, Piasecki employed 400 and won against all industry in a competition for a Navy development contract. This produced the XHJP-1, the famous

HUP, a 6-placer, ship-based rescue craft for the Navy, for the Army, Marines, French, and Canadian Navies.

Only one year later, the company had nearly doubled in size and moved into a new plant at Morton, Pennsylvania. The Air Force chose the PD-22, or H-21 "Work Horse," for arctic rescue work, and by 1950, Piasecki led the industry in the total number of military models on order.

For the Korean War, Piasecki went to full scale production of the HUP for the Navy. By 1952, the company's 5000 employees busily turned out both HUPs and H-25 *Army Mules* for the Army. The next year, the YH-16 first flew. This *Transporter* was the largest copter in the world, measuring 77½ feet long, and the Turbo-Transporter had a gross weight of 16 tons.

In January of 1953, Don Berlin came in as president and chairman of the board. Two years later, Piasecki left and formed a new company, Piasecki Aircraft Corporation. Berlin's Piasecki became known as the Vertol Aircraft Corporation in 1956, and the peak production which came that year totaled a backlog of $134 million.

Vertol merged with Boeing in 1960 to become

Bell's *JetRanger* (206A) was in commercial service by the end of the 60s with even wider acceptance expected in the 70s. The craft, in 1969, was used for charter and air taxi work, for powerline and pipe line patrols, as a corporation tool for moving executives and supplies, as an air-ambulance, for mapping, in the oil industry, and a variety of other unique duties. (Photo courtesy Bell Helicopter)

Boeing-Vertol Division with full production of 107-S's for the fledgling helicopter airlines and the YHC-1B *Chinook,* ordered by the Army, capable of lifting 2 to 3 tons of cargo or 32 fully armed troops.

In 1956, all of the producing copter companies had military backlogs of orders and simply could not supply the civilian market. The 3 certificated scheduled copter carriers threatened to go abroad for equipment. New York Airways had been moving passengers, mainly inter-airport, for 3 years and was ready to start routes in and out of downtown Manhattan.

Cleveland Air Taxi was handling over 1000 copter passengers each month. Chicago Helicopter Airways started passenger schedules in November of that year,

and their forecast of 300,000 passengers by 1960 was proven accurate. Los Angeles Airways, the first scheduled copter air mail service, started on October 1, 1947. LAA started air express in 1953 and passenger service in 1954. LAA coined the term "heliport" for the small patches of grass or concrete, all that was needed for copter landings and take-offs.

When the Sikorsky S-55s came into service, LAA, for instance, could increase their passenger and mail service. Bell, too, started concentrating on the civil market with developments of 2 utility models.

CAA records show that in 1956, about 140 helicopters were certificated for general aviation flying. During that year, 45,000 hours were flown primarily

Bell's Ag-5, an aerial applicator developed in the late 60s, came equipped with AgMASTER spray equipment that could easily be snapped on or off. (Photo courtesy Bell Helicopter)

The newest helicopter gunship, at the end of the 60s, Lockheed-California's U.S. Army *Cheyenne,* has greater speed (250 mph), firepower, weapon accuracy, and agility than any other helicopter gunship in the world. Built as a protector of troop-carrying Slicks and ground forces, the two-man *Cheyenne* has a swiveling gunner's station linked to rotating cannon turrets. Equipped with laser range-finding, which is tied to a fire control computer, the *Cheyenne* has pinpoint accuracy. The primary armament, which may be changed to fit the need, consists of 30mm cannons and 40mm grenade launchers, a far cry from a machine gun out of the door less than ten years earlier. (Photo courtesy Lockheed-California Co.)

for patrol and survey work. Operators and manufacturers were marking time for the magic year, 1960, when experts had predicted a mass use of copters.

Of course, these major companies were not the only ones developing whirly-birds. McDonnell, for instance, started in the field in 1944 with a Navy contract. Chief engineer, C. Yakhartchenko, was responsible for this 10-placer *Whirlaway* which flew in 1946. This was the world's first twin-engine copter and had non-intermeshing 40-foot diameter blades.

During the years between 1946 and 1951, McDonnell's St. Louis plant tested the XH-20 *Little Henry* powered by 2 simple ram-jets. In 1958, their *Flying Crane* became a test bed for other experiments and much research centered on a convertiplane for the USAF.

Kaiser Fleetwings built 2 flying "Twirlybirds" in 1944, and even earlier than that, Emile and Henry Berliner built a machine, in 1924, powered by a Bentley engine which did make a 1½ minute flight.

Republic Aviation Corporation began marketing the French "Alouette II" and "Djinn" and N. O. Brantly, through his Brantly Helicopter Corporation, certificated a co-axial rotored copter in 1946. The Brantly B-2 was delivered to the Army as the YHO-3BR in 1960 and production increased to 8 per month. This company was bought out by Lear, and early in 1969, Brantly was sold to a group near Boston who plan to reactivate production in the 70s.

And, there were others who pioneered rotor-craft developments for that magic year—1960.

Not only were designers pioneers, but so were some of the users. James S. Ricklef's Rick Helicopters, Incorporated showed faith by organizing, in 1948, a service specializing in mapping surveys, powerline patrol, agricultural uses, forest fire suppression, and general charter. By 1951, Rick was so successful it could buy out the copter division of Alaska Airlines. The following year, Rick purchased U.S. Helicopters, Incorporated in San Francisco to grow to one of the largest operators of helicopters in the world.

Another early user was Elynor Rudnick who formed Kern Copters, Inc. in Bakersfield, California in 1948. First, Kern answered the needs of farming then diversified into all types of use and spread from Alaska to New Mexico.

In 1949, Petroleum Helicopters, Inc. was born in Lafayette, Louisiana with 3 Bells and 7 men to service the petroleum industry. By the mid-50s, this company owned 14 Bells and Sikorskys, had 80 people on the payroll, and has been growing like the dickens ever since.

By the start of that magic date, 1960, records show that for every helicopter built, 7 lives were saved. But this was not the date for the mass acceptance of a civil copter. The true helicopter age came the following year: a brush-fire war in a country called Vietnam fanned into a full-scale conflict and was soon called "The Helicopter War."

That year, 1961, the Army and Navy ordered LOH (light observation helicopters) from Bell, Hiller, and Hughes. Nearly immediately, the U.S. military services called for heavier copters for moving troops and equipment, and eventually came the demand for gunships both to soften the enemy for advances and to protect the unarmed copters.

To quote General William C. Westmoreland, "Army Aviation . . . has made our conduct of this war possible." The imperative need of air mobility in that country with rough terrain and insufficient road or rail networks was answered by the utility peculiar to the helicopter. More than any other weapon, the copter permitted the Army to engage the Viet Cong in his own jungle.

Perhaps it sounds strange to talk this type air war as being Army, not Air Force, but this is the case. Army Aviation is young, really, no matter which birthdate you consider. Some claim this segment of the Army came to life on June 6, 1942, the day authorization came through to use aircraft for spotting targets.

Other official reports say Army Aviation started in 1947 when the Air Force became a separate service.

Make your own choice, but by the middle of the 1960's, Army Aviation had developed the Air Cavalry concept which fast replaced the need for tanks, trucks, and personnel carriers. The 1st Air Cav (Airmobile) Division was formed at Ft. Bragg, North Carolina. This was so successful that the 101st Airborne, in the late 60s, was reorganized to form the 2nd Air Cav Division in the early 70s.

Late in 1961, the Army's first copter wing was dispatched to Vietnam. Equipped with Vertol CH-21s and firing machine guns out of the door, the men of this wing quickly realized the need for gun platforms and for more copters. This formed the basic concept of airmobility, to move the troops on the ground and in the air with support from Army gunships.

An ordinary Army division of 18,000 men has a complement of 100 helicopters. By the end of 1967, the 1st Air Cav Division had 450. That same year, the Army counted 2200 aircraft in Vietnam, grown a 1000 by the start of 1969. These craft range from OH-13 observation helicopters to giant Sikorsky *Skycranes,* weight carrying Boeing-Vertol *Chinooks* capable of moving a payload of 24,000 pounds. In "starch-wing" craft, the Army counted 0-1 *Bird Dogs,* OV-1 *Mohawks,* Beech *Seminoles,* and deHavilland *Beavers* and *Otters* along with others used for cargo and troop transport, as well as reconnaissance.

Army reconnaissance pilots developed and perfected new systems of surveillance, yet the exciting airmobile concept comes from the combat active copters.

Army leaders found that a standard infantry division simply could not catch the Viet Cong and North Vietnamese in their jungle. When these leaders could bring in their own troops and firepower, by air, battles took on a different slant. U.S. troops no longer must march across a battle zone to meet the enemy. The dangers from mines, artillery, mortar fire, and ambush are being eliminated. Entire battalions, almost 800 riflemen, are commonly moved 100 or more miles during the night by copters to new and more profitable positions for the morning fight.

Army copters, which outnumber the total of all USAF and USMC whirlybirds in Vietnam, are used in heliborne assaults, to chase the enemy with firepower and men, as gunships, for reconnaissance, supply, and to position forces.

The Army has found that the copters, even at 800 to 2000 feet altitude, are less vulnerable than the old L-4 lightplanes previously used for artillery spotting. And, of course, there's the fantastic air medical evacuation system, called Dustoff. The death rate per 1000 wounded was reduced from 4.5 in World War II to 2.5 in Korea and to less than 1. in Vietnam. World War II casualties had no air evacuation directly from the battle areas, and only 15 per cent could be moved in Korea. In Vietnam, during this Helicopter War, 90 per cent of the wounded were moved directly from the battle zone to surgical facilities. The 100 Dustoff Army medical evacuation units counted a total of 322,000 wounded moved from 1962 until January 1, 1969.

The Army's assaulting copters use hit and run tactics. Rocket-armed gunships carry on aerial artillery by homing in on an infantry company's FM radio or on known terrain. In a trail formation, these copters zap targets marked by the infantry with red smoke and often only a few hundred yards away. If needed, the gunships call in strike planes from the USAF, and this joint effort proved most effective in softening the enemy lines.

The *HueyCobras* and older *Huey* gunships with their mixed armament loads of up to 2000 pounds fight the close support air war while the Air Force B-52s carry on the long range bombing effort and jet fighter/bombers hit troop and supply concentrations.

Ft. Rucker, the Army Aviation training headquarters, by 1968, was turning out 10,000 pilots and crewmen annually. About ½ of the 18,000 Army warrant officers on active duty are either aviators or in aviation related fields. From the 7 Army pilots who made the transition to copters in 1945, it's a tremen-

dous growth. In 1968, Rucker counted 6200 Army Aviation graduates and all but 600 of those went through rotary wing school. In 1969, Rucker forecasts graduates will be divided into 17,000 for aviation maintenance, 6900 rotary wing pilots and 600 fixed wing pilots; 95 per cent of these graduates will head directly for Vietnam.

In their copter history, the Army's Hughes OH-6A had logged 100,000 hours of combat flying by January 1, 1969. Their Sikorsky *Cranes,* in the 1st Air Cav, had rescued 400 downed aircraft, worth $200 million, and by 1980, the Army expects to double their number of copters and aircrews, likely having 18,000 men in Army Aviation.

For the Marines in Vietnam, their medium transport copters started operating in the Mekong Delta in mid-April, 1962. They fostered the use of helicopters in combat during the Korean War, and during Vietnam, their machines grew in size to the CH-53 *Sea Stallion* capable of airlifting 38 combat equipped troops in late 1968.

The big concentration of USAF helicopters in the Vietnam theatre was in the 3rd Aerospace Rescue and Recovery Group, at one of their 23 locations scattered across southeast Asia. By January 1, 1969, this group was credited with 2,202 rescues. Of those, 1,508 were "combat saves," meaning exposed to enemy fire. The group paid, in the same length of time, with 100 losses.

The USAF's rescue units used 3 copters, the HH-43 Kaman *Pedros,* HH-3E *Jolly Green Giants,* and the HH-53 *Jolly Green Buffs.* The drama of these rescues which, until 1969 started, ranged from 6 minutes time to pick up an F-4 pilot who "punched out" over the Gulf of Tonkin to 9½ hours to rescue 26 soldiers, is indeed thrilling. It would also fill a book all its own.

Born of air-sea rescue units in World War II, USAF rescue originally became Air Rescue Service in 1946, and ARRS (Aerospace Rescue and Recovery Service) in 1966. During those 20 years, the service saved 12,500 people from certain death and directly aided 55,000 more. In the next year, the refueling, in flight, of the *Jolly Green Giants* was perfected and opened unlimited fields for playing angel as ARRS had when astronauts splash down from the manned *Mercury, Gemini* and *Apollo* flights.

With rescue hoists for the sea, from the land, and now a four-pronged jungle penetrator plus the capability of landing on water or land, the copters of ARRS are true Guardian Angels.

As copters continued, late in the 60s, to prove their ultimate value in war, civil use grew. By 1969, police departments in 40 cities owned whirly-birds.

Bell's president, E. J. (Duke) Ducayet announced an 800 per cent increase in that company's commercial sales in the last 8 years of the 60s. Their 5-place turbine powered JetRanger counted 450 deliveries to customers in 33 countries between January, 1967 and January, 1969. Bell offered 5 different models in 1969 and announced that by 1970, the 212 Twin-Jet corporate copter would be available.

Brantly, as mentioned earlier in this chapter, was purchased by Aeronautical Research & Development Corporation (ARDC), and Roger P. Swanson, of that company, expects "a production build-up to one Brantly unit per day . . ." by 1971. Lear Jet, Brantly's previous owner, is developing a twin-turbine corporate copter as the 1960s come to a close.

Enstrom's F-28A, a 3-place civil copter, was made available to the public in 1969 with a price tag of $37,950, and Fairchild-Hiller, who had delivered over 150 FH 1100s by the end of 1968, continued commercial production of that craft.

Hughes offered private and corporate owners a choice of 3 models, and Sikorsky continued to produce certified scheduled passenger carriers.

At the end of the 1960s, Boeing and Messerschmitt agreed to give Vertol the rights to market and perhaps manufacture the German developed 5-place rigid rotor Boelkow BO-105.

The commercial growth of helicopters can be noted from the growth of active helicopter ratings in the United States which numbered 1,392 in 1965. This jumped to 2,573 ratings in 1967 and in that year, copter manufacturers delivered 443 civilian machines, an increase of 91 units over 1966's figures; 511 civil machines, worth $57 million, were sold in 1968, and the industry expects to place 545 civil copters in 1969, mostly 5-place, turbine-powered.

Late in the 60's, U.S. heliports/helistops numbered 1,892—a gain of 50 per cent since the mid-60's.

By March of 1969, U.S. Command stated that 2500 helicopters were in the Vietnam conflict, and if they were removed, 1 million added "trigger pullers" would be needed to do the same job.

There's no question that this is an expensive way to perfect a machine, yet the pay is difficult to gauge. Sikorsky, for instance, has awarded a total of 13,229 "Winged S" medals to officially recognized crewmen who have made helicopter rescues. Of these coveted Winged Ss 1,685 were presented in 1968 alone.

Over these past 20 years of helicopter growth, many of the same manufacturers have worked on developing STOLs (Short Take-Off and Landing) both for military uses and to off-set the time loss between city center and city center in urban areas. Some advocates believe these Vertical (V) and STOL crafts are the only answers to the crowded airport problem and to the time loss between airport and the middle of town.

These are not new ideas. In "tail-sitters", Convair built the *Pogostick* and Lockheed the XFV-1 for the Navy as test vehicles. The "tilt-wing" category found Hiller, Vertol, and Kaman building prototypes. Both Curtiss-Wright and Dornier believe in the "tilt propeller" concept of helicopter-type take-offs and fixed-wing type cruise. Fairchild, Robertson, and Ryan built machines which received vertical lift from the propeller slipstream deflected downward.

Believers in the ducted fan or ducted rotor theory include Collins, Chance-Vought, Goodyear, Piasecki, Rotovion, Vanguard, Bell, Doak, Ryan, Republic, and Sikorsky. Some of these experiments have progressed beyond the research tool stage, such as Lockheed's XV-4 *Humming Bird* which flew in July of 1967.

In the middle 60's, the U.S. government, through the military, spent over one-hundred million dollars a year on developing 14 of these V/STOL programs. Yet, by 1969, only the helicopter actually was in civil use.

The present decade, the 70's, doubtless will see STOLs come into their own. For the military, the development of the Air Force's light intra-theatre transport (LIT) may be the beginning of the answer. The picture is not too clear, though, as we enter 1969 for, as said, the government already has spent more than $500 million on V/STOL without too many tangible results.

In the civilian market, McDonnell-Douglas's Model 188 (the French built Breguet 941) is about the only really new airplane concept. Both Eastern and American Airlines have test-operated this craft, and it seems likely this 100-passenger, 400MPH STOL will be the first in the crowded northeast corridor from Washington to Baltimore, Philadelphia, New York and Boston.

The Helio *Courier,* a 6-place, single-engine, STOL can land and take-off in less than 150 yards and Robertson's conversions of single-engine Cessnas give them STOL possibilities.

In between, in size, comes Fairchild-Hiller's *Heli-Porter,* built under license from the Swiss *Pilatus,* with 50 delivered in the U.S. by the end of 1968.

The Short *Skyvan,* which carries 19 passengers in the commuter configuration, is in service as we come into 1970 as are deHavilland's *Twin-Otters* and *Buffalos.*

The commercial market again looks to the military for development and the 3 contracts let for LIT in 1969 to Boeing-Vertol, Ling-Temco-Vought, and McDonnell-Douglas may open wide the door of the copter's sisters, STOLs.

17. The Big Lift

In the surrender settlements after World War II Berlin, like Gaul, was divided into three parts. By easing off bits of the British and American sections, France became the third allied power to occupy and govern a German zone. The fourth was in the hands of the Soviet Union.

Those same agreements permitted the allies to supply their forces and the German citizens in their zones via roads, rails, canals, and three western air corridors. These crossed 110 miles of Russian-held land.

In February of 1948, the Czechoslovak government fell to Russian conquest and boosted the Russian appetite for more.

The Reds were dissatisfied with the reunification and free elections planned for the three allied zones of Germany (called, collectively, Western Germany), and under the pretext of disagreement with currency procedures, slapped restrictions on transportation through their zone. They walked out of a conference at Konmandatura, the headquarters of Allied Government for Berlin, with a *nyet* which became the standard Russian position.

General Lucius Clay, the American military governor in Germany, had 2 battalions, about 3,000 troops, in Berlin. Combined, the French and British troops totaled an additional 3,500. The Soviets had 18,000 soldiers in the city and another 300,000 spread through their East Zone surrounding Berlin. Justi-fiably, the Russian threats, and the odds, created tenseness.

On March 20, 1948, the Soviets stopped peaceful negotiations by storming out of the Allied Control Council for Germany. Leaders "back home" in the allied countries insisted the time had come to get the boys out of that cul-de-sac.

General Clay wired the Secretary of the Army, Kenneth Royall, "If we withdraw, our position in Europe is threatened . . . Communism will run rampant."

Soviet harassments increased, and the at-home "patriots" demanded a safe retreat (withdrawal, they called it) of the paltry 6,500 troops surrounded by 48,000. American voices soon made this harangue as much a part of the Cold War as Red aggression.

Our joint Chiefs of Staff warned that our forces were too weakened by demobilization for much of a show-down, which was exactly the way the Russians figured. President Truman, goaded by his military leaders to quit, reacted with action. When the arguments of his conferences were released, it came down to: "There was no discussion on that point (withdrawal), we were going to stay—period."

The Russians hadn't anticipated that backbone, so, they pushed a little harder. The Kremlin ordered a stop on all freight and parcel post service. Electric power into the allied zones was cut off. Efforts at negotiations continued, all to no avail. Simply, it

Allan (l) and Malcolm Loughead (r), aided by a
21-year-old draftsman-mechanic, John K. Northrop,
built this twin-hydroplane, F-1, in 1918. Financially
backed by Berton R. Rodman, the tiny Loughead
company in Santa Barbara, Calif. went out of business after WW-I when their single-place sport plane
failed to find buyers. The Lougheads changed their
name to Lockheed and, in 1926, returned to plane-
making with the Northrop-designed Lockheed *Vega.*
Lockheed-built airplanes today dominate the aircraft
inventory of the Military Airlift Command. (Photo
courtesy Lockheed Aircraft Corporation)

boiled down to the fact that the Russians wanted the
allies and their influence out of West Germany.

On June 24, 1948, the Soviet Union slammed shut
the open highways, canals, and rail lines. Only the
3 air corridors remained free. If the allies were to
foster freedom and stay in West Germany, the city of
Berlin and its two million citizens would have to
be supplied by air. Would the Germans, by our
neglect, be forced into the Russian fold by the bribe of
food, coal, and medical supplies? The decision came
down. No.

The original estimate called for 4,500 tons of supplies, daily, necessary for Berlin's living condition. As
an airlift, the figure was astronomical, and air leaders
said—impossible. The estimates were revised—4,500
tons? No, West Germany could not survive without
5,700 tons a day, 7 days a week! We had no choice,
according to General Albert Wedemeyer; either we
drop Germany, and a large part of Europe into the
Communist lap, or we make the airlift work.

General Clay called in Iron Pants LeMay, who,
with USAFE, had 100 war-weary C-47's in his com-

Part of MAC's story is the heritage of the WW-II Air Transport Command. And a part of ATC's story was made by women pilots. Mrs. Nancy Love (l) organized the Women's Auxiliary Ferrying Squadron (WAFS) as a small-scale experiment under ATC in Wilmington, Delaware. Mrs. Betty Huyler Gillies (r) was the first pilot sworn in on September 12, 1942. The WAFS job was the ferrying of aircraft from factories to training bases and ports of embarkation. Numbering only 50, the WAFS flew L-2's, PT-19's, L-4's, PT-26's, and BT-13's in the beginning, but were soon up-graded to fly nearly every aircraft then in Army service. Mrs. Gillies, for instance, flew *Thunderbolts, Mustangs,* and *Lightnings;* A-20's, A-30's, P-61's, C-45's, OA-9's, and this B-17. En route for foreign delivery of this B-17, Mrs. Love and Mrs. Gillies (with crew: Lt. R. O. "Pappy" Fraser, S/Sgt. D. A. Stover, T/Sgt. S. Weintraub, and T/Sgt. L. S. Hall) were halted at Goose Bay, Labrador, by order of Gen. Arnold who apparently did not want to risk U.S. women pilots in Europe and a shooting-war situation. Later, in October 1942, Jacqueline Cochran set up an air training section for women, and its graduates, along with the original WAFS, formed the WASPS—Women's Airforce Service Pilots. (Photo courtesy Fred Nelson)

mand. Within only four days, these lightweights loaded to capacity blasted aloft for the start of the LeMay Coal and Feed Company, code name "Operations Vittles."

That first rather unorganized day saw the old 47's move 80 tons of priority items over the heads of the Russian blockaders. From Rhein-Main AB 150 miles to Berlin's Tempelhof Aerodrome, the lumbering 47's re-opened the doors; only a dent in what was needed, but they put down the timbers of the *Luftbruecke,* air bridge.

In that same month of June was consummated a unique marriage, a joining of the Air Force's long range transports (ATC) with the U.S. Navy's NATS (Navy Air Transportation Service). This single non-combatant transportation organization known as MATS (Military Air Transport Service), under command of General Lawrence S. Kuter, received its first call-to-duty. The MATS heavy transports, particularly Douglas *Skymasters* capable of lifting 10 tons, homed in on Germany. Some from half-way around the world, the C-54's roared in. In fact, eventu-

WASPs Dorothea Moorman (l) and Mrs. Dora Dougherty Strothers (r) flew heavy aircraft including the B-29 *Superfortress*. About 140 WASPs specialized in fighter planes. The ladies' level of conduct was high, and they performed a vital service without some of the benefits accruing to other service personnel. They had no GI insurance, and 11 were killed in the ATC alone. The WASPs were dissolved in December 1944, on Miss Cochran's recommendation to General Arnold. (Authors' photo)

America's first tactical jet, the Lockheed XP-80 was first powered by a British engine, but more than 1400 production models were built around a General Electric engine. A *Shooting Star* won the world's first jet battle when it bettered a Russian-built MIG in Korea. Forerunner of Lockheed's supersonic F-104, the *Shooting Star* was the first jet plane produced in quantity and the first jet fighter in mass tactical operation in America. (Photo courtesy Lockheed Aircraft)

ally, 319 of these big boys out of a total active fleet of 400 served the airlift.

By the middle of July, MATS planes, supplemented by odd lots flown both by the Air Force and Navy, and 100 RAF transports, had upped Berlin's air delivery to 1,530 tons each day.

In August, General W. H. Tunner, famous for his success with the Hump airlift, took charge of the U.S. 1st Airlift Task Force soon to grow to the Combined Airlift Task Force of all American and British forces.

In this interval, the Soviets seemed to sense their ploy was back-firing. The German people, instead of turning to the Russians for help, were repulsed by the Communist show of power. Operation Vittles, with the allies making a supreme effort to cover the necessities and luxuries of life, was welcomed with friendliness and true appreciation.

And the airlift grew. The American *Skymasters* and the British *Yorks, Dakotas,* and C-47's, took off at 3 minute intervals, around the clock. They ignored the fog and thunderstorms in the narow 20 mile

A development of the F-80 *Shooting Star* is the Lockheed T-33 trainer first produced in 1948. The "T-Bird," in its first decade of life, was credited with training 90 per cent of the free world's jet pilots. Called by the Air Force, T-33A, by the Navy and Marines, the T-33B (TV-2), this two-place trainer served 23 friendly powers. (Photo courtesy Lockheed Aircraft)

corridors, and kept coming. The Soviets lashed out at this determination by creating radio interference, a major problem when navigation had to be so perfect. The airlift planes had to maintain a speed of exactly 170 miles per hour for they were only three minutes apart, at the take-off end. In the air, they were separated by only 500 feet of altitude.

Landing, only three minutes apart, a pilot often would be blinded by searchlights thrown aloft by the Soviets. Each airplane had to be handled with delicate precision for it was not only often overloaded, but it had to be flown into airfields—Gatow, Tegel, and Tempelhof—which were not overly large.

In the tight corridors, Soviet *Yaks* made a practice of buzzing the transports, even carrying out games of air-to-air gunnery. Still, Operation Vittles continued without let-up.

Each day, the Russians became more unhappy. The United States cocked the fist of SAC, the deterrent of atomic power, and ordered B-29's to Europe. For months, 60 of these bombers with their back-up of 75 *Shooting Star* jet fighters sat barely outside the Russian perimeter. They sat and waited, and the Soviets couldn't know whether they were "armed" (atomic or nuclear weapons) or not. Our stockpile of the "big" bombs was too low, then, but that word didn't get out.

The airlift continued with only harassments, not

In 1939, Daniel J. Haughton came to Lockheed as systems analyst. Famous planes such as the P-38 *Lightning* and the *Constellation* soon followed, until Lockheed Aircraft Corporation had sales of more than two billion dollars in 1966. By then, Haughton was president. In 1967, he succeeded Courtlandt S. Gross as board chairman. In that year, Lockheed faced turmoil after losing the supersonic transport contract to Boeing. Haughton (shown above), a Southerner who owns a farm outside of Atlanta, must steer the company, the biggest defense contractor in the world with a product mix of jet fighters and Polaris missiles, with numbers in between. He decided the company would re-enter the commercial transport field too, and in 1968 he announced Lockheed's L-1011 TriStar. (Photo courtesy Lockheed Aircraft)

all-out attacks, and by spring, an average day saw 8000 tons of supplies off-loaded in Berlin, this only a few months after 4,500 tons had seemed impossible. Later the average day could count on 10,000 tons. Berlin, indeed, was well supplied, and entirely by air.

Finally, the Soviets gave up and lifted the unsuccessful blockade in May of 1949. The Berlin Airlift continued until September 30 in order to rebuild a sizeable reserve.

The allies won the first round of the Cold War, but it was not inexpensive. In the first 14 months, 277,264 flights were made into Berlin. The British and American transports moved over 2.3 million tons of supplies in 500,000 flying hours. The cost to America came to $300 million and 35 American planes, 31 American lives were lost. Berlin received an overall average of 5,579 tons of survival supplies each day.

Reassured by the airlift, the Germans became staunch supporters of western freedom and they aligned behind NATO. Extraordinary efforts on the part of the allies, and the supreme price paid of a total of 68 German, American, and British airmen, brought lasting results. The West German Government was established under Dr. Konrad Adenauer, and MATS, made up of a bickering couple, settled down to maturity of purpose.

Both the USN and the USAF could only be considered a baby in the long range transportation field 8 years earlier, when World War II started. They were built on a nucleus of fledgling airline routes and equipment, which, itself, was young and struggling in 1940. Then, the total airline domestic routes measured only 37,500 miles and foreign routes totaled 46,000 miles, due mainly to expansion of Pan American, as told in an earlier chapter.

Scheduled transAtlantic passenger service was pioneered only in 1939 and trailblazed across the Pacific in 1940.

In 1941, General Robert Olds set up the Ferry Command from his obscure office in the basement of the Munitions Building in Washington. With help from General Arnold, the Ferry Command started a shuttle of American planes between the factories and the United Kingdom. This was soon nicknamed the "Arnold Line" and headed by Colonel Caleb Haynes and Major Curtis LeMay.

The first plane flown across the ocean by an American military man, as a ferry flight on the Arnold Line, was a Lockheed Hudson in July of 1941. At that time, we had barely a handful of 4-engine trained pilots. The United Kingdom really started this fly-it-yourself delivery when the RAF opened shuttles between the factories and Prestwick and hired civilians for the flying duties.

Under General Olds' prodding, Americans were starting ferry duties when we went to war on December 7, 1941. Suddenly, from a small group flying the Arnold Line, the Ferry Command was handed the problem of oceans and continents to cross before we could even reach our allies. China, for instance, was 13,000 miles away! The Ferry Command had only 11 B-24's in its inventory.

The U-2 (U standing for "Utility") "Sky Spy" was built by Lockheed in Clarence "Kelly" Johnson's super secret Skunk Works in an incredible 80 days. From 1956 until 1960 it flew over the world's countries unmolested; then Francis Gary Powers, in a U-2, was downed by a Russian surface-to-air missile. Premier Nikita Khrushchev walked out of a summit meeting in Paris, denouncing President Eisenhower. The many-faceted U-2 crisis followed. Originally, 38 U-2's were built, and by the start of 1969 the USAF's inventory counted 20 (18 had crashed). Two were flying out of South Vietnam's Bien Hoa airbase, keeping a careful eye on North Vietnam and Communist China. The other 18 are, for the most part, used as scientific-research craft studying tornados, hurricanes, and clear air turbulence. This particular U-2 shows a barber-pole-like gust probe on the nose as it heads for *Hi-Cat* —high altitude clear air turbulence above 55,000 feet. The nose boom is so sensitive even a man's breath will register. The Air Force sponsored *Hi-Cat* studies severe atmospheric motion over Puerto Rico, Alaska, and California. As for "Sky Spy" duties, the U-2's follow-ups are the ever-flying SAMOS photo satellites soon to be joined by Johnson's SR-71, also out of Lockheed. Working with him, incidently, is Francis Gary Powers, who test-flies U-2's but certainly, not over Russia. (Photo courtesy Lockheed Aircraft)

Herman R. (Fish) Salmon, Lockheed-California's chief engineering test pilot until his retirement in 1969, learned to fly at the age of 16. He joined Lockheed in 1940 and was among the first men to fly faster than sound and the first to fly on ram jet power. He made extensive contributions to aeronautical advances in early vertical-rising turbo-props, large commercial planes, and helicopters. No man has flown more different types of aircraft. (Photo courtesy Lockheed Aircraft)

American military might was forced to create an air transportation arm to deliver military aircraft, equipment, personnel, and cargo across often uncharted jungle and desert and vastness of oceans and the artic. The Ferry Command became ATC (Air Transport Command) on June 20, 1942. The U.S. Navy formed NATS at about the same time. Nowhere were we weaker than in the field of long range transports.

The Government purchased airline equipment, and ATC's commander, General Harold Lee George, took over all but 200 of the airline owned DC-3's. Before these could be put in service, the Army's transport fleet numbered, pathetically, 24 heavy aircraft. Four of these were Pan American acquired *Clippers,* five were C-75 *Stratoliners* from TWA, five more came from Consairways and were British B-17's, and the 10 B-24's that still were flyable. Later, two Martin Flying Boats were added to the list, a pitifully inadequate fleet.

From this beginning was hewn a mighty air armada. The airlines supplied a total of 324 of their aircraft, one-half their domestic fleet. They supplied pilots and executives, such as C. R. Smith and Robert Love, who knew the transportation field. They trained men, provided airbase facilities, and somehow managed to keep pace at home, in a war-producing country.

ATC (called "Allergic to Combat" by some fighter and bomber pilots) grew and perfected the blind landing system which made delivery of supplies in the Berlin Airlift possible. NATS and ATC, combined, made the first air evacuation of wounded on January 17, 1943, when they moved 17,000 wounded out of Karachi under constant attack.

They flew the vital supply routes over the Hump, and in the ATC, alone, trailblazed and manned 200,000 miles of routes around the world. ATC's eventual fleet of 2800 airplanes flew more than 600 million passenger miles per month. By the time Germany surrendered, ATC had 26 scheduled flights across the Atlantic, *each way,* each day. Thirty-eight ATC flights crossed the Pacific per day.

NATS covered an additional 70,000 miles of routes.

In the peak month, April, 1944, 2500 American military planes were delivered to forces overseas.

Basically, MATS, then, grew on the development of civilian aviation made in the middle 30's. The speeded-up technology of war demands, in turn, gave civilian aviation such gigantic advances as the jet engine, to name only one.

Serving in ATC were 205,000 military men and 108,000 civilians. Their final creation, in route structure, for post-war America was 35,000 miles of domestic and 148,900 miles of foreign routes.

MATS was not limited to war-time duty. Under its aegis was Air Weather Service (AWS). The Army's Medical Department created the first U.S. National Weather Facility in 1818. AWS has held this responsibility, war and peace, since 1937.

In the late 60's, AWS was made up of eight weather wings, 3 of which were stationed in Southeast Asia, along with Air National Guard and AF Reserve units. Eleven thousand weather service personnel man 400 weather stations in 29 countries and islands.

In days of war, AWS is particularly active. In Korea, for instance, only 24 hours after hostilities began, the first weather reconnaissance plane flew over the enemy. Naturally, much of the planning for

Lockheed's *Venturas* (military development of the Model 18 *Lodestar*), the PV-1's, were standard Navy patrol bombers in the Pacific from 1943 until the end of the war. There were 1,600 in service, and Lockheed continued the development for the Navy through the *Harpoons,* the *Neptunes,* to this model— the P-3 *Orion.* Based on the *Electra* transport airframe, the *Orions* entered production in 1961 and were delivered to the Navy starting in 1962. The latest model (1969), the P-3C, is equipped with data-processing systems for all major equipment involved with antisubmarine warfare. Two of the four turboprop engines can be shut down for longer range in search missions. Almost 300 *Orions* were in service with the U.S. Navy by the end of 1968. The new models are also joining the Royal New Zealand Air Force, Royal Australian Air Force, and Royal Norwegian Air Force. (Photo courtesy Lockheed Aircraft)

The Douglas C-124 *Globemaster,* with a 20-ton payload, came into MATS inventory in June, 1950. Utilized particularly as a missile mover, the *Globemaster*
also was used as a cargo airdrop carrier and for assault
drops of combat paratroopers. This particular craft
was used to transport the U.S. Army's 3rd Brigade
from Hawaii to Vietnam on December 24, 1965.
(Photo courtesy USAF)

Col. Allison C. Brooks, Commander of the Aerospace
Rescue and Recovery Service, and A3/C Donald Doll,
a pararescueman, are being picked up simultaneously
in a two-man pickup by the Fulton Skyhook system in
a Lockheed *Hercules.* Notice the V-shaped pick-up
arms now folded back along the nose of the C-130.
(Photo courtesy Lockheed-Georgia Co.)

In 1956, Lockheed produced the first F-104 *Starfighter,* the world's first Mach 2 fighter. The 1600-plus-mile-per-hour craft is programmed to remain a front line fighter in 14 nations of the Free World through the 1970s. A world-wide program produced 2400 of these planes by 1969. Italy, in the late 60s built 165 F-104S models to add to the earlier lines in the U.S., Canada, Japan, The Netherlands, Belgium, and West Germany. The stub-winged fighter carries a varied arsenal including rockets, bombs, missiles, and an aerial cannon, the M-61 *Vulcan.* (Photo courtesy Lockheed Aircraft)

Lockheed's wide-bodied jetliner, the L-1011 *TriStar,* will go into service in 1971 on Eastern, TWA, Delta, Northeast, Air Canada, and Air Holdings Ltd. of England. The 250–345 passenger airliner with three Rolls-Royce engines has a high-density seating, maximum payload of 87,000 pounds, nearly nine times as much as could be lifted by the largest weight-carrier on the Berlin Airlift. The 20-foot wide fuselage will carry eight passengers abreast, economy class, and six abreast, first class. The 178-foot length is longer than the total distance of the Wright brother's first powered flight. (Photo courtesy Lockheed Aircraft)

Air duct in tail of Lockheed TriStar for the big jet's
fuselage-mounted engine is 34 feet long. It will feed
a powerful river of air to one of three Rolls Royce
RB.211 engines, each of which has 40,600 lbs of thrust.
(Photo courtesy Lockheed Aircraft Corporation)

military moves, on the ground, in the air, and on the
sea depends on current and future weather conditions.

In a like way, space shots and safe recoveries depend
on forecasting.

The men of AWS have a motto—PRO BONO
PUBLICO—which means "For the good of the
public." In their C-130's, the Mighty *Hercules*
built by Lockheed, they live up to this creed by flying over 10 million miles of area reconnaissance missions each year in the chase for the "Big Blows," the
hurricanes and typhoons of the Atlantic and Pacific.

Your writers rode with the Hurricane Hunters in
their quest of a killer-storm called Hurricane *Betsy*
in 1965. In missions of 10 to 12 hours, a single
crew bores through the rivet-popping, death-defying,

magnificently violent eye-wall time after time. The
reason? First, they plot the direction of the killer so
the people on the ground can be warned in time to
move out of her path. And second, each piece of
knowledge gained on this monster which expends the
equivalent of 2½ times the power of a Hiroshima-
type A-Bomb *per second* just may be the one to finish
the puzzle of how to control the ladies.

AWS men fly the hurricane belt and the even
more deadly typhoons in the Pacific. When we asked
one of these men why they volunteer for such hazardous service, and without extra pay, he answered, "I
don't like to back-up for my pay check every month.
As a Hurricane Hunter, I can claim my pay with
pride."

ARRS's local base rescue teams fly Kaman *Huskies*. Statistics show that most air crashes are only a few miles from take-off and landing areas, and saving these lives is the primary duty of *Huskie* crews. In 1969, a new fire suppression kit (shown here) was added to the equipment. Capable of releasing 850 gallons of foam, few fires can blaze against this copter, so equipped. The down-wash of the copter blades has been used to save dozens of men from burning to death in crashes. (Photo courtesy USAF)

In 1969, AWS answered another duty, solar forecasting. From weather for medicine to weather for space in a century-and-a-half, that's the heritage of MATS's Air Weather Service.

In 1965, with the need for highly mobile forces in the "brush fires" starting in widely scattered areas of conflict, MATS's primary mission of scheduled flights transporting passengers and cargo changed. From the alphabet soup jargon of the military came a new name, MAC, Military Airlift Command, which from that year was on a par with other USAF combat elements.

Another part of the humanitarian aspects of MAC is the Air Rescue Service, which was organized in May, 1946. The British were the first to recognize the need to form an organization to rescue airmen early in World War II. In 1943, only 28 percent of the 8th AF crews "in distress" were rescued. By September, 1944, 90 percent of the AAF crews forced down in the sea in ETO were recovered!

By March, 1945, a total of 1,972 American airmen had been saved by British and American rescue units in the areas of the North Sea, English Channel, and other waters around Great Britain.

By the middle of 1968, ARRS (Aerospace Rescue and Recovery Service—another name change) was credited with 13,000 lives saved and they had directly aided more than 64,000 others. Under command of Colonel Allison C. Brooks, with headquarters in Orlando, Florida, ARRS's primary "starch-wing" plane, like that of the Hurricane Hunters, is the Lockheed *Hercules.*

That name "Lockheed" has been synonymous with smoothness of exterior design since the late 20's when their *Vega* was made famous by such pilots as Amelia Earhart and Wiley Post.

In June of 1938, Lockheed received their first really big military order. The British Air Ministry signed a contract for 200 airplanes, the largest order received by any American aircraft manufacturer since the end of World War I. This Model 14 became the famed RAF *Hudson,* which, ironically, was the only type plane being built by the nearly broke company, and that first Model 14 order came from Japan!

Before the end of World War II, Lockheed built 3,000 *Hudsons* which were so tough they earned a nickname, "The Burbank Boomerang," because they always came back from missions.

The first pure jet developed from the start for cargo, Lockheed's C-141 *StarLifter* holds the record as the first jet capable of paratroop drops. Cargo can be air-dropped at 230 mph, or the craft, with USAF cargo handling systems on the ground, can be unloaded and reloaded in 30 minutes. With 284 C-141's in MAC's inventory by the end of 1968, the Command's airlift capacity was four times as great as in 1961. (Photo courtesy USAF)

The USAF's XV-4B *Hummingbird II,* a vehicle for testing VTOL (vertical take-off and landing) designs, was built by Lockheed in 1968. The *Hummingbird II* differs from the I built for the army particularly in the engines. The II has six GE jet engines, four mounted vertically for direct lift and two mounted horizontally for lift-cruise. B. J. Dvorscak is test pilot. (Photo courtesy Lockheed-Georgia)

The late Robert Gross, wartime president of Lockheed Aircraft Corporation, Burbank, said, "The air industry was called upon to build thousands of something it had built only dozens of before," during World War II. And, Lockheed did. From the original Burbank plant, in shaky business since 1928, Lockheed turned out 19,000 military planes. P-38 *Lightnings,* in 18 versions, counted for more than one-half of that total. The *Lightnings* were the only American fighters in production at both the beginning and the end of the war.

Lockheed-Burbank's other 9,000 WW II models were the *Hudsons,* the *Ventura* and *Harpoon* for the Navy, the transports—the *Lodestar* and *Constellation,* and Boeing designed B-17's.

In the immediate post-war years, Lockheed developed America's first operational jet, the P-80 *Shooting Star,* which claimed its first victim in the first aerial jet fight, a MIG over Korea.

At this same time, the *Constellation* family grew into what was called the most graceful airplane in the air. The three-finned "Connie" spanned the transport time interval between the old and slow and few-seated DC-3 to the jet transports.

She had been on the drawingboards from the late 30's and was being built, primarily, at the request of

In the late 60s, Lockheed developed numerous designs for compound (winged) helicopters to study the feasibility of such craft as interurban transports. These two rigid-rotors (attaching blades to hub rigidly rather than flexibly), bottom, the Army-Navy XH-51A and top, five-place 286 are among the world's fastest and most maneuverable. The XH-51A has flown 302.6 mph, and the certificated 286 as fast as 206 mph. Lockheed's AH56A *Cheyenne* gunship compound helicopter designed for the Army ran into some performance problems in the spring of 1969. This culminated with the U. S. Army cancelling (May 19, 1969) the production contract of $875 million. (Photo courtesy Lockheed Aircraft)

Howard Hughes for his (then) TWA. Then, ATC took over all options on transport development. The first *Connie* was not test-flown until 1943. A total of 20 went to ATC, and they were flown throughout the remaining years of the war.

In September, 1945, in the effort to replenish their fleets, the airlines quickly ordered *Connies*. TWA, Pan Am, and Eastern signed contracts for $55 million worth of *Constellations*. Lockheed's post-war outlook couldn't have been brighter. TWA initiated the first

The world's largest aircraft in 1969, the C-5 *Galaxy*, a Lockheed-USAF development, first flew on June 30, 1968. The high flotation landing gear has 28 wheels and "kneels" that permits the main cargo floor to be lowered to truck bed height. Cruising over 500 mph, the C-5 is capable of taking off on a runway only 7,500 feet long even at gross weight of 728,500 pounds. The Military Airlift Command is the USAF operator. (Photo courtesy Lockheed Aircraft)

regular transAtlantic passenger flights by landplane with their *Constellations,* in 1946.

The family *Constellation* was produced through 1958 as an airliner and as a military craft.*

Lockheed redesigned the *Shooting Star,* and in a two-place configuration, it became the T-33 *"T-Bird,"* the first jet trainer; 5,691 *T-Birds* were built in this country and 656 more in Lockheed's Canada branch,

* The US Navy's hurricane hunter planes, called "Snowcloud," were *Constellations* as late as 1969. One of their reconnaissance 121's, a *Constellation* modified with sophisticated electronics and radar, was shot down by the North Koreans in the spring of 1969.

while Japan's factory turned out an additional 210.

As a follow-up in the fighter design, Lockheed's first triplesonic F-104 *Starfighter* flew in 1956, and by 1969, 2200 of these jets served in air force fleets of 14 nations.

The *Electra* followed the *Constellation* in the airline fleets in 1959. Many of those are still in service, in mid-1969, as freighters, but after that design, 9 long years passed before the company came out with a design that met the approval of the airline operators.

Perhaps the time expended on the concept of a supersonic transport (which lost out to a Boeing de-

Brigadier General Harold F. Funsch, MAC surgeon, is MAC's medical chief (1969). Referred to as "Mr. Airevac," General Funsch has insisted on patient comfort through World War II and the Korean and Vietnamese conflicts. With MAC's complements of intra and inter-theatre C-141's, and domestic C-131's, C-118's, and the new C-9's, any patient anywhere in the world can be at the treating U. S. medical facility within 36 hours. This has been General Funsch's objective. MAC airlifted a record number of patients in 1967, a total of 126,858. Of those, nearly 23,000 were battle casualties from the Pacific area. (Photo courtesy USAF)

sign) explains this delay. In 1968, though, Daniel J. Haughton, Chairman of the Board, introduced the brand new L-1011 *TriStar*. At a design range, the *TriStar* will carry 256 passengers and 5,000 pounds of baggage and cargo at a cruise speed of 569-MPH over 3,260 miles, non-stop. It is to be introduced into commercial service in 1971.

Lockheed has a product mix ranging from the jet transports and fighters mentioned, through missiles, oceanographic experiments, primary long-range anti-sub planes for the Navy, jet interceptors, the SR-71 strategic reconnaissance craft, and the U-2, plus the Army gunship helicopter, the *Cheyenne*. Most of these fall under the heading of Lockheed-California, while the total complex, counting almost 95,000 employees, ranging from the west coast to the east and some foreign subsidiaries adds research, ordnance, small business jets—and monster jets.*

* Lockheed's plants had a combined floor space of 15.7 million square feet in 1959. A 70 per cent increase was made in 10 years, and in 1969, total Lockheed floor area measured 26.4 million square feet. These plants included California's Rye Canyon Research Laboratory, Santa Cruz *Agena* test base, Sunnyvale's Missiles and Space Headquarters, Palo Alto's Research lab, Ocean Research Laboratory in San Diego, Lockheed's Propulsion plant at Redlands, with production at Potrero, Van Nuys—rotary wing craft production, Burbank—corporate headquarters, Lockheed-Georgia, Marietta, Georgia, McAlester, Oklahoma, Plainview, New Jersey, and servicing and shipbuilding facilities in many locations.

Lockheed-Georgia, under president T. R. May, is the birthplace of monster-jets. Basically, this plant came into the headlines with the C-130 *Hercules,* the world champion weight-lifter, in 1956. The Herky-Bird is the most widely used military transport in the world with 39 versions in the services of 15 nations. More than 1000 of these four-engine propjet transports had been produced by the start of 1969, and they were still rolling out of Lockheed-Georgia's plant.

The basic *Hercules* is 97.7 feet long, 38.4 feet high, and has a wingspan of 132.6 feet. The "E" model has a payload of 45,000 pounds and it serves

The McDonnell Douglas-built C-9 *Nightingale* brings jet speed and comfort to the MAC mission of airlifting sick and wounded between medical facilities. The first C-9 was delivered to MAC on August 10, 1968. A total of 12 of these flying hospitals, with built-in intensive care sections, will be operated by the 375th Aeromedical Airlift Wing, Scott AFB, Illinois. In wartime, MAC's Medical Evacuation units are augmented by Air Force Reserve units and Air National Guard's four squadrons. A modified version of the DC-9, the *Nightingale* can carry 40 ambulatory patients, 30 litter patients, or a combination of the two. (Photo courtesy USAF)

in every capacity from low-level assault to civilian airline airfreighter.

Two variants of the *Hercules* work with MAC's Aerospace Rescue and Recovery Service as air-snatch systems. One, the Fulton Skyhook, is a personnel pick-up. A "V" boom leads the 130's nose to connect into a cable suspended between a balloon in the air and a man on the ground or in the water below. After hooking the cable, the 130's interior equipment reels the man aboard.

The other air-snatch system is designed by All American Engineering, who pioneered the idea's use as a method to pick up mail bags with a moving plane in the late 30's. The modern version is a large trapeze suspended below and to the rear of a *Hercules*. A large number of successful air-to-air catches of data capsules, particularly from the *Discoverer* series of satellites, have been made.

ARRS utilizes the rescue virtues of the Sikorsky *Jolly Green Giant* and *Buff* helicopters, which, in combat conditions, are complete systems with hoists, with jungle penetrator seats, and with pararescuemen who are trained medics and SCUBA divers.*

ARS became an organized reality in March, 1946. During the Korean War, the service's 3rd Rescue Squadron evacuated more than 20,000 wounded men and is officially credited with saving 9,680 lives. At least 4 of our Korean aces were saved by the men of the 3rd.

More details of ARRS in combat were in an earlier chapter, but here, we want to add that the service was given world-wide space recovery responsibility during manned shots in 1961. ARRS took an active part in recovery of *Gemini* 3 (1964), *Gemini* 8 (1966), and all of the *Apollo* missions.

In the humanitarian sector of their missions, MAC, at the request of the French government, flew wounded Legionnaires out of Indochina; these men and planes brought earthquake victims out of Chile, Morocco, India, and Brazil. Following typhoons, they saved lives on Wake Island and Japan. When polio struck, MAC helped Argentina, and The Netherlands has reason to thank the Command for help when that country was hit by a disaster flood.

* These complete systems are a far-cry from the first major rescue mission in January, 1943. At that time, General Nathan F. Twining, then commander of the 13th Air Force, went down at sea with 14 companions between Guadacanal and Espiritu Santo. After six long days of floating, the men were found by a B-17 piloted by Frank F. Everest (now, a general). They were picked up by a Navy PBY.

On the side of their military duties, MAC has served the United Nations in the Korean War, Suez, Lebanon, Formosa, Congo, Cuba, India, and Vietnam. The airlift brought 9,700 Hungarian refugees to a haven in the United States.

Forty-three different nations have felt the helping hand of MAC, and to do this, plus their various other missions which range from Air Photographic and Charting Service to SAM (Special Air Missions, such as flying the president's aircraft) takes a variety of equipment.

For instance, in MAC's world-wide aeromedical airlift of the sick and injured, the basic aircraft was Lockheed's C-141 *StarLifter* powered by Pratt & Whitney turbofans, from the time of the first roll-out, 1963, until the McDonnell Douglas C-9 *Nightingale* flew in 1969.

Actually, the *Nightingale*, especially designed for this duty, replaces the air-evac prop planes entirely, and will lessen this duty for the *StarLifter*.

The *StarLifter* is not only a flying hospital but the backbone of MAC's cargo-troop carrier fleet. Through the late 60's, these 318,000-pound fanjets, made weekly trips around the world, evacuated both civilians and military men in distress; it was the first jet to drop paratroops, and holds records for heavy cargo drops. Only 14 squadrons of *StarLifters*, in 1967, had a capacity of 595 million ton miles a month, almost as much as the entire USAF fleet (638 million ton miles) in fiscal 1965.

The last *StarLifter* of the 285 unit order rolled out of Lockheed-Georgia. The long-range planning for this craft, however, means that no replacements are expected before 1975.

With the escalating brush-fire wars in Southeast Asia, three-quarters of the 1969 Defense Department budget was assigned to provide the supplies needed by men in combat. All of this fits under a broad term —logistics—which includes research and development, procurement, and dozens of like operations— but ends with MAC delivering. Into this part of logistics comes computers and palletized cargo, and the mightiest airplane of them all—the USAF/Lockheed C-5 *Galaxy* (named, as in the tradition of Lockheed, for a heavenly body.) This gigantic aircraft has a tremendous impact on all who see it— and on MAC.

When, about 30 years ago, headlines announced in amazement that it took only 38 B-18 bombers to move 400 men 400 miles, it's easy to see the tremendous interest in military airlift when the *Hercules* came out, in the 50's, with a payload of 8 tons. Then, along came the *StarLifter's* capability to fly 6,200 miles with 16 tons, twice the weight aboard a Herky-Bird. The jumbo C-5* moves 55 tons, about 3 times the payload of a C-141, 6,350 miles, non-stop. As an example, 100 *Galaxies* could deliver an entire Army division, 15,000 men and all of their organic equipment, from the United States to Europe in 24 hours.

The C-5's wing span is 223 feet, and its length—246 feet—is more than twice the distance of the Wright brothers' first flight in a powered aircraft. The top of the plane's tail soars 65 feet in the air. Powered by four GE jet engines creating 164,000 pounds of thrust, this jumbo is able to land on only a 4000 foot dirt runway. Just four of these crafts could replace the 14 *StarLifters* needed, daily, to supply the necessary 500 tons of cargo to Vietnam in 1968.

The commercial version of the C-5, designated the L-500, could be delivered by June, 1972. For specific duties, such as flying European automobiles to the American market, the L-500's 135 tons of allowable cargo weight with fuel to fly the Atlantic, is unsurpassed.

So goes Lockheed, whose sales in 1968 came to $2.22 billion. With total assets of $937 million and a year-end backlog of $4.76 billion, it's a long way from the near-bankrupt company of the 30's. Military orders are only a part of this back-log; orders for 181 commercial jumbo-jets, the *Tri-Star,* and sales of the corporate *JetStar,* will keep the company growing in what is hoped to be a peaceful decade—the 70's.

MAC continues to go—and grow. From the first aero medical evacuation in February, 1918, when one litter patient was flown out in a Curtiss JN-4, the humanitarian airlift covers the globe—by jet. More than 104,000 officers, airmen, and civilians serve in the Command; about 72,000 of those as assigned to the airlift, which, between 1964 and 1968, moved more than 6 billion pounds of cargo. That figure, alone, is more than the combined totals of supplies moved in the Hump operation, Berlin Airlift, and the total tactical airlift in Korea.

MAC makes nearly as many sorties (take-offs and landings) as all Air Force planes, combined, in Vietnam in 1969. General Howell M. Estes, Jr., the current comander, also administers the civil reserve air fleet (about 350 airplanes owned by the airlines) and the 250 transports of the Air Reserve forces. Exercise Big Lift indeed it is.

---

* In the spring of 1969, Defense Secretary Melvin Laird requested that Air Force Secretary Robert C. Seamans investigate the entire C-5 transport plane program. Secretary Laird said costs were running an estimated $2.1 billion higher than forecast four years ago. This breaks down to more than $35 million per unit, $10 million more than estimated in March, 1968. The Air Force originally ordered 58 of these planes and on January 16, 1969, exercised its option to buy 57 more, a total of 115. First deliveries were scheduled for June, 1969. Lockheed Board Chairman Haughton and President Carl Kotchian, in May of 1969, admitted the costs for the "first production run" would exceed the estimates, but that an exact price can't be set until the program has run out its four years of contract. Working on a costs-plus basis, there's no reason to think Lockheed is overcharging to increase its profits. *There will be little, if any, profit in the first run.* The higher costs, according to Mr. Kotchian, were due to abnormal inflation, the step-up in Vietnam fighting resulting in serious shortages and delays in supplies, and "Unanticipated design and manufacturing problems."

PROBLEMS, POLITICS
AND PROMISE

18. McNamara's Brand

The Convair F-111 is a remarkable airplane. Not the least of its several remarkable features is the fact that it actually flies. That it seems capable of performing at least one of the missions originally envisioned for it appears little short of miraculous when one considers that this craft is largely the product of an incredibly naive coterie of New Frontier/Great Society theoreticians led by an ex-Harvard economist. True, there had to be some honest-to-Pete aircraft engineers involved somewhere along the line, but they served more as extenuators than as innovators in the F-111 program. Ignored altogether were the air officers who asked for a new fighter plane in the first place, and who later had to make do with the bungled result.

The F-111 was conceived as a Tactical Fighter Experimental (TFX) craft in 1959 in the office of Air Force General F. F. Everest. General Everest had just taken over as chief of the Tactical Air Command (TAC) and foresaw a need for a new fighter-bomber that could sustain a speed of 800 mph for at least 400 miles at extremely low altitudes (low enough to slip under enemy radar screens). And since overseas bases would always be subject to political as well as physical obliteration, the proposed new plane should have a high altitude economy range of, say, 3,000 miles; enough to fly the Atlantic non-stop and without air-to-air refueling. Also desirable was a top speed in excess of 1,700 mph for air intercept of the best Soviet fighters likely to be operational in the late sixties and early seventies.

At that time, during the last two years of the Eisenhower Administration, U.S. policy for prevention of nuclear war with the Soviets was the promise of certain and massive U.S. retaliation should the Russians attempt a nuclear first-strike against America and her allies. In those saner times, no responsible U.S. leader was willing to gamble America's freedom —or existence—on a child-like faith in Russian pledges. In view of Soviet acts since WW-II one had to assume that, if Red Russia ever came to believe it could attack the United States with relative impunity, it would do so. Therefore, a clearly superior and well-balanced retaliatory strike-force was accepted as essential to the security of the U.S. during this time, and an aircraft possessing the performance parameters requested by TAC Headquarters would add the proper balance to America's new ICBM (Inter-Continental Ballistic Missiles) and high-altitude strategic bomber force.

Once TAC had decided upon the kind of airplane it needed to best fulfill its obligation to the nation's defense, normal procedures for its acquisition were set in motion: first, permission was obtained from Air Force Headquarters to proceed with the project; then Air Force Systems Command carried the ball until their slide-rule people pronounced the project feasible. Next, detailed specifications were drawn up to be sent to the various airframe manufacturers along with the request that each submit a specific design proposal. Normally, this would result in a number of different "paper airplanes," that is, drawings and definite proposals detailing how each plane-maker would meet the specifications and performance levels desired. Finally, all these designs would be evaluated according to what is known as the Systems Source Selection Procedure, which is a fancy way of saying that Air Force brass would get together and pick the design they liked the best and, through the Secretary of the Air Force and Secretary of Defense, ask Congress to fund it.

As we said, this is the way it would normally be done. But the original TFX concept never got this far because, late in 1960, President Eisenhower, unwilling to commit the next President (who would take office in January, 1961) to what could be regarded as a "lame duck" decision in the TFX matter, instructed the Air Force to delay its request for design proposals from the manufacturers in deference to the incoming administration.

And incoming with President John F. Kennedy was, of course, former economics professor Robert S. McNamara as the new Secretary of Defense.

Mr. McNamara was possessed of a tidy mind bounded by dollar signs, and it seemed ridiculous to him that the *last thing* the Air Force should ask when buying a new plane was its price. A weapons system, like anything else, should be "cost effective" (textbook terminology for "get your money's worth"); and besides, there surely had to be a more scientific means of choosing a new fighter airplane than reliance upon the collective judgment of a bunch of generals who had done their combat flying back in WW-II.

So, aided and abetted by President Kennedy, the new Secretary of Defense at once set about "restructuring" the Department of Defense to make it efficient, and as free as possible from military influence (which was one and the same thing in Secretary McNamara's view). "Efficiency" was the operative term and McNamara's chief selling point, because it implied good administrative practices and, as a corollary, reduced costs. But alas, history must record that McNamara's eager-eyed minions, though well supplied with exotic theories and properly benumbed by their obeisance to the computer, succeeded mostly in swelling the federal payroll, while achieving neither efficiency nor undisputed savings in seven years of experimentation and arbitrary civilian rule.* They

did, however, effectively wrest from military professionals the power of decision in weapons selection. And thereby hangs the tale of the F-111.

Now, while the Air Force was drawing up specs for its new TFX during the waning days of the Eisenhower Era, the U.S. Navy was also preparing to shop for a new fighter plane. The Navy's needs, of course, were quite. different from those of the Air Force. Primarily, the Navy's fighter must ride shotgun for the fleet. It must form a defensive perimeter, say 150 nautical miles in radius, and loiter at slow speeds and high altitudes while scanning the sky with radar to guard against enemy aircraft attack on the carrier force. To be truly effective, the Navy fighter should be able to remain on station (combat air patrol) for at least four hours at a time and still possess enough fuel to go out and meet an incoming enemy.

An important feature of the Navy fighter (indeed, its *raison d'etre,* and which gained for it the tentative name, *Missileer*) would be its long-range *Phoenix* air-to-air missile system, a very sophisticated marriage of an AIM-54 missile, AN/AWG-9 radar control and computer, plus the MAV-48A missile/bomb launcher. This ultra-advanced system could fire from extreme range at a radar-fixed target, track and destroy it, then (say its enthusiastic supporters) throw rocks at any survivors.

So, the Air Force TFX and the Navy *Missileer* programs were awaiting confirmation from President Kennedy's new Secretary of Defense when Mr. McNamara took possession of the Pentagon and informed its habitues that, henceforth, things were going to be different around there. He immediately looked at the TFX and *Missileer* requests and, on February 14, just three weeks after assuming office, ordered *all* the services (including the Army) to get together and agree upon a *single* tactical fighter design based upon the Air Force TFX concept.

This order was met with shocked silence from the services. The Air Force had asked for an offensive fighter; the Navy a defensive one. The Marines, which had asked for neither, were interested in airplanes only for close support of ground combat operations. And the Army, which had not owned a fighter airplane

---

* McNamara did close a number of military installations including Air Force bases. He also cancelled such major weapons systems as the *Skybolt* long-range nuclear-tipped air-to-surface

missile, the B-70 supersonic bomber and the Nike-Zeus antiballistic missile. Perhaps none of these weapons was/is essential to America's survival as a free nation. Perhaps. But such cancellations may represent a saving in the same sense that one saves money by cancelling a portion of his insurance. Time alone will determine whether or not the U.S. could afford these economies.

since the Air Force became a separate service in 1947, was puzzled as well as shocked because it was highly unlikely the Air Force would tolerate Army intrusion into a basic Air Force responsibility.

The Navy recovered first and, on March 9, flatly told the Department of Defense (DoD) that the Navy wanted no part of a multi-service TFX, adding that the F-4 *Phantom,* which it already had, was a better airplane for its purposes. And since the Navy makes such decisions for the Marines, that went for the Marines, too. The Army, perhaps not wishing to incur Air Force wrath, also allowed the Navy to speak for it. The Air Force, then headed by General LeMay, prudently held its fire. Clearly, if the Navy were able to successfully resist McNamara's naive order, the TFX program might go ahead as originally planned.

Meanwhile, Herbert F. York, first Director of Defense Research and Engineering under McNamara,

Secretary of Defense Robert S. McNamara (L) and Deputy Secretary of Defense Cyrus R. Vance face reporters in a 1967 news briefing. Mr. McNamara, a former economics teacher and president of Ford Motor Company, was clearly a patriotic and dedicated man in government service, but air historians cannot deal kindly with him. At best—that is, if the weaknesses he bequeathed us can be remedied in time—history may picture him as a sort of Ivy League Don Quixote tilting with windmill-powered computers. (Photo courtesy U. S. Army)

organized the Committee on Tactical Air. It now seems strange that Mr. McNamara should have permitted this committee to function, unless he was convinced that it would agree with his decision in the TFX matter. However, after studying the problem for a couple of months, the Committee on Tactical Air—attempting to arrive at the nation's tactical air requirements for the period 1962-1971—concluded that those aging generals and admirals had been right in the first place: the Air Force needed the TFX; the Navy needed its *Missileer*.

But Secretary McNamara had already made up his mind. Shortly *before* the Committee on Tactical Air issued its report (May 19, 1961), DoD cancelled the Navy's *Missileer* project. The Navy would take a compromised TFX or nothing.

Therefore, on May 31, Secretary of Navy John Connally wrote to McNamara saying the Navy was willing to fall into line on the question of a multi-service fighter, while at the same time suggesting that the Navy be allowed to run the program (you can't blame a guy for trying).

The Navy, of course, had no chance of directing TFX development, mainly because the Air Force would procure perhaps five times as many of the production airplanes as would the Navy; and when McNamara ordered, on June 7, 1961, that the TFX be developed as a joint Air Force/Navy venture, he gave the Air Force overall management authority. The Secretary of Defense had by that time modified his thinking to the extent that he no longer demanded that the plane also serve the Army and Marines. Still, Navy and Air Force requirements remained as incompatible as ever; and by late August the two services were convinced that they could never agree upon a single airplane design. If the Air Force were to get the speed it needed for its long-range low-level interdiction mission, the immutable laws of physics determined that the craft would have to be about 90 feet long and weigh about 90,000 pounds. These figures were dictated by 1) aerodynamic efficiency, 2) amount of fuel necessary and 3) sufficient structural strength to withstand flight loads incurred in the "thick" atmosphere of low altitude at supersonic speeds.

But the Navy insisted that the catapults on its carriers would not handle a 90,000-pound airplane, and most of the elevators that took its shipboard aircraft between hangar decks and flight decks would not accommodate a plane 90-feet in length. Besides, the Navy didn't need a plane all that strong or even that

fast. The Navy wanted a fighter that weighed not more than 55,000 pounds; was perhaps 50 feet in length and which possessed a relatively fat fuselage to hold a big radar dish. In other words, the Navy still held fast to its *Missileer* concept simply because that was what it needed. The Air Force was equally adamant regarding its needs; if the TFX were scaled-down, made lighter and fatter, it would not be capable of performing the primary mission required of it by the Tactical Air Command.

Nevertheless, on September 1, 1961, Secretary McNamara directly ordered the Navy and Air Force to settle upon a compromise fighter design and that was that.

In retrospect, it's difficult to conclude that McNamara was ever much concerned with the missions for which the Air Force and Navy had planned in drawing up specifications for their respective machines. If so, the mission of neither service was "cost effective" since each required a specialized machine—or, more properly, the specialized machines were not cost effective if each would fulfill the mission requirements of but a single service. In other words, Mr. McNamara was working from a very simple (and correct) assumption: two airplanes would cost twice as much to develop as one. Therefore as much as $500 million could be saved in research and development costs if one plane rather than two was developed because that amount was the "ball-park" estimate for R&D on each.

Another point should be considered: The services had fought McNamara every inch of the way; and if in the end he admitted they were right and that his "cost effective" theory was not applicable in the case of the TFX, his whole program for restructuring the DoD and proving that civilian thinking was superior to military thinking in the matter of weapons selection would be discredited, and that of course would make the less-than-humble Mr. McNamara and his "Whiz Kids" (a popular term for them at the time) look foolish indeed.

After McNamara's order of September 1, 1961, industry was asked for design proposals for the bi-service TFX. Initially, six prime contractors responded, though the field was soon narrowed to two, Boeing and General Dynamics (Convair Division), with Grumman participating as a sort of junior partner with the latter. Both Boeing and Convair chose a swing-wing design despite the fact that this principle was relatively undeveloped (NASA's swing-wing research craft, the X-5, had proven extremely unstable), because only by varying the wing's geometry in flight could the TFX come close to satisfying the widely diverse demands that would be placed upon it.

During 1962 four separate competitions between Boeing and Convair were conducted instead of the usual one, because both companies at first proposed designs that would not attain flying speed from carrier launch without unrealistic over-the-deck wind velocities (under battle conditions, it is often necessary to launch aircraft without turning a carrier directly into the wind), and because neither company offered cost estimates that were considered realistic by Secretary McNamara.

But at last, during the second week in November, 1962, the Navy and Air Force unanimously agreed upon a specific design proposal. Eight generals and three admirals, plus Chief of Naval Operations Admiral Anderson and Air Force Chief of Staff General LeMay, picked the Boeing design.

But apparently Mr. McNamara was out to prove something. On November 13, he announced that Convair, not Boeing, would be awarded the research and development contract for the TFX. The contract amounted to $439 million and included production of 22 airplanes. Agreeing with Secretary McNamara's decision (since they were also Kennedy appointees), were Secretary of the Air Force Eugene Zuckert and Secretary of Navy (since December, 1961) Fred Korth.

This astonishing decision appears less astonishing when one takes into account Mr. McNamara's determination, dedication, bull-headedness (pick the one you think most appropriate), and the fact—overlooked by most at the time—that the Boeing proposal better suited both Navy and Air Force because Boeing actually planned to build a different airplane for each. The Navy and Air Force versions of the Boeing design, while utilizing 60 per cent identical parts by number, used but 34 per cent identical structural parts by weight. Convair's two versions used 83.7 per cent identical parts by number and 92 per cent by weight. So, Boeing's design could hardly have constituted Mr. McNamara's idea of "commonality" between the Air Force and Navy versions of the TFX. Secretary McNamara himself suggested as much when he said, "My examination of the facts . . . convinced me that, as compared with the Boeing proposal, the General Dynamics proposal was substantially closer

to a single design . . . "* And that was the *only* reason for his decision that will survive a close study of the whole program. Suggestions that Convair won the prize because the (then) Vice President Lyndon Johnson was a Texan and Convair was a Texas company, or equally unprovable and perhaps politically-inspired charges, simply do not square with McNamara's character. Clearly, he is an obdurate and proud man—and an incorruptible one. His mistakes were mistakes of judgment, and admit to no moral indictment.

In January, 1965, the TFX prototype—by then called the F-111—tried out its swing-wing feature in flight for the first time and established that Convair engineers had solved the aerodynamic problems of the variable-geometry wing. Test pilots said they liked the airplane's handling qualities, and the Air Force managed to find some nice things to say about its step-child fighter, despite the fact that, due to the "commonality" requirement, the craft had been pared in weight to 72,000 pounds and in length to 73 feet. In truth, it was not the airplane the Air Force wanted. And it suited the Navy not at all. The Navy version was 6½ feet shorter in length, with a shorter, fatter nose holding a scaled-down radar dish, and its wing, extended, was 7 feet longer. Wingspan of both versions, wings folded for supersonic flight, was about 34 feet. The Air Force F-111A had a long needle nose to improve aerodynamic efficiency, while the Navy's F-111B possessed a hinged nose section which allowed an additional 5-foot reduction in overall length for carrier handling.

Actually, during the F-111's two year incubation period, the Navy seems to have concluded that there was no chance of obtaining a useful Navy fighter out of the program, and therefore allowed the Air Force to salvage whatever it could. There was simply no way to successfully mate a sports car and a four-ton truck. You could have one or the other, but not both in a pair of machines utilizing 90 per cent identical parts. The Navy, of course, paid lip-service to the program as long as Mr. McNamara remained in

* He went on to say, "I decided to select General Dynamics as the development contractor, since I concluded that it was best qualified to design the most effective airplane that could be produced at the least cost in the least time, to meet our military requirements." But this was a meaningless generalization. Certainly, General Dynamics' Convair Division, which can trace its airplane-building activity back to 1923, would be hard-put to match the successful Boeing military designs dating from that time.

Although the F-111 was expected by the Air Force to operate from unimproved airfields and thus greatly increase its flexibility, the Convair design placed air intakes close to the ground and directly in line with whatever foreign objects the dual nose wheels were likely to cast backwards for ingestion by the engines. Therefore, the F-111's much publicized short-field capability may have little actual value. (Photo courtesy General Dynamics)

office, because all things—both good and bad—come to the Navy via the DoD; and it must have been frustrating indeed that Mr. McNamara continued to run DoD under President Johnson after President Kennedy's tragic death in November, 1963, and then for another three years of LBJ's own administration.

Meanwhile, the F-111 test programs went ahead. Like all new designs this machine contained "bugs," and an almost predictable number of the planes were lost during the testing and early operational stages.

A total of 13 crashed amassing the first 25,000 hours of flying time, and some of them went unexplained, although some pilots suspected (perhaps wrongly) the plane's Terrain-Following Radar (TFR) system, an advanced radar-computer package designed to automatically fly the airplane, preferably at night or in bad weather, at extremely low altitudes following surface contours at a speed of 800 mph.

Also in the meantime, Secretary McNamara and his chief advisor, Assistant Secretary of Defense for Systems Analysis Alain C. Enthoven, pursued their cost effective doctrine by seeking other missions for the F-111. It wasn't necessary to look far because the Air Force would, by 1970, need a new strategic bomber to begin replacement of the intercontinental B-52 Models C through E which, due to anticipated metal fatigue, aggravated by low level operations, should be retired. And since McNamara had repeatedly refused to allow the Air Force to start development of its new Advanced Manned Strategic Aircraft (AMSA), and since at that late date (1965) such a craft could not possibly be developed and put into service by 1970, the Defense Secretary and his chief Whiz Kid determined that the F-111 would make a good strategic bomber. Accordingly, McNamara proposed that 210 of the strategic bomber versions be built at a cost of $8.3 million each. Designated the FB-111 (not to be confused with the Navy's F-111B), this stretched model would, the Defense Secretary assured the nation, be capable of carrying fifty 750-pound conventional bombs hung

The F-111A, operational with the Tactical Air Command, began its service life inferior in performance to the latest known Soviet fighter. Future air historians may regard the F-111 as symbolic of the enervating defense policies of the Kennedy/Johnson/McNamara years, a period during which huge sums were spent for defense while the nation's military strength, relative to that of the Soviets, eroded. (Photo courtesy General Dynamics)

beneath its wings (though the wings could not be folded), and would have performance "comparing well" with the B-52 ("There's no use trying," Alice said, "One can't believe impossible things." "I dare say you haven't had much practice," said the Queen).*

By the first of May, 1968, DoD had signed agreements in the amount of $4.5 billion and had issued checks totalling $2.9 billion for F-111 production. At that time, total planned procurement was 1,100

F-111A's, F-111D's and FB-111's for the Air Force; 270 of the F-111B's for the Navy, plus 24 F-111K's for Australia and 50 for Great Britain. At that point, 61 F-111A's had been built at a cost of $6.76 million each, and 4 F-111B's had been delivered at a cost of $8.1 million each, with contracts signed for more of the Navy versions in the amount of $376.4 million (Secretary McNamara originally estimated that the F-111 would cost $3.9 million each. By way of comparison, the F-4E *Phantom* cost $2.4 million each).

This was the situation as of May 1, 1968; but it

Alice in Wonderland; Lewis Carroll.

The FB-111 "strategic bomber." This version of the F-111 was picked by McNamara to replace B-52's Models C through F by the end of 1971. SAC's proud shield painted on fuselage of the FB-111 does not, of course, actually make it a strategic bomber; but since McNamara refused to allow development of the Air Force's Advanced Manned Strategic Aircraft, SAC must, for a few critical years at least, make do with McNamara's Brand. (Photo courtesy USAF)

was extremely tentative, and events of the previous five months would soon change the whole picture. In the first place, there was a new Secretary of Defense. Mr. McNamara, who had clearly become a political liability to President Johnson, had resigned suddenly in December, 1967. He was succeeded by Clark M. Clifford early in 1968.

Clifford, a Washington lawyer who knew his way around the Pentagon, had helped write the National Security Act of 1947, and had long been an advocate of superior U.S. offensive might as the best guarantee for world peace. Certainly, Secretary Clifford offered a sympathetic ear to the Navy in the F-111 matter; and after a decent interval solemnly acquiesced when the Congress—also well aware of the Navy's problem, largely through the investigation of Sen. Henry M. Jackson's National Security and International Operations Subcommittee—refused to vote money for the Navy's F-111B. Later, the Pentagon followed up, on July 10, 1968, officially announcing that General Dynamics had been ordered to stop all work on the F-111B (no decision was made at the time concerning the Air Force's 1,100 F-111's in three models, though Great Britain did wiggle out of her 50-plane order). The Pentagon spokesman did acknowledge, when questioned by aviation reporters, that the Navy had been considering design proposals for some months for a new Navy fighter known as the VFX (an updated *Missileer,* of course).

Two weeks later, the Navy said it had flown an F-111B onto the deck of the *Coral Sea* for 10 arrested landings and catapult take-offs. The test craft, however, had been stripped to 57,000 pounds for the trials, about 24,000 pounds under its combat-effective weight loaded with fuel and fully armed. These brief tests were evidently conducted to pin down performance figures in case the Navy was ever required to further defend its opposition to the commonality concept.

In the spring of 1969, the Navy chose Grumman's design proposal for its new VFX, labeled it the F-14A, and announced that it should be going to the fleet (Congress and President Nixon willing) as early as 1973—equipped with that lovely *Phoenix* missile system. The DoD budget for fiscal year 1970 contained $414 million for F-14A development.

The Department of Defense budget for FY 1970 also contained $175 million for initial development of the F-15, an honest-to-LeMay superiority fighter for the Air Force. But since the F-15 wasn't expected to be operational before 1975 (and since the American taxpayer has an awful lot of money invested in the F-111), the DoD budget also included $500 million for another 60 F-111's, which would give the Air Force a total of 391 such craft. Depending upon a number of things, including how the F-111's prove out in service, and such imponderables as the effect of aging flower child William Fulbright's televised inquisitions of the "Military-Industrial Complex," the Air Force indicated that it might later ask for additional F-111's.

To be sure, the F-111 falls short of all original design goals (except, perhaps, for un-refuelable range). Its actual performance figures are classified as this account is written; but it's no secret that it cannot carry a full bomb load above 30,000 feet; or that its low-level supersonic range is shorter than expected, and that it cannot dogfight the best contemporary Soviet fighters. True, the Air Force calls the F-111 a "fighter" airplane, but in reality it is a modern version of the WW-II Douglas A-26 *Invader* (called "B-26" after 1947). The F-111 is a ground attack aircraft; and most of the nice things AF pilots say about it are not directed at the airplane at all, but at its highly sophisticated avionics devices. During the spring of 1969, the F-111 was still undergoing modification (principally, strengthening of the wing carry-through structure) which would add more weight, and correspondingly subtract from its reported 1,600 mph maximum speed as well as other performance.

We should profit from this experiment in cost effectiveness, total civilian control and computerized analysis. There's nothing wrong with the idea that defense spending be carefully watched and our weaponry cost effective as long as our methods do not defeat our purposes. Cost effectiveness should be applied intelligently in weapons selection; so should the professional judgment of veteran military officers. We shall be able to take small comfort from the knowledge that the Soviet weaponry that clobbers us is not cost effective by our standards—and that we possess no effective counter measure for the same reason.

19. Air Power and the Flexible Response

U.S. air power was used in the Vietnam War much as WW-I generals employed it in France in 1918. At any time during the Vietnam conflict the world's mightiest air force and seaborne air-strike force could have, *with conventional weapons,* destroyed North Vietnam's ability to make war; and our Navy-Air Force team could have done so within a matter of weeks had it been allowed to pursue an overall air strategy for victory. Instead, Air Force and Naval air power was committed piece-meal against relatively insignificant logistics targets, in direct support of an endless and inconclusive series of ground actions, and as an extension of the artillery. General John J. Pershing could have planned as well fifty years before with a few squadrons of *Spads* and DH-4's.

This being true, there should be little wonder that an assortment of super-doves, elbowing one another for the spotlight on Senator Fulbright's TV Show, could assert that American air power had proved ineffective in stopping North Vietnam's infiltration of men and supplies into the South, and that bombing of the North could not force Ho Chi Minh to the negotiating table. And these political adventurers were correct because the Navy and Air Force air-strike capabilities were tightly fettered by the Kennedy/Johnson/McNamara doctrine known as "flexible response."

The theory of flexible response grew out of the negative reactions of well-meaning people to the Eisenhower-Dulles defense policy of massive nuclear retaliation. Flexible response was a simple proposition and a seemingly logical one (indeed, it still *sounds* logical, despite its failure in Vietnam), and its purpose was to give the United States a much wider range of action in dealing with brush-fire wars. It held that, through the build-up of a modern and varied mix of conventional weapons and forces, America would have alternatives for meeting aggression other than the very limited choices of massive nuclear retaliation or no retaliation at all. In short, the amount of force used by the U.S. should always be commensurate with the threat.

The original idea was not McNamara's. A number of respected leaders, including General Maxwell Taylor and General James Gavin, argued for a "limited war" capability long before McNamara became Secretary of Defense; but it was the Kennedy-McNamara team of Ivy League whiz kids that coined the term "flexible response," and then redirected U.S. policy toward a defense posture that, in the end, amounted to little more than Faith, Hope and Parity. By the time President Nixon took office early in 1969, faith in such a policy was dead; some hope remained that the U.S. would find a face-saving way out of Vietnam (though not among military leaders, who believed only a clear-cut military victory could provide that), and the Soviets had achieved parity with the U.S. in both first and second-strike nuclear capability.*

Perhaps the biggest flaw in the flexible response theory was simply that it did not take into account the average American's attitude toward war. All our history testifies that Americans unite in support of war only when convinced that our very survival is at stake or when embarked upon a righteous crusade with God firmly on our side. It was hard for the U.S. Government to make such an emotional pitch for a limited war with confused beginnings and the promise of an inconclusive end.

Also, inherent in the idea of flexible response was the fact that it was a policy of response, a reaction to moves initiated by the other side. In practice this meant the enemy chose the kind of conflict best suited to his resources, picked the areas of confrontation and decided the level of fighting. In other words, the war was fought on enemy terms and at his convenience. It is patently impossible to win such a war militarily; and when the enemy under such conditions also possesses a well-organized and well-disciplined quasi-political organization trained in the arts of propaganda and terror, and effectively infiltrates it throughout the disputed area, no stable political settlement—except in his favor—is likely; especially, when the defending government America attempts to support is corrupt and ineffective.

Given these ridiculous circumstances, a coalition of the faint-hearted, treasonable, mis-guided and just plain fed-up elements among us, some apparently believing Communism's dogma of the ant colony

---

* As of January 1, 1969, the U.S. possessed 1,054 ICBM's. At that time, lame duck Secretary of Defense Clark Clifford said Russia had over 1,000. A year earlier, Secretary McNamara had said the Soviets had 720 ICBM's and were adding to that arsenal at the rate of 380 per year. It therefore seems safe to assume that the Russians possessed at least 1,100 ICBM's as of January 1, 1969. It was known that a portion of this strike force had a re-load capacity, and that these missiles were ten times more powerful than U.S. ICBM's, the latter fact significant because such power could cripple U.S. hardened missile sites in a first-strike situation and therefore represent something more than an "over-kill" potential. On the above-mentioned date, America could count a numerically-superior intercontinental strategic bomber force: 646 (obsolescent B-52's and B-58's) to Russia's 150. The U.S. had 16 attack aircraft carriers in service; the Russians none. And though the U.S. had but 41 missile submarines to the Soviets' 100, the U.S. Polaris-armed subs did have an edge in total number of deliverable missiles. On the other hand, Russia had 25 surface-to-surface missile ships while America had none. Russia also had 62 ABM sites and the U.S. had none. All this was, of course, a far cry from the clear 5-to-1 nuclear advantage possessed by the U.S. when Eisenhower left office in 1961.

to be the wave of the future, fomented a serious division of the American People and probably rendered impossible the exercise of whatever limited options may have been left to newly elected President Nixon —except that of gradual disengagement and a pull-out of U.S. forces in Vietnam. Submerged somewhere among the obscene slogans of over-privileged young rebels and the pseudo-moralistic verbiage of leftist congressional leaders were the true issues: the security and vital interests of the United States. The Johnson Administration may have badly conducted America's confrontation with Communism in Vietnam; but nevertheless LBJ was attempting to serve his country's best interests.

The American presence in Vietnam was owed solely to the desire of several administrations—beginning with that of President Truman—to halt the spread of Communism before it engulfed, by aggression, subversion and other classical Communist means, the whole of Southeast Asia along with Australia and the Philippines. America had no other reason for sponsoring the Southeast Asia Treaty Organization (SEATO) and of course no territorial ambitions. It had seemed clear to President Truman and his Secretary of State James F. Byrnes in 1945, that if all Asia should fall to the Reds, then Japan, Australia and the Philippines must perforce seek accommodation with the Communists—assuming these peripheral nations were spared outright invasion. In either case, the Free World's western frontier would be the West Coast of the United States. In other words, since a stand-off with the Soviets was necessary somewhere along the line in order to stop their avowed intention of spreading the questionable joys of Stalinism throughout the world, better make that stand as far as possible from American shores.

Therefore, America aided the French in France's "re-colonization" of Indo China (Laos, Cambodia and Vietnam) at the end of WW-II. President Truman not only viewed French control of that portion of Southeast Asia as a barrier to Soviet expansion, but probably would have backed the French there in any event because French participation was essential to the formation of the North Atlantic Treaty Organization (NATO) which was then in the planning stage (NATO became fact in 1948). So, although the Truman Administration had already spoken out against foreign domination of such small countries as Laos, Cambodia and Vietnam, Truman found the Soviet threat in Europe to be of such immediacy, and NATO of such importance, he was forced to compromise with one injustice in order to foil a far greater one.

Meanwhile, a typical Communist organization, originally formed in 1930 by Ho Chi Minh, and which had ineffectually opposed French rule before WW-II in the area now known as North Vietnam, gained strength during the war by playing-down its Red leadership and recruiting non-Communist peasants for guerilla action against Japanese occupation forces—an activity in which the Viet Minh, as they called themselves, were aided by the American OSS force ("Wild Bill" Donovan's Office of Strategic Services, organized during WW-II under President Roosevelt, was the parent of the CIA). Later, during the early fifties, the Viet Minh, with Soviet and Red Chinese money and arms, fought to expel their French masters, a task they accomplished in 1954 after the famed seige of the French garrison at Dienbienphu.

Following the French defeat in North Vietnam, a multi-nation conference in Geneva produced the Geneva Accords, agreements that formally established conditions for a cease-fire in Indo China. This instrument provided for the independence of Laos,

Douglas AD *Skyraiders* of the Vietnamese Air Force fold wings for parking as they return from an air strike against Viet Cong positions. *Skyraider* deliveries to the U. S. Navy began in 1946 and production continued for ten years for a total of about 3,150 AD's of 29 different models. Engine is the Wright R-3350. (Photo courtesy USAF)

The ageless C-47 *Gooney Bird* fights its third war for the USAF in Vietnam. This one is dropping psychological warfare leaflets inviting the invader to surrender. Using the leaflets as safe conduct passes, 1,600 of the enemy defected in a single month. (Photo courtesy USAF)

Cambodia and Vietnam, while a political dividing-line was drawn at the 17th Parallel across Vietnam in recognition of centuries-old differences between the 18 million people of the North, traditionally ruled from Hanoi, and the 16 million people of the South whose emperors had ruled from Hue before the French arrived. A provision of the Geneva Accords made mandatory free elections throughout Vietnam by July, 1956, at which time the North and South were to be united under a single government. This stipulation embarrassed the U.S. and prevented the U.S. from becoming a signatory to the Geneva Accords, because America well knew that the Viet Minh would have agents in every hamlet to insure Ho Chi Minh's election.

This, then, was the political bucket of eels America inherited in Vietnam after French collapse. But since the original reason for U.S. involvement remained as valid as ever, the American Government—by then in the hands of President Eisenhower and his Secretary of State John Foster Dulles—supported the formation of the Diem Government in South Vietnam, convinced that Ngo Dinh Diem was the only man on the scene with sufficient following to successfully resist Red subversion and eventual takeover by Ho's gang. Diem probably had another appeal to the U.S., it being that his new regime—which took power from the anemic government of Bao Dai (established in office by the departing French) in a relatively-bloodless *coup d' etat*—had

A flight of B-57 *Canberra* TAC bombers start engines with explosive cartridge charges that permit operation from forward airfields with a minimum of ground support equipment. *Canberras* were 1951 British (English Electric) designed, built in U.S. by Martin. (Photo courtesy USAF)

not signed the Geneva Accords and could therefore ignore the "free election" bit until Ho's guerillas in the South were rounded up and something akin to a real choice between Communism and a republican form of government could be offered the people of Vietnam.

However, Diem, though he did effectively fight Communism for a time, proved to be a despot of another color; and in 1963 President Kennedy appeared less than grieved when the Diem Government fell with Diem's assassination, and a military junta led by General Duong Van Minh assumed power. Other *coups* and political intrigues followed as prominent South Vietnamese sought power,

although all were anti-Communist. During this period, the U.S. continued to spend money in South Vietnam and sent military advisers to help train the South Vietnamese Army, a policy that was justified by requests for such aid from each succeeding Saigon government—none of which could have survived without American help (nor could Ho Chi Minh's government in the North have survived without Soviet and Red Chinese aid had Ho been subjected to similar aggression from the South).

Undisguised aid to South Vietnam by the U.S. and several other Free World nations resulted from the SEATO pact signed at Manila on September 8, 1954. The Southeast Asia Treaty Organization—

Ling Temco Vought F-8D *Crusader* of VF-124 Squadron is caught an instant before catapult launch from the carrier *Constellation*. This carrier saw action in the Gulf of Tonkin, and her pilots carried out many air strikes over Vietnam. (Photo courtesy LTV by Arthur Schoeni)

formed while the French were pulling out of Southeast Asia—was a mutual defense society intended to discourage Red aggressions against Thailand, Pakistan, the Philippines, Australia and New Zealand, all of which were members, as well as Cambodia, Laos and "the free territory under the jurisdiction of the State of Vietnam" (South Vietnam), who were not members because of possible conflict with the Geneva Accords. Cambodia, Laos and South Vietnam could, according to the SEATO agreement, ask for SEATO help in case of armed attack. South Vietnam, of course, did so. Cambodia and Laos did not; evidently preferring Communist infiltration.

India and Burma remained aloof from SEATO, clucking their tongues righteously while receiving a measure of SEATO protection without expenditure or commitment on their part.

Early in 1961, Ho Chi Minh announced that, on the previous December 20, he had formed the National Liberation Front (Viet Cong), and then began escalating his war against the South. The Viet Cong, organized around hard-core Red guerillas of the old Viet Minh, murdered 1,719 and kidnapped 9,688 South Vietnamese during the next year. About 6,200 of Ho's men invaded the South that year, and this escalation of the war by the North continued

USAF's 4503rd Tactical Fighter Squadron, the Skoshi Tigers, was equipped with the Northrop F-5 *Freedom Fighter*. One of them is pictured dropping three general purpose bombs on Viet Cong positions in March 1966. The F-5 was conceived as an economical all-purpose fighter for NATO countries. (Photo courtesy USAF)

USAF C-123 *Provider* lifts-off from 1,900-ft. landing strip at Chi Lang, Vietnam, carrying South Vietnamese troops to a battle area, October 1966. (Photo courtesy USAF)

Convair F-102 *Delta Daggers* over Southeast Asia.
First plane to employ the NACA-discovered "area
rule" principle in fuselage design—after the prototype
of this intended supersonic fighter failed to achieve
Mach 1. The "bargain-priced" F-106 pushed as a substitute for a true air-superiority fighter, evolved from
this 1955 craft. (Photo courtesy USAF)

B-52 raids on Viet Cong strongholds in South Vietnam
began in June 1965. On July 7, 28 *Stratofortresses,*
modified to carry "iron bombs" instead of nuclear
weapons, dropped 540 tons of such explosives in War
Zone D, 30 miles from Saigon. (Photo courtesy USAF)

355

Air Force Chief of Staff Gen. John P. McConnell (L) congratulates Sgt. Mack, Spring Lake, N.C., after presenting him and Capt. Glenn, Fayetteville, N.C., with the Silver Star and Distinguished Flying Cross for heroism during the 1967 Battle of Dak To in South Vietnam. (Photo courtesy USAF)

throughout the sixties. It was matched by the "flexible response" of the Johnson Administration.

In July, 1964, President Johnson ordered the U.S. military mission in South Vietnam increased from 16,000 to 21,000 men (American forces in Vietnam numbered 685 in 1954; 2,000 in mid-1961, at which time President Kennedy had been in office 5 months, and 15,000 in 1963 when Johnson became President). Then, on August 2, 1964, North Vietnamese torpedo boats launched an attack upon the U.S. destroyer *Maddox* in the Gulf of Tonkin, and two days later struck again at the *Maddox* and the destroyer *Turner Joy.* The American vessels suffered minor damage and probably destroyed a pair of North

Vietnamese torpedo craft. In other circumstances that probably would have ended the matter (the Soviets, North Koreans and Red Chinese, both before and after the Tonkin Gulf incidents of 1964, fired upon or seized U.S. ships and planes without suffering armed retaliation), but President Johnson viewed the Tonkin Gulf attacks as a calculated test of American will by the North Vietnamese, and a challenge that could not be ignored if the SEATO guarantees were to remain credible. Also, the military position of South Vietnam (and U.S. assisting forces) should be considerably improved if the U.S. Air Force and Navy air power were loosed against military targets in the North—a move now conveniently justified, the Presi-

The Attack Carrier *USS Forrestal* (CVA-59) in the Gulf of Tonkin, July 29, 1967. (Photo courtesy U.S. Navy)

dent believed, in retaliation for Ho's attacks on U.S. ships.*

At 11:30 PM on the night of August 4, 1964, President Johnson told a nationwide TV audience that American air strikes against North Vietnamese gun boats and supporting facilities were under way. On the following day, the President asked Congressional support for "all necessary action to protect our armed forces and to assist nations covered by the SEATO treaty." Congress at once obliged with a resolution which specifically held that the President was authorized to "take all necessary steps, including the use of armed force, to assist any member or

protocol state of the Southeast Asia Collective Defense Treaty (original term for the SEATO document) requesting assistance in defense of its freedom." That was the precise wording, and the resolution contained no qualifying phrase. It was adopted by a vote of 466-to-0 in the House; 88-to-2 in the Senate. So, "Johnson's War," as the conflict in South Vietnam was to become known, clearly had a lot of god-fathers.

However, as we have seen, the key escalations of that war were made by Ho Chi Minh's National Liberation Front between December, 1960, and August, 1964. At the end of that time, the NLF had approximately 115,000 men in the South—which had murdered an estimated 5,587 and kidnapped an estimated 26,504 South Vietnamese civilians. In the face of these figures, whatever "escalation" the U.S.

* Ho admitted the August 2nd attack, saying it was a response to assaults against the North by South Vietnamese gun boats. He denied the August 4th attack, and Ho's U.S. apologists inferred that it was an LBJ invention.

Flight deck safety man gives all clear signal to catapult officer (not in picture) as Douglas A-4 *Skyhawk* awaits launch from Attack Carrier *USS F.D. Roosevelt* in the Gulf of Tonkin. (Photo courtesy U.S. Navy)

Grumman A-6A *Intruder* leaving deck of aircraft carrier is a low-altitude attack craft with all-weather capability. Crew has an integrated display system which enables them to "see" target area at night or in obscuring weather. Performance classified at this writing. (Photo courtesy Grumman Aircraft Engineering Corp.)

North American F-100 *Supersabre* flown by 1st Lt. Ben J. Briggs of Greenville, S.C., is shown during one of three attacks made by Briggs on a Viet Cong base camp, April 15, 1966. (Photo courtesy USAF)

induced into the conflict at that point in an attempt to halt the butchery would seem to be morally suspect only by Red sympahizers or the poorly informed.

Actually, a sustained air attack against North Vietnam (albeit one limited to indecisive targets) was not begun until March, 1965. In the meantime, President Johnson may have hoped that the initial air strikes in August, 1964, along with his mandate from the Congress, would serve to sufficiently impress Ho Chi Minh that a speedy settlement might be effected. Also, the 1964 Presidential Campaign was in progress and voters were obviously sensitive about the Vietnam issue. Up until that time, relatively few Americans had been in combat in South Vietnam (between January 1, 1960 and January 1, 1965 a total of 255 U.S. servicemen were killed while on

base defense duty or serving as advisers to South Vietnamese Army units).

But on the night of February 7, 1965, a large force of Viet Cong made a surprise attack on the American compound at Pleiku, killing 8 Americans and wounding 126. This resulted in immediate U.S. reprisal against the North with air strikes directed at military targets. And when the Viet Cong attacked American barracks twice more during the succeeding five days, U.S. jet fighters returned to North Vietnam each time in retaliation. Meanwhile, infiltration of men and supplies from North Vietnam into the South had reached alarming proportions (during the first 6 months of 1965, North Vietnamese units in the South more than doubled); therefore, early in March, in response to this continued escalation of the war, U.S. air strikes against the North were begun on a sustained basis, aimed primarily at the "Ho Chi Minh Trail" and other invasion routes. So, just which side did the "escalating" would seem to depend upon which side the appraiser favored—*The New York Times,* Senator Fulbright and the Students for a Democratic Society notwithstanding.

Criticism at home and perhaps the off-chance that Ho might negotiate caused President Johnson to try a 5-day pause in the bombing of the North beginning May 12, 1965. When it proved unproductive the strikes were resumed, and during the following month B-52 raids on Viet Cong positions in South Vietnam were begun. Late in July, Johnson announced that the U.S. forces in South Vietnam would be increased from 75,000 to 125,000 in response to North Vietnam's continuing troop build-up in the South.

During the next few months, as targets in the North were selected by the White House a few at a time, Air Force and Navy planes hit some installations of tactical and even strategic value, including tire and truck factories, arms plants and military barracks. On December 15, a strike was mounted against the electric power plant at Uongbi, 14 miles from Haiphong. Nevertheless, truly vital targets such as Haiphong Harbor (through which 70 per cent of Ho's military supplies passed) and the Red River Dam network (the key to North Vietnam's agricultural base), were regarded in Washington as "all-out-war" targets, and therefore not to be considered within the framework of flexible response.

Between December 24, 1965 and January 31, 1966, another fruitless bombing halt was tried; and when it produced no reaction—except stepped-up in-

Republic F-105 *Thunderchief* pilots over North Vietnam being led by F-100 *Supersabre* use F-100's radar monitoring equipment to pin-point cloud-obscured target. These craft struck at targets in the north from bases in Thailand before President Johnson halted such action in a futile attempt to negotiate a cease-fire. (Photo courtesy USAF)

The UH series of Bell helicopters is tri-service and is operational with military forces of more than 30 foreign nations. The Marine Corps version, the UH-1E, in combat in Vietnam, carries an assortment of weapons, rescue hoists, for its role as assault transport, armed escort craft, and rescue/evacuation vehicle. (Photo courtesy Bell Helicopter Company)

A development of the UH-1B, the *HueyCobra* broke speed records with a sustained level cruise of 200 mph in 1965. The next year the U.S. Army ordered 320 *HueyCobras,* the first copter designed as an aerial weapons platform. By October 1967, *HueyCobras* were zapping the Viet Cong and North Vietnamese invaders in Vietnam. This shark-mouthed *HueyCobra* has just loosed a rocket (extreme left) at the enemy below. (Photo courtesy U.S. Army)

Time exposure taken during the February 1968 Battle of Bien Hoa Air Base as enemy troops attempted to over-run American positions. Flares dropped by AC-47 drift above while *HueyCobra's* path may be traced by bursts of mini-gun fire concentrated on ground target. Enemy was stopped by Air Force 3rd Security Police Squadron and Vietnamese forces on ground and the death-spitting *HueyCobras* in the air. Enemy left 153 dead behind. (Photo courtesy USAF)

filtration of troops from the North—the Johnson Administration responded with more troops from the U.S. Thus, the pattern of escalation continued. By August 1, 1966, the enemy had increased his forces in the South to 282,000, while maintaining a monthly infiltration rate of approximately 5,000 men from the North. At that same time, American forces in South Vietnam totaled 267,000 men (South Vietnam's Army had about 275,000 regulars plus 340,000 ill-trained reserves. Australia, New Zealand and South Korea had a total of 29,150 men in South Vietnam).

But slowly, it became clear that flexible response was in fact not too flexible. At least, it was not as

Kaman HH-43 *Huskie* equipped with a fire bottle is first on scene as an A-1E *Skyraider* (originally AD-5) crash lands at Da Nang. *Huskie* has a top speed of 120 mph. (Photo courtesy USAF)

Sort of a poor boy's counterinsurgency airplane is the Cessna T-37 *Tweety Bird* jet trainer, all dressed up in battle fatigues, tip tanks, and packing side arms (in this case, wing-mounted rockets). As an honest-to-Pete warplane, the *Tweety Bird* is known as the A-37. (Photo courtesy USAF)

363

Modified Cessna *Superskymaster* in battle dress is the O-2A serving in Vietnam as a spotter or FAC (Forward Air Controller) craft. FAC pilots, flying "low and slow" (ly) search out the enemy, mark his position with smoke rockets, then call down and direct fighter-bomber strikes against him. FAC crews take a lot of enemy ground fire for their pains and are highly respected by friend and foe alike. (Photo courtesy USAF)

long as the U.S. remained determined to contain the conflict and minimize chances of provoking a direct confrontation with the Soviets and/or the Red Chinese. America therefore found itself trapped— by its own policies—in a protracted war of attrition that offered no promise of military victory and little chance of political solution short of an ignominious (however disguised) compromise with Communist aggression. President Johnson undoubtedly saw that his only choices were all-out conventional war—the unleashing of U.S. air power against the North with no vital strategic or tactical targets off-limits—or a gradual disengagement of U.S. forces coupled with massive arms aid to South Vietnam and the hope

the South Vietnamese could hold back the Reds while negotiating a settlement that did not lead to a Viet Cong seizure of power in Saigon.

But in the end, Johnson failed to make a choice. Instead, he made concessions to the enemy in a futile bid to reach a political agreement denying Ho Chi Minh the objectives the Red leader had sought. Since Ho had not had his arm sufficiently twisted, there was of course no reason for him to give up his objectives in the South, and whatever was to be done toward resolving the Vietnam problem was therefore left up to the next President, Richard Nixon.

Johnson's first major concession to the Reds was offered on March 31, 1968, when he announced that

80 per cent of the area north of the 17th Parallel (containing 90 per cent of all North Vietnamese people) would henceforth be spared further aerial attack by U.S. forces. At that time, all major railroad bridges in North Vietnam were down or damaged beyond use; war material could move southward only at night, and even then the trucks were in constant danger from U.S. night fighters. All consumer goods, including food, were strictly rationed; and 300,000 people, counting many Red Chinese "volunteers," were fully employed in road and rail repair. The bombing of the North, limited as it had been, had done much damage to the enemy's war machine. Therefore, Ho must have indeed been grateful to gain respite from further destruction when the only cost to him was that of maintaining a North Vietnamese "negotiating" team in Paris—which had small reason to seriously negotiate in the face of such an encouraging sign.

Although the limited bombing halt failed—for six months—to produce any meaningful dialog between the combatants' representatives in Paris, President

USAF Capt. Ed P. Larson of Puyallup, Wash. paddles toward an AF Grumman HU-16 *Albatross* amphibian that rescued him and his electronics officer, Capt. Kevin A. Gilroy, Menlo Park, Calif. on August 30, 1966, after the F-105 *Thunderchief* they were flying was hit by ground fire north of Hanoi and the U.S. airmen ejected over the South China Sea. Rescue was made through a hail of fire coming from nearby Red-held islands. (Photo courtesy USAF)

(about \$4.3 billion worth, to say nothing of the crews), while the total cost of the Vietnam War averaged about \$2 billion per month for the years 1966 through 1968 inclusive. Of the fixed-wing aircraft lost, 1,246 fell to hostile action—327 over the South, 919 over the North—and 1,247 were lost to operational accidents. Of the 982 helicopters lost to enemy action all but 10 went down over South Vietnam; 1,293 helicopters were destroyed in non-combat operations (again, the above figures are for the period January 1, 1961 to January 1, 1969). As for enemy casualties, the Viet Cong and North Vietnamese Peoples Army apparently lost 500,000 men during the above-mentioned period. When Italian Journalist Oriana Fallaci asked North Vietnam's De-

Thirsty Navy *Phantom* F-4 fighter refuels over the Gulf of Tonkin from Douglas KA-3B *Skywarrior* after a mission over North Vietnam. Both aircraft were operating off the carrier *USS Kitty Hawk,* March, 1968. (Photo courtesy U.S. Navy)

Johnson, under extreme pressure from a menage of home-front dissidents, and possibly influenced by a desire to salvage a Democratic victory in the 1968 Presidential Election, halted *all* bombing of North Vietnam on November 1st. He said at the time that Ho had agreed to some reciprocal measures of de-escalation. If Ho did so, there was never any evidence of it.

And that was the situation as President Nixon took office on January 20, 1969. More than a half-million U.S. troops were then in South Vietnam, and American combat deaths were approaching the 33,000 mark to equal our losses in the Korean War of the early fifties. Between January 1, 1961 and January 1, 1969, the United States lost a total of 4,768 aircraft in Vietnam; 2,493 fixed-wing and 2,275 helicopters

Scratch one North Vietnamese MiG. This is how it looks through the gunsight of an F-105 *Thunderchief* as 20-mm round explodes port wing tank of enemy fighter at almost point-blank range over North Vietnam. Victorious American pilot was identified only as "Major Kuster." (Photo courtesy USAF)

This Russian-built North Vietnamese surface-to-air missile (SAM) which missed its target was photographed by the pilot of an RF-101 *Voodoo* near Hanoi in June 1967. (Photo courtesy USAF)

fense Minister Vo Nguyen Giap if that figure, claimed by the Americans, was correct, Giap replied, "That's quite exact."*

The morality of America's confrontation with Communism in South Vietnam is defensible if we believe that the Red conspiracy is a grave threat to freedom and social justice throughout the world. However, the manner in which that confrontation was conducted would seem to possess little defense, either morally or militarily. The gradualism of flexible response wasted American lives, enemy lives and the lives of innocent civilians while hindering rather than hastening a conclusion of the conflict.

A dangerous side effect of the Vietnam War and the Kennedy/Johnson/McNamara Era has been the unreasoned blame for·those blundering years that has attached itself to that portion of U.S. industry which supplies America's military hardware, and to the U.S. military forces. Biased and sketchily researched news stories offered by major television networks and some newspapers have conspired with the artful dema-

goguery of the leftist Congressional leaders to provoke public resentment and distrust of a "Military-Industrial Complex" that is supposedly bent upon fleecing the U.S. taxpayer on the one hand while pushing us into a nuclear war of annihilation on the other (Eisenhower, before his death, on at least two occasions tried to correct the misinterpretation of his "warning" against a Military-Industrial Complex).

The truth is, charges of "excess profits" in defense spending are easily refuted by the actual figures. Net profit after taxes (percentage of sales) for the entire aerospace industry averaged exactly 2.28% for the years 1960-1965 inclusive, which was lower than any other segment of U.S. industry—and a principal reason aerospace companies long ago began diversifying into other markets.

And it is well to remember that, since 1961, weapons selection and defense spending have been further beyond military control than at any time in recent history. The TFX, Sheridan tank, M-16 rifle, etc., were approved by appointed civilians in the DoD and funded by the U.S. Congress. It is therefore ironic that suspicion and blame should be directed at the

* *Time,* April 18, 1969.

RADAR

BAMBOO MATTING

McDonnell-built RF-101 *Voodoo* reconnaissance photo of a SAM sight in North Vietnam, August 16, 1965. (Photo courtesy USAF)

U.S. Army Capt. Gerald O. Young, the first living helicopter pilot to be awarded the Congressional Medal of Honor, flew a *Jolly Green Giant* 118 hours on 60 missions during his three months at Da Nang. He rescued 11 people before his copter crashed. He was the only member of his crew to survive. (Photo courtesy Sikorsky Aircraft)

Receiving the U.S. Air Force Distinguished Flying Cross from Brig-Gen. Don F. Smith is 2nd Lt. Dinh Cam Bao, a FAC with the Vietnamese Air Force. Lt. Bao was cited for heroism for saving two companies of Vietnamese Army soldiers and their American advisers from being over-run and annihilated by a battalion of North Vietnamese in February 1968. Looking on is Lt. Col. Nguyen Huy Anh of the VNAF, Binh Thuy Air Base Commander. (Photo courtesy USAF)

In a near-vertical dive this *Skyraider* pilot aims his demolition and fragmentation bombs on a Viet Cong installation in the dense jungle area of Phuoc Tuy Province in South Vietnam. (Photo courtesy USAF)

369

least culpable. Industry did as it was asked; the military did as it was ordered.

America owes to both establishments not abuse, but appreciation. We are particularly indebted to our airmen who, frustrated by a policy in Vietnam they could scarcely comprehend, nevertheless did as our airmen have always done: they fought and died for freedom, and obeyed their Commander in Chief. As they themselves sometimes put it, they "kept the faith." The rest of us will learn to do the same; or lose that freedom.

Authors' note: The above was written in April, 1969, at which time the Vietnam War seemed far from ended. But whenever and however the end comes, this account should remain relevant.

20. The Crowded What?

On Saturday, July 13, 1968, a clot finally formed in the hardening arteries of America's air traffic system. The restriction was at a single airport, John F. Kennedy International, Long Island, New York; but circulation was affected in the system's extremities as is usual in such cases. And although the patient was (and continues to be) mainly attended by quacks, primarily concerned with expanding their own "practices," it is still alive and functioning—to a degree— as this is written.

That fateful Saturday came at the apogee of the tourist season, when hordes of New Yorkers jammed the Van Wyck Expressway bent on jetting to Cleveland or Washington or even all the way to Chicago (which is an impressive safari for the native of Fun City who believes—if he's ever thought about it— that the Kiowa Indian Reservation begins just beyond the Hudson). Anyway, these would-be air travelers were unaware that a great mass of hot, stagnant air, which had been building up from Boston to Cape Hatteras for almost a week, had absorbed tons of pollutants and reduced visibility to 2½ miles all the way up to 10,000 feet altitude. That in turn meant that all aircraft in the area must proceed under instrument flight rules (IFR) and be under "positive control" of ground controllers. But there is obviously a limit to the number of aircraft that can be so controlled, the principal limiting factors being the number of runways available for landings and take-offs,

and the efficiency of the controlling human/electronic system. At the end of the sixties, both were generally inadequate at major airports (along with ground access systems) for efficient airline operations, and particularly so at JFK International.

Although JFK possessed parallel runways, they were not designed for simultaneous instrument approaches. Under instrument conditions, controllers at the time were safely handling about 23 take-offs and 23 landings (or a mix totalling 46 aircraft movements) per runway per hour, spacing the movements about 80 seconds apart. So, clearly, given the conditions prevailing in the NYC area on that week-end, airliners operating from JFK could expect to be delayed in direct proportion to the number scheduled in excess of about 46 per hour. A check of the airline schedules revealed that as many as 87 airline departures and arrivals per hour were actually scheduled.

It should be noted at this point that at least two other runways at JFK were not in use because of "noise abatement" restrictions. In short, JFK International was and is severely limited in the number of airline flights it could and can handle because of an inadequate configuration for instrument approaches, inadequate ground-handling facilities for the processing of passengers, and an outmoded air traffic control system.

Another contributing factor to the air traffic mess during the summer of 1968 may have been a deliber-

During the Great Air Traffic Mess of mid-1968, TV's Johnny Carson, faced with tightly-scheduled appearances on both East and West Coasts, solved his problem by renting a Lear Jet and by-passing congested air terminals. He's pictured here explaining his dilemma to Lear Jet's Director of Public Relations, James R. Greenwood. (Photo courtesy Lear Jet Industries)

Turbo Commander built by North American Rockwell's Aero Commander Division in Bethany, Okla., is a 285 mph business plane with a range of 1,100 miles and ceiling of 30,000 feet. (Photo courtesy North American Rockwell)

Cessna *Cardinal* is a four-place personal and business
craft that sells for about $15,000 (depending upon
avionics desired). This gen-av aircraft has a top speed
of 144 mph and may safely operate from the smallest
airports. Engine is 150-hp Lycoming 0-320-E2D.
(Photo courtesy Cessna Aircraft Company)

TV star Hugh Downs is a licensed pilot and uses his
Cessna as a business machine, as do many other en-
tertainers to whom time is money. Downs, like Arthur
Godfrey, has proven an effective goodwill ambassador
for general aviation. (Photo courtesy Cessna Aircraft
Company)

UNITED STATES DEPARTMENT OF JUSTICE

$10,000 REWARD $10,000
HIJACKING OF AIRLINERS

The Attorney General of the United States hereby offers a reward of Ten Thousand Dollars ($10,000.00) for information leading to the arrest and conviction of anyone for violating any federal statute in any actual, attempted, or planned hijacking of aircraft.

As used in this offer, "hijacking" means the use of force, threats, or other means in illegally obtaining control of an aircraft of United States registry, or of any aircraft while in or over United States territory, for purposes which include the unauthorized removal of such aircraft from the United States or the unauthorized prevention of its return to the United States. This offer is made pursuant to Title 18, United States Code, section 3059.

Anyone having any information which he or she believes may be of the kind described above should give such information promptly to the nearest office of the Federal Bureau of Investigation.

August 4, 1961
at Washington, D. C.

Attorney General

Original poster sent to all airports in August 1961 by U.S. Attorney General Robert Kennedy, informing public of new law designed to combat hijacking of airliners to Cuba following Fidel Castro's alliance with Russia. As nearly as your authors could discover, no such reward had been paid as of June 1, 1969. (Author's photo)

ate slow-down by air traffic controllers. We say "may have been," because this is impossible to prove. The controllers are charged with the responsibility of *safely* moving air traffic as efficiently as possible. They have a handbook to guide them. Still, theirs is a "judgment" situation. It is often possible for experienced controllers to cut corners and speed traffic with total safety, especially in good weather. But if they choose to space aircraft farther apart under certain conditions, who can—or should—question whether these professionals are acting for any reason other than

the air travelers' best interests? Such acts did, however, contribute to the JFK bottleneck, dramatized the system's weaknesses, and resulted in significant (though needed) additions to the FAA controller force.

The air traffic delays that occurred elsewhere about the nation on that week-end were directly tied to the situation at JFK, because those were airliners with JFK as a destination. There was no reason to take-off from Miami or Chicago bound for JFK if one could not land when he got there.

All of the above could have been reported quickly and simply by the various news media at the time had it not been that these truths were clouded by misleading statements from those most guilty of creating the mess. Both the airlines, who had shamelessly over-scheduled in a scramble for the passenger's dollar, and the Federal Government, which has controlled, built, maintained, regulated and dictated the air traffic system in the United States since 1926, shifted the blame from themselves. It was not hard to do because they had a convenient whipping-boy all set up by years of airline propaganda.*

* The airlines speak with a single voice, that of Stuart Tipton, President of the Air Transport Association (ATA). All U.S. domestic airlines of any significance are members of ATA, and it constitutes one of the most effective pressure groups on Capitol Hill.

Both the airlines and the U.S. Department of Transportation (into which the morale-poor Federal Aviation Administration had been crammed by Lyndon Johnson) allowed that much of the air traffic muddle would magically clear if it weren't for all those privately owned general aviation airplanes cluttering up the air. This theme was picked up by newspapers and TV newscasters and other instant experts including those in the Congress (Senator Jack Javits, an alleged Republican from New York, was an example). The only thing wrong with that theory was that gen-av aircraft—that is, all aircraft except airliners—made up exactly 7 per cent of the air traffic at JFK, and most of that miniscule 7 per cent were air taxis delivering paying passengers to Big Brother.

General aviation airplanes are used for family vacations, too. This California couple is loading their *Piper Cherokee* for a trip into Baja California. Anticipating unimproved landing fields, they have included a spare tire in baggage compartment. (Photo courtesy Don Downie)

Senator Barry Goldwater, a veteran flyer, has long owned a private airplane. During the late 40s, it was a *Navion* shown here on an improvised airstrip in an isolated section of Arizona. *Navion* was originally designed by North American. (Photo courtesy Don Downie)

The truth was, and remains, that no gen-av pilot in possession of his senses flies into JFK (or any other major air terminal) unless he has a compelling and legitimate reason for doing so. To eliminate gen-av from JFK, or to assign priority to airliners over gen-av aircraft there, could not significantly ease the congestion. Gen-av aircraft simply were not there in the first place.

Well, why then, if "all those privately owned planes" weren't responsible for the problem at JFK, should the airlines and the Department of Transportation want to blame them? Why should DoT foster a rule (effective June 1, 1969) giving the airlines

priority over gen-av aircraft at five major air terminals in the U.S., priorities that entirely eliminated all but scheduled air carriers from JFK, La Guardia, Newark, O'Hare and Washington National during peak traffic hours?

Most people in general aviation believe the airlines and DoT took advantage of a situation (ironically created by the airlines and DoT) to establish forever the precedent that public air transportation should have priority and a favored status over private air travel. There was nothing new in this concept. The airline-Federal Government alliance has resulted in favored treatment for the public air carriers since the Kelly

General Aviation is also forest fire-fighting and aerial survey. These Beechcraft C55 *Barons* patrol valuable timberlands in the Western States and perform para-cargo drops. (Photo courtesy Beech Aircraft Corporation)

The Flying Farmers are another segment of general aviation and, as in other roles, the airplane pays its way down on the farm. This one is a 1962 Model Cessna 180, which has a cruising speed of 162 mph. (Photo courtesy Cessna Aircraft Company)

Twin-engined Piper *Navajo* above Navajo country in
Arizona as seen from rear window of sister craft. This
meeting was planned. One seldom sees another aircraft in flight above most of the U.S. The sky is not
crowded. (Photo courtesy Don Downie)

Bill (H.R. 7064) of 1925 established the U.S.
domestic airline industry and financed it with the
taxpayers' money (via air mail subsidies several times
that of actual air mail revenues).* Direct subsidy payments were no longer necessary to the
major airlines after WW-II (about a dozen feeder
airlines are still subsidized by the government,
though such payments are gradually declining),
nevertheless, the airlines are provided with a
multi-billion dollar air traffic control and weather
service at taxpayer expense, and of course they build
none of the multi-million dollar terminals or runways
constructed for their benefit (though they do pay
rental and landing fees). True, gen-av pilots also
use the air traffic control system and the posh airports
to a degree; however, neither the ATC system nor
the big air terminals were built for gen-av, and the
private or business plane could do very well with a
lot less. If it weren't for airline requirements, runway
thickness, for example, could be reduced by 65 per

cent with a proportionate decrease in cost. But the
fact that these *are* public facilities built with public
funds should be guarantee enough that all segments
of aviation enjoy equal access to them.

General aviation did possess such rights until the
system broke down after air transportation's rapid
growth (38 per cent per year) overtook the aging
air traffic control system and under-built ground facilities. The patch-work "solution" that was imposed
was based upon the premise that the airlines "produced the greatest good for the greatest number" (as
opposed to general aviation), and therefore general
aviation should be restrained from interfering with
the air carriers' dividends or Divine right to the
airways.

But the airlines' claim (echoed by the DoT) that
they produce the greatest good for the greatest number may also be in error. In 1968 general aviation,
serving *all* the nation's 9,000 airports (as opposed to
a total of 515 served by the airlines), carried more
than half of all air travelers. So, it is possible to ask,
just *which* half of the air-traveling public constitutes

* See chapters 12 and 21 of *Command the Horizon.*

378

the "greatest good?" Obviously, neither. Both the airlines and gen-av serve a basic need, and in terms of public service one is as important to America's total transportation system as the other.

There were two other reasons why the general public (almost half of which had never flown as of 1969) tended to side with the airlines and rendered it politically safe for the Federal Government to favor the big air carriers over all other segments of aviation. First, the belief had been fostered, largely by the news media, that airliners were flown only on instrument flight rules (IFR) and were always under "positive control" from the air traffic controllers, while gen-av airplanes were flown only under visual flight rules (VFR) and were loosely supervised if at all during flight. The truth was and is that there is but a single set of air regulations which apply equally to all aircraft whether they be airliners, private, commercial or military. The airlines, military and gen-av aircraft alike fly IFR or VFR as weather and visibility conditions dictate (*any* pilot who is not instrument-rated must remain on the ground when conditions are IFR). And all gen-av aircraft are operated under exactly the same degree of "positive control" in high-density areas and under IFR as the airlines. All gen-av aircraft must adhere to exactly the same rules under VFR conditions as the airlines.

Secondly, the general public had become convinced

Still another use for gen-av aircraft is duty with the U.S. Border Patrol. Here, a Piper *Super Cub,* a souped-up version of the venerable J-3, is flying over the Mexican Border City of Juarez, Mexico (note bull ring at lower right). (Photo courtesy Don Downie)

ACTIVE AIRMEN

ANALYSIS BY YEAR BY CLASS OF CERTIFICATE

Year	Students	Private	Commercial	ATR	Other	Total
1957	98,498	124,799	70,813	13,964	1,138	309,212
1958	103,456	140,573	93,126	15,840	1,370	354,365
1959	107,815	139,804	93,815	16,950	1,491	359,875
1960	99,182	138,869	89,904	18,279	1,828	348,062
1961	93,973	144,312	92,976	19,155	2,444	352,860
1962	95,870	149,405	96,047	20,032	4,617	365,971
1963	105,298	152,209	96,341	20,269	4,583	378,700
1964	120,743	175,574	108,428	21,572	4,724	431,041
1965	139,172	196,393	116,665	22,440	6,100	479,770
1966	164,536	205,787	119,854	21,760	6,500(E)	518,437
1967	181,287	253,312	150,135	25,817	7,380	617,098
1970*	224,000	298,000	179,000	31,000	8,000	740,000
1975*	320,000	403,000	243,000	41,000	10,000	1,017,000
1980*	460,000	552,000	332,000	57,000	14,000	1,415,000

ANALYSIS OF GENERAL AVIATION USERS
AIRCRAFT
1953-1980

AIRCRAFT

Year	Business	Commercial	Instruction	Personal	Other	Total
1953	18,220	7,090	5,440	29,260	1,030	61,040
1954	18,570	7,850	4,720	29,350	690	61,180
1957	21,520	8,800	5,680	29,850	670	66,520
1961	20,728	10,999	6,095	41,706	1,104	80,632
1963	20,793	11,548	6,121	44,860	1,766	85,088
1964	21,127	11,979	6,855	46,721	2,060	88,742
1965	21,650	11,355	8,034	51,093	3,310	95,442
1967*	30,100	14,449	14,155	62,540	956	122,200
1980*	58,435	29,415	30,616	139,510	2,024	260,000

* Estimate based upon FAA projection.

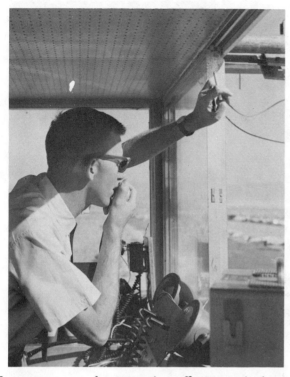

Key component of present air traffic system is the man in the tower. Pressures on him can be extreme. Future system must relieve him of such tasks as may be automatically performed via taped information, including initial individual voice-contacts with each incoming aircraft. (Photo courtesy Don Downie)

Cessna's entry in the "Biz-jet" market is the Cessna Fanjet 500, announced in October 1968, with deliveries promised in 1972. It is priced at $590,000. FAA estimates 2,600 pure jets in the gen-av fleet by 1975. (Photo montage courtesy Cessna Aircraft Company)

Turbo-charged Cessna 310 is popular business aircraft owned by many small corporations. Cruising speed is 260 mph at 20,000 ft. with a range of 1,500 miles. List price is $83,950. (Photo courtesy Cessna Aircraft Company)

Grumman *Ag-Cat* is only biplane in production during recent years, the biplane configuration being well-suited to dusting and spraying chores. These and other agricultural planes greatly increase U.S. food yield—and farming profits. (Photo courtesy Robert T. Smith)

Cessna 150 is a two-place sport/trainer and excellent low-priced personal plane inexpensive to maintain and easy to fly. Priced at $7,295 (floats extra), it was out-selling all other airplanes in the world at the end of the 60s. (Photo courtesy Cessna Aircraft Company)

(again, mostly via inaccurate news reporting) that the sky was crowded—principally by a lot of those "uncontrolled" little "Piper Cubs" flying around for fun and getting in the airliners' way. The truth was that, at the end of the sixties, all U.S. civil aircraft, including the (approximately) 2,500 domestic airliners, could fly at the same altitude, at the same time, above the State of Arizona and each would have a square mile of airspace. Since the airspace over Arizona comprises less than 4 per cent of the U.S. total, since no more than half of the 125,000 gen-av planes are ever in the air at one time and since airplanes, operating in the third dimension, separate by height as well as by width and breadth, this

example should prompt the question, "So where was the 'crowded sky'?" Obviously, it did not exist—except in the immediate vicinities of a handful of metropolitan airports where inadequate facilities and airline over-scheduling during peak hours artificially created it.

Eventually—say, in another decade or so—the sky could become "crowded" in places if air travel continues its current growth rate and if principal cities, aided by the government and the "aviation users' tax," fail to add more runways intelligently positioned, and if the air traffic control system is not restructured.

Four basic steps appear necessary if air transportation is not to be permanently restricted. These suggestions have come from various segments of the aerospace industry, and there seems no major divergence of opinion on them:

1) Increase the total number of runways at major airports that can be used simultaneously. The effectiveness of this kind of planning is illustrated by the Opa Locka, Florida Airport, which has three usable parallel runways, and though its tower operates but 16 hours per day, this general aviation facility counted 596,949 landings and take-offs in 1967, compared to 451,533 for JFK International. Opa Locka's hourly average was 102 aircraft movements, vs. 52 for JFK.

2) Improve and simplify the air traffic control system.
   a. Encourage development of an electronics package that provides a visual read-out of traffic instructions on plane's instrument panel, thus greatly reducing the load on voice radio.
   b. Provide separate radio frequencies and

The Texas-built Mooney *Statesman,* flying over Guadalupe Peak (8,751 ft; a fact that surprises most people who think of Texas as flat country). The four-place *Statesman* is an aerodynamically efficient design that gets 178 mph out of its 180-hp Lycoming engine. Today's Mooneys can trace their ancestry back to the Alexander *Eaglerock* biplanes of 1927 at which company young Al Mooney got his start as an airplane designer. Mooney left the current Mooney Aircraft Company in 1959 after designing the Mooney Mk.20. (Photo courtesy Mooney Aircraft Company)

GENERAL AVIATION AIRCRAFT
POPULATION OF ELIGIBLE AND ACTIVE FLEET
—HISTORICAL AND PROJECTED—

	Single Engine Recip.		Multi-Engine, Reciprocating To 12,500 lbs.				Multi & Single Engine Turbine Turboprop						Avg. Yearly	
	1-3 Place	4+ Place	To 600 hp	Over 600 hp	Over 12,500 lbs.	Total	Under 12,500	Over 12,500	Pure Jet	Total	Rotor	Other	Total	Incremental Change
1955	35,740	19,240				3,342					237	231	58,790	—
1956	35,358	22,805				4,183					283	257	62,886	4,096
1957	35,898	23,751				5,036					344	260	65,289	2,403
1958	35,522	26,170				5,416					439	292	67,839	2,550
1959	34,543	27,301				6,034					525	324	68,727	888
1960	33,472	34,829				7,243					634	371	76,549	7,822
1961	32,800	38,206				8,241				160	798	427	80,632	4,083
1962	32,341	41,120				8,973				213	967	507	84,121	3,489
1963	30,977	42,657				9,450				245	1,171	588	85,088	967
1964	30,367	45,777				10,338				306	1,306	648	88,742	3,654
1965	31,364	49,789				11,403				574	1,503	809	95,442	6,700
1966	35,681	52,940				12,671				915	1,622	877	104,706	9,264
*1967	39,010	57,887				13,842				1,030	1,716	915	114,400	9,694
**1967	41,760	61,319	10,423	2,864	1,222	14,509	475	323	787	1,585	1,875	1,152	122,200	—
1970	48,700	69,800	13,500	3,900	1,150	18,550	950	500	1,300	2,750	2,400	1,400	143,600	7,133
1975	55,400	98,200	19,500	6,200	800	26,500	2,400	1,000	2,600	6,000	4,200	1,700	192,000	9,680
1980	58,700	143,900	26,000	8,700	500	35,200	4,800	1,900	4,900	11,600	8,700	1,900	260,000	13,600

* Estimate of FAA Count.
** Revised Data Based on Study.

In 1968, Windecker Research, Inc. of Midland, Texas, announced a test program for their *Eagle I,* a four-place all-plastic airplane constructed of Fibaloy, a Dow Chemical material (not a thermoplastic) that offers an unusual strength-to-weight ratio and is said to resist fatigue much better than aircraft metals. FAA certification of the *Eagle I* was expected early in 1969. (Photo courtesy Windecker Research, Inc.)

Beechcraft *King Air* 100, a pressurized turboprop corporate aircraft can carry six executives 800 miles nonstop at a cruising speed of 287 mph. It is, in effect, a compact company-owned airliner; it possesses far greater flexibility than an airliner, and is capable of operating from any 2,500-ft. airstrip. It sells for $565,-000. (Photo courtesy Beech Aircraft Corporation)

ECONOMIC IMPACT OF GENERAL AVIATION*

(millions of dollars)

	1967	1975	1980
Total Production (Retail Prices)	667.5	1,547.9	2,306.0
Used Aircraft Transaction Costs	22.0	54.0	86.0
Operator's Costs of Operating Aircraft	683.1	1,491.0	2,488.0
Pilot's Wages—Administrative	521.0	941.0	1,139.0
Manufacturer's Investment	66.0	153.9	230.6
Investment by Dealers/Distributors	25.1	50.0	68.8
Investment by other FBO's	31.8	69.4	115.8
Government Expenses	218.0	465.6	695.5
	2,234.5	4,772.8	7,129.7

* These figures include only direct impact. The multiplier factor effect on the economy is not included in this estimate.

Corporate *King Air* 100's cockpit is airline configured as are most corporate-owned aircraft. To the layman standing in line at an airline ticket counter, this aircraft may be "one of them little twin-motored Piper Cubs;" but such gen-av craft are as well equipped as the airliner, and flown by a professional equally as competent as the 727 captain. (Photo courtesy Beech Aircraft Corporation)

separate airport traffic patterns for different aircraft categories.

   c. Establish separate approach and departure routes and altitudes for different category aircraft in congested areas.

3) Add new satellite airports in congested areas.

4) Improve ground transportation facilities to eliminate ground bottlenecks—between satellite airports, between airports and town, and between airports and outlying high-population areas. An example of a good beginning is the special train of Cleveland's Transit Electric Line which links the downtown Public Square with Cleveland-Hopkins Airport. The 19-mile 20-minute ride costs 35¢ and carries 4,000 people per day. The trip by taxi requires an hour, and costs $6 plus tip, while the airport limousine is $1.65 and an hour's time.

Some other, obvious things should be done, including the removal of *all* flight training (airline, private and military) from congested airports, the spreading-out of the now bunched airline schedules and installation of instrument approach and loading facilities at satellite airports.

Finally, as all gen-av pilots know, once you escape from that tiny block of airspace best described as a funnel's neck leading to or from one of the twelve or fifteen major airports in America, you may fly for hours across the nation without ever encountering another airplane. There's an awful lot of uncrowded sky out there (in 1969 America's civil aircraft population was about equal to the automobile population of 1906). However, until and unless the government-favored airlines can be induced to match their schedules to the facilities available, all private, business and commercial flying to and from some large metro-

ESTIMATED

DISTRIBUTION

OF THE

GENERAL AVIATION

FLEET

IN THE TOP 75

STANDARD

METROPOLITAN

STATISTICAL

AREAS (SMSA's)

PRESENT AND POTENTIAL

SMSA Area	Number of Active Registered Aircraft				
	1967	1970	1975	1980	Differential 1967 1980
New York	2,196	2,740	3,800	5,300	3,104
Chicago	2,883	3,560	4,900	6,700	3,817
Los Angeles	4,596	5,670	7,700	10,600	6,004
Philadelphia	1,348	1,730	2,500	3,700	2,352
Detroit	1,746	2,400	4,000	6,500	4,754
Boston	814	1,100	1,800	2,800	1,986
San Francisco	2,037	2,740	3,700	5,200	3,163
Pittsburgh	719	920	1,300	1,900	1,181
St. Louis	1,114	1,350	1,800	2,400	1,286
Washington, D.C.	1,507	2,040	3,300	5,200	3,693
Cleveland	792	1,000	1,400	2,000	1,208
Baltimore	598	810	1,300	2,100	1,502
Newark	606	800	1,200	1,900	1,294
Minneapolis	855	1,020	1,400	2,000	1,145
Houston	1,501	1,830	2,400	3,200	1,699
Buffalo	294	390	600	900	606
Milwaukee	655	770	1,000	1,200	545
Cincinnati	426	560	800	1,200	774
Paterson	541	630	1,000	1,500	959
Dallas	1,390	1,650	2,200	2,800	1,410
Seattle	1,122	1,310	1,700	2,100	978
Kansas City	1,088	1,340	1,800	2,400	1,312
San Diego	982	1,170	1,500	2,000	1,018
Atlanta	1,087	1,340	1,800	2,400	1,313
Indianapolis	804	980	1,300	1,700	896
Miami	1,009	1,270	1,800	2,600	1,591
Denver	1,023	1,230	1,600	2,100	1,077
New Orleans	403	540	800	1,300	897
Portland	1,136	1,300	1,600	1,900	764
San Bernardino	1,029	1,170	1,500	2,000	971
Tampa	466	670	1,100	1,900	1,434
Columbus	527	660	900	1,300	773
Rochester	344	440	600	900	556
Dayton	577	660	800	900	323
Louisville	252	350	600	1,100	848
Birmingham	267	390	700	1,100	833
Providence	128	180	300	500	372
San Antonio	473	600	900	1,300	827
Anaheim	985	1,170	1,500	1,900	915
Hartford	287	390	700	1,100	813
Memphis	590	750	1,000	1,500	910
Phoenix	1,010	1,160	1,400	1,700	690
New Haven	161	240	400	800	639
Albany	232	320	500	900	668
Bridgeport	274	350	600	900	626
San Jose	1,142	1,430	2,000	2,800	1,658
Toledo	345	440	600	900	555
Sacramento	828	970	1,200	1,600	772
Jersey City	46	60	100	100	54
Akron	314	410	600	800	486
Worcester	84	150	300	700	616
Norfolk	105	130	200	300	195
Gary	195	230	300	400	205
Fort Worth	774	920	1,200	1,500	726
Syracuse	284	370	500	800	516
Springfield	421	470	600	700	279
Greensboro	404	460	600	700	296
Oklahoma City	673	800	1,000	1,300	627
Youngstown	240	290	400	500	260
Allentown	197	220	300	300	103
Nashville	237	310	500	900	663
Grand Rapids	349	450	600	800	451
Omaha	406	480	600	800	394
Jacksonville	200	300	600	1,200	1,000
Salt Lake City	348	460	700	1,100	752
Richmond	190	290	500	900	710
Tulsa	553	630	800	900	347
Flint	335	410	500	800	465
Wilmington	366	440	600	700	334
Wichita	868	930	1,100	1,200	332
Harrisburg	194	280	500	800	606
Knoxville	215	300	500	700	485
Fresno	478	580	800	1,100	622
Mobile	148	230	400	700	552
Honolulu	182	270	500	900	718
SMSA Total	53,995	67,400	94,700	134,300	80,305
SMSA's Not Listed	68,205	76,290	97,300	125,700	57,495
Total Fleet	122,200	143,690	192,000	260,000	137,800
Top 75 SMSA % Of Total	44.2%	46.9%	49.3%	51.7%	58.3%

Note: Cities are ranked by population.

politan airports is going to suffer some curtailment and loss of business. And most av-people believe the situation will get worse before it gets better.

Note: In addition to the authors' own experiences, and interviews with such knowledgable people as a veteran pilot-official of the Atlanta FAA Regional Office, we also referenced material provided by Frank Hedrick and Leddy Greever; Frank Kingston Smith of the National Aviation Trades Association; the Aerospace Industries Association; a special report by R. Dixon Speas Associates for the Utility Airplane Council; *Flying* magazine; booklets of the Air Transport Association of America, and a special report by Kent Boyd. We do not mean to imply, however, that any of the above necessarily endorse the authors' presentation.

The Cessna *Skylane* is a four-place personal and business craft with a cruising speed of 162 mph at 6,500 ft. and a 695-mile normal range. It consumes 13–14 gal. of fuel per hour under such conditions. Overall cost of operation for planes of this class compares favorably with most automobiles when computed upon a seat/mile basis. Price is $19,950. (Photo courtesy Cessna Aircraft Company)

Bellanca 260C is an unusual four-placer in that it trades conventional metal wing and aluminum skin for extra performance. Plastic-impregnated Dacron covering is expected to last life of the plane, however, and plywood-covered spruce wings, specially treated with resin to prevent deterioration are said by Bellanca to be stronger than metal. Plane cruises at 190 mph with 260-hp, has excellent short-field capability. (Photo courtesy Chuck Wolfe)

21. Dr. Goddard and Charlie Brown

Modern rocketry was conceived October 19, 1899. That was the day the basic idea came to seventeen-year-old Bob Goddard as he pruned a cherry tree in the yard of the family home in Worcester, Massachusetts. Now the fact that it was a cherry tree must not arouse suspicion that this account is a folklore-type put on like that other cherry tree bit. Honest, we're telling it like it was. Bob Goddard, until his death in 1945, always celebrated October 19 as the anniversary date of his life's work. He had read a science-fiction story about space flight earlier that day —more than four years before the Wright brothers' first powered flight—and from that moment Robert H. Goddard dedicated himself to the development of a new science that would ultimately take man to the moon and beyond.

After high school, Goddard attended Worcester Polytechnic Institute and faced up to the fact that math, his weakest subject, must somehow become his strongest one. Countless nights of study plus extra coaching from a dedicated professor eventually dispelled the mysteries of mathematics, allowing its precise beauty to unfold and its "knowns" and "unknowns" to line up in orderly ranks like perfectly drilled soldiers to serve the cause for which Bob Goddard had drafted them. During this period, too, Goddard authored a paper suggesting the possibility of employing radioactive material as a fuel for deep space flight. The idea was ridiculed then; but such engines would appear on U.S. drawing boards fifty years later.

Following graduation, Goddard accepted a teaching slot at W.P.I. while attending nearby Clark University where he earned first his Master's degree, then his PhD. He then moved on to Princeton as a research fellow; but a year later was told by his doctor that he was so seriously infected with tuberculosis that he had not long to live. He went to bed as ordered, but refused to quit his work. If he must die soon, then all the more reason to carry his computations as far as possible. Perhaps someone else would take it from there.

But as the weeks passed, and the sheets of paper covered with odd mathematical symbols and formulae piled up beside his bed, Dr. Bob Goddard grew stronger rather than weaker. At the end of a year (1912), doctors pronounced the TB arrested—while in the meantime Goddard received patents upon a multi-stage rocket system that was to provide the basis for our manned space vehicles of the nineteen-sixties and seventies.

During the next four years, Goddard served as an assistant professor at Clark and spent most of his salary on experiments with small rockets. He knew of course that really significant progress would require significant money, so he authored another paper, ex-

Dr. Robert H. Goddard, Father of Modern Rocketry, began his work before WW-I, fired the world's first liquid-fueled rocket March 16, 1926. Aided by Charles Lindbergh's intervention on his behalf, Goddard, with Guggenheim grants, made significant progress during the 30s. (Photo courtesy U.S. Information Agency)

plained the nature of his work, progress to date, and sent copies to several non-profit scientific organizations in a bid for money to continue his experiments. Two months later, in January, 1917, the Smithsonian Institution provided a $5,000 grant in what its trustees surely must have regarded as a long shot of imposing proportions.

Nevertheless, when America entered WW-I three months later and Goddard's design work on a liquid-fueled rocket was halted, the Smithsonian prodded the Army into asking Goddard to produce a small battlefield rocket. That request resulted in a shoulder-fired weapon intended for the Infantry which was demonstrated at Aberdeen Proving Ground Novem-

ber 7, 1918. However, by that time the war was almost over and Dr. Goddard's unlikely looking contraption was shelved until, a quarter-century later, someone began casting about for a weapon American G.I.'s could use against Hitler's *Panzers* in WW-II. Goddard's old drawings were unearthed, and the 2.36-in. anti-tank rocket launcher that grew from them is best remembered by its more common name, the *Bazooka*.

At the end of WW-I, Goddard returned to Clark University as a full professor and in his spare time resumed work on his liquid-fueled rocket design. It was a slow process. In 1924 he married the secretary and former Clark honor student that he'd hired

Double-sonic Lockheed NF-104 *Starfighter,* specially modified with a rocket booster in its tail, orients future space pilots as it zooms trainees into a ballistic trajectory more than 100,000 feet up. Reaction controls similar to those used in Apollo spacecraft provide flight control experience required of men in space. Maj. James G. Rider, inset, beside the 6,000-lb. rocket booster in *Starfighter's* tail, heads flight operations at Edwards Air Force Base, home of the Aerospace Research Pilot School. (Photo courtesy Lockheed Aircraft Corporation)

Gemini command module, made by McDonnell Aircraft Corp. America's Gemini program of two-man earth-orbit space shots began in March 1965. By the time Gemini 12 flew in November 1966, the Soviet's demonstrated space technology had been eclipsed in all areas of accomplishment by U.S. astronauts. (Photo courtesy McDonnell Douglas)

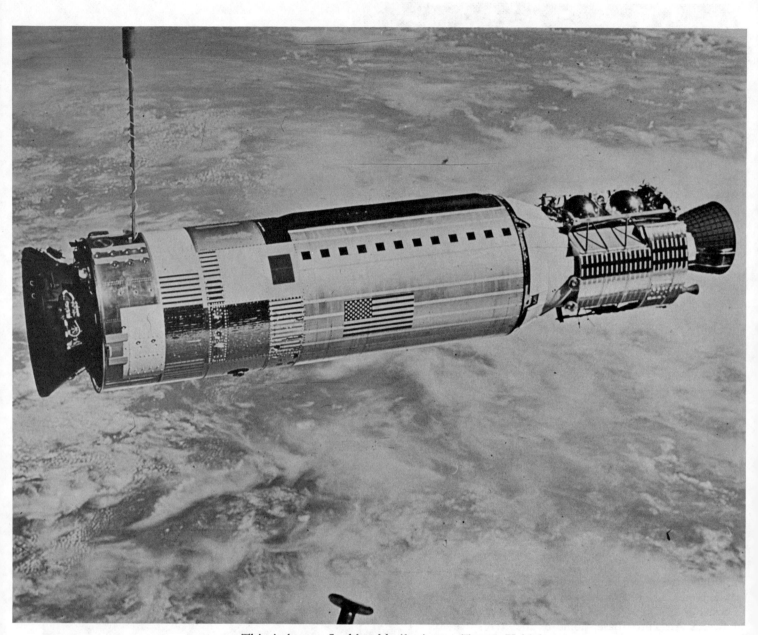

This is how a Lockheed-built Agena Target Vehicle appeared to Gemini astronauts as they approached for docking. Space docking, extra-vehicular activity and orbit manipulation were among new space skills acquired during Gemini flights. (Photo courtesy Lockheed Missiles & Space Company)

to type his notes. Then at last, on March 16, 1926, Dr. Bob Goddard tested the world's first liquid-propelled rocket. That forerunner of all space vehicles to come was ten feet in length and it soared 184 feet during a 2½-second burn. The flight was witnessed by Goddard's wife Esther, Henry Sachs, a machinist who aided in the rocket's construction, and Professor Percy Roope of Clark's physics department.

But the actual birth of modern rocketry was not announced to the world at large. Dr. Goddard sent a detailed report to the Smithsonian (which included photographs taken by his wife), and officials there decided not to tell the press of an event that might well rank with the Wright brothers' first flight in potential importance. The Smithsonian had good reason for such caution. A good deal of undeserved ridicule had attached itself to that august institution following the failure of a flying machine designed

This photo, taken atop the huge assembly building, shows Apollo-Saturn rocket at Kennedy Space Center as the 363-foot space vehicle and its launch umbilical tower move out of the assembly building headed for launch pad on the crawler-transporter. (Photo courtesy North American Rockwell)

F-1 rocket engines, each developing 1,500,000 pounds of thrust, are installed in S-1C first stage of the Saturn 5 booster. The S-1C stage is Boeing-built, the F-1 engines come from North American's Rocketdyne Division. (Photo courtesy North American Rockwell)

by Smithsonian Secretary Professor Langley in 1903. And when Goddard's first paper on his work (the one that fostered Smithsonian backing) had been released in 1920 and generated only scorn and disbelief, the Smithsonian decided it would be best to wait for a truly spectacular success before inviting more public derision.

Goddard tested two improved rockets during the next three years, then, on July 17, 1929, "spectacular success" of a sort was achieved—unintentionally—and the press, then as now a reflector of popular prejudice, blinded itself with ridicule and failed to perceive the significance of what it reported. On that day, Goddard launched a 55-lb rocket 11½-ft. in length fueled with 14 lbs of gasoline and 11 lbs of

LOX (liquid oxygen). It flew from a converted windmill tower, a distance of 171 feet, at an altitude of 90 feet with an 18-second burn. Most importantly, its gyro guidance system and on-board instrument package worked perfectly. Unfortunately, the vehicle's thunderous and fiery flight, from America's Launch Complex No. 1 (located on Aunt Effie Ward's farm near Auburn, Mass.), panicked the gentle folk of the neighborhood and brought police, firemen, sheriff and countless small boys to investigate. As a result, newspapers jibed that the professor's "moon rocket" had missed its target by approximately 239,000 miles, and the state fire marshal forbid any more nonsense of that kind.

Goddard appears to have possessed a great capacity

for absorbing ridicule without allowing it to affect his normal good humor. And that should be a good clue to his personal philosophy: although he was sure that history would absolve him, most men prefer the accolades while they are still alive to enjoy them. But Goddard, if hurt or discouraged by public reaction to his work, never outwardly showed it. He seemed a happy man. Esther too was content. She know little about rocketry, less about the exotic mathematics that occupied her husband's evenings; but she had total faith in her mate and bore the calumny quite as cheerfully as did he.

The storm of disparagement in the newspapers that followed the noisy shot of July 17, 1929, turned out to be the ill wind that blew in someone good—that someone being Charles A. Lindbergh, the man who, two years earlier, had parlayed guts, ability and a bold concept into the beginning of a transportation revolution. Lindbergh spent an afternoon with the Goddards and apparently concluded that the easygoing professor had a similar parlay, including a concept of far greater potential. The famed flyer pledged his support; and Lindbergh's support at that time was the next best thing to an endorsement personally proffered by the Good Lord Himself—at least in aviation circles. Therefore, on April 5, 1930, God-

The Saturn 5 second stage S-II is built by North American's Space Division and its five J-2 hydrogen-fueled engines come from Rocketdyne. The J-2's generate 200,000 pounds of thrust each. (Photo courtesy North American Rockwell)

Third stage of the mighty Saturn 5 booster system is called (confusingly) the S-IVB stage. It is made by McDonnell Douglas and has a single Rocketdyne J-2 engine of 200,000 pounds thrust. The S-IVB was also used by the less powerful Saturn IB booster for earth orbital missions. The S-IVB served as the second stage in Saturn 1B. (Photo courtesy North American Rockwell)

dard received word that Lindbergh had talked with Daniel Guggenheim and Guggenheim had agreed to furnish $50,000 for rocket research over a two-year period. If Goddard were able to report reasonable progress at the end of that time, a like amount would be waiting for further experiment.

This was the opportunity Goddard had waited for. The Smithsonian had done the best it could with its limited resources, but the Guggenheim grants (continued by Daniel's son Harry through the Guggenheim Foundation after the elder Guggenheim's death) allowed truly meaningful research in the field of rocketry during the thirties.

The Goddards immediately moved to New Mexico. There, in desolate Eden Valley some 15 miles northwest of Roswell, a number of rockets were fired, each a little more advanced than the one preceding it. By March, 1935, a 75-lb rocket exceeded Mach 1 while climbing beyond a mile in height and flying 9,000 feet down-range. There were many failures, of course, but Goddard learned from each; and he made his research "cost effective" by obtaining as much multiple data as possible per shot. He fired rockets with a cluster of four engines, with gyro-controlled gimbal-mounted tails, and with steering vanes positioned within the exhaust stream. In 1938, he made a series

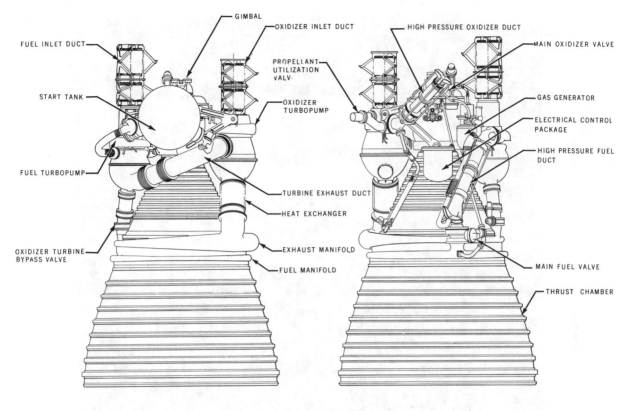

GIMBAL
OXIDIZER INLET DUCT
HIGH PRESSURE OXIDIZER DUCT
FUEL INLET DUCT
MAIN OXIDIZER VALVE
PROPELLANT-
UTILIZATION
VALV·
START TANK
GAS GENERATOR
OXIDIZER
TURBOPUMP
ELECTRICAL CONTROL
PACKAGE
HIGH PRESSURE FUEL
DUCT
FUEL TURBOPUMP
TURBINE EXHAUST DUCT
HEAT EXCHANGER
OXIDIZER TURBINE
BYPASS VALVE
EXHAUST MANIFOLD
MAIN FUEL VALVE
FUEL MANIFOLD
THRUST CHAMBER

J-2 ROCKET ENGINE

of demonstrations for the National Aeronautic Association, and although those representatives—as most others of the scientific world—were impressed, it seems clear in retrospect that no one in America then knew quite what to do with Dr. Goddard's fire-tailed birds.

In Germany, however, there were men who knew exactly what they would do with such vehicles.

The original impetus for rocket development in Germany appears to have possessed three legs: first, there was the Versailles Treaty of 1919. Born of French vindictiveness in particular and Allied stupidity in general, this document was designed to punish Germany for her role in WW-I and to insure that she never again should have sufficient military strength to threaten Europe. Among other things, Germany was allowed no air force while her other conventional armaments were severely restricted and carefully monitored. Therefore, in the late twenties, the clandestine German General Staff became interested in rockets as a form of extra-long-range artillery. Such weapons could be made secretly and outside conventional arms factories. Secondly, the Germans had some rocket-oriented people of their own, including

Hermann Oberth (actually, a Rumanian) who had been corresponding with Dr. Bob Goddard and who had authored a book in 1923, *The Rocket Into Interplanetary Space* which, along with the published Goddard papers, formed the basis for liquid-propelled rocket development in Germany.* Another German rocket expert was the now little-known Major General Wolfgang von Chamier-Glisczinski who would head-up the initial German effort in this field at Kummersdorf. He is believed to have died in an Allied bombing raid during WW-II. Better known are General Walter Dornberger, a WW-I veteran and ballistics specialist who would command the secret rocket research center at Peenemunde, and his rocket technician Wernher von Braun. Von Braun, building upon the disciplines of Goddard and Oberth, would soon far surpass those pioneers.

So, Germany had good reason to begin serious rocket research, capable men for the task, and Goddard's sound foundation upon which to build.

* A contemporary of Goddard and Oberth was Konstantin E. Tsiolkovsky of Russia who worked independently of them, but whose work was similarly eclipsed by German progress in the late thirties.

Control panel of Apollo command module has 250 switches and controllers. Panel shows 137 quantity measurements and records 142 events. (Photo courtesy North American Rockwell)

The Peenemunde facility became operational in 1937, and two years later a von Braun rocket attained an altitude of 5 miles. Steady progress during the next four years culminated in the 5½-ton V-2 (called the A-4 by its designers) which, on October 3, 1943, left the earth's atmosphere and flew a distance of 124 miles.

At the end of WW-II, Germany's 10-year lead in liquid-fueled rocketry passed to the U.S. and Russia when the victors scrambled madly about the prostrate Reich shanghaiing German rocket scientists. The U.S. got von Braun, Dornberger and a few others, though most disappeared into Stalin's Russia.

During the years immediately following WW-II, America's rocket program was limited to the firing of captured V-2's (under the direction of von Braun) at White Sands Missile Test Center near Alamagordo, N.M., and a sort of half-hearted effort at producing short-range artillery rockets (the *Corporal,* which eventually went into large-scale production in 1953)

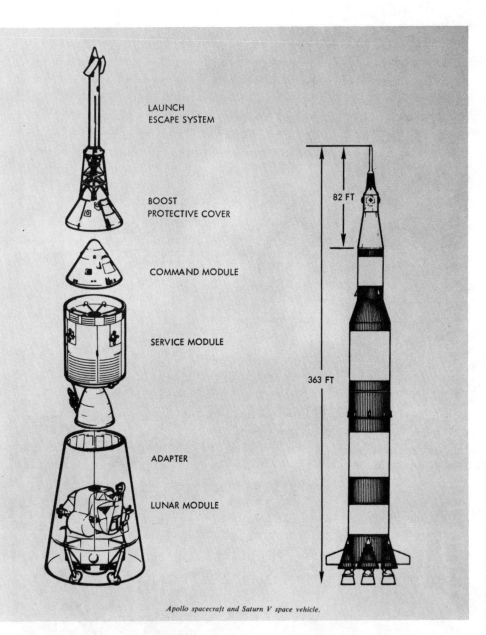

LAUNCH
ESCAPE SYSTEM

BOOST
PROTECTIVE COVER

COMMAND MODULE

SERVICE MODULE

ADAPTER

LUNAR MODULE

82 FT

363 FT

Apollo spacecraft and Saturn V space vehicle.

SATURN V

LAUNCH ESCAPE SYSTEM
NORTH AMERICAN AVIATION-SPACE DIVISION
LAUNCH ESCAPE MOTORS-LOCKHEED AIRCRAFT CORP.
LAUNCH JETTISON MOTORS-THIOKOL CHEMICAL CORP.

APOLLO COMMAND MODULE
NORTH AMERICAN AVIATION-SPACE DIVISION

APOLLO SERVICE MODULE
NORTH AMERICAN AVIATION-SPACE DIVISION

LUNAR MODULE ADAPTER
NORTH AMERICAN AVIATION-SPACE DIVISION

LUNAR MODULE
GRUMMAN AIRCRAFT AND ENGINEERING CORP.

INSTRUMENT UNIT
IBM/MANNED SPACE FLIGHT CENTER

S-IVB
McDONNELL DOUGLAS CORP.

1 J-2 ENGINE
NORTH AMERICAN AVIATION-ROCKETDYNE DIVISION

S-II
NORTH AMERICAN AVIATION-SPACE DIVISION

5 J-2 ENGINES
NORTH AMERICAN AVIATION-ROCKETDYNE DIVISION

S-IC
BOEING COMPANY

5 F-1 ENGINES
NORTH AMERICAN AVIATION-ROCKETDYNE DIVISION

Astronaut Thomas Stafford flew a 17-earth-orbit mission with Walter Schirra in Gemini 6, a 47-orbit flight with Eugene Cernan in Gemini 9, and commanded the 8-day deep-space flight to the moon in Apollo 10. (Photo courtesy NASA)

Astronaut Frank Borman flew the Gemini 7 rendezvous mission in December of 1965, and the historic Apollo 8 flight three years later that took man, for the first time in history, from the dominating influence of earth's gravity to that of another heavenly body. (Photo courtesy NASA)

Astronaut James Lovell first went into space with Frank Borman in Gemini 7 (for 220 earth-orbits), returned in November 1966, aboard Gemini 12, and during Christmas of 1968 orbited the moon in Apollo 8 with Borman and William Anders. (Photo courtesy NASA)

and an anti-aircraft rocket (*Nike-Ajax,* operational in 1953). Meanwhile, the U.S. felt secure with its monopoly of the atomic bomb and superior jet air power, and development of Air Force missiles was largely limited to unmanned miniature jet airplanes such as *Matador* and *Snark.* But the Soviets produced an A-bomb in 1949, the "cold war" developed in the meantime, and the Korean War followed in 1950. These things, plus the fact that Stalin had boasted of Russia's coming ICBM's, moved a frugal-minded Eisenhower Administration and cautious Congress to a leisurely program of medium-range rocket building, and emerging from this was the *Redstone* and *Jupiter,* direct descendents of the German V-2.

By 1951, when the *Redstone* project was born, knowledgable aerospace people—led by Major General Donald L. Putt and Brigadier General John W. Sessums, Jr.—had rejected the conclusions of several high-level committees that recommended no immedi-

ate work be done on long-range ballistics missiles, arguing that the Russians were already far ahead in this field and that America must not delay its own ICBM program. In 1953, when Air Force Secretary Harold Talbot and his Chief of Research and Development Trevor Gardner joined the minority crusade, others in the executive branch, as well as in Congress, began to listen. However, another year passed before America's ICBM program received top priority from the White House. By then, the Soviets had detonated 14 nuclear devices and that, taken together with sound evidence of Soviet ICBM development, at last sparked a crash program in America for acquisition of a 6,000-mile ballistics-missile booster.

Born of this activity was the *Atlas,* designed and built by Convair (largely because Convair had produced an improved version of the V-2 for Air Force tests back in 1947). The 100-ton, 80-foot *Atlas* first flew in June, 1957, and became operational in

Artist's drawings provided by North American Rockwell depict Apollo 11's lunar landing mission from lift-off to splashdown. Follow sequence left-to-right top, left-to-right center and left-to-right bottom on each of these four pages.

Giant booster undergoes last-minute checks before launch

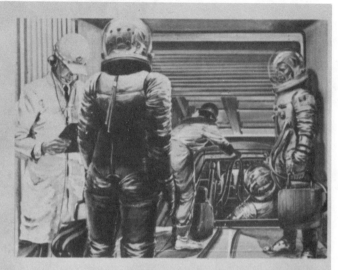

Astronauts enter CM from service tower after final checks

Saturn V lifts Apollo spacecraft off pad at Cape Kennedy

Saturn V second stage ignites as the first stage falls away

Second stage is jettisoned and third stage is ignited

Third stage pushes spacecraft out of earth's orbit

Adapter panels are opened and CSM separates

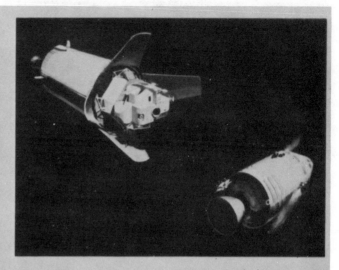

CSM turns around to get into position for docking

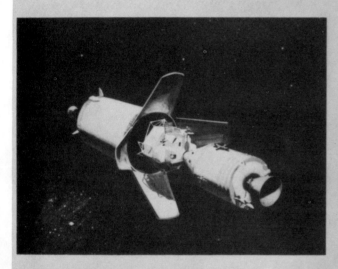

Command module docks with LM

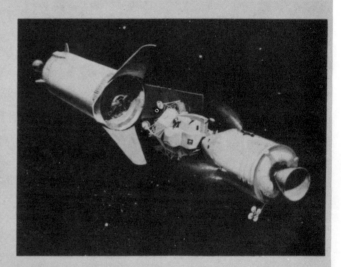

After docking, spacecraft leaves third stage behind

SM engine fires to put spacecraft in orbit around moon

LM separates from CSM to begin descent to moon

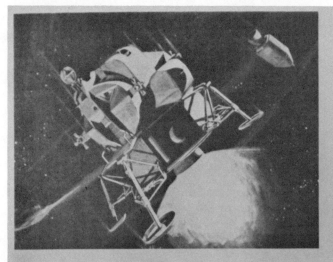

LM engine fires while CSM remains in orbit

Two astronauts guide LM to landing on lunar surface

Astronaut gathers soil samples from the lunar surface

Astronaut explores surface of moon

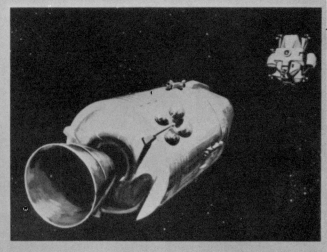

Engine fires to lift LM ascent stage off moon and into orbit

Astronauts in LM line up their craft for docking with SC CSM

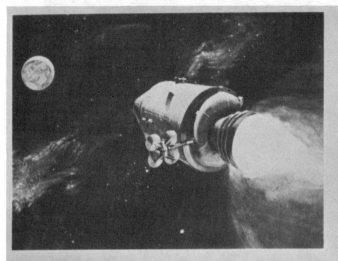

SM engine fires to start homeward journey; LM stays behind

SM is jettisoned as CM prepares for entry into atmosphere

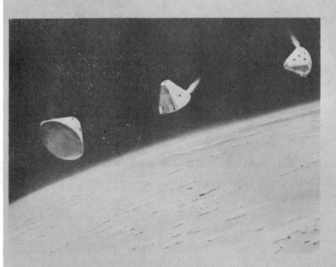

Pilot orients CM so base heat shield takes friction heat

Drogue parachutes are deployed for initial slowing of CM

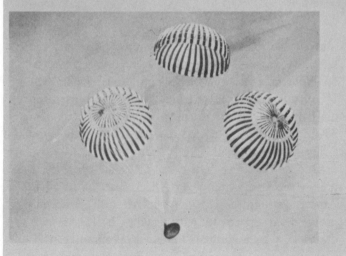

Main parachutes are deployed to lower CM safely to surface

Recovery forces move in as the CM floats in water

Artist's concept shows how SERT-II spacecraft, scheduled for launch late in 1969, will resemble a great bird with panels of solar cells for "wings." Wings, of course, are useless in airless space; cells will convert sun's rays into electrical power for the spacecraft, which uses a Lockheed Agena space vehicle to test experimental space engine developed by NASA. (Photo courtesy Lockheed Aircraft Corporation)

September, 1959. By March of 1962, 119 *Atlases* had been fired, with the Air Force terming 80 completely successful, 25 partially successful (meaning they came un-glued in flight but provided useful data), and 14 unsuccessful. In November, 1961, an *Atlas* booster rocketed a chimpanzee named Enos twice around the earth in a prelude to the Project Mercury manned orbital flights; and on February 20, 1962, an *Atlas-Mercury* launch vehicle boosted Astronaut John H. Glenn, Jr., into America's first manned orbit of the earth.

Due to America's late start in the "space race," the Soviets got thar fustest with the mostest. On October 4, 1957, Russia's 184-lb *Sputnik* 1 was lofted into earth orbit to become the world's first artificial satellite. *Sputnik* 2, weighing 1,121 pounds, followed on November 3rd carrying a dog named Laika. The U.S. managed to get its first satellite into earth orbit on January 31, 1958, when a *Jupiter C* booster sent 31-lb *Explorer 1* into space—to discover the Van Allen Radiation Belt.

During the next four years, Russian space technology repeatedly humbled the U.S. space effort while America struggled to catch up. Actually, America's progress in space rocketry, taken by itself, was dramatic (if the dismal *Vanguard* program can be forgotten). First, a number of *Explorers*, and then the *Thor-Agena*-boosted *Discoverer* series performed increasingly useful tasks, radioing back to earth all sorts of data about their space environment, while providing experience for launch and recovery crews and almost daily discoveries to aid scientists and designers. American aerospace engineers sometimes designed new hardware from knowledge gained but a few days, or even hours before. As one young engineer recalled, "We were designing parts we didn't even have names for—sure were a lot of 'gizmos' in some of those early birds." After a few seconds' pause, he added, "A lot of prayers, too."

In October, 1958, the National Aeronautics and Space Administration (NASA) was created from that venerable well-spring of aviation technology, the National Advisory Committee for Aeronautics (NACA, founded in 1915), and NASA became the official agency for all exploratory and scientific programs in space as well as in the air. Therefore, in 1961 when newly elected President Kennedy challenged the Soviets to a race for the moon, America had an experienced and capable organization to call its space shots, plus a youthful and innovative engineering force to create the pioneering hardware.

And it should not be forgotten that it was John F. Kennedy and the pulse-quickening spell of his challenge—to America as well as to the Soviets—that gained Congressional allegiance and appropriations (ultimately exceeding $25 billion) for man's greatest scientific adventure.

Since we seem prone to remember our presidents

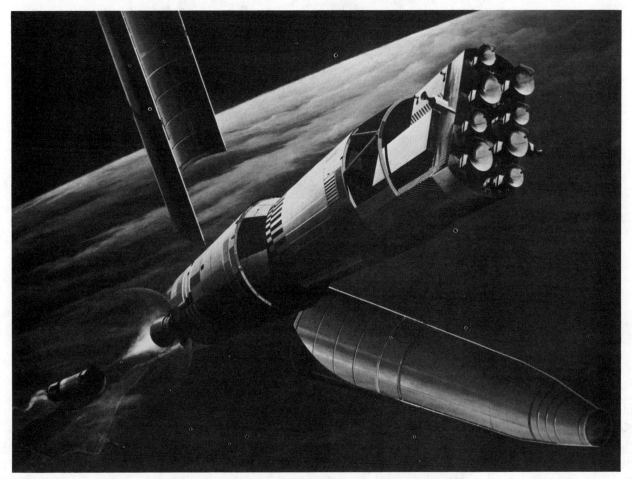

Artist's concept shows Lockheed-designed satellite that could relay international telephone calls and TV programs in near future. Satellite, bristling with antennas, is seen emerging from protective shroud aboard Agena upper stage and second stage of booster. Such a device could relay scores of TV shows and thousands of phone calls at once. (Photo courtesy Lockheed Aircraft Corporation)

Lockheed's Reginald Kearton displays model of re-usable space vehicle proposed as a solution to space cost problems. Big auxiliary fuel tanks, forming a "V" into which the space vehicle is neatly wedged, would supply fuel for lift-off and ascent. Once in space, the tanks would be dropped. At mission's end, the space-craft, containing engines and other expensive and complex equipment along with its passengers, would re-enter the atmosphere and glide like an airliner to a horizontal landing at a spaceport landing strip. (Photo courtesy Lockheed Aircraft Corporation)

for a single, significant deed unique to each, John Kennedy will undoubtedly be identified by school children 100 years hence as the Chief Executive who directed this nation to summon the stars. That should be quite enough, whatever his other, less inspired judgments, to assure his place in history beside Washington, Jefferson and Lincoln.

On April 12, 1961, less than three months after Kennedy took office, Soviet Cosmonaut Yuri Gagarin rode *Vostok 1* in an orbit around earth to become the first man in space. Then, on May 5 and July 21,

Alan Shepard and then Virgil Grissom made 300-mile sub-orbital flights in *Mercury-Redstone* vehicles to become the first Americans in space. These relatively modest shots were followed, on August 6, 1961, by Soviet Cosmonaut Gherman Titov's 17-orbit flight in *Vostok 2*. As previously noted, it was not until the following February that U.S. Astronaut John Glenn made America's first orbital flight. A brief study of the accompanying table will quickly reveal both U.S. and Russian progress in manned space exploration as of mid-May, 1969 (appropriately, as these words are written your authors must pause to watch the first live, color television transmission from space, courtesy of the Apollo 10 crew on their way to the moon).

Launch Date	Project	Crew	Mission
4/12/61	USSR Vostok 1	Yuri Gagarin	1 orbit
5/15/61	US Mercury-Redstone	Alan Shepard	1 sub-orbit
7/21/61	US Mercury-Redstone	Virgil Grissom	1 sub-orbit
8/ 6/61	USSR Vostok 2	Gherman Titov	17 orbits
2/20/62	US Mercury-Atlas 6	John Glenn	3 orbits
5/24/62	US Mercury-Atlas 7	Scott Carpenter	3 orbits
8/11/62	USSR Vostok 3	Andreyan Nikolayev	64 orbits
8/12/62	USSR Vostok 4	Pavel Popovich	48 orbits
9/ 3/62	US Mercury-Atlas 8	Walter Schirra	6 orbits
5/15/63	US Mercury-Atlas 9	Gordon Cooper	22 orbits
6/14/63	USSR Vostok 5	Valery Byovsky	81 orbits
6/16/63	USSR Vostok 6	Miss Valentina Tereshkova	48 orbits
10/12/64	USSR Voskhod 1	Vladimir Komarov Konstantin Feoktistov Boris Yegorov	16 orbits
3/18/65	USSR Voskhod 2	Pavel Belyayev Alexei Leonov	17 orbits
3/23/65	US Gemini-Titan 3	Virgil Grissom John Young	3 orbits
6/ 3/65	US Gemini-Titan 4	James McDivitt Edward White	62 orbits
8/21/65	US Gemini-Titan 5	Gordon Cooper Charles Conrad	128 orbits
12/ 4/65	US Gemini-Titan 7	Frank Borman James Lovell	220 orbits
12/15/65	US Gemini-Titan 6	Walter Schirra Thomas Stafford	17 orbits
3/16/66	US Gemini-Titan 8	Neil Armstrong David Scott	6½ orbits
6/ 3/66	US Gemini-Titan 9	Thomas Stafford Eugene Cernan	47 orbits
7/18/66	US Gemini-Titan 10	John Young Michael Collins	46 orbits
10/12/66	US Gemini-Titan 11	Charles Conrad Richard Gordon	47 orbits
11/11/66	US Gemini-Titan 12	James Lovell Edwin Aldrin	63 orbits
4/23/67	USSR Soyuz 1	V. Komarov killed on landing	18 orbits
10/11/68	US Apollo-Saturn 7	Walter Schirra Donn Eisele Walter Cunningham	163 orbits
10/25/68	USSR Soyuz 2	crew not announced	Rendezvous with Soyuz 3; 4-day flight
10/26/68	USSR Soyuz 3	Georgi T. Beregovoy	7-day deep space flight & moon orbit
12/21/68	US Apollo-Saturn 8	Frank Borman James Lovell William Anders	7-day deep space flight & moon orbit
1/14/69	USSR Soyuz 4	Lt. Col. Vladimir Shatalov	Rendezvous, docking and crew-change in space with Soyuz 5. 4-day flight.
1/15/69	USSR Soyuz 5	Lt. Col. Boris Valyno Lt. Col. Yevgeny Khrunov Alexei Yeliseyev	
3/ 3/69	US Apollo-Saturn 9	James McDivitt Russell Schweickart David Scott	10-day earth orbit to test moon-landing craft
5/18/69	US Apollo-Saturn 10	Thomas Stafford Eugene Cernan John Young	8-day deep space flight, moon orbit & moon landing craft test
7/16/69	US Apollo-Saturn 11	Neil Armstrong Michael Collins Edwin Aldrin	Moon landing July 20, 1969

The Mercury series put Americans in space much as the wood-and-cloth airplanes of 1910 put us into the air. Then Project Gemini brought muscle and sophistication to our new space technology. A whole set of new space disciplines was mastered while engineers perfected vastly more powerful boosters and U.S. astronauts logged hundreds of hours in space learning to rendezvous with sister ships, control and change orbit, and accustom themselves to the hostile environment. Meanwhile, great numbers of unmanned craft were lofted into earth, moon and solar orbits to probe and measure and sample the unknown as a prelude to manned exploration, and to serve the workaday world.

Although men had become "experienced" in space flight as 1968 drew to a close, none had yet left earth orbit to venture into deep space. Therefore, a century or so from now historians will probably pin-point a moment in December of that year as the single most significant moment in the story of mankind. It was 10:41 A.M. (EST), Saturday, December 21, 1968 Anno Domini, when the crew of *Apollo 8* slipped the bonds of earth's gravity and whipped out of earth orbit bound for the moon.

The Lunar Landing Program had been suggested by NASA back in July, 1960, and a feasibility study conducted by several aerospace companies was handed to President Kennedy in mid-May, 1961. The President presented the plan to Congress on May 25th, along with his famous commitment to put Americans on the moon by the end of the decade. The people's representatives promised the money and the first engineering contracts were let in 1962. Eventually, more than 20,000 companies and 300,000 people contributed to the Apollo-Saturn Lunar Landing Program (*Apollo* was the designation given the 4-unit spacecraft itself; *Saturn* was the booster system). On February 26, 1966, the first unmanned *Apollo* was flight tested, sent aloft by a *Saturn* 1B booster (*Apollo* used the smaller 1B first-stage booster of 1,600,000-lbs thrust for earth orbital missions. *Saturn 5,* the big first-stage booster used for lunar missions, has 7,500,000 lbs of thrust).

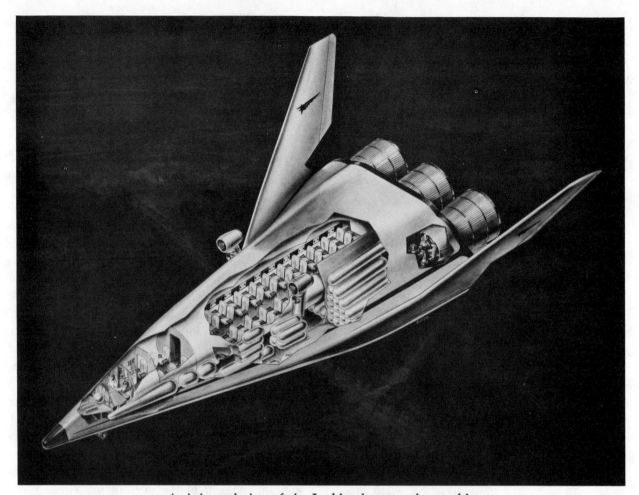

Artist's rendering of the Lockheed-proposed re-usable spacecraft returning to earth after jettisoning its empty fuel tanks. Craft is modeled after a "lifting body" vehicle, a wingless aircraft shaped to provide lift enough to support its weight in a high-speed glide. Late in '68 and early in '69 Northrop's lifting body, the HL-10, a small, single-place test model, was successfully flown. (Photo courtesy Lockheed Aircraft Corporation)

On January 27, 1967, three astronauts (Virgil Grissom, Edward White and Roger Chaffee) died in an accident at Kennedy Space Center during a pre-launch test when the pure oxygen atmosphere of their *Apollo* Command Module (CM) was ignited by a short in the electrical system. This tragedy set back the program by many months (during which time Soviet Cosmonaut Komarov was killed returning from orbit), but on November 9, 1967, a second unmanned *Apollo,* this one hurled far out into space by the mighty *Saturn 5,* made a re-entry into earth's at-

mosphere at almost 25,000 mph to prove its ability to safely return a crew from the moon. Another unmanned test of the *Apollo-Saturn 5* on April 4, 1968, was not altogether successful; but *Apollo 7,* with ill-tempered Walter Schirra, Donn Eisele and Walter Cunningham aboard, flew a 163-orbit mission in October, 1968 to dispel any lingering doubts about the CM and provided appropriate ruffles and flourishes for *Apollo 8*'s grand entry.

Apollo 8, commanded by AF Colonel Frank Borman with Navy Captain James Lovell and AF Major

Following cancellation of USAF's manned orbiting laboratory program in June 1969, America's remaining hope for putting an orbital workshop in space rested with NASA as part of the Apollo Applications Program. The NASA concept is the use of an S-IVB Saturn booster stage converted to a two-story experimental laboratory after using up its fuel achieving orbit; and an Apollo command module, launched separately, to take crews to and from the space station. (Photo courtesy McDonnell Douglas)

William Anders making up the balance of the three-man crew, thundered aloft from Kennedy Space Center's Launch Pad 39A at 7:51 A.M., December 21, 1968 ("thundered" really isn't the word; nor is there one to adequately convey the all-pervading sound of a *Saturn 5* booster at lift-off. It is louder than anything in history except nuclear blasts, the Krakatau volcano and the Great Siberian Meteorite of 1908). The giant space machine—weighing 6.2 million pounds, half again as much as a Navy destroyer—lifted itself on a pedestal of fire and then lanced gracefully into the east-

ern sky. At an altitude of 42 miles, 152 seconds after lift-off, its first stage cut off and tumbled into the Atlantic Ocean. Two seconds later, the five J-2 engines of the second stage ignited for a 300-second burn, taking the astronauts to an altitude of 122 miles before it too cut off and was discarded. Three seconds after that, the third stage began a 142-second burn to place *Apollo 8* in orbit 118 miles above earth at a speed of almost 17,500 mph.

The spacecraft orbited while its crew made final checks of all systems. Then, at 10:19 A.M., the history-making order came from Houston's Manned Spacecraft Center: "*Apollo 8,* you are go for TLI."*

"Roger, understand," replied Major Anders.

Twenty-two minutes later (10:41 A.M., EST), in the pre-dawn darkness over Hawaii, the third stage was re-ignited for a 302-second burn to fling *Apollo 8* into deep space at a speed of 24,196 mph, the fastest man had ever traveled.

"You're on your way," exulted Christopher Kraft, Jr., NASA Flight Director. "You're really on your way!"

Twenty-five minutes later, explosive bolts separated the *Saturn 5* third stage from the command and service modules and the third stage, containing a model of the lunar landing craft, was abandoned. On future moon missions, beginning with *Apollo 10,* the lunar module (LM) would be extracted from the third stage booster at this point and, coupled to the nose of the command module (CM) would accompany the astronauts into moon orbit from where it would serve as the commuter vehicle between the moon's surface and the orbiting CM above.

During the next 53 hours *Apollo 8* coasted toward its rendezvous with the moon, gradually slowed by earth's gravitational pull. On Monday morning Houston Control reminded Borman, Anders, and Lovell that they had just two more shopping days 'till Christmas, at which time they were approximately 200,000 miles from the nearest shopping center; and at 3:30 P.M., EST, the astronauts passed that point in space, 214,000 miles from earth, where the pull of the moon's gravity became stronger than that of earth's. By then slowed to 2,217 mph, their speed began to increase as *Apollo 8* was drawn toward the moon.

The spacecraft passed behind the moon at 4:49 A.M. the next morning which was Tuesday, Christmas Eve. Ten minutes later, with its service module engine pointing forward, a 240-second burn slowed *Apollo 8* from 5,758 mph to 3,643 mph, thus balancing its speed with the moon's gravitational pull to achieve an eliptical lunar orbit 194.5 miles at apogee and 69.6 miles at perigee.† Later, after transmitting to earth live

TV pictures of the moon, the crew refined their orbit to a circular 69.5 miles above the lunar surface with a short corrective burn of the service module (SM) engine.

During their ninth lunar orbit at 9:34 P.M. on Christmas Eve, the astronauts began a second telecast to earth and greatly moved millions of their distant fellowmen with a strangely appropriate reading of the first ten verses from the Book of Genesis.

A few hours later, at 12:42 A.M. on Wednesday, Christmas Day, *Apollo 8* circled behind the moon on its final orbit while the world anxiously waited, unable to communicate with the astronauts for the 43 minutes they were on the moon's far side. If the SM's engine should fail to re-start or properly burn, Borman, Anders and Lovell would be stranded in moon orbit with no chance of rescue before their life-support systems were exhausted. But half-way around the moon's backside the faithful SPS engine in the service module exploded to life upon command. It burned, just as it was supposed to do, for 198 seconds, thrusting the spaceship to an escape velocity of nearly 6,000 mph. And when *Apollo 8* came speeding around the moon's horizon at 1:25 A.M., Captain Lovell radioed happily to earth: "Houston, this is *Apollo 8.* Please be informed there is a Santa Claus."

The rest was anti-climactic. At 12:30 P.M. on Christmas, the spacecraft again reached the "equigravisphere" and then earth's gravity again became dominant pulling the astronauts homeward at an ever-increasing speed.

Apollo 8 streaked into the fringes of earth's atmosphere 34 hours and 58 minutes later, on Friday, December 27, 1968. Re-entry, beginning at about 400,-000 feet, was made at a 7-degree angle, 1,600 miles from the landing zone, in order to dissipate as much of the spacecraft's 24,630-mph velocity as possible before encountering the thicker air at lower altitudes. Still, *Apollo 8* arced earthward like a great meteor as air friction built up a temperature of nearly 5,000 degrees F on its ablative heat shield (Colonel Borman later described re-entry as "like being inside a neon tube"). In the command module the temperature remained 70 degrees, although the astronauts were subjected to deceleration forces of about 7 G's.

At 23,000 feet the two 16½-ft. stabilizing parachutes opened, slowing the CM to 300 mph. A minute later the three orange-and-white 83-ft. main 'chutes released automatically at 10,000 feet; and at 10:51 A.M., EST, Friday, December 27, 1968, *Apollo*

---

* Translunar injection (TLI) results when just the right amount of thrust is applied, at just the proper moment during earth orbit, to propel the spacecraft from orbit onto an intercepting course for the moon.

† Actually, the terms "apogee" and "perigee" are properly applied only to the orbits of objects circling earth. In lunar orbit, the high point is the "apocynthion," and the low point the "pericynthion."

8 splashed into the Pacific Ocean 1,450 miles southwest of Hawaii and three miles from the carrier *Yorktown* to complete a 537,000-mile journey into the future.

Just three months later, on March 3, 1969, *Apollo 9* flew a 10-day earth orbital mission to test the lunar module, the space taxi that would ferry astronauts between the moon's surface and the command module orbiting above. Astronauts Lt. Col. James McDivitt and Russell Schweickart (a civilian) spent six hours in the LM at distances up to 113 miles from Lt. Col. Dave Scott in the command module as both craft orbited earth. Having thus proved that America's system of space-docking, space transfer of crews between vehicles, and particularly the reliability of the bug-like LM itself, the U.S. was ready to take the LM into moon orbit with the *Apollo 10* command module for a final test prior to an actual moon landing.

Apollo 10 left Planet Earth just before noon on Sunday, May 18, 1969. Its journey to the moon was very similar to that of *Apollo 8*, except that *Apollo 10* had farther to travel (the moon's orbit about earth is an elliptical one), and it took along the lunar module after extracting it from the top of the expended third-stage booster following the TLI burn.

For the *Apollo 10* mission the command module had the radio-call code name of "Charlie Brown," and the lunar excursion module "Snoopy" (after cartoon characters drawn by Charles Schulz and especially enjoyed by aerospace people because of Snoopy's imaginary adventures as a WW-I flying ace). *Apollo 10* was commanded by AF Colonel Thomas Stafford and crewed by Navy Commanders Eugene Cernan and John Young.

Apollo 10 reached the moon and achieved lunar orbit at 4:45 P.M., EDT, Wednesday, May 21. Meanwhile, Stafford, Cernan, and Young repeatedly treated earthlings back home to live color telecasts extemporaneously narrated in high good humor. At mid-afternoon on Thursday, Stafford and Cernan entered Snoopy and un-docked from Charlie Brown. Then they fired Snoopy's lower-stage engine in a braking maneuver that placed them in an eliptical orbit with a pericynthion of just 9.4 miles above the moon's surface. After two such revolutions and a total of 8 hours in Snoopy, Stafford and Cernan maneuvered the LM back to the circular orbit 69 miles above the moon where John Young manned the CM alone. Snoopy's lower stage, mounting its four landing legs, was left behind.

Young expertly nudged Charlie Brown's docking probe into Snoopy's matching aperture and the two craft locked together once again. Then Stafford and Cernan re-entered Charlie Brown, Snoopy was again released, and sent away to an uncertain fate, while the crew of *Apollo 11* settled down for another 36 hours of data-collecting in moon orbit before blasting away on their 54-hour trip back to earth.

Another Apollean step had been taken into the universe.

Less than two months later, on Wednesday, July 16, 1969, *Apollo 11* left earth to carry out the first lunar landing mission. In command was civilian astronaut Neil Armstrong (a former Navy flyer). His crew was AF Lt. Col. Michael Collins, pilot of the *Apollo 11* Command Module, and AF Colonel Edwin "Buz" Aldrin, Jr. At 9:32 A.M., EDT, Launch Control announced: "Lift off. We have a lift off!" And the great space machine rose majestically from Cape Kennedy and streaked through filmy stratus clouds into space.

Four days later, Sunday, July 20th at 1:50 P.M., EDT, Neil Armstrong radioed to earth that the Lunar Module "Eagle" had separated from the Command Module "Columbia" three minutes previously as *Apollo 11* was about to emerge from behind the moon. Then, at 3:08 P.M., again behind the moon, Eagle's descent-stage engine fired for 29.8 seconds in a braking burn that lowered the space taxi containing Armstrong and Aldrin into an orbit with a pericynthion of 9.8 miles above the lunar surface. From that point in space and time, highlights from the Eagle's log were as follows:

4:00 P.M.: "Eagle, this is Houston . . . you are go for powered descent."

4:06 P.M.: Eagle's altitude is 50,000 feet, 260 miles from the landing site. It's lower-stage engine is ignited to slow the craft and control its descent. "Everything looking good," Houston reports.

4:10 P.M.: Altitude, 33,500 ft.

4:12 P.M.: Altitude, 21,000 ft. Speed, 820 mph.

4:14 P.M.: Altitude, 4,200 ft. "You're go for landing," Houston says.

4:15 P.M.: Altitude, 750 ft. Speed, 15 mph. Descent engine continues its burn. Then, a few seconds later at 350 ft., Armstrong quickly switches to semi-automatic control and instructs Eagle's on-board navigation computer to change course as it becomes evident that the automatic landing system is about to land them inside a rock-strewn crater the size of a football field. He chooses a touch-down spot which is later fixed at about four miles beyond the programmed site. It is within an area known to astronomers as "Mare Tranquillitatis," the Sea of Tranquility.

4:17 P.M.: Altitude 40 ft. Speed, 1.5 mph. "Picking up some dust," Armstrong reports. Altitude, 5 ft., and a light on the instrument panel flashes as one of the antenna-like sensors extending from Eagle's landing legs contacts the moon's surface. Aldrin shuts off the descent engine and Eagle touches down so gently a cupful of coffee would not slosh over had the astronauts had time for it.

"Houston, Tranquility Base here," Neil Armstrong reports in a voice barely containing his elation, "The Eagle has landed."

10:51 P.M.: Following a rest period, a light supper, and time-consuming preparations for the "extra vehicular activity" (EVA), Mission Commander Armstrong emerged from Eagle and descended its ladder.

10:56 P.M.: EDT (Sunday, July 20, 1969): Neil Armstrong realized one of man's oldest dreams when he placed his foot on the lunar surface. "That's one small step for a man, one giant leap for mankind," he said quietly to uncounted millions of earthlings who were witnessing the event via live television.

11:11 P.M.: Buzz Aldrin emerges from Eagle to join Armstrong on the moon's surface.

12:58 P.M.: After working with Armstrong to set up several scientific experiments, plant (and salute) the American Flag, and gather rocks and lunar dust samples, Colonel Aldrin re-enters Eagle.

01:10 A.M. (Monday, July 21): Neil Armstrong re-enters Eagle after transferring the moon booty to Aldrin inside the LM.

01:54 P.M. (that afternoon): Following several hour's rest and a careful check-out of the Eagle's systems, Armstrong and Aldrin blast off from the moon's surface, leaving Eagle's descent-stage behind, and rendezvous in moon orbit with Mike Collins in the *Apollo 11* Command Module.

12:55 A.M. (Tuesday, July 22): Collins fires *Apollo 11*'s Service Module engine in a two-minute, 28-second burn to leave lunar orbit and return to earth.

12:50 P.M. (Thursday, July 24): *Apollo 11* splashes down in the Pacific 915 miles southwest of Hawaii and 13 miles from the awaiting aircraft carrier *Hornet*.

The three astronauts were quarantined for three weeks after their return while doctors made certain that no strange new malady had been brought back from the moon. Then, on August 13, after a day spent relaxing with their families, Armstrong, Aldrin and

Collins good-naturedly began that part of the mission for which they were the least prepared: subjection to the adulation of their proud fellow Americans.

But even before *Apollo 11*'s crew was released from quarantine, NASA Administrator Dr. Thomas O. Paine was outlining the space agency's plans for the future: Three additional *Apollo* shots were authorized by the Congress, but Dr. Paine wanted six more besides those. And NASA plans were well along for an earth-orbiting space station in which many astronauts could work for extended periods (in July, 1969 design contracts in excess of $5 million were let by NASA for the first 12-man space station).

Also envisioned was the development of re-usable space vehicles with aerodynamic qualities allowing them to glide to spaceport landings upon returning from a mission. This advance alone would greatly reduce costs by eliminating the expensive recovery system of the sixties.

A further economy would be realized with development—targeted for 1977—of a nuclear engine (NERVA) for space travel.

November, 1981, was the tentative date set for launch of the men-on-Mars mission. The Mars vehicle would be launched from an earth-orbiting space station and would be gone for two years during which time it would spend some two and a-half months in Mars orbit and would send a six-man team of astronauts to explore the Martian surface for as long as six weeks.

Dr. Paine estimated the cost of this twelve-year program (which included many unmanned space shots) at about $6 billion per year. This compared with a 1969 NASA budget of $3.8 billion.

Meanwhile, other space scientists were suggesting that NASA include, during the late seventies, an unmanned deep space probe or two that would make the "grand tour:" One spacecraft could be sent past Jupiter, Saturn, and Pluto; the other would fly past Jupiter, Uranus, and Neptune. These projects will be possible because the planets of this solar system will be so aligned during this period that the space vehicles may employ the gravitational pull of each planet in turn to fling the probes toward the next. Since the planets will not be lined up in this order again for 175 years, U.S. scientists are loath to pass up such an opportunity. Using this technique, we can reach Pluto in only eight years, they say. Otherwise, a normal powered flight would require 41 years to traverse that 3.7 billion miles.

Other, less incredible space missions are programmed for the seventies. In 1971, two more unmanned *Mariners* will return to Mars and orbit the Red Planet for sixty days of picture-taking. In 1973 a pair of unmanned *Vikings* are scheduled to soft-land instrument packages on Mars. In 1972–73, two *Pioneer* unmanned spacecraft will explore the asteroid belt beyond Mars. Also during the early seventies NASA wants to send unmanned craft to Mercury and Venus.

Yes, it will all cost money. NASA spent in the neighborhood of $25 billion between 1961 and 1970. We cannot resist pointing out, however, that the U.S. taxpayer anted up just five times that much during the same period for interest on the national debt.

Anyway, assuming sound leadership during the seventies, the pace of America's space programs will be determined by her national will. Our aerospace industry, our engineers, scientists, and astronauts have dramatically demonstrated their fantastic potentials. Now it is up to the people and the Congress to support the proper exploitation of this unmatched national resource—in the name of peace and for all mankind.

Bibliography

Books

Aerospace Industries Association of America, Aerospace Yearbooks, 1964–1967. Washington, D.C.

AFROTC Headquarters. 1958. *Foundations of Air Power.* USAF, Maxwell AFB.

Air Force Magazine Editors. 1959. *Space Weapons.* Frederick Praeger. New York.

American Heritage Publishing Company. 1962. *The History of Flight.* New York.

Army ROTCM 145–20, *American Military History.* U.S. Army, 1954.

Art, Robert J. *The TFX Decision.* Boston: Little, Brown & Co., 1968.

Birdsall, Steven. *B-24 Liberator:* New York: Arco Publishing Co., 1968.

———. *B-17 Flying Fortress:* New York: Arco Publishing Co., 1965.

Boyington, Col. Gregory. *Baa Baa Black Sheep.* New York: G. P. Putnam's Sons, 1958.

Bridgeman, William, with Jacqueline Hazard. *The Lonely Sky:* New York: Henry Hall & Co., 1955.

Bruno, Harry. *Wings Over America.* New York: Robert M. McBride & Co., 1942.

Brophy, Arnold. *The Air Force:* New York: Julian Messner, Inc., 1957.

Caidin, Martin. *The Night Hamburg Died:* New York: Ballantine Books, 1960.

Chivers, Sydney P. *Flying Tigers.* Cleveland: Challenge Publications, Inc., 1953.

Christy, Joe and Shamburger, Page. *Aces and Planes of WW-I.* E. Norwalk, Connecticut: Sports Car Press Ltd., 1968.

Churchill, Winston. *The Second World War* 6 vols. New York: Houghton, Mifflin Co., 1948.

Cleveland, Reginald. *The Coming Air Age:* New York: McGraw Hill, 1944.

Cowburn, Philip. *The Warship in History:* New York: Macmillan Co., 1967.

Maynard, Crosby. *Flight Plan for Tomorrow.* Santa Monica, California: Douglas Aircraft Co., 1966.

Crossfield, Scott and Blair, Jr. Clay. *Always Another Dawn.* New York: World Publishing Co., 1960.

Delear, Frank. *The Miracle of the Helicopter.* Bridgeport, Connecticut: Sikorsky Aircraft Company, 1961.

Duke, Neville. *Sound Barrier:* New York: Philosophical Library, 1955.

Fleming, Peter. *Operation Sea Lion:* Simon & Schuster, New York: 1957.

Flight Year, Inc., Los Angeles, California, 1953.

Freudenthal, Elsbeth. *The Aviation Business.* New York: Vanguard Press, 1940.

Futrell, Robert. *The USAF in Korea:* New York: Duell, Sloan & Pearce, 1961.

Gallico, Paul. *The Hurricane Story:* Garden City, New York: Doubleday & Co., 1960.

Giap, Gen. Vo Nguyen. *People's War, People's Army.* New York: Frederick Praeger, Inc., 1968.

Gurney, Gene, Col., USAF. *Test Pilots.* New York: Franklin Watts, Inc., 1962.

———. *The War in the Air.* New York: Crown Publishers, 1962.

Haggerty, James J. and Smith, Warren R. *The Air Force.* Washington and New York: Books, Inc., 1966.

Johnson, Robert and Caidin, Martin. *Thunderbolt.* New York: Rinehart & Co., 1958.

Joubert, Sir Philip, Air Chief Marshal, RAF. *Rocket.* New York: Philosophical Library, 1957.

Juptner, Joseph. *U.S. Civil Aircraft.* vols 1 and ·4. Fallbrook, California: Aero Publishers, 1962, 1967.

Kantosha. *Japanese Military Aircraft in the Pacific War.* Tokyo, 1956.

Kirk, John and Young, Robert. *Great Weapons of WW-II.* New York: Bonanza Books, 1961.

LeMay, Curtis E., Gen., USAF. *America Is in Danger.* New York: Funk & Wagnalls, 1968.

La Farge, Oliver, Lt. Col., USAF. *The Egg and the Eagle.* Boston: Houghton Mifflin, 1949.

Lockheed-California Company. *Lockheed Horizon #7.* Burbank, California, 1969.

Miller, Ed Mack. *Men of Contrail Country.* Englewood Cliffs, New Jersey: Prentice-Hall, 1963.

Moore, Samuel Taylor, Col., USAF. *U.S. Air Power.* New York: Greenberg: Publisher, 1958.

Morris, Lloyd and Smith, Kendall. *Ceiling Unlimited.* New York: Macmillan Co., 1960.

Payne, L.G.S., Air Commodore, RAF. *Air Dates.* New York: Frederick Praeger, 1957.

Peaslee, Budd J. *Heritage of Valor.* New York: J. B. Lippincott Co., 1964.

Robertson, Bruce. *Air Aces of the 1914–1918 War.* Letchworth, Herts, England: Harlyford Publications, Ltd., 1959.

Rust, Kenn C. *The 9th Air Force in WW-II.* Fallbrook, California: Aero Publishers, Inc., 1967.

Scott, Robert L. Jr., Gen., USAF. *Boring a Hole in the Sky.* New York: Random House, 1961.

————. *God is My Co-Pilot.* New York: Ballantine Books, 1943.

Shamburger, Page and Christy, Joe. *Command the Horizon.* New York and London: A. S. Barnes and Co., 1968.

Shrader, W. A. *Fifty Years of Flight.* Canoga Park, California: Eaton Mfg. Co., Canoga, 1953.

Sikorsky, Igor I. *The Story of the Winged-S.* New York: Dodd, Mead & Co., 1967.

Sims, Edward H. *The Greatest Aces.* New York: Harper & Row, 1967.

Smith, Henry Ladd. *Airways Abroad.* University of Wisconsin Press, 1950.

Smith, Robert T. *Staggerwing.* Media, Pennsylvania: Stephen Maney, 1967.

————. *Guide to Air Traffic Control.* E. Norwalk, Connecticut: Sports Car Press, Ltd., 1965.

Smith, S. E. *The U.S. Navy in WW-II.* New York: William Morrow & Co., 1966.

Snyder, Louis L. *The War, 1939-1945.* New York: Julian Messner, Inc., 1956.

Swanborough, F. G. *Vertical Flight Aircraft of the World.* Fallbrook, California: Aero Publishers, 1964.

Sunderman, James, Col., USAF. *World War Two in the Air.* 2 vols. New York: Franklin Watts, Inc., 1962.

Tuleja, Thaddeus. *Climax at Midway.* New York: W. W. Norton & Co., 1960.

Ulanoff, Stanley. *MATS,* Franklin Watts, 1964.

USAF Report on the Ballistic Missile. Garden City, New York: Doubleday & Co., 1958.

U.S. Civil Aircraft Register. U.S. Govt. Pntg. Office. Washington D.C., 1968.

U.S. Naval Aviation 1910–1960 NAVWEPS-00-80P-1, U.S. Gvt. Pntg. Office, Washington, D.C., 1960.

Yeager, Charles E., Major, USAF, with William Lundgren. *Across the High Frontier.* New York: William Morrow & Co., 1955.

Magazines, Journals, and Newsletters:

Aero Album. Fallbrook, California: Aero Publishers, fall, 1968.

Aerospace Historian, 6, no. 1; 7, no. 1. Bolling AFB.

Aerospace International. Washington, D.C.: USAF Association, July-August, 1967.

Aerospace Industries Association. *Working Press Memos.* Washington, D.C., most issues refer to 1966-1968.

Aerospace Safety. USAF, Norton AFB. March, 1969.

Air Classics Magazine. Most issues refer to Jan. 1965 through June 1969. vol. 5, no. 5, Canoga Park, California: Challenge Publications.

Air Force and Space Digest. May, Sept., 1964; Sept., 1965; Sept., 1966; Sept., 1967; August, Sept., 1968; March, 1969, Washington, D.C.

Air Power Historian. July, 1965. Maxwell AFB.

Air Progress. June, 1968; May, 1969, New York.

American Aviation. July, 1964. Washington, D.C.

American Aviation Historical Society Journal 9, no. 1; 9, no. 3; 9, no. 4. Los Angeles, California.

American Helicopter Society Newsletter. March, Sept., Oct., Nov., Dec., 1961. New York.

American Helicopter Society Journal 1, no. 1. New York.

Air Transport Association of America. *Keeping Aircraft Apart.* Washington, D.C.

Collins Radio Co. *Collins Signal.* Spring, 1963. Dallas, Texas.

FAA Aviation News. Dec., 1968. Washington, D.C.

Flying. June, 1953, March, 1957, Jan., 1959, Feb., 1964. New York.

Indicator, monthly newsletter of National Aviation Trades Association. Jan.–May 1969. Washington, D.C.

National Geographic. Feb., 1935, March, 1969, Washington, D.C.

News Releases. USAF, Hdqrs. 7th AF, June, 1968 through June, 1969. Tan Son Nhut Air Base, Republic of Vietnam.

Rendezvous, Bell Aerosystems Co. 4, no. 4. Buffalo, N.Y.

Sport Aviation. June, 1961. Hales Corners, Wisc.

Other sources included a special report by the R. Dixon Speas Associates commissioned by the Utility Airplane Council of the Aerospace Industries Association, The Magnitude and Economic Impact of General Aviation, 1969; and a portion of Chapter 12 in this book previously appeared in Air Progress Homebuilt Annual, 1966, written by same authors. We're grateful to Conde Nast Publications, Inc., for permission to draw upon that story for this work.

Index

429